Globe Law
and Business

The Global ESG Handbook

A Guide for Practitioners

Consulting Editor **Paul Davies**

Consulting editor
Paul Davies

Managing director
Sian O'Neill

The Global ESG Handbook: A Guide for Practitioners
is published by

Globe Law and Business Ltd
3 Mylor Close
Horsell
Woking
Surrey GU21 4DD
United Kingdom
Tel: +44 20 3745 4770
www.globelawandbusiness.com

The Global ESG Handbook: A Guide for Practitioners

ISBN 9781787429765
EPUB ISBN 9781787429772
Adobe PDF ISBN 9781787429789

DISCLAIMER
This publication is intended as a general guide only. The information and opinions which it contains are not intended to be a comprehensive study, or to provide legal advice, and should not be treated as a substitute for legal advice concerning particular situations. Legal advice should always be sought before taking any action based on the information provided. The publisher bears no responsibility for any errors or omissions contained herein.

Table of contents

Preface

Paul Davies
Latham & Watkins

This handbook has been prepared in order to bring together a number of the legal trends that commercial lawyers and ESG practitioners now have to address on a daily basis. Throughout, we have aimed to present the dynamic and ever-evolving nature of the ESG landscape, which is continuously shaped by regulatory changes and emerging trends. Given the rapid rate of the evolution of these trends, it is inevitable that since the writing of this handbook there have been a number of developments that are not directly reflected in the text – although the themes identified throughout remain relevant and current. In addition, since this hand's completion, there have been two notable regulatory developments which it would be remiss not to acknowledge.

On 6 March 2024, nearly two years after the proposed rules were first released, the US Securities and Exchange Commission adopted final rules requiring registrants to disclose certain climate-related information in registration statements and annual reports. The final rules scale back many of the items that would have been required by the proposed rules, while still requiring extensive climate-related disclosure from many companies. Following adoption, the rules have been immediately subject to legal challenges, making the final position of the rules subject to a level of uncertainty.

In the European Union, on 24 May 2024 the European Council formally adopted the Corporate Sustainability Due Diligence Directive (CSDDD), marking the last step in the decision-making process. This followed extended negotiations and revisions from the provisional agreement of the European Council and European Parliament. The CSDDD will require in-scope companies to conduct due diligence to identify and assess environmental and human rights issues across their value chain, and to take steps to prevent and eliminate them (and will therefore likely have significant impact throughout the value chain).

There are a number of other developments that postdate the preparation of this handbook and there will no doubt be many more in the coming months and years.

Acknowledgements

I would like to express my gratitude to everyone who contributed to the creation of *The Global ESG Handbook*. I have been fortunate to have the support of many superb individuals and teams who have been instrumental in shaping it. My appreciation extends to all the authors (and, in turn, no doubt the many others that supported them) who have shared their expertise and insights on ESG issues – your contributions have been essential in making this a comprehensive resource. I am grateful to the team at Globe Law and Business for their professionalism and support in making this publication possible.

I am thankful to my colleagues Michael Green and James Bee for their consistent support – their guidance has been greatly appreciated and has significantly contributed to the development of this work. Special thanks to Samantha Banfield for her excellent coordination and valuable input throughout. Her efforts have been crucial in bringing this handbook together. Lastly, I thank my ESG co-chairs, Sarah Fortt and Betty Huber, for their thorough edits and support. Their attention to detail and understanding of ESG have undoubtedly enhanced the quality of this handbook.

To everyone involved, your hard work and dedication have been invaluable.

Finally, thanks to my wife and children for their enduring patience.

What is ESG?

Paul Davies
Latham & Watkins

1. Introduction

Environmental, social and governance (ESG) considerations have seen an exponential rise in prominence in recent years. Initially brought into focus within the asset management and investment community, ESG concerns have since broadened to become a focal point for a diverse array of stakeholders, including corporations, policymakers, courts and the general public across the world. The COVID-19 pandemic has only served to amplify this trend, spotlighting specific ESG issues related to the pandemic, while also perpetuating the global re-evaluation of corporate purpose.

This shift in perspective was encapsulated in August 2019, when the Business Roundtable released a statement redefining the purpose of a corporation,[1] including the promotion of an economy that serves all citizens, as opposed to shareholders only.

Nevertheless, the rapid development of ESG has not been without its challenges. Complex trade-offs involving global equity and energy security have fuelled scepticism as to the efficacy and merit and value of ESG as a concept, scepticism which has been louder in certain jurisdictions and regions than others. However, as with any evolving and maturing idea, it is to be expected that ESG will face numerous challenges, and be required to adapt and adjust over coming years.

This handbook aims to explore some of these challenges, while also highlighting areas where ESG is poised to develop further. It seeks to provide a comprehensive overview of the current market landscape, offering insights into the dynamic interplay between ESG factors and the broader socio-economic environment.

2. What is ESG?

ESG is an umbrella term which represents the non-financial factors that

---

1   "Business Roundtable Redefines the Purpose of a Corporation to Promote 'An Economy That Serves All Americans'" (Business Roundtable, 19 August 2019), www.businessroundtable.org/business-roundtable-redefines-the-purpose-of-a-corporation-to-promote-an-economy-that-serves-all-americans.

investors, businesses and other stakeholders consider in their investments, analyses and decision-making processes. In the investment community, ESG has largely supplanted CSR (corporate social responsibility), which represents a firm's sustainability efforts and its practices and policies which seek to have a positive impact on the environment and on society in general. ESG was originally created by the financial sector to quantify and measure firms' sustainability practices, but recent years have seen a growth in the breadth and number of stakeholders showing interest in ESG, and companies are now focusing on these issues from a reputational perspective and as part of their social licence to operate.

While different people and different institutions have varying definitions of exactly what issues fall within the scope of ESG, environmental factors typically involve a firm's impact on the environment, such as carbon emissions and resource usage. Social factors relate to how the firm treats stakeholders such as its employees, local communities, customers and society in general. Governance factors include: a firm's policies and procedures; its ability to avoid corruption, bribery and other fraud; and the independence and structure of its board of directors. Different ESG factors may be more relevant for some industries and firms than for others, and the importance of certain factors may change over time. In recent years, corporate stakeholders have increasingly focused on climate change, DEI (diversity, equity and inclusion) and a firm's health and safety measures in light of the COVID-19 pandemic.

Although there is no universal definition of what qualifies as ESG, factors include but are not limited to the elements in Figure 1.

3. Why does ESG matter?

The legal landscape is rapidly evolving to reflect the importance of ESG considerations, with regulatory frameworks around the world developing to incorporate ESG principles. Non-compliance can lead to significant repercussions, as evidenced by the proliferation of ESG-related enforcement actions and private litigation. In the United States, for instance, the Dodd-Frank Act of 2010 as amended, the Foreign Corrupt Practices Act of 1977 as amended and recent SEC proposals underscore the necessity of ESG disclosures, ranging from supply chain transparency to climate risk and greenhouse gas emissions. Similarly, in the United Kingdom and Europe, the development of ESG taxonomies and the European Union's recent roll-out of the Corporate Sustainability Reporting Directive (CSRD) are the latest harbingers of the transition from soft law to hard law in ESG matters, with stringent disclosure requirements and cross-jurisdictional mandates becoming the norm.

ESG performance can also be an important determinant in an entity's ability to secure financing. Investors and financial institutions, stewarding trillions in capital, increasingly prioritise ESG metrics when assessing the risk and growth

Figure 1. What qualifies as ESG?

Environmental	Social	Governance
• Climate change and greenhouse gas (GHG) emissions • Energy efficiency • Resource depletion, including water and raw materials • Waste and pollution • Deforestation • Biodiversity	• Human rights and working conditions (including slavery and child labour) • Diversity, equity and inclusion (including anti-discrimination) • Impact on local communities, including indigenous people • Conflict zones and conflict minerals • Health and safety • Customer privacy and security	• Corporate governance and oversight • Risk management • Executive pay • Fraud, anti-bribery and anti-corruption controls • Political lobbying and donations • Board independence, diversity and structure

potential of investments. The surge in sustainable investments and the prevalence of ESG reporting among S&P 500 and Russell 1000 companies[2] reflect the financial sector's increasing focus on such issues. Entities with robust ESG strategies may find it easier to attract investment, as they are perceived to be better prepared to navigate future challenges and capitalise on opportunities. Conversely, those with poor ESG records may face divestment and a shrinking pool of willing investors.

Nevertheless, the complexity of the ESG landscape is compounded by the diverse perspectives of its stakeholders, with each participant group, jurisdiction and market bringing its unique view to bear on what exactly 'ESG' entails. What constitutes responsible environmental conduct, social responsibility, or effective governance can vary significantly from one country to another; influenced by cultural norms, legal systems, economic priorities and societal expectations. For example, the emphasis on environmental issues might be more pronounced in countries severely affected by climate change, while social issues such as labour rights might take precedence in regions with a history of labour exploitation. Similarly, governance concerns may differ in markets with

---

2   From the G&A Institute "2023 Sustainability Reporting in Focus" report, 98% of S&P 500 and 90% of Russell 1000 publish sustainability reports.

varying levels of regulatory enforcement and transparency standards. The challenge lies in navigating the variegated definitions of the 'E', the 'S' and the 'G', and the potential for conflicting regulatory demands.

Stakeholders, ranging from consumers and employees to regulators and non-governmental organisations, also bring unique viewpoints to the table, influencing "why ESG matters" on a case-by-case basis. A consumer group's focus on ethical sourcing may drive a company's social ESG efforts, while investor pressure for transparency and accountability may shape governance initiatives. As such, entities must traverse this landscape with a nuanced and adaptable ESG approach, tailored to the specificities of each market and stakeholder group they engage with.

The very presence of these complexities stands testament to the fact that ESG considerations have become an enduring feature of the global business landscape. Stakeholders must cultivate a deep and actionable understanding of ESG, not only to mitigate risks and fulfil legal obligations, but also to harness opportunities for sustainable growth and long-term value creation.

4. Overview of *The Global ESG Handbook*

This handbook is structured to provide a holistic view of ESG issues, guiding readers through each component and their interconnections. The flow of the book aims to build a comprehensive understanding of ESG, starting with foundational concepts and moving towards more complex applications and global perspectives.

In the first part of the book, the chapters provide a comprehensive overview of the ESG landscape, illustrating the relevance, application and significance of these principles across the contemporary business world. "Energy transition and climate issues" by Andrew Angle, Aiste Brackley and Mark Lee from ERM, addresses the global shift toward renewable energy, highlighting both the challenges and opportunities this transition presents. This is applied in practice in the chapter "Addressing human rights risks in global supply chains" by Mariana Abreu, Ian Barclay and Stuart McLachlan of Anthesis Group and Amandine Bressand of ISEAL, which tackles managing sustainable supply chains across a range of topics, from ethical sourcing and labour rights to the environmental repercussions of supply chain operations, emphasising the critical role of due diligence and the transformative power of technology in fostering transparency and accountability.

In "The S in ESG", Sarah Fortt and Betty Huber from Latham & Watkins turn the spotlight on the social aspects of ESG. They dissect how companies are addressing pressing issues such as human rights, employee relations, community impact and the pursuit of diversity and inclusion. This discussion sets the stage for "ESG reporting" where Fortt and Huber are joined by James Bee, Paul Davies and Michael Green, offering a comprehensive look at ESG disclosure practices. They outline the existing frameworks and standards, the role of third-party assessments and the ongoing challenges companies encounter in delivering meaningful ESG information to their stakeholders.

The next chapters maintain this focus on the relevance of ESG considerations for key stakeholders. In "ESG corporate issues: shareholder activism", Elina Tetelbaum and Carmen Lu from Wachtell, Lipton, Rosen & Katz, alongside Desi Baca, Lawrence Elbaum and Patrick Gadson from Vinson & Elkins in "Shareholder activism: case studies", explore the growing influence of investors in shaping corporate environmental and social policies. This theme of ESG integration continues in "ESG corporate issues: M&A" with Rachel Barrett, Dearbhla Cantwell and Vanessa Havard-Williams from Linklaters examining how ESG considerations are becoming increasingly integral to the mergers and acquisitions process, from due diligence to valuation and post-merger integration.

The book then shifts to specific practice areas, to build an understanding of the real-world industry application of ESG considerations. Paul Davies and Michael Green from Latham & Watkins, in "ESG in private equity", analyse how ESG criteria are being incorporated into investment decisions within the private equity sector. They discuss the motivations, measurement challenges and the sustainable benefits that ESG-focused investing can yield. On the finance side, Helene Banks, Gregory Battista, Patrick Gordon and Meghan McDermott of Cahill Gordon & Reindel, in "The basics of ESG finance", introduce readers to the financial products and services designed to support ESG objectives, including innovative instruments that fund sustainable development and reward ESG achievements. This focus is further expanded in "Global obstacles and opportunities for regulated financial institutions" by Nicola Higgs, Anne Mainwaring and Gary Whitehead from Latham & Watkins, who delve into the regulatory environment of ESG in the financial sector, discussing compliance challenges and the potential for regulatory harmonisation.

The book then presents a mosaic of ESG global perspectives, with insights from Robin Hulshizer and Sophie Lamb KC looking at global litigation trends; Edward Kempson, Chidi Onyeche, Kathleen Teo and David Ziyambi from Latham & Watkins on Africa; Farhana Sharmeen, also from Latham & Watkins, on Asia; Christine Covington and Kate Gill-Herdman from Corrs Chambers Westgarth on the Australia and New Zealand region; and Milenko Bertrand-Galindo, Paula Errázuriz Sotta and Bernardita Salvatierra Riquelme from Bertrand-Galindo Barrueto Barroilhet on Latin America. Each author provides a regional analysis of ESG challenges and initiatives, reflecting the diverse approaches and developments across continents.

Lastly, the book assesses the way in which the market is responding to these shifts in the ESG terrain. In "ESG in the insurance sector", Daniela Bergs and Thomas Kelly from Howden examine how the insurance industry is responding to ESG, developing aligned products and managing associated risks. Kristina Wyatt from Persefoni, in "How technology is transforming ESG reporting", highlights the role of technology in enhancing ESG data collection, analysis and reporting, thereby improving ESG performance. The final chapter, "What's next for ESG? Leading perspectives on the future development of ESG", considers forward-looking perspectives on ESG, with contributions from: Reena SenGupta (RSGI Limited); Ruth Knox and Sabrina Zhang (Paul Hastings); Helene Banks and Gregory Battista (Cahill Gordon & Reindel); Glenn O'Halloran (Howden); Jonathan Friedman (Anthesis Group); Aiste Brackley (ERM); and Cornelia Gomez (General Atlantic). The chapter identifies the drivers of change and sets expectations for the evolution of ESG strategies and practices from various sector-specific angles, including the legal sector, insurance, finance and private equity.

5.   Conclusion and looking forward

The multifaceted nature of ESG requires a multidisciplinary understanding. It cuts across diverse areas such as environmental law, energy regulation, corporate governance and anti-corruption measures. Practitioners in this evolving field must be adept at juggling various considerations, often simultaneously, to ensure that their organisations or clients not only comply with current standards but are also well-positioned for future developments.

This handbook aims to be a valuable resource for those navigating this complex ESG terrain, offering guidance and insights to help balance the many 'spinning plates' of ESG practice.

Energy transition and climate issues

Andrew Angle
Aiste Brackley
Mark Lee
ERM Sustainability Institute

1. Introduction

Climate targets are proliferating as companies and governments react to the increasing impacts and urgency of climate change. However, the Paris Agreement goals look increasingly challenging, and climate-related events, such as the wildfires, droughts and heatwaves in Europe, North America and Asia, show that even less than 1.5°C of warming presents potential material risk.

While increasing climate ambition and target setting from companies and governments is positive, doubts about implementation feasibility are rising given the scale of the task. The International Monetary Fund estimates that US$6–10 trillion in additional public and private investment (equivalent to 6–10% of global GDP) is needed in the next decade alone to reach net zero emissions by 2050, demonstrating the magnitude of the transformation that would be required.[1]

Decarbonisation of the global economy will require companies to fundamentally rethink how they do business. It is therefore critical that boards and corporate leaders up and down value chains possess the climate-related expertise necessary to imagine and enact change. Board oversight of climate topics is becoming more common within the largest global corporations and some other leading companies. According to one study, 90% of the world's 166 largest corporate greenhouse gas (GHG) emitters now have some level of board oversight of climate change. CDP added a new question to its 2022 climate change questionnaire asking companies to disclose if at least one board member has climate-related competence, another sign of increasing expectations. Companies are likely to be cautious in claiming they already have the required knowledge and skills, especially given that the 2022 Taskforce on Climate-Related Financial Disclosures (TCFD) Status Report found that only 29% of TCFD-aligned disclosures report on board climate oversight. This wariness is understandable; after all, no one has previously led an organisation, let alone the global economy, all the way through decarbonisation to net zero.

---

[1] F Jaumotte and G Schwerhoff, "Reaching Net Zero Emissions" 29 July 2022, www.imf.org/en/Blogs/Articles/2021/07/22/blog-reaching-net-zero-emissions.

2. Climate uncertainties

2.1 Financial risk and opportunity

Beyond risk, the private sector's understanding of climate-related financial opportunities is improving. According to one study, transitioning to renewable energy could save up to US$12 trillion globally by 2050; similarly, CDP found that European companies investing in emissions-reduction initiatives expect bottom-line contributions of more than €40 billion (US$39.8 billion) from associated cost savings.[2,3] In many cases, simple steps such as implementing energy efficiency measures can significantly improve the bottom line. For example, IBM implemented 936 energy conservation projects in 2021 that saved US$9.9 million.[4]

2.2 Policy

In a recent survey of US-headquartered companies conducted by ERM and the Environmental Defense Fund (EDF), half of respondents identified policy and regulation as the external drivers most able to accelerate corporate decarbonisation.[5] While policies and regulations are changing, they are not evolving at the speed required to turbocharge transformation of the global economy.

Globally, 151 of 198 countries have set net zero emissions targets covering 88% of global emissions as of February 2024.[6] The United States passed the Inflation Reduction Act of 2022 (IRA), which may contribute to the country reducing its GHG emissions by half from 2005 levels by 2030 and reaching net zero by 2050.[7] In Europe, the European Union passed the European Climate Law, which affirmed its aspiration to achieve climate neutrality by 2050, while China has committed to reach net zero before 2060.[8,9]

To ensure accurate and verifiable progress, regulators and policymakers also increasingly target greenwashing by organisations. Greenwashing techniques

---

2   R Way *et al*, "Empirically grounded technology forecasts and the energy transition", 13 September 2022, www.cell.com/joule/fulltext/S2542-4351(22)00410-X.

3   Oliver Wyman, "Doubling Down: Europe's Low-Carbon Investment Opportunity", February 2020, www.oliverwyman.com/content/dam/oliver-wyman/v2/media/2020/February/Doubling-down_Europes_low_carbon_investment_opportunity.pdf.

4   International Business Machines Corporation (IBM), "IBM 2021 ESG Report", www.ibm.com/impact/files/reports-policies/2021/IBM_2021_ESG_Report.pdf.

5   A Angle and M Lee, "Net Zero: Obstacles and Catalysts for Business Climate Action, www.sustainability.com/thinking/net-zero-obstacles-and-catalysts-for-business-climate-action/.

6   Data Explorer, https://zerotracker.net/.

7   117th Congress, H R 5376 – 117th Congress: Inflation Reduction Act of 2022, www.congress.gov/bill/117th-congress/house-bill/5376.

8   European Commission, "European Climate Law" https://climate.ec.europa.eu/eu-action/european-green-deal/european-climate-law.en.

9   People's Republic of China, "China's Achievements, New Goals and New Measures for Nationally Determined Contributions" https://unfccc.int/sites/default/files/NDC/2022-06/China's%20Achievements%2C%20New%20Goals%20and%20New%20Measures%20for%20Nationally%20Determined%20Contributions.pdf.

include misleading consumers and investors with false or unsubstantiated sustainability claims, using offsets or renewable energy certificates of questionable quality, setting long-term net zero targets that exclude Scope 3 emissions or lack concrete intermediate targets, and executive performance bonuses tied to soft and insignificant ESG targets. The global trend towards mandatory ESG disclosures and specification of what counts as a sustainable activity puts increasing pressure on companies, making greenwashing practices a punishable offence with potential financial and legal repercussions.

2.3 Energy security and equity

Preventing disruption from global warming and ecosystem collapse is the leading driver for countries and corporations to accelerate decarbonisation. But geopolitical considerations also play an increasingly important role. Both the war in Ukraine and the recently intensified Israeli–Palestinian conflict did and have the potential to profoundly destabilise fossil fuel supply and prices. It is a stark reminder that fossil fuels are the Achilles heel for many economies that make the upscaling of renewable alternatives more desirable.

On the other hand, it is becoming clear that rapid growth of renewable capacity creates new dependencies, notably on a handful of countries that produce and process the critical minerals vital for the renewable energy transition. China, already the indispensable country for solar panels and electric vehicle (EV) battery components, also accounts for 60% of global production and 85% of the processing capacity of critical minerals.[10]

Diverging priorities and outlooks between developed nations, on the one hand, and middle-income and developing countries on the other, is another important factor influencing the global speed of decarbonisation. Many developing and middle-income countries feel they should be granted more leeway to continue using fossil fuels than rich nations since the latter group heavily relied on fossil energy for centuries to build its current wealth.

Many developed nations agree in principle but have been slow to deliver on promises to support decarbonisation in developing nations. Their decade-old pledge to provide US$100 billion annually for this purpose has yet to be fulfilled. The Loss and Damage Fund agreed upon during the climate summit in Egypt in 2022 has also come to a standstill, further fuelling disappointment among developing and middle-income countries.[11] It's also clear that public funds from rich countries alone won't be enough and will have to be complemented by significant private capital flows. In 2030, developing

---

10   B Glaser and A Wulf, "China's Role in Critical Mineral Supply Chains", 2 August 2023, www.gmfus.org/
      news/chinas-role-critical-mineral-supply-chains.
11   V Volcovici, "Countries deadlocked on 'loss and damage' fund as UN climate summit nears", 23 October
      2023, www.reuters.com/sustainability/cop/countries-deadlocked-loss-damage-fund-un-climate-summit-
      nears-2023-10-23/.

countries, excluding China, will need US$2.8 trillion a year to keep decarbonisation in line with the Paris Climate Agreement.[12]

2.4   Technology

Scaling uptake of the most advanced decarbonisation technologies available today and rapidly innovating others will be key to meeting corporate climate commitments. However, most companies lack the knowledge required to integrate existing solutions into their operations, and they can struggle to raise funds to develop technologies that are not yet available.

Rapidly falling costs and increasing demand help make the business case for the use of low-carbon technologies. For instance, in 2021, the cost of electricity produced from solar photovoltaics fell by 13% from 2020, by 15% for onshore wind and by 13% for offshore wind.[13]

In addition to renewables, hydrogen is another technology with potential to play an important role in the green energy transition. Worth US$1 billion in 2021, the green hydrogen market is projected to grow to US$72 billion by 2030.[14] This rapid growth signals significant market opportunities and could make decarbonisation easier for companies in hard-to-abate sectors like steel. For example, multinational steel manufacturer ArcelorMittal is looking to replace the natural gas used in the traditional iron-making process with hydrogen, which, if produced from a net zero process, would enable net zero production.[15]

Despite costs falling and markets growing, decarbonisation technology investment must increase precipitously. The World Economic Forum found that investments in breakthrough technologies such as bioenergy; carbon capture, utilisation and storage (CCUS); and hydrogen must be 10 times larger in 2030 than in 2020 if the world is to achieve net zero by 2050.[16]

Partnerships will be key to scaling investments in breakthrough technologies. In Europe, groups of companies are creating 'industrial clusters' to pool resources and expertise to support CCUS and hydrogen technology development.

---

12   The World Bank, "What You Need to Know About How CCDRs Estimate Climate Finance Needs", 13 March 2023, www.worldbank.org/en/news/feature/2023/03/13/what-you-need-to-know-about-how-ccdrs-estimate-climate-finance-needs.

13   International Renewable Energy Agency, "Renewable Power Remains Cost-Competitive amid Fossil Fuel Crisis", 13 July 2022, www.irena.org/news/pressreleases/2022/Jul/Renewable-Power-Remains-Cost-Competitive-amid-Fossil-Fuel-Crisis.

14   Straits Research, "Green Hydrogen Market Size is projected to reach USD 72 billion by 2030, growing at a CAGR of 55%: Straits Research", 29 June 2022, www.globenewswire.com/news-release/2022/06/29/2471419/0/en/Green-Hydrogen-Market-Size-is-projected-to-reach-USD-72-Billion-by-2030-growing-at-a-CAGR-of-55-Straits-Research.html.

15   ArcelorMittal, "Climate Action: Technology pathways to net-zero steel", https://corporate.arcelormittal.com/climate-action/ technology-pathways-to-net-zero-steel.

16   World Economic Forum, "Financing the Transition to a Net-Zero Future", October 2021, www3.weforum.org/docs/WEF_Financing_the_Transition_to_a_Net_Zero_Future_2021.pdf.

3. A blueprint for action

3.1 Introduction

In an age of climate uncertainty, there are big questions, including: What new financial risks and opportunities will emerge? Which types of disclosures will investors demand next? What other leadership expectations will stakeholders – from consumers and employees to citizens and communities – demand the private sector embrace to help address climate change? How fast will government policy evolve and how hard will it be to comply? What geopolitical events will speed or slow progress? And what technologies will scale quickly and cheaply enough to be implemented globally?

There are other uncertainties and questions beyond those discussed here – not least which climate-related events might cause cascading and potentially irreversible impacts, like the melting of permafrost or the collapse of a major ice sheet in Antarctica or Greenland – but the six presented here were chosen because of their near-universal relevance to businesses of all sizes and in all geographies today.

This section outlines how companies can best prepare themselves to navigate uncertainty and offers companies a framework for climate issues. This framework can help companies address climate strategy and goals, through opportunity prioritisation and operational implementation, product and service redesign and portfolio adjustment, and digital enablement and the change management necessary to support employees and maintain a resilient culture.

With so many factors driving business decarbonisation and the landscape shifting rapidly, developing a comprehensive and effective decarbonisation plan – and putting it into practice – requires significant commitment, resources, innovation, and time on the part of business leaders. The framework proposes companies prepare to meet uncertainty through six response elements as shown in Figure 1.

Figure 1: Six response areas[17]

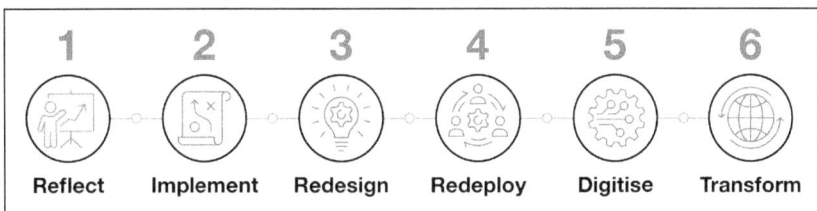

| 1 | 2 | 3 | 4 | 5 | 6 |
| Reflect | Implement | Redesign | Redeploy | Digitise | Transform |

---

17   A Angle, A Brackley, A Delpon Fuentes and M Lee, "The Decarbonization Imperative: An Executive Primer", www.sustainability.com/globalassets/sustainability.com/thinking/pdfs/2022/the-decarbonization-imperative.pdf.

3.2 Reflect

Robust analysis of where a company is and reflection on where it wants to go is at the core of setting strategy.

Decarbonisation strategies set end goals regarding climate change and chart how the company will get there. While strategy-setting is unique to each company, a well-planned and executed process usually involves, amongst other things:

- assessing climate-related risks and opportunities;
- setting climate goals; and
- designing a climate strategy and define overarching principles to guide your approach.

Key components of the assessment phase are landscape analysis and peer benchmarking, which are both effective tools for identifying the areas where a company is already leading and the gaps where action is needed the most. Scenario analysis of climate-related risks and opportunities is also essential to prepare for setting strategy.

These activities help lay the groundwork for setting comprehensive, science-based goals, which are at the core of strong decarbonisation strategy. Robust climate goals should be informed by the latest science, include all value chain emissions and define interim targets in addition to long-term commitments. Unfortunately, corporate net zero commitments often don't meet these criteria. For instance, according to a recent analysis of 150 of the largest corporate GHG emitters, only 13% have set medium-term targets that are aligned with the International Energy Agency's 1.5°C scenario and cover all material emissions. Just 35% have comprehensive net zero by 2050 or sooner commitments that cover all GHG emissions including Scope 3.[18]

"Robust climate goals must be informed by the latest science, include all value chain emissions and define interim targets in addition to long-term commitments."

The use of high-quality and rigorously vetted offsets also needs to be incorporated into goal-setting efforts. While offsets should never dilute efforts to decarbonise value chains, investment in carbon credits such as Natural Climate Solutions (which deliver social and biodiversity benefits in addition to addressing carbon) will be essential for achieving emissions reduction targets on a global scale.[19]

The process of designing a robust strategy rests heavily on goals but must also include detailed roadmaps that will help translate strategy into action on the

---

18   Climate Action 100+, "Climate Action 100+ Net Zero Company Benchmark 2.0 2023 Results", October 2023, www.climateaction100.org/wp-content/uploads/2023/10/2023-Key-Findings.pdf.

19   A Brackley *et al*, "Natural Climate Solutions and the Voluntary Carbon Market: A Guide for C-suite Executives", September 2022, www.wbcsd.org/contentwbc/download/14832/210827/1.

ground as well as more holistic principles to underpin a company's approach to climate. For instance, Japanese automobile manufacturer Nissan Motor Corporation strives to achieve a "symbiosis of people, vehicles and nature" with its overarching environmental philosophy encompassing three major action areas: energy (higher efficiency and renewable), resources (reduced use and recycling) and social and economic activities (within levels nature can absorb).[20]

An essential element of climate strategy design is its alignment with the core corporate strategy. However, it is also a step that many companies find difficult. Developing and delivering a climate strategy that connects climate goals with broader business objectives is the step that companies most struggle with on their net zero journey. In many cases, aligning the two might require entirely reimagining the business model.

While complicated, if the process is done right, it can deliver many benefits. For instance, Italian power company Enel has transformed its business model into one that produces more than 50% of its electricity from renewables after predominantly using fossil fuels throughout its history. With 56 gigawatts of installed capacity, Enel is one of the world's largest private renewables utilities, operating in more than 30 countries on five continents.[21]

3.3   Implement

After the reflect phase has enabled risk and opportunity assessment, goal setting and strategy design, companies should focus on implementation.

Translating strategy into action is not simple. ERM research with EDF indicated that 92% of surveyed companies reported facing challenges when putting net zero commitments into practice. In fact, most businesses struggle to translate high-level strategy and commitments into operational plans and actions on the ground, with only 19% of surveyed companies reporting they had launched a fully costed and fully funded decarbonisation effort.[22]

Many factors determine how successful businesses are at operationalising decarbonisation strategy and goals. To achieve desired outcomes, companies need to produce detailed roadmaps and implementation plans that can be embedded across all core business functions and operations. Crucially, all these efforts must receive adequate resources and investment.

It's critical to have the full view of emissions and then identify and implement measures to effectively reduce them to target levels. We would recommend emphasising the following steps:

20   Nissan Motor Corporation, "Sustainability Report 2022", www.nissan-global.com/EN/SUSTAINABILITY/LIBRARY/SR/2022/ASSETS/PDF/SR22_E_All.pdf.

21   Enel Green Power, "Enel Green Power sets new records in 2022 for renewable capacity built and under construction, energy generated and projects developed worldwide", 30 January 2023, www.enelgreenpower.com/media/press/2023/01/new-records-2022-renewable-capacity.

22   A Angle and M Lee, "Net Zero: Obstacles and Catalysts for Business Climate Action", www.sustainability.com/thinking/net-zero-obstacles-and-catalysts-for-business-climate-action/.

- conducting a GHG emissions inventory;
- prioritising decarbonisation opportunities;
- implementing decarbonisation action plans; and
- publishing climate-related disclosures.

Companies should first conduct a GHG emissions inventory to determine their baseline emissions. Using the results, they can identify and prioritise decarbonisation opportunities.

As companies sort decarbonisation choices, they must remain cognisant of their emissions profile (ie, which Scope composes most of their emissions). For most companies, the largest emissions will be Scope 3, which average 11.4 times greater than Scope 1 and 2 emissions combined.[23,24] However, reducing Scope 3 emissions is one of the biggest climate action challenges companies face, due to lack of control.

"In a survey of US companies, 92% of respondents reported facing challenges when putting net zero commitments into practice."[25]

While decarbonisation across all Scopes is challenging, especially for companies with complex supply chains and those in hard-to-abate industries, developing and implementing comprehensive decarbonisation action plans can make the process easier. For instance, Holcim, a Swiss-based building materials and aggregates company, began its Scope 3 decarbonisation journey in 2020 by quantifying and categorising its Scope 3 emissions. From this data, the company created specific action plans to operationalise these commitments such as optimising shipping routes and loads and replacing fossil fuels with alternative biofuels.[26] Together, these actions will help the company achieve net zero Scope 3 emissions by 2050.

With assessment converted to operational roadmaps and plans, companies need to develop systems to track and report progress in ways that meet the climate-related disclosure expectations of regulators, investors and other stakeholders. One of the most widely used frameworks for climate-related disclosures is TCFD, whose recommendations are tailored to help companies publish "decision-useful, forward-looking information" in their financial reporting.[27]

---

23   CDP, "CDP Technical Note: Relevance of Scope 3 Categories by Sector CDP Climate Change Questionnaire", https://cdn.cdp.net/cdp-production/cms/guidance_docs/pdfs/000/003/504/original/CDP-technical-note-scope-3-relevance-by-sector.pdf?1649687608.

24   CDP, "Engaging the Chain: Driving Speed and Scale CDP Global Supply Chain Report 2021", February 2022, https://cdn.cdp.net/cdp-production/cms/reports/documents/000/006/106/original/CDP_SC_Report_2021.pdf?1644513297.

25   A Angle and M Lee, "Net Zero: Obstacles and Catalysts for Business Climate Action", www.sustainability.com/thinking/net-zero-obstacles-and-catalysts-for-business-climate-action/.

26   Holcim Ltd, "Holcim's Net-Zero Journey – Climate Report 2022", www.holcim.com/sites/holcim/files/2022-04/08042022-holcim-climate-report-2022.pdf.

27   The Task Force on Climate-related Financial Disclosures, "TCFD Recommendations", www.fsb-tcfd.org/recommendations/.

3.4   Redesign

Redesigning products and services is a critical step in achieving effective decarbonisation of the private sector and reaching global net zero emissions goals.

Figure 2: Proposed approach for designing products aligned with circular principles[28]

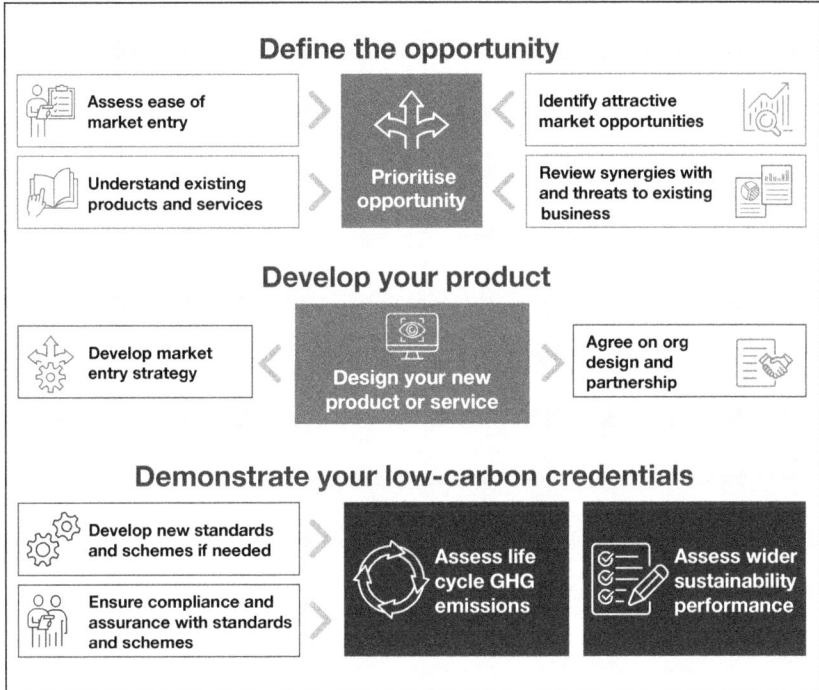

Define the opportunity

Assess ease of market entry	Identify attractive market opportunities
Understand existing products and services	Review synergies with and threats to existing business

Prioritise opportunity

Develop your product

Develop market entry strategy	Agree on org design and partnership

Design your new product or service

Demonstrate your low-carbon credentials

Develop new standards and schemes if needed	Assess life cycle GHG emissions
Ensure compliance and assurance with standards and schemes	Assess wider sustainability performance

According to the Ellen McArthur Foundation, more than 45% of global emissions are associated with making products, meaning circular economy approaches will be critical to reducing the carbon footprint associated with manufacturing.[29] Redesigning the ways we produce and consume, however, will take time. As companies redesign their businesses, they must consider that mainstream adoption of low-carbon products and services may be slow. They also must be open to embracing the new ways of working that will be required to align their portfolio with their climate commitments and develop the kinds of partnerships needed to scale action.

---

28   A Angle, A Brackley, A Delpon Fuentes and M Lee, "The Decarbonization Imperative: An Executive Primer", www.sustainability.com/globalassets/sustainability.com/thinking/pdfs/2022/the-decarbonization-imperative.pdf.

29   Ellen MacArthur Foundation, "Completing the Picture – How the circular economy tackles climate change", www.ellenmacarthurfoundation.org/completing-the-picture.

The three-step process in Figure 2 above helps guide companies' redesign efforts:

- identify and prioritise climate-related market opportunities;
- develop new products or services to meet identified market opportunities; and
- demonstrate your low-carbon credentials.

To begin, companies must identify and prioritise attractive climate-related market opportunities, a process that should consider the ease with which a company can enter the identified market, and how well identified opportunities align with a company's business model and existing products and services. After identifying such opportunities, companies should develop their new climate-related products or services accompanied by an effective market entry strategy.

While all sectors will have to develop new products and services through a climate impact lens, redesign is especially important for companies in hard-to-abate sectors like cement, steel and energy. Because of the nature of their operations, these sectors' future viability relies disproportionally on their ability to transform their business model away from carbon-intensive products and processes. According to the Ellen McArthur Foundation, when applied to four key industrial materials (eg, cement, steel, plastic and aluminum), circular economy strategies could help cut their emissions by 40% by 2050.[30]

Many companies in hard-to-abate sectors are already reimagining their products and services for decarbonisation. Dow aims to use circular solutions to support its goal to reduce GHG emissions by 15% by 2030 from a 2020 baseline and achieve carbon neutrality by 2050. Dow's solutions centre on using fewer resources to manufacture its products, partnering to reduce waste by rethinking business models, and working with customers to design products to extend their life.[31]

"While all sectors will have to develop new products and services through a climate impact lens, redesign is especially important for companies in hard-to-abate sectors like cement, steel and energy."

In another hard-to-abate industry, aluminium producer Novelis's use of recycled aluminium helps it reduce emissions across its value chain as it works toward carbon neutrality by 2050 or sooner. Currently, 57% of its inputs are recycled aluminium, which uses 5% of the energy used to create primary

---

30   Ellen MacArthur Foundation, "Completing the Picture – How the circular economy tackles climate change", www.ellenmacarthurfoundation.org/completing-the-picture.
31   Dow Corporate, "Reducing emissions", https://corporate.dow.com/en-us/science-and-sustainability/ commits-to-reduce-emissions-and-waste.html.

aluminium, and emits as little as half a ton of carbon dioxide compared to the four to 20 tons of carbon dioxide needed to produce equivalent primary aluminium.[32]

After identifying market opportunities and developing new products and services, companies will need to demonstrate their low-carbon credentials by validating that these offerings contribute to decarbonisation. The most direct way to do so is using assurance standards and schemes such as Carbon Trust's Product carbon footprint label, which confirms that a company is tracking and reducing a product's emissions.[33]

3.5 Redeploy

In addition to reflection, implementation and redesign, many companies will need to revise their approach to capital projects and readjust their corporate structure and holdings through mergers, acquisitions and divestments.

Although frequently associated with heavy industry, capital projects matter to companies in all sectors and can be thought of as any project involving significant investment, a long lifespan and complex development. These characteristics mean that such projects generally take time to implement, making it imperative that companies revise approaches now to ensure their capital projects align with their decarbonisation commitments and avoid carbon lock-in.

While critically important, revising approaches to capital projects and readjusting corporate structures and holdings in line with decarbonisation plans is challenging. Only 5% of the over 150 Climate Action 100+ focus companies have committed to align their capex strategies with their climate commitments.[34] Surmounting this requires acting with climate in mind across four redeployment-focused steps:

- plan and design capital projects for climate-related risks;
- build capital projects in a way that minimises emissions and increases climate resiliency;
- operate capital projects in an emissions-efficient manner and reduce end-of-life climate impacts; and
- readjust your corporate structure and holdings for decarbonisation through mergers, acquisitions and divestments.

To achieve the level of decarbonisation required, capital investment will need to rise precipitously.

According to the International Energy Agency (IEA), decarbonisation-related

---

32   Novelis, "Sustainability", www.novelis.com/sustainability/.
33   Carbon Trust, "Assurance and certification: Product carbon footprint label", www.carbontrust.com/what-we-do/assurance-and-certification/product-carbon-footprint-label.
34   Climate Action 100+, "Climate Action 100+ Net Zero Company Benchmark shows an increase in company net zero commitments, but much more urgent action is needed to align with a 1.5°C future", 30 March 2022, www.ceres.org/news-center/press-releases/climate-action-100-net-zero-company-benchmark-shows-increase-company-net.

capital investment must grow from approximately US$2 trillion today to close to US$5 trillion by 2030 and US$4.5 trillion by 2050 if the world is to achieve net zero emissions by 2050. These investments will likely fund a major uptick in capital deployment for specific technologies. For example, the IEA says that renewables as a total share of global electricity generation must rise from 29% in 2020 to nearly 90% by 2050.[35]

Companies will also want to consider emissions and climate resiliency from the very initial stages of planning and design. New capital deployment, including for renewable energy sites, requires careful assessment of social and environmental impacts. Once a project is operational, there is a need to continue efforts to minimise day-to-day emissions through operational efficiency measures. Companies also need to anticipate the end of a project's lifecycle and develop decommissioning strategies that reduce end-of life climate impacts.

"[T]he IEA says that renewables as a total share of global electricity must rise from 29% in 2020 to nearly 90% by 2050."

For many companies, rapidly delivering on decarbonisation commitments and avoiding climate-related risk will also require adjusting their corporate structure and holdings, specifically through mergers and acquisitions of low-carbon assets as well as thoughtful divestments of carbon-intensive or climate-vulnerable assets. For successful implementation of capital projects as well as portfolio adjustments, financial institutions have critical roles to play. Many financial institutions are accelerating funding for projects that reduce emissions. For instance, Bank of America has set emissions reduction targets for its financing activities in the auto manufacturing, energy and power generation sectors.[36]

Divestments of carbon-intensive or climate-vulnerable assets can help companies and investors reduce their climate change contributions and exposures. However, divestments can simply pass contributions and exposures on to the next organisation, where they may not be managed well. To avoid this compounding overall climate impact while reducing it for one company, the Glasgow Financial Alliance for Net Zero (GFANZ) encourages companies and investors to pursue managed phaseout of carbon-intensive assets by retiring them before the end of their lifecycle rather than selling them into situations where they continue high carbon operation.[37]

35   International Energy Agency, "Net Zero by 2050 – A Roadmap for the Global Energy Sector", October 2021, https://iea.blob.core.windows.net/assets/deebef5d-0c34-4539-9d0c-10b13d840027/NetZeroby 2050-ARoadmapfortheGlobalEnergySector_CORR.pdf.

36   Bank of America, "Bank of America Announces 2030 Financing Activity Targets as Part of Net Zero Commitment", 13 April 2022, https://newsroom.bankofamerica.com/content/newsroom/press-releases/ 2022/04/bank-of-america-announces-2030-financing-activity-targets-as-par.html#.

37   Glasgow Financial Alliance for Net Zero, "The Managed Phaseout of High-emitting Assets", June 2022, https://assets.bbhub.io/company/sites/63/2022/06/GFANZ_-Managed-Phaseout-of-High-emitting-Assets_June2022.pdf.

3.6   Digitise

Digital tools will play a critical role in achieving global emissions goals by helping to optimise operations, maximise energy efficiency gains, and support performance tracking, among many other ways.

According to the World Economic Forum, digital technologies could deliver one-third of the emissions reductions required by 2030 to keep the world on track to limit global temperature rise to well below 2°C.

Digital tools support corporate climate action in many ways. Digital tools are often facilitators of climate action rather than direct solutions, enabling more efficient decarbonisation by improving existing processes and efforts. Digital solutions facilitate and accelerate decarbonisation in multiple ways, such as by:

- enabling more efficient decarbonisation by optimising operations;
- improving assessment of company exposure to climate-related risks and opportunities; and
- supporting climate-related performance tracking and disclosure.

"ERM's emissions.AI tool can help companies optimise their energy use, lowering emissions and their associated costs by as much as 7.5% annually."

Digital tools excel at helping companies reduce emissions through optimisation of operations. Developing a digital decarbonisation plan is foundational to realising this benefit. That plan will outline and explain the role digital will play in reducing emissions and pinpoint the parts of operations and geographical locations where the most emissions reductions can be achieved.

For example, one such tool for carbon-intensive companies is 'emissions.AI' developed by ERM. The tool helps to identify hidden operational inefficiencies using engineering-first principles, analytics and artificial intelligence that, when addressed, can help companies optimise their energy use, lowering emissions and their associated costs by as much as 7.5%.[38]

Digital tools can also help companies assess their exposure to climate-related risks and opportunities as part of scenario analysis. For example, ERM's Climate Impact Platform uses predictive analytics to help companies assess how vulnerable its assets are to climate change.

In addition to enabling more direct corporate climate action, digital tools play essential roles in supporting climate-related performance tracking and disclosure. The growing carbon accounting software industry is helping companies more accurately track and manage emissions as they decarbonise. Tracking emissions through these software platforms also makes climate-related disclosure easier by aggregating data from across an organisation in one place.

---

38   ERM, "emissions.AI for complex facilities", www.erm.com/service/digital-services/emissions-ai/.

3.7   Transform

The transformation required to achieve decarbonisation goals is as much about people and culture as products and services or practices and processes.

Even with a climate strategy, implementation plan, revised product portfolio, new thinking about capital and digital tools in place, most companies will need to undergo significant transformation to thrive in the future low-carbon economy.

To effectively transform organisational culture and guide their people through the challenges of the net zero transition, companies need to embrace change management best practices to:

- incorporate decarbonisation into governance;
- address climate-related knowledge and skills gaps among employees; and
- support employees and partners through the transformation.

By preparing a structured approach for addressing governance- and culture-related change, companies will be better positioned to quickly decarbonise and seize value creation opportunities. Well-designed change programmes define how change will occur (eg, integrating decarbonisation thinking into broader business strategy), how change will be implemented (eg, redesigning the organisational structure to deliver decarbonisation) and how change will be embedded (eg, by defining the actions core business functions need to take to achieve decarbonisation commitments). Additionally, for change to take hold, companies must mobilise their workforce by engaging them in the decarbonisation journey and leveraging their expertise to scale impact.

It is also important for companies to incorporate decarbonisation into governance to ensure appropriate oversight of implementation of climate commitments. While the board of directors is ultimately responsible for governance, the exact structure and form of climate governance mechanisms will vary depending on company size and circumstance, and there are also critical management roles associated with governance.

As one example of how climate-related governance can work, Dow created a global programme management office (PMO). Dow's PMO has four governance tracks: Scope 1 and 2 emissions, Scope 3 emissions, product benefits, and new ventures. The PMO also is responsible for enabling platforms (eg, initiatives that ensure consistent climate-related communications, metrics and reporting) that help the tracks work in concert.[39] Dow's Climate Steering Team, which comprises business presidents and functional leaders, oversees both the PMO and the enabling platforms. To ensure consistent progress, Dow based the PMO's structure on other existing governance structures so that climate could be governed within their organisational matrix.

---

39   A Sundareshwar and A Angle, "From Promise to Action on Net Zero – An Interview with Dow", www.sustainability.com/thinking/an-interview-with-dow/.

Figure 3: Blueprint for Action: What to Prioritise[40]

Blueprint for Action: What to Prioritise

Reflect

Set interim and long-term climate commitments in line with the Paris Agreement's 1.5°C ambition.

Design a decarbonisation strategy that outlines how you will achieve your climate commitments, defines how you will approach decarbonisation, and aligns with your overall business strategy.

Implement

Operationalise strategy and goals with the help of detailed roadmaps and implementation plans.

Conduct a comprehensive GHG emissions inventory and prioritise and pursue reduction opportunities based on abatement effectiveness as well as economic and technological feasibility.

Redesign

Identify attractive climate-related market opportunities for existing and new products and services.

Develop a product or service to meet identified opportunities and create a market entry strategy.

Redeploy

Develop a capital project deployment strategy that accounts for physical and transition climate-related risks, minimises emissions, and reduces end-of-life climate impacts.

Adjust your portfolio through low carbon-focused mergers and acquisitions and divestments of carbon-intensive or climate-vulnerable assets in ways that align with your climate strategy.

Digitise

Optimise operations for emissions reductions and energy efficiency gains with digital tools.

Improve climate-related planning and disclosure by using digital tools to assess your exposure to climate-related risks and opportunities.

Transform

Incorporate climate action into corporate governance by establishing clear structures and processes for decarbonisation.

Equip employees with the climate-related knowledge and skills needed to support decarbonisation through targeted education and training.

"In addition to strong governance, companies must equip their workforces with climate-related knowledge and skills to maximise the impact of their decarbonisation-focused business transformation."

---

40   A Angle, A Brackley, A Delpon Fuentes and M Lee, "The Decarbonization Imperative: An Executive Primer", www.sustainability.com/globalassets/sustainability.com/thinking/pdfs/2022/the-decarbonization-imperative.pdf.

TCFD provides clear guidance on climate-related governance outlining the roles that board members and management should play in managing associated risks and opportunities.[41] In addition to strong governance, companies must equip their workforces with the climate-related knowledge and skills needed to maximise the impact of their decarbonisation-focused business transformation. Companies should concentrate on expanding knowledge through education efforts so employees understand what decarbonisation will require from them. For instance, insurance company AXA has established a 'Climate Academy' which aspires to train all its employees on climate-related issues.[42]

Companies must also help employees manage the workplace disruption wrought by transformation. Supporting employees is critical to maintaining cohesive corporate culture and building internal buy-in for climate action, for instance, when fears of job transfers and/or layoffs grow within companies preparing to decarbonise. Support involves retraining employees for the new roles suited to the low-carbon economy. For example, Danish energy company Ørsted recently partnered with North America's Building Trades Unions (NABTU) to construct offshore wind farms using union workforces.[43] Through the partnership, Ørsted will train and create apprenticeships to equip union contractors and subcontractors involved in its projects with the skills required to be successful in the offshore wind industry.

4.   Conclusion

This chapter emphasises the importance of private sector action to help address the climate crisis, explores information and knowledge gaps that cause hesitation, and presents a blueprint for the kinds of corporate reaction and response required to create momentum.

With multiple milestones critical to keeping the ambition of the Paris Agreement in reach so near, acknowledging the gravity of the moment is increasingly straightforward for many leaders across all sectors of society.

Grappling with the uncertainties accompanying the drivers that shape the financial risk and opportunity aspects of climate change is more difficult, but critical to progress on the climate agenda and to the future success of individual companies and their leaders. Business leaders need to grasp that the uncertainties discussed in this chapter will shape the future context in which companies decarbonise.

The points above – the notions that addressing the climate crisis and

---

41   The Task Force on Climate-related Financial Disclosures, "TCFD Recommendations", www.fsb-tcfd.org/recommendations/.
42   AXA, "Making AXA's employees pioneers to fight climate change", 25 October 2021, www.axa.com/en/magazine/axa-employees-and-climate-change.
43   Ørsted, "North America's Building Trades Unions and Ørsted Agree to Build an American Offshore Wind Energy Industry with American Labor", 5 May 2022, https://us.orsted.com/news-archive/2022/05/national-offshore-wind-agreement.

business as a growing concern are now wholly intertwined, and that climate uncertainties are shaping the future – give reason for optimism. Those that embrace this change – including the framework – will have the opportunity to support the low-carbon energy transition while also building the adaptability and resilience their organisations will need to survive it.

This will demand new approaches to strategy and goal setting, operations, product and service portfolios, capital expenditure and digital solutions. It also requires tremendous care managing the profound change that transformation will impose on leaders at all levels of corporations, from boards and the ranks of senior executives to operational and frontline workers. However, the years and decades ahead will not be tranquil either; they will be some of the most tempestuous, difficult, dynamic and competitive that the private sector has ever experienced, making business leadership's understanding and application of climate an essential competency.

While the urgency of the climate emergency and the scale and pace of change needed mean business leaders must increase climate knowledge and understanding rapidly, the same factors convey why business action cannot be delayed. Companies must start on the decarbonisation journey immediately, even if they are unsure of the specific path they will take and where it will ultimately lead.

We urge every company to embrace the imperative to apply the framework outlined in this chapter – or another – and commence the work of future-proofing their business against the impacts of the low-carbon transition while contributing to development of the net zero economy targeted by 2050.

Addressing human rights risks in global supply chains

Mariana Abreu
Ian Barclay
Stuart McLachlan
Anthesis Group
Amandine Bressand
ISEAL

1. Rights and risks at stake

1.1 Human rights risks in global supply chains

(a) Introduction

When considering the complexities of global supply chains there are a myriad of issues to consider across the ESG spectrum. On the environmental side, for example, biodiversity issues in supply chain considerations are increasingly important due to the direct and indirect impacts that global supply chains (GSC) can have on ecosystems, species diversity and natural habitats. Further, the issues brought forth by climate change give rise to challenges, impacting the stability, efficiency and sustainability of global supply chains. Whilst these topics and other issues are undoubtedly important when considering supply chain issues, this chapter is dedicated to addressing the relationship between supply chains and human rights.

Thirteen years after the adoption of the UN Guiding Principles on Business and Human Rights (UNGPs), the private sector faces increased scrutiny over its ESG performance. Increased convergence between international voluntary standards and emerging regulations on supply chain due diligence, like the proposed EU Corporate Sustainability Due Diligence Directive[1] (CSDDD), prompts companies and investors to address their adverse risks and impacts on universal human rights[2] in GSC.[3]

---

1   Proposal for a Directive of the European Parliament and of the Council on Corporate Sustainability Due Diligence and Amending Directive (EU) 2019/1937, COM/2022/72 final, 2022/0051 (COD).

2   Universal human rights are defined in the International Bill of Rights, which consists of the 1948 Universal Declaration of Human Rights (UDHR), the International Covenant on Economic, Social and Cultural Rights (ICESCR), the International Covenant on Civil and Political Rights (ICCPR) and its two optional protocols. International labour standards applicable to GSC also include the International Labour Organisation (ILO) Declaration on Fundamental Principles and Rights at Work (amended in 2022), made of 11 conventions on principles of free association and collective bargaining, abolition of forced and child labour, elimination of discrimination and the principle of a safe and healthy working environment.

The attribution of corporate responsibility to human rights impacts in GSC concerns direct and indirect business relationships[4] distributed across large networks of suppliers. The supply chain of a large multinational company may comprise tens of thousands of direct suppliers alone. As such, managing risks tied to these business relationships requires effective data collection, reliable risk assessments and actionable enforcement measures that are met with the practical challenges of scalability, methodology and leverage.

Relevant to both corporates and global investors, this chapter offers practical insights on key aspects of the UNGP-aligned Human Rights Due Diligence (HRDD) process applied to upstream supply chain risks. The first section defines human rights risks in GSC and their implications for businesses and investors. The second section provides a blueprint for effective risk assessment amidst practical limitations specific to GSC. The third section shares best practices for the integration of HRDD findings, with a focus on supplier engagement.

(b) *Managing interrelated supply chain risks*

Companies manage a broad range of supply chain risks to ensure the uninterrupted provision of goods and services, from economic disruptions, geopolitical instability, environmental and climate change, to global labour shortages. Addressing human rights risks in GSC must therefore be considered as part of a comprehensive supply chain risk management process, with the important distinction that managing human rights risks considers the risks to people rather than to the business.

Major vulnerabilities of GSC management include a company's foreign dependencies via its supply network, with risks of global disruptions observed during the COVID-19 pandemic. As a result, companies seek greater visibility over their supply network to manage operational and strategic risks as well as ESG-related risks.[5] Companies may, for example, pursue the reshoring of previously foreign suppliers to domestic locations to limit foreign dependencies and increase the resilience of supply networks against transnational disruptions.[6]

Furthermore, assessing a company's human rights footprint requires a

---

3   GSC thereafter refers to a company's upstream supply chain, which encompasses all the activities related to, and the entities involved with the various stages of its production process, including the extraction, sourcing, supply, manufacturing, production, transportation and storage of raw materials, products and services required for its operations. (Council of Supply Chain Management Professionals – CSCMP).

4   Business relationships means a company's direct or indirect business partners and entities in its value chain, and other non-state or state entities directly linked to business operations, products or services (UNGP 13 Commentary).

5   LM Ellram, WL Tate and KJ Petersen, "Offshoring and reshoring: an update on the manufacturing location decision', *Journal of Supply Chain Management*, 49(2) (2013), pp14–22.

6   NA Choudhary, M Ramkumar, T Schoenherr, NP Rana and YK Dwivedi, "Does Reshoring Affect the Resilience and Sustainability of Supply Chain Networks? The Cases of Apple and Jaguar Land Rover", *British Journal of Management*, 34 (2023), pp1138–1156, https://doi.org/10.1111/1467-8551.12614.

holistic view on ESG-related risks and impacts. Given the interdependency of universal rights, a company's adverse impact on the environment or biodiversity may have a human rights impact on communities. For example, a chemicals factory may contaminate local water sources on which neighbouring communities rely to live, or the commercial development of an area may cause biodiversity loss through land use change, which in turn affects the livelihoods of farming and fishing communities.[7]

(c) **Rights-holders subject to adverse impact**

Over one in five employments worldwide are estimated to be linked to GSC,[8] located in jurisdictions with very different human rights protection provisions. Rights-holders in GSC include workers formally employed across tiers of the supply chains, as well as contracted, subcontracted, unlawfully employed and forced or exploited labour. When assessing the impact on workers' rights, the entire employment lifecycle, from recruitment practices, working conditions and relocation, to employment termination should be considered.

According to the International Bill of Human Rights, consisting of the UN Declaration of Human Rights (UDHR), the International Covenant on Economic, Social and Cultural Rights (ICESCR) and the International Covenant on Civil and Political Rights (ICCPR), rights of workers include: the right to health (UDHR 25, ICESCR 12); the right to work and to just and favourable conditions of work (UDHR 23 and 24, ICESCR 7); the right to safe and healthy working conditions (UDHR 23, ICESCR 7); freedom of association and collective bargaining (UDHR 20, ICCPR 2 and 23, ICESCR 8); freedom of assembly (UDHR 20, ICCPR 21); and the right to equal pay for equal work (UDHR 23, ICESCR 7). Salient human rights risks for GSC workers include: exploitative labour practices, such as forced labour; debt bondage; labour exploitation for personal or commercial gains amounting to modern slavery; sexual and gender-based violence; and human trafficking.[9]

Beyond workers involved in the production of goods and services, rights-holders in GSC include communities affected by business activities, such as the residents of areas close to these operations. Implications on the rights of communities include land-related violations, impact on health due to contamination of their living environment and infringements on social and cultural rights. Certain rights-holders, such as children, women, migrant

---

7   R Panwar, H Ober and J Pinkse, "The uncomfortable relationship between business and biodiversity: Advancing research on business strategies for biodiversity protection", *Business Strategy and the Environment* (2022), pp1–13, https://doi.org/10.1002/bse.3139.

8   International Labour Organization (ILO), *World Employment Social Outlook* (2015); See also: ILO, *Integrated Strategy on Fundamental Principles and Rights at Work 2017–2023* (2019).

9   Forced labour is embedded in international rights including the: "right to freedom from forced labour and servitude" (UDHR 4, ICCPR 8), "right to freedom of movement" (UDHR 13, ICCPR 12); and "right to freedom from torture and other cruel or degrading treatment or punishment" (UDHR 5, ICCPR 7).

workers and indigenous peoples, are subject to vulnerabilities recognised in international law.[10]

(d) Scrutiny over forced labour in GSC and sector-wide risks

The number of individuals subject to modern slavery has significantly increased in recent years, rising to 50 million people in 2021.[11] Among them, 28 million were deemed subject to forced labour, including 17.3 million working in the private sector and 3.9 million in forced labour imposed by a state.[12] Well-documented cases of systemic forced labour in GSC, often picked up in mainstream media and political circles, include child-labour in the Democratic Republic of the Congo providing cobalt for phones and electric vehicles, Uyghur minorities in forced labour in the Xinjiang region of the People's Republic of China linked to the solar industry and migrant construction workers subject to labour exploitation on infrastructure projects like the 2022 FIFA Men's World Cup in Qatar.[13]

In response, the last decade has seen a raft of new legislation aimed at companies to ensure they address modern slavery and forced labour in their supply chains.[14] Trade-based legislations focused on import bans have also increased scrutiny over risks of forced labour, as seen with the Uyghur Forced Labor Prevention Act 2022 (United States).[15] The expectations and enforcement mechanisms of these laws is also increasing amidst new supply chain due diligence laws (see section 1.2 (a)).

We also note that patterns of human rights adverse impacts in GSC may occur at sector levels. The Organisation of Economic Cooperation and Development (OECD)'s sectoral guidance for investors and corporates calls for scrutiny in: (i) the extractive sector and mining, oil and gas industries; (ii) mineral supply chains and conflict minerals; (iii) garment and footwear supply

---

10   See UN Convention on the Rights of the Child; Convention on the Elimination of All Forms of Discrimination Against Women (CEDAW); Convention on the Elimination of Racial Discrimination (CERD); and ILO Convention 169 on Indigenous and Tribal Peoples.

11   ILO, WalkFree, International Organization for Migration (IOM), "Global Estimates of Modern Slavery: Forced Labour and Forced Marriage" (2021), www.ilo.org/wcmsp5/groups/public/—-ed_norm/—-ipec/documents/publication/wcms_854733.pdf.

12   *Ibid.*

13   N Elbagir, D van Heerden and E Mackintosh, "How child labour is prevalent in cobalt mines", CNN, (May 2018); Business & Human Rights Resource Centre (BHRRC), "China: 83 major brands implicated in report on forced labour of ethnic minorities from Xinjiang assigned to factories across provinces", (March 2020), www.business-humanrights.org/en/latest-news/china-83-major-brands-implicated-in-report-on-forced-labour-of-ethnic-minorities-from-xinjiang-assigned-to-factories-across-provinces-includes-company-responses/; BHRRC, "Labour rights and the Qatar World Cup 2022", (March 2023), www.business-humanrights.org/en/big-issues/major-sporting-events/labour-rights-and-the-qatar-world-cup-2022/.

14   See, for example, the UK Modern Slavery Act 2015, Australia's Modern Slavery Act 2018 and Canada's Fighting Against Forced Labour and Child Labour in Supply Chains Bill 2020.

15   See EU Parliament, Directorate General for External policies, "Trade-related policy options of a ban on forced labour products", www.europarl.europa.eu/RegData/etudes/IDAN/2022/702570/EXPO_IDA(2022)702570_EN.pdf; EU COM(2022) 453, "Proposal for a regulation on prohibiting products made with forced labour on the Union market."

chains; (iv) the financial sector; and (v) the agricultural supply chain.[16] Other industries are increasingly being scrutinised, including e-commerce and telecommunication services.[17] Conflict-affected areas are also subject to particular considerations and often present associated patterns of risks such as sexual and gender-based violence (UNGP Principle 7). An example of the systemic overlap of human rights risks is described in the OECD Due Diligence Guidance for Responsible Supply Chain of Minerals from Conflict-Affected and High-Risk Areas.

1.2   Implications on material risks to businesses

(a)   *Regulatory frameworks for human rights due diligence*

Corporate and investor responsibility to respect human rights in GSC is formalised in international voluntary standards like the UNGPs and the OECD Guidelines for Multinational Enterprises on Responsible Business Conduct[18] ('OECD Guidelines'). The OECD Guidelines, first adopted in 1976, were last revised in June 2023 to include updated recommendations for responsible business conduct across areas that include supply chain due diligence. Other notable frameworks include sustainability indices, corporate and investor performance standards (see section 1.2 (b)) and increasingly national regulations focused on supply chain due diligence. Importantly, new legislative frameworks affecting GSC establish the correlation between corporate responsibility and adverse impact through indirect business relationships.[19]

Adding to pre-existing requirements on responsible sourcing for high-risk products,[20] and modern slavery and forced labour laws mentioned in section 1.1(d), the number of national supply chain due diligence laws mandating HRDD across GSC is increasing. While thresholds of scope vary, mandatory HRDD is a common feature of national laws like Germany's Supply Chain Due Diligence Act 2022, Norway's Transparency Act 2022, Japan's Guidelines on Respecting Human Rights in Responsible Supply Chains 2022, France's Duty of

---

16   See OECD sector guidelines at: https://mneguidelines.oecd.org/sectors/.

17   See suggested amendments to proposed EU CSDDD listing high-risk sectors at: www.europarl.europa.eu/doceo/document/TA-9-2023-0209_EN.html.

18   Leading standards for responsible business conduct on human rights, namely the UNGPs and the OECD Guidelines, spell out expectations for the private sector that include a formal policy commitment, having an HRDD process in place and enabling or providing adequate access to remedy (UNGPS Principles 17–21). See also Organisation of Economic Cooperation and Development, OECD Guidelines for Multinational Enterprises on Responsible Business Conduct, (Paris, revised June 2023).

19   Business relationships are defined as the "relationships with business partners, sub-contractors, franchisees, investee companies, clients, and joint venture partners, entities in the supply chain which supply products or services that contribute to the enterprise's own operations, products or services or which receive, license, buy or use products or services from the enterprise, and any other non-State or State entities directly linked to its operations, products or services" (OECD Guidelines for Multinational Enterprises, revised June 2023).

20   Several countries require annual reporting on sourcing practices of high-risk products. See the US Securities and Exchange Commission (SEC)'s Dodd-Frank Consumer Protection Act, mandating listed companies to disclose the use of 'conflict minerals' in production processes.

Vigilance Law 2017 and proposed legislation in Austria, the Netherlands, Brazil and beyond. If it comes into effect, the proposed EU CSDDD will compel all EU member states to adopt national mandatory HRDD laws, with implications on suppliers globally.

Common elements of national mandatory HRDD laws include: (i) the creation of supervisory authorities to monitor HRDD practice and act in cases of non-compliance; (ii) the creation of mechanisms for third parties to make complaints and/or obtain information from companies; and (iii) a requirement that companies publish information about their HRDD process. The HRDD process, both its methodology and scope, must be tailored to the circumstances and context of a business' operations and supply chain (eg, sector(s) of activities, locations, regulatory landscape, etc).

(b) *Considerations for investors*
Standards that guide investor scrutiny on human rights issues include the International Finance Corporation's Performance Standards (IFC-PS) and the upcoming Corporate Sustainability Reporting Directive (CSRD) replacing the EU's current Non-Financial Reporting Directive (NFRD). The UN-supported Principles for Responsible Investment (PRI), an international network of ESG-conscious institutional investor signatories, has furthermore set standards for responsible investment related to human rights. In June 2023, PRI published a UNGP-aligned technical guide for HRDD, with considerations around data collection, leverage, portfolio concentration and the nature of actions required in various stages of an investment.[21]

Risk management and reporting for the financial sector increasingly requires HRDD in various investment areas, from private equity and credit investments, corporate mergers and acquisitions to initial public offerings. An investor's risk management measures will ultimately vary based on leverage and data accessibility constraints (see section 3.2).

(c) *Financial, legal and reputational risks to businesses*
Risks to rights-holders are increasingly recognised as a material corporate governance issue.[22] Among fiduciary implications, failure to comply with mandatory HRDD may lead to sanctions,[23] import bans, costly interruptions of business services, large fines and the prospect of class-action lawsuits, not to

---

21   PRI, "How to identify human rights risks: A practical guide in due diligence" (5 June 2023), www.unpri.org/human-rights/how-to-identify-human-rights-risks-a-practical-guide-in-due-diligence/11457.article.

22   J Ruggie, C Rees and R Davis, "Ten Years After: From UN Guiding Principles To Multi-Fiduciary Obligations", *Business and Human Rights Journal* 6(22) (2021), pp179–197.

23   US Department of Commerce, "Commerce Adds NSO Group and Other Foreign Companies to Entity List for Malicious Cyber Activities" (3 November 2021), www.commerce.gov/news/press-releases/2021/11/commerce-adds-nso-group-and-other-foreign-companies-entity-list.

mention the reputational damage. Failure to address adverse human rights impact in GSC can therefore lead to significant legal fees and remediation costs, and result in huge value destruction for corporations and their shareholders.

Clauses of civil and criminal liability tied to corporate laws on business conduct are also being considered in pending regional and national legislation.[24] Given the rise of cross-border human rights litigation and the influence of bodies like the International Criminal Court,[25] concepts of corporate criminal responsibility are becoming better established in certain domestic legal systems.[26]

Looking at reputational risks, public disclosure of a company's adverse social impact damages its societal standing with implications that range from talent attraction and retention[27] to social licence to operate.[28] Consumer purchasing decisions are influenced by social justice, good governance and environmental stewardship, and a reduction in a company's publicly recognised ESG performance may lead to a decline in sales.[29] Similarly, a loss or exclusion from the Dow Jones Sustainability Index might have financial repercussions such as exclusion from certain investment funds or higher borrowing costs.[30]

2. Identifying human rights impact through HRDD

2.1 Prioritising salient human rights risks in GSC

(a) Initial risk assessment and risk-rating

Given the number of rights-holders and business relationships involved in GSC, GSC-focused HRDDs may require risk-based prioritisation (UNGP

---

24   Ongoing 2023 EU trilogue negotiations will determine civil liability implications of EU's CSDDD. See also comparative table of corporate due diligence laws and legislative proposals in Europe (22 March 2022): https://corporatejustice.org/publications/comparative-table-corporate-due-diligence-laws-and-legislative-proposals-in-europe-2/.

25   See A Ramasastry and RC Thompson, "Commerce, Crime and Conflict: Legal Remedies for Private Sector Liability for Grave Breaches of International Law", (FAFO, 2006).

26   J Zerk, "Corporate liability for gross human rights abuses", (Office of the UN High Commissioner for Human Rights, 2013), www.ohchr.org/sites/default/files/Documents/Issues/Business/Domestic LawRemedies/StudyDomesticLawRemedies.pdf.

27   See N Aminudin, "Corporate social responsibility and employee retention of 'green' hotels", *Procedia-Social and Behavioral Sciences* 105 (2013), pp763–771; IA Zainee F and Puteh, "Corporate social responsibility impact on talent retention among Generation Y", *Revista de Gestão* 27(4), (2020), pp369–392, https://doi.org/10.1108/REGE-06-2019-0070.

28   H Lee and T-H Rhee, "How Does Corporate ESG Management Affect Consumers' Brand Choice?" 15(8) (2023) *Sustainability* Article 6795, DOI 10.3390/su15086795.

29   S Frey, J Bar Am, V Doshi, A Malik and S Noble, "Consumers care about sustainability and back it up with their wallets", McKinsey (6 February 2023) www.mckinsey.com/industries/consumer-packaged-goods/our-insights/consumers-care-about-sustainability-and-back-it-up-with-their-wallets; K Alldredge, A Grimmelt and M Toriello, "Understanding the ever-evolving, always-surprising consumer", McKinsey (31 August 2021) www.mckinsey.com/industries/consumer-packaged-goods/our-insights/understanding-the-ever-evolving-always-surprising-consumer.

30   N Denuwara, A Kim, V Atree *et al*, "Corporate economic performance and sustainability indices: a study based on the Dow Jones Sustainability Index", *SN Bus Econ* 2(77), (2022), article 77 https://doi.org/10.1007/s43546-022-00251-0.

Principle 17). To prioritise high-risk areas, a supply chain risk assessment will first require desktop research analysis, accounting for sector and country risk in scope, as well as the review of a company's human rights-related policies. Policies and procedures that relate to risk management practices of a company's business relationships are particularly relevant to analysing systemic GSC risks (eg, procurement and purchasing policies and supplier code of conduct).

Assessing the human rights risk-levels of a large supplier base will then entail analysing supplier spend analytics to prioritise risk assessment on top-spend suppliers and/or suppliers corresponding to a high-risk profile.[31] An investor's risk assessment process follows a similar logic, with extensive guidance on relevant indicators and data source provided in the June 2023 PRI technical guidance.[32] Risk-rating formats vary and could include 'risk heat maps' to visualise risks based on a colour-coded split of risks.

For a high-level risk screening of a company's supplier base, digital tools may be used to aggregate relevant supplier information and streamline data collection. This process may rely on software-based solutions for data collection and authentication of data (see section 2.2). The use of questionnaires and sustainability performance assessments as well as social audit reports may also be used as part of an initial screening.

(b) Saliency mapping

After conducting an initial risk assessment through comprehensive public record research and document review, tools like saliency mapping are useful to identify priority issues. A UNGP-aligned saliency mapping considers the severity of actual and potential human rights impacts combined with the likelihood of the adverse impacts occurring.

Severity of risks considers scale (how serious is the impact), scope (how widespread is the impact) and irremediability (how easily prior enjoyment of the rights can be restored to those impacted) (UNGP 14 Commentary). Saliency mapping requires analysing risk severity and likelihood to paint a picture of various risk levels across a company's GSC. From there, a tailored approach is developed based on each risk level, which may warrant further due diligence in high-risk areas, such as a particular jurisdiction or raw material.

Findings from a saliency mapping are weighed against a company's management practices, attribution and leverage. Current management examines policies and practices that are already in place; attribution qualifies

---

31   A supplier risk exposure profile should account for a suppliers' location(s), sectors, product risks, nature of services provided, etc.

32   PRI, "How to identify human rights risks: A practical guide in due diligence" (5 June 2023), www.unpri.org/human-rights/how-to-identify-human-rights-risks-a-practical-guide-in-due-diligence/11457.article.

the link to the harm (namely, the distinction between cause, contribution and direct link) (UNGP 17); and leverage refers to the ability of a business enterprise to effect change.[33] All these factors inform the development of an action plan that will define the immediate, short- and long-term measures for mitigation and remediation of risks and the impact identified.

(c)   *Due diligence on high-risk areas through impact assessments*
An initial risk assessment highlights risk areas emerging from business relationships that warrant further due diligence. To adequately gauge human rights risks in these areas, the UNGPs recommend assessing adverse impacts drawing on meaningful consultation with potentially affected groups (UNGP 18). Such assessments include a Human Rights Impact Assessment (HRIA), a human rights-based methodology used to analyse adverse risks and impacts on rights-holders through stakeholder engagement with rights-holders (eg, workers, local community members, consumers and others).[34]

While more costly than a survey-based data collection, meaningful engagement of rights-holders is key to understand their perspectives in the context of their day-to-day experiences. This process in turn leads to an accurate account of actual and potential impact that can inform targeted mitigation measures.[35] HRIAs conducted on suppliers will typically involve site visits (eg, supplier site), individual and group interviews with rights-holders on site, interviews with selected members of the supplier management team and visual assessments on site. Human-rights based principles apply to engagement with rights-holders. For example, workers attending group interviews must be paid at their normal rate for time spent participating in interviews, and managers are to be excluded from interviews. Group interviews are supplemented by individual interviews to corroborate findings.

2.2   Practical challenges for human rights risk assessments in GSC

(a)   *Addressing the lack of visibility in lower tiers of the supply chain*
Given that GSC are fragmented in complex networks of multi-tier suppliers, based in distinct jurisdictions, a challenge of HRDD lies in gaining visibility into direct and indirect business relationships. Digital supply chain risk management solutions can increase transparency and streamline the collection

---

33   Shift, Global Compact Network Netherlands, Oxfam, *Doing Business with Respect for Human Rights*, (2nd edn, 2016), pp62–76, https://shiftproject.org/resource/doing-business-with-respect-for-human-rights/.
34   The Danish Institute for Human Rights, "Human Rights Impact Assessment Guidance and Toolbox" (2016, revised 2020), www.humanrights.dk/tools/human-rights-impact-assessment-guidance-toolbox/introduction-human-rights-impact-assessment.
35   HRDD case studies suggest that insufficient engagement with rights-holders can significantly flaw the HRDD findings. Similarly, risk assessments that fail to verify a company's human rights policies and processes against actual practices will not uncover actual risks and impact. Such gaps may be addressed through HRIAs.

of data from suppliers through tools like surveys and self-assessment questionnaires. Software-based supply chain mapping tools increasingly offer risk-tracking screening based on risk profiling and adverse media searches.[36] On a product-level, product compliance software solutions can help companies align with a multitude of ESG compliance requirements (eg, material compliance, waste compliance, origin compliance).

Risk factors relevant to HRDD can be integrated in software-based supply chain risk management systems to effectively collect data pertinent to certain aspects of supplier risks, so long as the risk assessment is supplemented with a tailored risk analysis that places the risks to rights-holders (rather than material risks) at the heart of the risk management process.

(b) Implementation challenges of traceability solutions for HRDD

Given that sustainability requirements affect a company's entire value chain (ie, from the sourcing of raw materials to a product's end-of-life), companies may adopt system-wide traceability solutions to efficiently collect, track and report information relevant to multi-jurisdictional ESG due diligence. Traceability systems, at times supported by AI and blockchain technology, can help address human rights risks by tracking information relevant to areas like responsible sourcing (eg, collecting trusted records for the provenance of physical good, supplier site locations, or certification statuses that can inform a risk assessment on labour practices).[37] Traceability systems nonetheless vary in their ability to support in-depth HRDD, as they vary greatly in both the means and end of collecting data.

Government policies and industry initiatives are accelerating the use of digital product passports (DPP) to digitalise value chain and product information data.[38] Some of these tools offer opportunities to increase supply chain traceability and transparency and may help companies improve their HRDD process as they comprehensively map their supply chains. Certain DPP already embed human rights and child labour indices among their performance

---

36   H-T Liao and C-L Pan, "The Role of Resilience and Human Rights in the Green and Digital Transformation of Supply Chain", (IEEE 2nd International Conference on Technology, Engineering, Management for Societal impact using Marketing, Entrepreneurship and Talent, India, (2021), pp1–7, doi: 10.1109/TEMSMET53515.2021.9768730.

37   W Crumpler, "The Human Rights Risks and Opportunities in Blockchain," Center for Strategic & International Studies (December 2021), https://csis-website-prod.s3.amazonaws.com/s3fs-public/publication/211214_Crumpler_HumanRights_Blockchain.pdf?VersionId=arkH_fAUfQAlZExHYUfrq6Wks9.SPwN; World Economic Forum, "Digital Traceability: A Framework for More Sustainable and Resilient Value Chains" (September 2021), www3.weforum.org/docs/WEF_Digital_Traceability_2021.pdf; PlanetGOLD, GEF Initiative, "Supply Chain Technology Solutions for planetGOLD projects" (20 September 2021) www.planetgold.org/sites/default/files/Supply%20Chain%20Technology%20Report_final.pdf.

38   In March 2022, the EU Commission proposed a series of legislations to increase the sustainability of physical products in the EU market, including a Regulation on Ecodesign for Sustainable Products (ESPR). ESPR introduces the use of digital product passports (DPP), a traceability centralising standardised information on a product's lifecycle. Certain industries are considered particularly mature to implement DPP, including apparel, consumer goods and battery technology (see for example the July 2023 adoption of the EU Batteries Regulation prescribing the use of a DPP).

indicators, thereby supporting the tracking of human rights data.[39] Yet, current versions of these tools largely rely on self-reporting mechanisms which cannot replace the meaningful collection and verification of a supplier's human rights track record.[40] In addition, infrastructure and data-related hurdles like the cost of implementing and running traceability technology (eg, hardware, software and training) and voluntary data sharing across company borders remain significant barriers to implementing such traceability solutions.[41]

(c)   *Qualitative data at scale: limitations of self-assessment and social audits*
Using evidence-based online platforms that rate supplier sustainability through automated processes is an appealing approach for scalable risk identification. Given the need to streamline data collection, supplier risk assessments rely heavily on self-assessment questionnaires as the primary means to collect information used in the onboarding of suppliers and in the risk management process that follows. Yet, the viability of findings gathered through such tools has been questioned by several credible experts in this field due to methodological limitations known as 'social desirability bias' and 'supplier assessment fatigue'.[42]

Aggregating qualitative data on human rights risks across large supplier networks represents a challenge of scalability that favours the use of replicable supplier self-assessments. Social audits may be effective in some circumstances and improve sustainable supply chain management.[43] There remains limitations to this approach, including problematic incentives that compromise the integrity of their findings and the lack of transparency regarding the data collection methodology.

As such, best practice recommends exercising scrutiny over the means of self-assessments, limiting those to initial risk prioritisation, random sampling of high-risk counterparties and complementing questionnaires with in-depth impact risk assessment and physical investigation led by trained human rights practitioners on high-risk supplier sites.

---

39   See, for example, different iterations of the 'battery passport', like the Global Battery Alliance's concept proof of a battery passport embedding human rights and child labour indices.

40   For limitations on certain software-based solutions, see: C-H Tsai and C-F Lin, "Shedding New Light on Multinational Corporations and Human Rights: Promises and Limits of 'Blockchainizing' the Global Supply Chain" 44 *Mich J Int'l Law*, 117 (2023), https://repository.law.umich.edu/mjil/vol44/iss1/4.

41   World Economic Forum, "Digital Traceability: A Framework for More Sustainable and Resilient Value Chains" (September 2021), www3.weforum.org/docs/WEF_Digital_Traceability_2021.pdf.

42   EcoVadis, "Reducing Survey Fatigue with Smart & Scalable Supply Chain CSR Solutions" (April 2017), https://resources.ecovadis.com/suppliers/reducing-survey-fatigue-scalable-supply-chain-csr-solutions; IJ Fraser, M Müller and J Schwarzkopf, "Dear supplier, how sustainable are you? A multiple-case study analysis of a widespread tool for sustainable supply chain management" 28(3-4) *NachhaltigkeitsManagementForum* (2020), pp127–149, doi: 10.1007/s00550-020-00507-z.

43   RM Locke, *The promise and limits of private power. Promoting labor standards in a global economy*, (Cambridge University Press, 2013); JL Short, MW Toffel, AR Hugill, "Monitoring global supply chains", 37(9) (2016) *Strategic Management Journal*, pp1878–1897, https://doi.org/10.1002/smj.2417; C Terwindt and A Armstrong, "Oversight and accountability in the social auditing industry: the role of social compliance initiatives", 158(2), (2019) *Int Labour Rev*, pp245–272, https://doi.org/10.1111/ilr.12143.

(d)   *GSC risk assessment in challenging jurisdictions*

Certain jurisdictions impose limitations to field-based risk assessments. Conflict-affected areas, or countries with pervasive surveillance where civil society cannot freely operate, severely restrict site access, and raise safety risks for impacted rights-holders and HRDD practitioners. At all times, the principle of 'do no harm' should apply, meaning that HRDD practitioners should minimise any unintended negative impact that their engagement with rights-holders may cause.

Where opportunities for safe on-the-ground engagement are limited, HRDD professionals and investigators should first leverage publicly available information through in-depth desk-based research, well beyond a simple internet engine search. Research must be conducted in all relevant languages and consider the full spectrum of open-source intelligence including social and traditional media, blogs, NGO reports, available court records and employee review websites, as well as the analysis of meta data of photographic and satellite imagery. HRDD data collection in GSC may be complemented through local partners and expert enquiry, as site visits may be more safely conducted by local organisations. Findings may also be triangulated or complemented by obtaining insights from external experts. Barriers to access information must be explicitly stated in the HRDD reporting, along with measures taken to overcome these obstacles and any potential limitations faced in the process.

3.   Acting on HRDD findings in GSC

3.1   Implementation at supplier level

(a)   *Tailored mitigation and remediation plan*

After identifying where human rights risks and impacts occur in the GSC, the next step in the HRDD process is to effectively prevent or mitigate identified risks and support access to remedy for impacted rights-holders (Figure 1). While earlier stages (namely policy gap analysis against relevant industry standards, human rights saliency mapping, supplier risk ratings and determining areas for further due diligence) may be conducted in-house depending on capacity and resources, an in-depth due diligence (eg, HRIAs) and the development of a mitigation and remediation plan generally require independent third-party experts, due to their impartiality and specific skillset applicable to human rights assessments.

Figure 1. UNGP framework for human rights impact remediation based on attribution

How is the company or investee connected to the harm?		Cause	Contribute	Directly linked
Has the harm already occurred?	No, it's a risk	**Prevent** the impact	**Cease contribution** and **mitigate** harm using leverage	Use leverage to **prevent or mitigate**. As a last resort, end the relationship
	Yes, it's an impact		Ensure grievance mechanisms are established and provide **remedy** to affected individuals	**Support access to remedy**

A human rights risk mitigation and remediation plan for GSC (hereafter referred to as 'HRDD mitigation plan') should include tailored actions and KPIs needed to prevent, mitigate and remediate salient risks or impacts identified at the level of the business relationships at stake. Best practices recommend including a supplier engagement plan to manage risks at third-party level and guide existing and future engagement with business partners and suppliers.[44]

Tailored supplier recommendations should be based on prior assessment of supplier policies and procedures in place (eg, supplier policies on health and working conditions), and must furthermore be congruent with business constraints imposed on suppliers. Companies must, for example, acknowledge how pressure to deliver goods or services at reduced costs or constrained turnaround times might increase human rights violations at supplier level.[45]

Importantly, a HRDD mitigation plan should account for the leverage that the company has over third parties involved. Where a company has no leverage or ways to engage with a third party, it should consider seeking alternatives and ending its business relationship if necessary,[46] while demonstrating ongoing efforts to mitigate risks while the relationship is maintained (UNGP 19). In most cases the company will be able to increase its leverage through targeted supplier engagement.

---

44   See S Lees, UNDP Business and Human Rights, "Training Facilitation Guide Human Rights Due Diligence", p64, www.undp.org/sites/g/files/zskgke326/files/2021-09/UNDP-RBAP-Human-Rights-Due-Diligence-Training-Facilitation-Guide-2021.pdf.

45   S Ponte, *Business, Power and Sustainability in a World of Global Value Chains* (Zed Books Ltd, 2019).

46   The outcome of a risk assessment on a business relationship will depend on various factors. See Shift, Global Compact Network Netherlands, Oxfam, "Doing Business with Respect for Human Rights", (2nd edn, 2016), pp62–76, https://shiftproject.org/resource/doing-business-with-respect-for-human-rights/.

(b)   *Effective supplier engagement*

Looking ahead, supervisory authorities enforcing HRDD may scrutinise whether multinational companies are merely pushing compliance constraints onto their suppliers and contactors instead of building capacity for shared accountability. Pressure exerted by businesses' demands on suppliers may clash with policies of responsible supplier conduct (eg, requiring fair wages, minimal overtime) and thus structurally constrain supplier compliance below tier one.[47] In this context, close cooperation with direct suppliers helps leverage legal enforcement mechanisms for the purpose of a balanced supplier engagement plan.

Best practice calls companies and investors to constructively engage with suppliers (eg, training and awareness raising) to understand supplier limitations and provide effective technical support. Certain companies have, for example, developed a dedicated supplier engagement platform to centralise policies relevant to responsible sourcing and supplier conduct (eg, code of conduct), as well as provide technical support opportunities.[48]

Obstacles to enacting change in a company's supplier engagement strategy include the divide between, on the one hand, purchasing teams driven by commercial imperatives, and on the other hand, compliance and ethics teams familiar with risk factors addressed in HRDDs. Emerging best practice suggests bridging the gap through legislative means, internal capacity building and the integration of human rights-related requirements into procurement contracts.

3.2   Considerations for investors

To implement effective risk management processes, investors are encouraged to obtain data relevant to human rights risks throughout the investment process, as a means to adequately incentivise investees.[49] Investors can thereafter use their investment decisions, stewardship of investees and dialogue with policy makers and other stakeholders to act on a HRDD's findings.[50] While prioritisation in human rights risk assessments follows the same logic as with companies,[51] measures for mitigation and remediation will vary based on the

---

47   R Locke *et al*, "Beyond corporate codes of conduct: Work organization and labour standards at Nike's suppliers" 146(1–2) (2007) *International Labour Review*, pp21-40; P Ngai, "Global Production, Company Codes of Conduct, and Labor Conditions in China: A Case Study of Two Factories" 54 (2005) *The China Journal*, pp101–113.

48   See, for example, Ikea's IWAY standards at: www.ikea.com/global/en/our-business/how-we-work/iway-our-supplier-code-of-conduct/#:~:text=IWAY%20is%20the%20IKEA%20way,providers%20that%20 work%20with%20IKEA.

49   PRI, "What data do investors need to manage human rights risks?" (November 2022), www.unpri.org/ human-rights/what-data-do-investors-need-to-manage-human-rights-risks/10856.article.

50   PRI, "Why and how investors should act on human rights", (October 2020), www.unpri.org/human-rights/why-and-how-investors-should-act-on-human-rights/6636.article.

51   Namely, investors prioritise action on risks based on severity and leverage, after assessing their attribution to the impact in GSC. This may be through causation (eg, where the investor holds a controlling stake in an investee company), contribution (eg, through an investment activity that induces an adverse impact from an investee company or project) and direct linkage (eg, through the activities, products or services of an investee company or project).

investment instrument, stages and leverage available to influence an investee (eg, equity investors may have direct mechanisms through proxy voting rights, while private equity investors, even when they are in a minority, may hold board positions or other rights allowing them direct influence).[52]

Where leverage in some cases may be limited, PRI calls on investors to increase it through collaboration with other investors. Where an investor is unable to alter an investee's behaviour, with no prospect for improvement, the severity of human rights impact and the human rights consequences of divesting must be considered to decide whether to stay invested.[53]

4.   Conclusion

Features of GSC, including geographically dispersed production and competition among export manufacturers, unfortunately increase the chances of poor working conditions on production sites and heighten the risks of labour exploitation.[54] This chapter highlights the human rights risks in GSC in the context of regulatory developments and the implications for material risks to businesses and investors. The UNGP-aligned HRDD process has the potential to become an effective way to assess, mitigate and prevent potential and actual adverse impact occurring in GSC, if widely adopted.

With recent development of laws and proposed regulations relating to HRDD, companies will be required to identify and address human rights risks and impacts in their upstream supply chains. Given the implications on materials and compliance described in this chapter, companies must as an absolute minimum engage in meaningful supply chain due diligence processes, abiding by clear standards of practice with primacy to rights-holders. For companies wanting to lean into the changing regulatory and enforcement environment, amidst increasing expectations from investors and end customers, an in-depth HRDD including HRIA on high-risk areas or businesses will continue to be best practice.

---

52   PRI, "Why and how investors should act on human rights", (October 2020), www.unpri.org/human-rights/why-and-how-investors-should-act-on-human-rights/6636.article.
53   *Ibid.*
54   R Mares, "Corporate transparency laws: A hollow 'victory'?" *Netherlands Quarterly of Human Rights* 36(3) (2018), pp189–120.

The S in ESG

Sarah E Fortt
Betty M Huber
Latham & Watkins

1. Introduction

Of the three pillars of ESG, 'social' – the 'S' – is often considered by some to be the most recent to take centre stage. In reality, its roots lie deep in fundamental principles of corporate governance and stakeholder engagement. Some aspects of the S in ESG have been standard practice for decades, and other aspects are either novel or newly invigorated, stemming from cultural shifts, increasing stakeholder scrutiny or regulatory developments that require companies to examine their social footprint. Ultimately, the social facets of ESG build on the foundations of corporate or business ethics, social responsibility and compliance programmes that addressed issues such as non-discrimination in the workplace and respect for human rights in labour practices, among other topics.

Because some social issues are wrapped up in the current public discourse and political debate, they can be controversial. However, this chapter eschews editorialising about the reasons why organisations might enact social programmes, and instead focuses on consumer, investor and regulator sentiment toward social initiatives, as well as the trends, opportunities and challenges that organisations should consider in this area. As stakeholders scrutinise companies' corporate practices, value chains and regulatory compliance, corporations will need to evolve their policies, practices and governance structures to keep abreast of best practices.

To start, this chapter addresses challenges and trends in this developing practice area. The extent to which regulators have been involved in the topic varies across jurisdictions. Further, analysing social factors is often qualitative, presenting measurement and reporting difficulties. Yet, perhaps the greatest challenge, and opportunity, facing organisations with social initiatives and obligations is the cultural pressure that these programmes inherently press against. It is perhaps an unavoidable fact and, therefore, an unavoidable challenge that social efforts abut moral questions regarding equity, equality and society. On the one hand, the S can be about reducing reputational and compliance risks by enforcing corporate codes of conduct, treating people equitably, and complying with regulation; on the other hand, the S can be about making a difference, creating change and promoting justice. For many companies, some combination of the two approaches is where they find their sweet spot. However one approaches the S in ESG, strategies must account for political, cultural, regulatory and business contexts.

After discussing trends and challenges, this chapter will address five key focus areas of the S in ESG, describing each focus area individually and demonstrating the interconnection between key focus areas. The 'social' in ESG is not a monolith and spreads in many directions, with offshoots that diverge, intertwine and converge, often merging with the environmental and governance branches. The five key focus areas considered in this chapter are: (i) diversity, equity and inclusion (DEI); (ii) workplace investigations, including racial equity audits; (iii) human rights and supply chain transparency; (iv) 'do no significant harm' criteria; and (v) shareholder proposals. Each focus area provides a lay of the land, guidance on best practices and forward looking statements about likely developments in each space at the time this chapter was written.

2.   Current trends and challenges

Recent societal movements have reignited public discourse regarding various social matters as well as stakeholders' expectations that businesses play a role in creating and responding to social change and political debates. The S in ESG has been defined many different ways over the years, and has included matters such as labour standards, human rights, pay equity, social issues, workplace diversity, supply chain, data security and privacy. Today, in the context of ESG, we tend to think of the S in terms of social factors that may pose a risk to an organisation's financial performance or long-term value. An organisation's social footprint includes its customers, employees and the communities in which it does business and which are impacted by its business. Therefore, given the breadth of stakeholders included in the organisation's social footprint and the breadth of potential issues involved, the S in ESG can create both significant opportunities and significant risks for the organisation.

2.1   The range of approaches and views

Organisations are increasingly making voluntary disclosures on social issues. Third-party voluntary disclosure frameworks include the Sustainability Accounting Standards Board (SASB) (now part of the IFRS Foundation, and the Global Reporting Initiative (GRI)), among others, as convergence of metrics remains a challenge. Many organisations are working together to drive convergence around ESG standards, including organisations such as the ESG Data Convergence Initiative, which brings together general partners (GPs) and limited partners (LPs) around standardised ESG metrics in private markets.[1]

---

1   ESG Data Convergence Initiative, www.esgdc.org/our-goal/.

These voluntary disclosures implicate many of the topics covered in this chapter such as internal controls spanning DEI efforts and racial equity audits, third-party monitoring under supply chain transparency initiatives and analysis of potential adverse effects of business activities under the 'do no significant harm' principle of the European Union. To both protect against competing and potentially conflicting regulatory requirements and show responsiveness to social issues, organisations are creating their own internal frameworks covering strategy, risk management and disclosures. In this way, many companies are focused on improving their practices to better reflect their strategy and values or to meet the expectations of stakeholders like customers, employees and investors. In the United States, there is a rich history of shareholder activism on social matters, such as the response to corporate activities in South Africa during apartheid and, more recently, the focus on creating more diverse pipelines or assessing human rights risks in response to stakeholder pressures.

At the same time, social matters, particularly in the US, can be politically charged, with various shareholders staking out opposing positions on a wide range of issues. While many of these topics have always been part of the political discourse, attention to them has arguably become more noticeably polarising in the US in recent years. This tension was striking during 2023, which has featured shareholder proposals, public campaigns, boycotts and litigation with opposing aims, with some, for example, pushing for robust diversity, equity and inclusion practices on one hand and others pushing for the dismantling of the same on the other hand. These developments are continuing into 2024, and are likely to continue for some time.

2.2 The complexity of measuring and reporting

Another set of challenges for the social dimension of ESG includes measurement and reporting. There is no uniform framework to create consistency with respect to reporting on many of the different social aspects in the ESG movement; by comparison certain frameworks for essential environmental and governance matters may be considered more developed. For example, the Task Force on Climate-Related Financial Disclosures (TFCD) has issued detailed recommendations to assist corporations in providing "clear, comparable and consistent information about the risks and opportunities presented by climate change".[2] The TFCD provides climate-related recommendations pertaining to governance, strategy, risk management, and metrics and targets for organisations across all industries.[3] Similarly, the Taskforce on Nature-related Financial Disclosures (TNFD) provides

---

2   Task Force on Climate-related Financial Disclosures, Recommendations of the Task Force on Climate-related Financial Disclosures (2017), https://assets.bbhub.io/company/sites/60/2021/10/FINAL-2017-TCFD-Report.pdf, at 2.

3   *Ibid.*

recommendations to aid organisations in their assessment, management and disclosure of nature-related issues, while the Greenhouse Gas (GHG) Protocol provides the global standards for companies and other organisations to measure and manage their GHG emissions. Governance has been the topic of regulatory requirements for a long time, with corporate governance frameworks, such as the UK Cadbury Code in 1992, which evolved to the UK Corporate Governance Code, the OECD Principles of Corporate Governance first published in 1999, and the US Sarbanes-Oxley Act of 2002, in place for decades. By contrast, reporting on social issues remains somewhat voluntary and *ad hoc*, though regulations and frameworks are quickly evolving. This lack of standardisation can engender incomparability between companies within and across industries.

The lack of standardisation can also arguably facilitate 'social washing', which occurs when companies either actively seek to or inadvertently portray themselves as better social actors than they are in reality.[4] Social washing manifests itself in many ways, including obscuring accurate, negative information, or disseminating inaccurate, positive information.[5] Similar to the increased focus on greenwashing, the increased focus on social washing, coupled with greater regulatory scrutiny of even voluntary ESG disclosures, has resulted in the need for any public statements regarding ESG to be evaluated for potential regulatory and reputational risks. ESG disclosures, including disclosures regarding social matters, can also introduce the possibility of legal liability for material misstatements or omissions in securities offerings documents under the US Securities Act of 1933, for fraud or deception in connection with the sale or purchase of a security under the US Securities Exchange Act of 1934, or under US state consumer protection laws.[6] These suits have largely been unsuccessful to date,[7] but are likely to continue. Some courts have deemed particular statements and disclosures immaterial puffery or made without the required scienter; others have determined that ESG risk disclosures cannot be misleading.[8] However, the potential costs of litigation, coupled with the likelihood that these lawsuits are likely to continue, means that ESG disclosures, even if voluntarily made, warrant internal controls analogously to those adopted for required financial disclosures.

2.3   Emerging regulatory considerations

At the same time, regulators are taking considerable action around the world to promote disclosures relating to the S of ESG. Such disclosure requirements

---

4   Dean Emerick, "What is social washing?", ESG: The Report, Sustainability, www.esgthereport.com/what-is-social-washing/.
5   *Ibid.*
6   James J Park, "ESG Securities Fraud" (25 April 2023), *Wake Forest Law Review* (forthcoming), UCLA School of Law, Law-Econ Research Paper No 23-02, 17–29 https://ssrn.com/abstract=4428212.
7   *Ibid.*
8   *Ibid.*

include expected Securities and Exchange Commission (SEC) Rules, the Nasdaq Board Diversity Rule, the Sustainable Finance Disclosure Regulation, the EU Corporate Sustainability Reporting Directive and China's Voluntary Guidance for Enterprise ESG Disclosure, among others. These regulatory developments reflect the movement of ESG, broadly speaking, from a regime based on private ordering and soft law to one with hard law requirements, which could present challenges for companies navigating numerous and potentially conflicting requirements globally.[9]

Moreover, the breadth of new rules also includes those aimed at corporate practices with many regulations being particularly concerned with supply chains such as the US Uyghur Forced Labor Prevention Act, the proposed EU Corporate Sustainability Due Diligence Directive (CSDDD), the UK Modern Slavery Act, the French Duty of Vigilance law and the German Supply Chain Due Diligence Act.[10] As the regulatory landscape rapidly evolves, failure to comply with its requirements, or providing inaccurate or incomplete information, can result in legal liability, including fines and other penalties such as loss of goodwill or reputational damage. These developments serve to further underscore the importance of implementing internal controls around social-related disclosures, even if they are currently made voluntarily they may become subject to regulation in the future.

2.4 The E and S intersection

Finally, the emergence of a positive feedback loop between environmental and social impacts is a force-multiplier of social considerations.[11] In fact, there is a growing awareness of the intersectionality between environmental and social matters, which comes with additional complexities for organisations to navigate as calls for global progress on environmental issues, including climate change, become louder and more insistent. For example, climate change-driven loss in biodiversity can have severe impacts on the livelihoods of people in the affected communities.[12] Relatedly, the health effects of climate change are not borne equally across racial lines.[13] However, even beyond questions regarding the historical inequities of global development and resource allocation, the

---

9   Paul Davies, Sarah Fortt and Betty M Huber, "ESG Insights: 10 Things That Should Be Top of Mind in 2023", Environment, Land & Resources (2023), www.globalelr.com/2023/01/esg-insights-10-things-that-should-be-top-of-mind-in-2023/.

10   *Ibid.*

11   International Regulatory Strategy Group and KPMG, "Accelerating the S in ESG – A Roadmap for Global Progress on Social Standards", (June 2021), https://assets.kpmg.com/content/dam/kpmg/uk/pdf/2021/06/irsg-kpmg-accelerating-the-s-in-esg-report.pdf, 10.

12   Paul Davies, Sarah Fortt and Betty M Huber, "ESG Insights: 10 Things That Should Be Top of Mind in 2023", Environment, Land & Resources (2023), www.globalelr.com/2023/01/esg-insights-10-things-that-should-be-top-of-mind-in-2023/.

13   See, eg, Alique G Berberian, David JX Gonzalez and Lara J Cushing, "Racial Disparities in Climate Change-Related Health Effects in the United States", *Curr Environ Health Rep* (2022) 9(3), 451–464, www.ncbi.nlm.nih.gov/pmc/articles/PMC9363288.

decisions organisations make today about their business strategies and market engagement can have immediate knock-on effects that implicate both the organisation's impact on the environment and the climate, and its impact on the people within and around its business functions. Companies navigating the complex and growing array of social issues will need to prioritise what is material for their organisations and in their industries, while considering all stakeholders' interests.

Despite these difficulties, and perhaps in certain regards because of them, effective analysis of social risks and opportunities often requires analyses that run deeper than the surface requirements of existing frameworks or regulation. The need for deeper analysis is one reason for recent increases in corporate audits regarding social issues, including racial equity audits, which serve to evaluate the disparate impact of a company's operations on individuals of different races. Another example of deeper analysis is supply chain audits, which help to identify potential incidents of modern slavery, human trafficking, child labour and other issues through supplier questionnaires and due diligence.[14] Engaging third parties to help evaluate these aspects, where possible, builds credibility and reduces the existence or perception of social washing.

3.   Key focus areas

3.1   Diversity, equity and inclusion

While diversity, equality and inclusion (DEI) factors are not new in business culture and decision making, they have received increased attention given the spotlight on the S of ESG since 2020 following the murder of George Floyd. Today, rules are being enacted across jurisdictions to solidify and standardise DEI-related disclosures. Formal rules follow a 'comply or explain' model for diversity reporting; however, the current frameworks only serve as a starting point for further scrutiny and accountability. In addition, an emerging backlash to DEI efforts, particularly in the US, has created increased complexity and risk for companies navigating their diversity-related initiatives, goals and efforts.

In the US, Nasdaq's Board Diversity Rule, which is being phased in through 2026, follows the 'comply or explain' model; it does not impose board diversity mandates or quotas.[15] Further, the SEC has two rules in the proposal stage on its agenda: the Corporate Board Diversity Rule (3235-AL91) and Human Capital

---

14   Natalie Runyon, "How companies are measuring the impact of their 'social' issues", Thomson Reuters (2022), www.thomsonreuters.com/en-us/posts/news-and-media/how-companies-measure-social-impact/.

15   The rule is being challenged in court by think tank the National Center for Public Policy Research and the Alliance for Fair Board Recruitment, whose arguments include that the rule violates the equal protection clause of the Fifth Amendment by encouraging discrimination on the basis of sex and race. A Fifth Circuit panel rejected the petitioners' claims in October 2023. However, the Alliance for Fair Board Recruitment and the National Center for Public Policy Research have petitioned for review.

Management Disclosure Rule (3235-AM88).[16] In the United Kingdom, the Financial Conduct Authority (FCA) has announced a finalised rule covering diversity and inclusion on company boards and executive committees. This rule also requires companies to 'comply or explain' whether they have met the specific board diversity targets.[17] Companies are also required to publicly disclose annual numerical diversity data and explain their approach to collecting these data.[18]

Beyond regulatory requirements, corporate practices and disclosures around DEI have experienced significant evolution from 2020 with events spurring dialogue around DEI issues, including regarding the role that corporations have to play in creating equitable and inclusive societies. Examples of corporate progress include the addition of 'equity' and 'belonging' into DEI language, the expansion of DEI teams and their influence, and corporations exploring further areas of DEI impact such as supply chain improvement and public advocacy.[19] A 2023 report found that chief diversity and inclusion officers were the C-suite position with most significant hiring growth of approximately 169% from the period of 2019 to the end of 2022.[20,21] The global DEI market is projected to reach US$15.4 billion by 2026.[22] Regulators globally are also mandating increased transparency on DEI disclosures such as supply chain considerations, diversity and pay equity.[23]

While appetite for both formal and informal DEI initiatives continued to increase through most of 2022, in the second half of 2022 and to date, a

---

16 Agency Rule List Fall 2023, Securities and Exchange Commission, www.reginfo.gov/public/do/eAgendaMain?operation=OPERATION_GET_AGENCY_RULE_LIST&currentPub=true&agencyCode=&showStage=active&agencyCd=3235&csrf_token=E6F3961DF6A851BB0824D1A65D1A666308C96C8FDEB51D00FF1395A6E0479C6216C83BC0CB8D496CF11C5DD4F896AE25C386.

17 Financial Conduct Authority Policy Statement, "Diversity and Inclusion on Company Boards and Executive Management", PS 22/3, (April 2022), www.fca.org.uk/publication/policy/ps22-3.pdf.

18 Financial Conduct Authority Press Release, "FCA Finalises Proposals to Boost Disclosure of Diversity on Listed Company Boards and Executive Committees", (20 April 2022), www.fca.org.uk/news/press-releases/fca-finalises-proposals-boost-disclosure-diversity-listed-company-boards-executive-committees.

19 "Corporate Progress and Action on Diversity, Equality and inclusion" The SustainAbility Institute by ERM (September 2021), www.sustainability.com/globalassets/sustainability.com/thinking/pdfs/2021/ermsi-corporate-progress-and-action-on-dei-sept21.pdf.

20 LinkedIn report – George Anders, "Who's vaulting into the C-suite? Trends changed fast in 2022", (1 February 2023), www.linkedin.com/pulse/whos-vaulting-c-suite-trends-changed-fast-2022-george-anders/.

21 See also "This You? Diversity Matters, Part II: So You've Hired a Chief Diversity Officer, Now What?", (23 November 2020), www.yahoo.com/video/diversity-matters-part-ii-ve-173438326.html?guccounter=1&guce_referrer=aHR0cHM6Ly93d3cuZ29vZ2xlLmNvbS8&guce_referrer_sig=AQAAAKnsl7bOv5ypm7HDds11U8D-wOCKOEAZbSsMPzEf556Dnc3c7HJpCUIqFwNOsuxYId12Glyky192oQg9wqtWa0BZf4RMZ2tPts6FlX9Bodq4j6pzrr_4-ltopiS-1YQQYyEUEUrl7e18tx2oAkv6eNmrVmsqwi6AdClEvw78INS1.

22 Global Industry Analysts Inc, "With Global Spending Projected to Reach $15.4 Billion by 2026, Diversity, Equity & Inclusion Takes the Lead Role in the Creation of Stronger Business", PR Newswire, (3 November 2021), www.prnewswire.com/news-releases/with-global-spending-projected-to-reach-15-4-billion-by-2026—diversity-equity—inclusion-takes-the-lead-role-in-the-creation-of-stronger-businesses-301413808.html.

23 Moreover, in the US, "[o]ver the past 18 months, companies have increasingly moved to provide disclosures on their workforce demographics, notably publishing their EEO-1 reports, in part due to pressure from investors, including the NYC Comptroller, institutional pension funds and large asset managers last year", Adam Emmerich, David Silk and Sabastian Niles, "Combatting Racial Inequality: A Two-year Retrospective", Harvard Law School Forum on Corporate Governance, (8 July 2022), https://corpgov.law.harvard.edu/2022/07/08/combatting-racial-inequity-a-two-year-retrospective/.

pushback on DEI efforts in both the legislative and judicial branches, as well as in public discourse has grown.[24] The Supreme Court's June 2023 decision in *Students for Fair Admissions, Inc v President and Fellows of Harvard College* prohibiting the consideration of race in college admissions[25] is having ripple effects in public discourse and in litigation trends, and public campaigns against companies that are perceived to have misjudged certain stakeholders' positions on DEI matters have become more commonplace.[26] In August 2023, the American Alliance for Equal Rights, a conservative organisation founded by Edward Blum who had previously founded Students for Fair Admissions, filed a lawsuit against Fearless Fund, an Atlanta-based venture capital fund that invests in black women business owners, alleging racial discrimination.[27] A number of other lawsuits, public campaigns and US Equal Employment Opportunity Commission claims have focused on 'reverse' discrimination claims as well. For example, the American Alliance for Equal Rights has also sued a number of law firms for their diversity fellowships.[28] Brands have been the subjects of backlash in response to their LGBTQ+-friendly marketing.[29] State legislatures continue to propose anti-ESG legislation that explicitly or implicitly prohibits DEI programmes, spending and training.[30,31] While anti-DEI trends are likely to continue for some time, companies continue to make progress on their DEI-related goals and efforts behind the scenes.

3.2   Workplace investigations

Investigations are a powerful tool for enforcers of laws, regulations and corporate codes of conduct to unveil malfeasance, find the root cause of noncompliance and identify opportunities to enhance internal controls. In

---

24   Sarah E Fortt, Danielle Conley, and Nineveh Alkhas, "Diversity Matters: The Four Scary Legal Risks Hiding in Your DEI Program", Reuters, (15 June 2023).

25   Note the decision would allow the use of race in limited circumstances/insofar as it impacted the applicant's individual experiences.

26   See generally, *Students for Fair Admissions, Inc v President and Fellows of Harvard College*, 600 US 1 (2023); Fidan Ana Kurtulus, "The Impact of Eliminating Affirmative Action on Minority and Female Employment: A Natural Experiment Approach Using State-Level Affirmative Action Laws and EEO-4 Data", working paper University of Massachusetts Amherst and Harvard Law School, (30 October 2012).

27   Nate Raymond, "Conservative activist behind US affirmative action cases sues venture capital fund", Reuters, (2 August 2023), www.reuters.com/legal/conservative-activist-behind-us-affirmative-action-cases-sues-venture-capital-2023-08-02/.

28   Douglas Belkin and Erin Mulvaney, "Activist Behind Supreme Court Affirmative Action Cases Is Now Suing Law Firms", *The Wall Street Journal*, (updated 22 August 2023), www.wsj.com/us-news/edward-blum-lawsuits-affirmativeaction-law-firms-b8871ab1.

29   Stefan Sykes, "Boycotts rarely work — but anti-LGBTQ+ backlash is forcing companies into tough choices", CNBC, (22 June 2023), www.cnbc.com/2023/06/22/the-business-of-boycotts-what-can-corporate-america-do.html.

30   Casey Harper, "States Push Back Against Diversity, Equity, Inclusion in Universities", *Washington Examiner*, (1 June 2023), www.washingtonexaminer.com/news/states-push-back-against-diversity-equity-inclusion-in-universities.

31   Furthermore, challenges exist beyond the DEI programmes themselves, such as concerns with collecting and tracking data given the data protection laws existing in Latin America, Africa, and the General Data Protection Regulation (GDPR) in the European Union. Companies may nonetheless continue to ask employees to disclose voluntarily in line with efforts to improve internal diversity.

many jurisdictions, employers have broad discretion to investigate employee conduct internally, retaining discretion over when and how to involve outside experts or government authorities. The rigour of these investigations, the enforcement of their substantive determinations and the robustness of their documentation are especially important in the wake of the #MeToo Movement.[32] Since 2017, companies have been broadening the scope of allegations and behaviours that are subject to investigation, and have increasingly begun demanding representations and warranties concerning sexual harassment from counterparties.[33]

This broader range of behaviours that may give rise to an investigation now includes not only alleged statutory and regulatory noncompliance and potential violations of codes of conduct, but also corporate culture violations and workplace misconduct such as bullying.[34] This is at least in part because, after the corporate reputational and business damage that misconduct by high profile individuals has caused, investigations professionals have reassessed the evidentiary thresholds and best practices for allocating resources to investigations.

Incentives to properly scope and resource internal investigations are myriad. For example, a well-conducted investigation with meaningful consequences for misconduct can reinforce an effective and compliance workplace culture and garner goodwill with the public, stakeholders and regulators; it also can help preserve confidentiality and attorney-client privilege. In addition, the prospect of external investigation and penalties, regulations on the treatment of whistleblowers and, increasingly, representations to counterparties about corporate officers' history of compliance also provide an incentive for companies to conduct effective and thorough internal investigations. Moreover, the US Department of Justice (DOJ) considers the rigour of internal investigations among other factors when assessing penalties for noncompliance or even whether to conduct its own, potentially more far reaching, investigations.[35] The DOJ also considers remedial actions taken to address the root cause of an issue and prevent it from reoccurring.[36] Regardless of DOJ

---

32 See, *Marchand v Barnhill*, 212 A 3d 805, 824 (Del 2019) (directors have a fiduciary duty to monitor and respond to "mission critical" risks); *In re McDonalds Corp Stockholder Deriv Litigation*, CA No 2021-0324-JTL (Del Ch 2023) (officers have a fiduciary duty to monitor and respond to risks, including, for a hospitality company, the proper conduct of investigations and remedial actions required by law); see also William R Baker *et al*, *Delaware Chancery Court Extends Oversight Duties to Non-Director Corporate Officers*, Latham & Watkins LLP (3 February 2023), www.lw.com/admin/upload/SiteAttachments/Delaware-Chancery-Court-Extends-Oversight-Duties-to-Non-Director-Corporate-Officers.pdf.

33 Kathleen Healy and Rebecca Zech, "Worklife 2.0: International trends on workplace investigations", Freshfields Bruckhaus Deringer, (7 October 2022), https://riskandcompliance.freshfields.com/post/102hyni/worklife-2-0-international-trends-on-workplace-investigations.

34 *Ibid*.

35 See, Assistant Attorney General for the Criminal Division, Leslie R Caldwell, "Remarks by Assistant Attorney General for the Criminal Division Leslie R Caldwell at the 22nd Annual Ethics and Compliance Conference" (1 October 2014); see also, Federal Sentencing Guidelines (1991); DOJ Evaluation of Corporate Compliance Programs (2020).

36 See, Federal Sentencing Guidelines, above n 35; DOJ Evaluation of Corporate Compliance Programs, above n 35.

guidance, organisations should engage legal investigators in certain circumstances such as when, after a preliminary internal investigation, there is a credible claim against an officer.[37] Engaging outside legal expertise minimises the appearance that the officer may influence the investigation into their conduct.[38] It may behove the organisation to make certain results of a high profile investigation public when the investigation concludes, including any disciplinary actions and actions to address root causes.[39]

Investigations often arise from whistleblower tips, whether someone blows the whistle internally, to regulators, or in the public forum. Whistleblower protections vary by jurisdiction and industry, with societal and corporate norms also affecting employees' willingness to speak up. Whistleblower protections are especially broad in the EU. Under the EU Whistleblower Directive, many types of reporters can be whistleblowers, and whistleblowers enjoy a presumption that detrimental actions by employers are retaliatory.[40] The UK takes a similar consolidated approach to EU whistleblower protections, but confines the definition of 'whistleblower' to workers generally.[41] Protections in the US exist on both the federal and state level and broadly protect against retaliation.[42] Cultural attitudes towards whistleblowing are relatively positive in these regions. In Asia Pacific, whistleblower protections vary, and cultural attitudes towards whistleblowers have historically been negative, which can undermine trust in internal investigations and enforcement mechanisms and result in lower levels of reporting.[43] In addition to statutory whistleblower protections, the ways in which organisations conduct investigations and safeguard confidentiality can engender a culture of speaking up or, alternatively, undermine trust in the corporation's ability to manage issues internally.[44] Generally, organisations should be careful to treat whistleblowers equitably, ensure the confidentiality of investigations, and have investigations policies and procedures based on regional regulatory requirements and issue-specific criteria at the ready.

---

37 Geoffrey P Miller, *The Law of Governance, Risk Management and Compliance* (3rd edn, Aspen Publishing, 2019).

38 *Ibid.*

39 *Ibid.*

40 Directive 2019/1937 of the European Parliament and of the Council of 23 October 2019 on the Protection of Persons who Report Breaches of Union Law [2019] OJ L305/44; "The EU Whistleblower Directive; what does it mean for you?", Deloitte, www2.deloitte.com/nl/nl/pages/finance/articles/the-eu-whistleblower-directive-what-does-it-mean-for-you.html.

41 Press release, "Government reviews whistleblowing laws" (27 March 2023), www.gov.uk/government/news/government-reviews-whistleblowing-laws.

42 See generally, Michael Delikat and Renée Phillips, *Corporate Whistleblowing in the Sarbanes-Oxley/Dodd-Frank Era* (2nd edn, Practising Law Institute, 2022).

43 See "Asia: managing workplace investigations (part 1 of 2)", Herbert Smith Freehills LLP (14 December 2020), www.lexology.com/library/detail.aspx?g=2d730e5c-1b9b-4622-9e4e-129c93695ce0; "Asia Pacific investigations capability survey", Deloitte (2021), www2.deloitte.com/content/dam/Deloitte/sg/Documents/financial-services/sea-fa-asia-pacific-investigation-capability-survey-hires.pdf.

44 See, Kathleen Healy and Rebecca Zech, "Worklife 2.0: International trends on workplace investigations", Freshfields Bruckhaus Deringer (7 October 2022), https://riskandcompliance.freshfields.com/post/102hyni/worklife-2-0-international-trends-on-workplace-investigations.

Increasingly, corporations are policing each other's investigation practices. Since the #MeToo Movement, so-called 'Weinstein representations' have become commonplace in some M&A contracts.[45] These representations declare that since a certain date no corporate officers or executives have been implicated in allegations of sexual harassment or misconduct.[46] Some of these clauses go further and require that the company not be party to a settlement agreement regarding covered behaviour.[47] Regardless, the US Speak Out Act limits the enforceability of pre-dispute non-disclosure and non-disparagement clauses covering sexual assault and sexual harassment allegations.[48] Another recent US act amended the Federal Arbitration Act to afford putative sexual assault and sexual harassment plaintiffs subject to arbitration agreements an opportunity to bring their claims in court.[49] Representations and warranties relating to other types of investigations – such as workplace discrimination investigations – have not become common practice yet. Instead, specific social representations and warranties tend to appear based on idiosyncratic deal risk factors. Even so, organisations should consider whether additional representations and warranties might be advantageous based on their codes of conduct, DEI commitments and business strategy.

Racial equity audits and civil rights audits represent companies' efforts to assess some of their most challenging social issues.[50] Broadly speaking, racial equity and civil rights audits consist of investigations into companies' practices, policies, products and services to identify inequities[51] experienced by internal and external stakeholders. While the scope of racial equity and civil rights audits can be bespoke to a specific company's process, stakeholders may include shareholders, employees, customers, suppliers and the communities in which companies operate, and the scope of the review may include a review with respect to any protected classes, including race, ethnicity, gender and LGBTQ+ status.[52] These audits are also designed to help organisations develop a plan to meet their racial justice and civil rights goals and mitigate inequities identified

---

45   See generally, Anna Windemuth, "The #MeToo Movement Migrates to M&A Boilerplate", 129 Yale L J 488 (2019); see also, Amelia Miazad, "Sex, Power, and Corporate Governance", 54 Univ Cal Davis 1913, 1980-84 (2021); Matthew Jennejohn *et al*, "Contractual Evolution", 89 Univ Chicago L Rev 901, 951–954 (2022).

46   See, Matthew Jennejohn *et al*, above, n 45, at 951.

47   See, Anna Windemuth, above, n 45, at 517–518.

48   See, Paul Davies *et al*, "ESG Insights: 10 Things That Should Be Top of Mind in 2023", Latham & Watkins LLP (5 January 2023), www.globalelr.com/2023/01/esg-insights-10-things-that-should-be-top-of-mind-in-2023/.

49   *Ibid.*

50   Betty M Huber *et al*, "Measuring the Impact: Key Considerations for Your Firm's DEI Programs and Racial Equity Audits", 7 PLI Current: *The Journal of PLI Press*, 3 (2023), www.lw.com/admin/upload/SiteAttachments/Measuring-the-Impact-Key-Considerations-for-Your-Firms-DEI-Programs-and-Racial-Equity-Audit.pdf.

51   Claudia B Dubon *et al*, "Racial Equity Audits: A new ESG initiative The Harvard Law School Forum on Corporate Governance" (2021), https://corpgov.law.harvard.edu/2021/10/30/racial-equity-audits-a-new-esg-initiative/.

52   Laura W Murphy, "The Rationale for and Key Elements of a Business Civil Rights Audit" (2021), www.civilrightsdocs.info/pdf/reports/Civil-Rights-Audit-Report-2021.pdf.

as a result of the audit.[53] Demands for these audits have risen sharply – by nearly 300% between 2021 to 2022[54] – in the years since the murder of George Floyd,[55] including at major technology companies. Racial equity and civil rights audits have often been prompted by shareholder proposals requesting that the company undertake such an initiative,[56] however, in 2022, 2023 and into 2024, companies were proactively undertaking such reviews. Critically, however, the recent push back to diversity-related efforts in the wake of the Supreme Court's June 2023 decision in *Students for Fair Admissions, Inc v President and Fellows of Harvard College*, some companies are taking a quieter approach to diversity-related initiatives and efforts, including racial equity and civil rights audits. While many companies continue to advance their diversity-related efforts internally, many are reevaluating their external disclosures and statements as the number of anti-diversity proposals, campaigns and lawsuits increases throughout the US.

3.3 Human rights and supply chain transparency

Even though various components of the S of ESG are recently in focus due to current events, some components – such as the need to ensure that organisations' activities do not involve abuses of human rights – have relatively long histories.[57] For example, broad investor appetite for socially responsible investments was first whetted in the 1990s and the UN began developing principles around human rights disclosures in the mid-2000s.[58] The chapter "Addressing human rights risks in global supply chains" goes deeper into the specifics of human rights risks in global supply chains and how to mitigate those risks and prevent violations of human rights. However here, the focus is on recent developments in this space, which have centered on due diligence of, reporting on and safeguarding of human rights practices throughout organisations' supply chains.

Indeed, the global supply chain became top of mind during the COVID-19 pandemic when unpredicted demand and supply chain challenges created significant issues. Recent regulatory developments in the US and EU have kept supply chain considerations top of mind for ESG practitioners. This changing landscape has meant that, in addition to supply chain resiliency, human rights and labour practices are salient, particularly for businesses with complex supply chains, including manufacturers and certain retailers.[59] Public scrutiny of labour practices

---

53   Dubon *et al*, above, n 51.
54   Alex M Whitebrook, "Racial Justice audits set to rise in 2023, Minerva Analytics (2023), www.manifest.co.uk/racial-justice-audits-set-to-rise-in-2023/.
55   Huber *et al*, *supra* above, n 50, at 5.
56   Dubon *et al*, above, n 51.
57   George Lawton, "A timeline and history of ESG investing, rules and practices", TechTarget (7 April 2023), www.techtarget.com/sustainability/feature/A-timeline-and-history-of-ESG-investing-rules-and-practices.
58   *Ibid.*
59   See, David W Simon *et al*, "Keeping the 'S' in ESG: Human Rights & Supply Chain", Foley & Lardner LLP (29 March 2023), www.foley.com/en/insights/publications/2023/03/keeping-s-esg-human-rights-supply-chain.

has increased in parallel, with producers, investors and consumers all becoming more sensitive to supply chain disruption in addition to labour practices.

Although entering the spotlight only recently, global supply chains have been subject to US labour regulation since at least the early 20th century.[60] In Europe, the EU and some member states are developing and implementing supply chain transparency obligations, such as the proposed CSDDD and the enacted Corporate Sustainability Reporting Directive (CSRD), on a swathe of companies whose businesses touch their jurisdictions.[61] Much of the new and emerging supply chain transparency regulation has a global impact, extending beyond single jurisdictions or individual corporations to include organisations' supply and value chains worldwide; even the slightest nexus to the regulating jurisdiction can bring a company's operations under scrutiny.[62] Corporates should aim to meet the most stringent applicable regulations and engage experts to navigate the web of regulations.

In the US, the Tariff Act of 1930 prohibits the importation or sale of products made with forced labour, which is effected through Withhold Release Orders.[63] Lately, the US has ratcheted up its human rights labour protections. For example, in 2016, the Trade Facilitation and Trade Enforcement Act of 2015, which closed enforcement loopholes, enabled the first seizure of goods connected to forced labour by US Customs and Border Protection in 15 years.[64] In 2021, a bipartisan US Congress condemned foreign forced labour by enacting the Uyghur Forced Labor Prevention Act.[65] The Act imposes a rebuttable presumption that manufacturers in Xinjiang use forced labour in manufacturing goods and prohibits importation by virtue of Section 307 of the Tariff Act of 1930 if any part of a good is produced in Xinjiang absent a rebuttal by the importer.[66]

---

60   Compare the Tariff Act of 1930 with the Uyghur Forced Labor Prevention Act (2021).
61   See, eg, European Parliament Press Release, "MEPs Push Companies to Mitigate Their Negative Social and Environmental Impact" (1 June 2023); Proposed Corporate Sustainability Due Diligence Directive (EU Commission, 2022); Corporate Sustainability Due Diligence Directive Negotiating Position (EU Council, 2022); Directive 2022/2464 of the European Parliament and of the Council of 14 December 2022 Amending Regulation 537/2014, Directive 2004/109/EC, Directive 2006/43/EC and Directive 2013/34/EU, as Regards Corporate Sustainability Reporting [2022] OJ L322/15; Supply Chain Due Diligence Act (Germany, 2023); Stefan Bartz *et al*, "How Germany's New ESG Law Will Affect Suppliers Globally", Latham & Watkins LLP (21 February 2023), www.lw.com/admin/upload/SiteAttachments/How-Germany%E2%80%99s-New-ESG-Law-Will-Affect-Suppliers-Globally.pdf.
62   See, Paul Davies *et al*, "ESG Insights: 10 Things That Should Be Top of Mind in 2023", Latham & Watkins LLP (5 January 2023), www.globalelr.com/2023/01/esg-insights-10-things-that-should-be-top-of-mind-in-2023/.
63   See, David E Bond *et al*, "Supply Chain Compliance with Human Rights and Environmental Obligations", White & Case (24 February 2023), www.whitecase.com/insight-alert/supply-chain-compliance-human-rights-and-environmental-obligations.
64   See, David W Simon *et al*, "Real ESG Enforcement Mechanisms: Restrictions on Imports of Goods Made With Forced or Child Labor", Foley & Lardner LLP (19 December 2022), www.foley.com/en/insights/publications/2022/12/real-esg-enforcement-mechanisms-restrictions.
65   See, Fadel Allassan, "Biden signs historic bill punishing China for Uyghur genocide", Axios (23 December 2021), www.axios.com/2021/12/23/biden-signs-uyghur-forced-labor-bill.
66   See, Paul Davies *et al*, "US Government Publishes Uyghur Forced Labor Prevention Act Enforcement Strategy", Latham & Watkins LLP (12 July 2022), www.lw.com/en/people/admin/upload/SiteAttachments/Alert%202973.pdf.

In the EU, the CSDDD would subject in-scope companies' global chain of activities to due diligence for adherence to international human rights standards.[67] The proposed directive would require due diligence and reporting for actual and potential adverse human rights (and environmental) impacts by in-scope companies' suppliers with 'certain relationships' and would obligate covered entities to address any actual adverse human rights impacts.[68] In addition to the CSDDD, the CSRD imposes ESG reporting obligations on many companies, even outside the EU, whose business touches the EU, including an obligation to report on matters relating to workers in the value chain.[69]

Another proposal in the EU would prohibit the placement of products made with forced labour into the EU market.[70] If adopted, the CSDDD and the forced labour proposal would set regulatory floors for member states, but jurisdictions could impose additional, more stringent regulations on affected entities – that is, the exact scope and impact of both CSDDD and the forced labour proposal depend first on the results of negotiations among EU political institutions and second on how each EU jurisdiction implements the final directives.[71] Germany has already gone a step further in addressing supply chain considerations. Germany's Supply Chain Due Diligence Act (Lksg) covers the supply and value chain of companies of certain sizes based in Germany, regardless of whether their products or services are actually placed in the jurisdiction.[72] Obligations under the law differ depending on whether a supplier is a direct supplier or an indirect supplier to an in-scope company, although the law's effects will likely trickle down to indirect suppliers.[73] The UK has also demonstrated a renewed focus on human rights issues in the supply chain in recent years, but its Modern Slavery Act 2015 requires attestations on steps taken to "deal with modern slavery risks" in the supply chain rather than due diligence to guarantee that the supply chain is free of forced labour.[74] France has also waded into these regulatory waters.[75] These laws and regulations are components of a multifaceted expansion of

---

67   See, Paul Davies *et al*, above, n 62; Proposed Corporate Sustainability Due Diligence Directive (EU Commission, 2022).

68   See, David E Bond *et al*, above, n 63.

69   See, Paul A Davies *et al*, "The EU Corporate Sustainability Reporting Directive—How Companies Need to Prepare", Latham & Watkins LLP (27 January 2023), www.lw.com/admin/upload/SiteAttachments/Alert%203059.pdf.

70   See, Paul A Davies *et al*, "European Commission Proposes Legislation to Prohibit Products Made or Imported With Forced Labour", Latham & Watkins LLP (15 September 2022), www.globalelr.com/2022/ 09/european-commission-proposes-legislation-to-prohibit-products-made-or-imported-with-forced-labour/.

71   See, Paul A Davies *et al*, "European Parliament Agrees Position on Corporate Sustainability Due Diligence Directive", Latham & Watkins LLP (15 June 2023), www.globalelr.com/2023/06/european-parliament-agrees-position-on-corporate-sustainability-due-diligence-directive/.

72   See, David E Bond *et al*, above, n 63 (noting that the Lksg applies to companies with at least 3,000 employees from 1 January 2023 and to companies with at least 1,000 employees from 1 January 2024).

73   See Stefan Bartz *et al*, above, n 61.

74   UK Government Home Office, "Guidance: Publish an annual modern slavery statement" (last updated 28 July 2021), www.gov.uk/guidance/publish-an-annual-modern-slavery-statement.

75   See, Paul Davies *et al*, "ESG Insights: 10 Things That Should Be Top of Mind in 2023", Latham & Watkins LLP (5 January 2023), www.globalelr.com/2023/01/esg-insights-10-things-that-should-be-top-of-mind-in-2023/.

human rights protections in global value chains with implications for cross-border trade, especially in countries that are long on manufacturing. For instance, the 2016 and 2019 trade agreements between Vietnam and the US and the EU, respectively, required Vietnam to conform its labour regulations to ILO principles as well as to enhance enforcement of labour standards.[76]

In response to these developments, the ABA Business Law Section has released model contract clauses to protect workers in international supply chains and to institutionalise practices that support positive labour practices.[77] Affected companies can manage their human rights and forced labour risks by leveraging these models as well as their own existing compliance processes, such as evaluations of third-party intermediaries for compliance with anti-corruption laws.[78] Finally, companies with exposure to these regulations are incorporating relevant representations and warranties into their contracts and disclosures. These provisions will likely become boilerplate both for companies within the scope of the laws discussed above and companies seeking to minimise related risks.

Altogether, supply chain transparency regulations beg the question of how far down the value chain organisations need to go to satisfy their due diligence obligations.[79] Consensus is elusive for now, but organisations should know their counterparties and ensure that those counterparties know their counterparties in turn. Furthermore, organisations should document their compliance, including their due diligence, to minimise their reputational and compliance risks.

3.4 'Do no significant harm' criteria

The 'do no significant harm' (DNSH) principle is a core idea throughout the 'alphabet soup' of the EU ESG disclosure regime. It is an underlying force of the European Green Deal and is laid out in European legislation, including the Sustainable Finance Disclosure Regulation (SFDR) and the EU Taxonomy Regulation (EU Taxonomy), and requires forthcoming European Commission initiatives to abide by this principle.[80]

---

76 See "United States-Viet Nam Plan for the Enhancement of Trade and Labour Relations" (2016), https://ustr.gov/sites/default/files/TPP-Final-Text-Labour-US-VN-Plan-for-Enhancement-of-Trade-and-Labour-Relations.pdf; Peter Liddell and Neeraj Bansal, "Rethinking supply chains in Asia Pacific", KPMG (October 2021).

77 Working Group to Draft Model Contract Clauses to Protect Human Rights in International Supply Chains, ABA Business Law Section, "Balancing Buyer and Supplier Responsibilities: Model Contract Clauses to Protect Workers in International Supply Chains", Version 2.0, 77 *The Business Lawyer* 115, 177–182 (2022).

78 See, David W Simon *et al*, "A New Year for Human Rights Compliance Resolutions", *Industry Today* (4 February 2022), https://industrytoday.com/a-new-year-for-human-rights-compliance-resolutions/.

79 See, Paul A Davies *et al*, "European Commission Proposes Legislation to Prohibit Products Made or Imported With Forced Labour", Latham & Watkins LLP (15 September 2022), www.globalelr.com/2022/09/european-commission-proposes-legislation-to-prohibit-products-made-or-imported-with-forced-labour/ (comparing differences in language between legislation proposed by the EU Commission and the EU Council on supply chain disclosures).

80 *Do No Significant Harm Handbook*, Maples Group, ELS Europe, Frankfurt School FS-UN Collaborating Centre, 6 (November 2021), www.fs-unep-centre.org/wp-content/uploads/2021/11/Do-No-Significant-Harm-Handbook.pdf.

DNSH takes a holistic approach to safeguarding against investments that focus on specific environmental or social objectives to the detriment of others, or without consideration of other adverse impact indicators. For example, SFDR, Article 2(17) provides for the DNSH principle in defining an investment as 'sustainable' if it furthers an environmental or social objective, accounts for Principle Adverse Effect indicators (PAI), and does not significantly harm any other environmental or social objective all the while practising good governance.[81] While the principle is primarily attributable to the EU, US-based organisations should consider DNSH due to potential ripple effects of business decisions and activities.

In practice, the DNSH principle means that any Article 8 or Article 9 financial product must conduct a DNSH test. Article 8 financial products, those that promote an environmental or social goal, must explain how adverse social and environmental impact indicators are taken into account.[82] Article 9 financial products, those that have a sustainable investment objective, must ensure that any 'sustainable investments' align with Article 18 of the EU Taxonomy, which sets forth the DNSH principle.[83,84]

Jurisdictions utilising the DNSH principle expand beyond the EU and include Mexico, the UK, Canada, Chile and Singapore, among others, though most remain focused on environmental objectives at present. For example, Singapore's DNSH principle focuses on mitigating adverse impacts of climate change mitigation activities on the other four environmental objectives of the taxonomy, namely climate change adaptation, protection of ecosystems and biodiversity, promoting resilience and circular economy, and pollution prevention and control.[85] Incorporation of social objectives outside the EU remains a large potential area for growth, however, one example of early steps includes Mexico, which finalised its Sustainable Taxonomy in March 2023 with

---

81   Consolidated questions and answers (Q&A) on the SFDR (Regulation (EU) 2019/2088) and the SFDR Delegated Regulation, Commission Delegated Regulation (EU) 2022/1288, JC 2023 18, (17 May 2023), www.esma.europa.eu/sites/default/files/2023-05/JC_2023_18_-_Consolidated_JC_SFDR_QAs.pdf.

82   Lewis Davison, Fiona McNally, Charlotte North, "ESG: EU Regulatory Challenge and Its Implications", Harvard Law School Forum on Corporate Governance (18 February 2023), https://corpgov.law.harvard.edu/2023/02/18/esg-eu-regulatory-change-and-its-implications/.

83   David Henry Doyle, "A Short Guide to the EU's Taxonomy Regulation", S&P Global (12 May 2021), www.spglobal.com/esg/insights/a-short-guide-to-the-eu-s-taxonomy-regulation.

84   The DNSH principle further applies in the EU Taxonomy which applies to environmentally sustainable economic activities. The EU Taxonomy is rooted in two key ideas: an activity must (i) contribute to one or more of the six environmental objectives listed in the EU Taxonomy; and (ii) do no significant harm to any of the other objectives while respecting human rights and labour standards. For each activity, Technical Screening Criteria outline the conditions for an activity to be considered as significantly contributing to a sustainability objective, as well as the thresholds for compliance with DNSH.

85   Paul A Davies, Farhana Sharmeen, Michael D Green and James Bee, "Singapore's Green Finance Industry Taskforce Launches Final Consultation on Green and Transition Taxonomy", Latham & Watkins Environmental, Land & Resources (2 March 2023), www.globalelr.com/2023/03/singapores-green-finance-industry-taskforce-launches-final-consultation-on-green-and-transition-taxonomy/#:~:text=%E2%80%9CDo%20No%20Significant%20Harm%E2%80%9D%20Criteria,-The%20consultation%20also&text=The%20DNSH%20would%20require%20companies,mitigation%20measures%20to%20protect%20biodiversity.

a substantial focus on both social and environmental factors. Mexico's Taxonomy provides a clear framework on what is considered 'sustainable', although this framework only applies to environmental objectives for now.[86]

Until there is a common reporting standard for ESG data, reporting and disclosing social-related risks and return will remain a challenge. However, the proposed amendments and current trends signal a push for more detailed disclosures to improve the information available to investors and the accountability of managers. In anticipation of finalised and uniform disclosure standards, screening broadly and carefully for potential adverse impacts of operations, assets and investments today will create a smoother path in the future.

3.5 Shareholder proposals

(a) *Social proposals*

Social issues have long given rise to a significant proportion of the ESG shareholder proposals submitted to companies each year. The specific subject matter of socially-oriented shareholder proposals varies widely but broadly pertains to human capital management or social policy issues.[87] Human capital management looks inward at companies' leadership, personnel and employment practices. Examples include proposals pertaining to diversity at the board, executive, or workplace levels.[88] Proposals for racial equity audits have also emerged as a core topic of human capital management shareholder proposals since 2020.[89] Social policy proposals look outward at the effects of companies' activities and operations. Examples include proposals on political contributions and lobbying, as well as attention on climate-related political spending.[90] Proposals focusing on human rights and public health matters are also prevalent.[91]

The subjects of shareholder proposals also continue to change quickly and are subject to legal and political developments. In the 2023 proxy season alone, more than 30 shareholder proposals were filed relating to companies' responses to the Supreme Court's decision to eliminate the Constitutional right to an abortion in June of 2022.[92] Abortion-related proposals concerned not only

---

86 Austin Pierce, "Mexico's New Sustainable Taxonomy – Voluntary for Now, but Designed to Expand", Latham & Watkins Environment, Land & Resources (4 April 2023), www.globalelr.com/2023/04/mexicos-new-sustainable-taxonomy-voluntary-for-now-but-designed-to-expand/.

87 Matteo Tonello, "Shareholder Voting Trends (2018-2022)", The Conference Board, www.conference-board.org/pdfdownload.cfm?masterProductID=40063.

88 *Ibid.*

89 *Ibid.*

90 *Ibid.*

91 *Ibid.*

92 Carrie Byrnes and Megan Juel, "Investor Proposals Show Abortion A Rising ESG Concern" Law360 (2023), www.law360.com/articles/1590830/investor-proposals-show-abortion-a-rising-esg-concern.

human capital management matters, such as employee healthcare and other benefits, but also social policy issues, such as political spending and data privacy. This development additionally demonstrates how even one topic can cut across different facets of an organisation and its operations.[93]

Finally, so called 'anti-ESG' shareholder proposals have become significantly more common in recent years, nearly quadrupling over the past nine years.[94] The overwhelming majority of such shareholder proposals has been directed at certain social issues: two-thirds of such proposals oppose diversity initiatives and another quarter of proposals oppose certain political activity.[95] Despite the rapid increase in such proposals, however, they have often been excluded from proxy votes altogether.[96] When they are not excluded, anti-ESG proposals on average receive below the threshold level of support (5%) required for eligibility for resubmission in the following year's shareholder vote.[97,98]

(b) Shareholder proposal legal frameworks

In the US, the legal framework governing shareholder proposals is Rule 14a-8 of the Securities Exchange Act of 1934.[99,100]

The relevant bases for excluding proposals under Rule 14a-8 have their own precedent, subject to complex and layered guidance issued by the Commission's staff over time, as well as precedent responses from the staff concurring with or indicating that the staff cannot concur with exclusion of the underlying proposals. In recent years, the Commission has scrolled back guidance that would permit more proposals to be excluded, and has also begun interpreting the rules underlying exclusion more narrowly, resulting in more proposals being included in proxy statements over the past few proxy seasons.

Additionally, the SEC has proposed amendments to several other bases for

---

93   *Ibid.*
94   Heidi Welsh, "Anti-ESG Shareholder Proposals in 2023", The Harvard Law School Forum on Corporate Governance (2023), https://corpgov.law.harvard.edu/2023/06/01/anti-esg-shareholder-proposals-in-2023/.
95   *Ibid.*
96   *Ibid.*
97   *Ibid.*
98   An anti-ESG shareholder proponent has filed a suit against the SEC, alleging the Commission is engaging in unlawful viewpoint discrimination in violation of the First Amendment. Specifically, the suit alleges the SEC is barring companies from excluding shareholder proposals that concern sexual orientation and gender identity discrimination while allowing organisations to exclude identically worded shareholder proposals that would have prohibited discrimination on political ideology grounds. The litigation is ongoing at time of writing. Sarah Jarvis, "5th Circ. Urged To Undo SEC Ruling On Ideological Bias Proxy", Law360, (17 July 2023), www.law360.com/articles/1700309.
99   Shareholder Proposals, 17 CFR § 240.14a-8 (2020). Specifically, Rule 14a-8 "addresses when a company must include a shareholder's proposal in its proxy statement" by establishing shareholder eligibility requirements for submitting shareholder proposals, substantive bases on which the company can exclude shareholders' proposals, and procedural requirements governing shareholders' submission and companies' exclusion of proposals. Rule 14a-8, and particularly its grounds for excluding shareholder proposals, has and will continue to evolve rapidly.
100   SEC Commissioner Hester Pierce described the current proposed efforts to amend recently adopted rules as "regulatory whiplash": Hester M Pierce, "U-Turn: Comments on Proxy Voting Advice", *Newsroom* (2022), www.sec.gov/news/statement/peirce-statement-proxy-voting-advice-071322.

excluding shareholder proposals.[101] Specifically, the Commission has proposed modifying three of the bases for exclusion of shareholder proposals, including the substantial implementation under Rule 14a-8(i)(10) basis, the duplicative proposal basis under Rule 14a-8(i)(11) and the resubmission basis under Rule 14a-8(i)(12).[102] If adopted, these amendments would likely have the effect of making exclusion of shareholder proposals – including socially-oriented ones – even more difficult for companies.

Shareholder proposals of all kinds are significantly less prevalent in Europe than in the US. In one recent proxy season, there were fewer than 20% as many European shareholder proposals as American ones.[103] One important reason for this disparity is that Europe has significantly higher capital eligibility requirements – typically 5% of a company's equity[104] – for submitting shareholder proposals as compared to the US, where proposals can be submitted by shareholders holding as little as $2,000.[105] Other reasons include ownership structures that afford controlling shareholders substantial voting power and greater opportunities for the shareholders to interface more with the board before the annual meeting.[106] In other parts of the world, ownership thresholds tend to range between the US approach and the European approach. For example, in China, the ownership threshold to be eligible to submit shareholder proposals is 3% – not quite as high as it is in Europe, but still significantly higher than in the US.[107]

4.   Conclusion

While the S in ESG is already entwined in longstanding business ethics and compliance, the rules of the game are nonetheless dynamic and changing as regulators across the globe contemplate or enact new requirements. For the S in ESG, this includes a range of items focused not only on disclosure but also on business conduct, including labour practices across the supply chain. Moreover, debates on businesses' impact on society and politics have galvanised stakeholders who are raising their concerns and pressing for action, which often includes conflicting opinions. In fact, the S in ESG may be uniquely controversial given the propensity of social issues to strike a chord and,

---

101   Rule 14a-8 Amendments, Reginfo.gov, www.reginfo.gov/public/do/eAgendaViewRule?pubId=202310& RIN=3235-AM91.
102   *Ibid.*
103   Barbara Novick *et al*, "Europe's listed companies: Their governance, shareholders and votes cast", BlackRock (February 2020), www.blackrock.com/corporate/literature/whitepaper/viewpoint-europe-listed-companies-governance-shareholders-votes-cast-february-2020.pdf.
104   Paul Oudin and Sophie Vermeille, "Shareholder Proposals and Boards' Veto Power", Oxford Business Law Blog (13 September 2022), https://blogs.law.ox.ac.uk/oblb/blog-post/2022/09/shareholder-proposals-and-boards-veto-power.
105   Shareholder Proposals, 17 CFR § 240.14a-8(b)(i)(A) (2020).
106   Novick *et al*, above, n 103.
107   Jan Holthuis and Li Jiao, Shareholder Activism in China: Overview Change Practical Law (2022), https://uk.practicallaw.thomsonreuters.com/w-013-1127?transitionType=Default&context Data=(sc.Default).

particularly in the US, a backlash. It is within this context that businesses should be prepared to respond to scrutiny from stakeholders including regulators, customers, employees and the communities where businesses operate or the communities affected by such operations.

As demonstrated in this chapter, the S in ESG presents significant risks and strategic opportunities including ones that warrant the attention of the board. On the one hand, increasing regulation and public scrutiny mean businesses may have to navigate complexity, and failure to meet expectations can lead to legal liabilities or allegations of social washing, or impact a business's social licence to operate. On the other hand, businesses that carefully consider and govern their approach to social matters may be able to reap benefits like consumer trust, better employee retention, or opportunities linked to the business's unique industry and strategy. Going forward, the companies that navigate the S best will thoughtfully evaluate their social goals, policies, programmes and reporting, authentically tying them to their strategic objectives and mission.

ESG reporting

James Bee
Paul Davies
Sarah E Fortt
Michael D Green
Betty M Huber
Latham & Watkins

1.   Introduction

ESG reporting is an area that has grown significantly in both importance and complexity over recent years. As interest in, and appreciation of, the key role of ESG has developed, corporates, investors and regulators among others have realised the importance of high quality, reliable and comparable information about the ESG performance of entities being available.

ESG reporting has a long history. In many cases, public disclosure of ESG information started as a way by which companies that wished to publicise certain ESG-related messages to investors and customers could voluntarily highlight relevant efforts and achievements. As a result, much of this early ESG reporting was led by marketing and public relations teams, was not standardised, and was often subject to limited internal control procedures within disclosing entities.

However, as investors in particular became increasingly focused on the economic and societal impacts of companies' ESG performance, it was acknowledged that being able to compare the information provided by companies was a vital part of such information becoming decision-useful. This led to the development of standardised voluntary frameworks, which companies could use as the basis of preparing their ESG disclosures. Such voluntary frameworks played a key role in the development of more sophisticated ESG reporting, and a number of the more successful ones (including the Global Reporting Initiative (GRI), the Sustainability Accounting Standards Board (SASB) Standards and the recommendations of the Taskforce on Climate-Related Financial Disclosures (TCFD) – see below for further information) gained considerable traction in the market.

The popularity of these voluntary frameworks led to a significant number of different frameworks being developed and published, covering a broad range of ESG topics, sectors and focuses, with the effect of creating an 'alphabet soup' of different acronyms and standards by which companies could report. Different investors and stakeholders had their own preferences as to which voluntary standard(s) companies should be reporting against, meaning that a number of companies found that they were being asked to report against multiple different frameworks, leading to an unnecessary impact on company time and resources.

As a result, we have more recently seen broad calls for standardisation that are beginning to be considered. The development of the International Sustainability Standards Board (ISSB) and the publication of its first set of standards, and also specific regulatory action being taken in a number of jurisdictions (much of which is based on pre-existing voluntary frameworks), both in relation to corporate disclosures and disclosures in relation to the ESG characteristics of financial products, are all arguably focused on improving reporting standardisation, as are other initiatives. This chapter will discuss some of the key initiatives taking place in this regard across the globe, including in the United States, European Union, United Kingdom and elsewhere, which seek to ensure that investors and broader stakeholders in these jurisdictions have access to high-quality ESG information from companies that is comparable and decision-useful. However, it goes without saying that, with so many jurisdictions seeking to introduce their own mandatory standards, each of which may have differing focuses with respect to areas such as the definition of materiality and the scope of ESG issues covered, many multinational companies and investors are at risk of finding themselves in a similar position as before, with companies reporting in different ways on different topics and the results not being as comparable as hoped. Moreover, it is possible that comparability is a red herring and, given the complexity of the topics underlying ESG reporting, transparency is the best that can be hoped for and should be the main ambition of ESG-related reporting.

The EU is generally viewed as being the jurisdiction globally that is advancing the promulgation of regulations in relation to mandatory ESG disclosures most rapidly. The backbone of a number of these proposals has been the European Green Deal, announced by the Commission in December 2019, which set out a policy roadmap for making the EU's economy sustainable in the long term. The policies that have subsequently been developed and enacted by the EU in furtherance of the aims of the Green Deal include a number that are directly relevant to the ESG reporting obligations of companies and financial institutions operating in the bloc. An overview of the some of the most important of these is provided below.

2. European Union

2.1 CSRD: Overview

The EU has had mandatory ESG reporting legislation in place for a number of years. In particular, the Non-Financial Reporting Directive (NFRD) was adopted in 2014 and introduced certain, high-level reporting requirements for a relatively small number of large, listed companies. As part of the Green Deal, the EU committed to review and revise the NFRD, and the result of such review was the enactment of the Corporate Sustainability Reporting Directive (CSRD).

The CSRD amends and expands on the NFRD, both considerably broadening the scope of the companies required to provide sustainability[1] disclosures and also introducing considerably more detailed disclosure requirements for those companies that are in scope.[2]

The reporting requirements under CSRD apply to EU entities that are: (i) 'large undertakings'; (ii) parent companies of large groups; and/or (iii) 'small and medium-sized undertakings which are public interest undertakings'. Companies based outside the EU may also be in scope to the extent that they have securities listed on a regulated EU exchange or subsidiary companies/branches located in the EU. 'Large undertakings' are EU companies that meet at least two of the following three thresholds:

- balance sheet total: €25 million;
- net turnover: €50 million; or
- average number of employees during the financial year: 250.

The CSRD also applies to EU parent companies of large corporate groups, which are groups of companies that meet the above thresholds on a consolidated basis.

Organisations with parent companies based outside of the EU may also be subject to reporting requirements in relation to their entire global corporate group, and not just their EU operations. Such companies would be required to disclose certain information if the global group has generated a net turnover within the EU of €150 million for two consecutive financial years and either:

- has an EU subsidiary that is a large undertaking or public interest entity with securities listed in the EU; or
- has a branch in the EU that generated €40 million net turnover in the preceding financial year.

Such disclosure requirements are not due to enter into force until 2028 (with first reports being issued in 2029).

2.2   CSRD European sustainability reporting standards

The CSRD itself lays out only very high level reporting requirements. The more granular detail on the sustainability information that in-scope companies will be required to report will be set out in EU sustainability reporting standards

---

1   The EU uses the term 'sustainability' as opposed to ESG in its legislative initiatives.
2   Directive 2013/34/EU of the European Parliament and of the Council of 26 June 2013 on the annual financial statements, consolidated financial statements and related reports of certain types of undertakings, amending Directive 2006/43/EC of the European Parliament and of the Council and repealing Council Directives 78/660/EEC and 83/349/EEC Text with EEA relevance [2013] OJ L182/19 https://eur-lex.europa.eu/legal-content/EN/TXT/PDF/?uri=CELEX:32013L0034&from=EN.

(ESRS). The first set of ESRS were adopted by the Commission on 31 July 2023, which consists of a combination of 'cross cutting' and 'topical' ESRS, that apply to all large in-scope entities across sectors, and will form the basis of the initial reporting under CSRD.

Figure 1. Structure of the ESRS

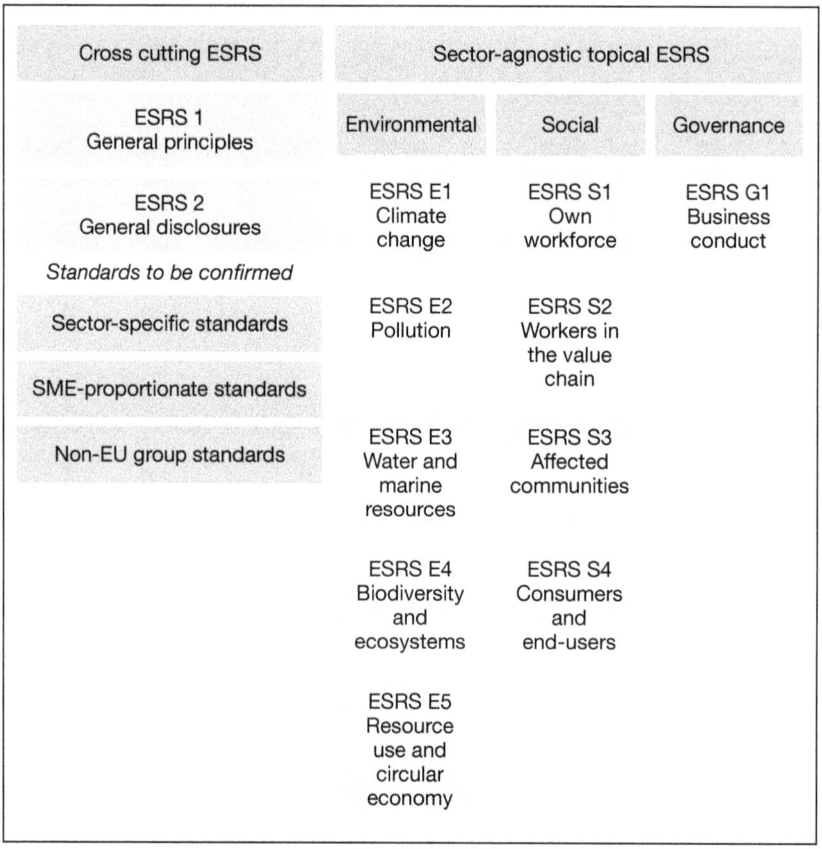

Cross cutting ESRS	Sector-agnostic topical ESRS		
ESRS 1 General principles	Environmental	Social	Governance
ESRS 2 General disclosures	ESRS E1 Climate change	ESRS S1 Own workforce	ESRS G1 Business conduct
Standards to be confirmed	ESRS E2 Pollution	ESRS S2 Workers in the value chain	
Sector-specific standards			
SME-proportionate standards	ESRS E3 Water and marine resources	ESRS S3 Affected communities	
Non-EU group standards	ESRS E4 Biodiversity and ecosystems	ESRS S4 Consumers and end-users	
	ESRS E5 Resource use and circular economy		

Additional sets of ESRS, including sector-specific ESRS and SME standards, are due to be provided in future years. The deadline for such standards to be adopted was initially 30 June 2024 (which remains the case for the SME standards), although European Commission and the European Financial Reporting Advisory Group (EFRAG) announced in October 2023 that publication of the sector-specific ESRS would be delayed by two years until June 2026, with public consultations on initial drafts commencing in 2024.

2.3   CSRD: Key aspects

Certain key aspects of CSRD include:

- *Double materiality:* Under CSRD, companies must not only disclose sustainability-related information that is 'material' for their business results and operations (ie, financial materiality), but also information that is 'material' to the company's impact on society (ie, impact materiality). This represents a notable departure from the concept of materiality as it has traditionally been understood by many across the corporate reporting landscape, and is an area where EU legislation departs noticeably from other jurisdictions and voluntary standards.
- *Value chain reporting requirements:* Under CSRD, companies are required to report material information not only regarding the reporting company and its subsidiaries, but also about its value chain, ie, direct or indirect business relationships, which in many cases will require detailed value chain due diligence to be undertaken by the reporting company.
- *Assurance of CSRD reporting:* The CSRD requires that companies must obtain a third-party verification as to the company's compliance with the reporting requirements thereunder. This requirement will initially be on a 'limited assurance' basis, but will in time be raised to a 'reasonable assurance' basis.

Given the acknowledged complexity of the materiality assessment process and incorporation of value chain information into CSRD reporting, EFRAG has been tasked with producing formal implementation guidance to assist undertakings with their CSRD obligations in these two areas. In December 2023, EFRAG published its first ESRS Implementation Guidance documents for public feedback, with an additional publication covering the detailed ESRS datapoints with accompanying explanatory notes.

2.4   SFDR and fund-naming proposals

The Sustainable Finance Disclosure Regulation (SFDR), a key aspect of the EU's Action Plan on Sustainable Finance, has introduced various disclosure-related requirements for financial market participants and financial advisers at entity, service and product level. The SFDR aims to increase transparency on sustainability within financial markets in a standardised way, thereby reducing the risk of greenwashing and ensuring comparability between regulated investment products. It requires, among other things, that certain asset managers and institutional investors disclose the principal adverse impacts of their investment decisions on sustainability factors at entity level as well as for certain financial products.

The SFDR requires, subject to certain requirements: (i) pre-contractual disclosures; (ii) website disclosure; and (iii) periodic disclosures of sustainability-related information. At a product level, the SFDR requires the providers of financial products to classify their products into one of three categories: (i) products which promote environmental or social characteristics (otherwise known as 'Article 8 products'); (ii) products which have a sustainable investment objective ('Article 9 products'); and (iii) other products ('Article 6 products').

The exact nature of the disclosures required under the SFDR differ depending on the nature of the product being provided, with additional disclosures being required for Article 8 and Article 9 products compared to Article 6.

For financial advisers, required disclosures include: (i) information about policies on the integration of sustainability risks into the investment advice; and (ii) consideration of principal adverse impacts on sustainability factors in the investment advice, in each case, on a 'comply or explain' basis.

In January 2023, Regulatory Technical Standards (RTS) to the SFDR entered into force. Those RTS contain templates that entities subject to SFDR shall use to disclose relevant information. The RTS also contains a statement for presenting key performance indicators (KPIs) in relation to any identified adverse impact.

Certain market participants and commentators have acknowledged that there have been challenges with the implementation of the SFDR, and that has been recognised by the European Commission's publication of two consultation documents (one public and one targeted) in September 2023, which revealed that the Commission is looking at potential issues with the implementation of the SFDR and considering the establishment of a new product categorisation system to supplement or replace aspects of the SFDR.

In addition, in November 2022, the European Securities and Markets Authority (ESMA) published a specific consultation paper on guidelines for naming funds using ESG-related terms, in an attempt to ensure that funds that were marketed using ESG terms met certain relevant standards. At the time of the consultation, ESMA indicated that final guidelines were to be issued by Q3 2023, but this timeline was ultimately delayed.

2.5 Taxonomy

The Taxonomy on Sustainable Finance (the 'Taxonomy') establishes a classification system for 'environmentally sustainable activities', which has applied in certain respects since January 2022.

In order for an activity to be considered 'environmentally sustainable', and therefore Taxonomy-aligned, it must: (i) make a substantial contribution[3] to one or more of the six environmental objectives set out below; (ii) do no significant harm to any of the other environmental objectives; (iii) be carried out in

---

3   Subject to certain conditions, so-called 'enabling activities' or activities that directly enable activities that contribute substantially to the environmental objectives can be considered Taxonomy-compliant.

compliance with certain the minimum safeguards;[4] and (iv) comply with the relevant technical screening criteria (TSC). The Taxonomy establishes the following six environmental objectives:

- climate change mitigation;
- climate change adaption;
- sustainable use and protection of water and marine resources;
- transition to a circular economy;
- pollution prevention and control; and
- protection and restoration of biodiversity and ecosystems.

While the Taxonomy Regulation itself only contains a high-level description of environmentally sustainable activities, it is the TSC that contain the detailed criteria pursuant to which an activity can be assessed as to whether it meets the requirements under the Taxonomy in relation to both: (i) making a substantial contribution; and (ii) doing no significant harm to relevant environmental objectives. As noted above, the Commission is required to adopt TSC for all of the six environmental objectives, but to date only the TSC on climate change mitigation and climate change adaption have been formally adopted. However, in April 2023, the Commission issued a consultation on the TSC for the remaining four environmental objectives which will, once adopted, provide that relevant criteria are available for all aspects of the Taxonomy.

While being primarily a classification framework, the Taxonomy also contains certain disclosure requirements for corporates that will be subject to CSRD. Such companies will be required to disclose the proportion of Taxonomy-aligned turnover, capital and operating expenditure. Such disclosure obligations have been further clarified in the Article 8 Delegated Act, which was adopted by the Commission in July 2021 and sets out the different KPIs and forms of disclosure to be used by in-scope entities.

3. United States

In contrast to the European approach, traditionally the US does not rely primarily on a 'line item' based approach to disclosure, but on its 'principles-based' disclosure regime to provide investors and other stakeholders with relevant and material information. While some investors and stakeholders may have concerns that principles-based disclosure requirements, without more specific product relevant information, may not produce the disclosures and information that investors may need, others fear what an abandonment or divergence from the principles-based approach will mean for the complexity

---

4   'Minimum safeguards' refers to international frameworks in relation to corporate conduct and human rights, such as the OECD Guidelines for Multinational Enterprises, the UN Guiding Principles on Business and Human Rights or the International Bill of Rights.

and costs associated with compliance. Parties will need to analyse the effects of the US approach on disclosure (as well as consider the specific requirements of US Regulations SK and S-X, including the SEC's proposed climate disclosure proposal described below) to determine, on relevant transactions, how to navigate the different approaches and resulting disclosures, and how these differences might affect a company's specific reporting structures, offerings and liability. This is particularly important considering that there is some opposition in the US, including in the US Congress, to any mandatory ESG-related disclosure requirements, particularly those that are not directly related to the issuer's financial performance or its ability to repay its debts.

In March 2022, the US Securities and Exchange Commission (SEC) proposed rules that would require registrants, including both domestic and foreign private issuers, to include climate-related information in registration statements and annual reports.[5] The proposed rules would require significant, detailed new narrative disclosures in the body of annual reports and prospectuses as well as new disclosures in the audited notes to annual financial statements and, for certain companies, a new attestation report by an independent outside expert relating to additional quantitative disclosures on GHG emissions. The proposed rules are modelled in part on the TCFD recommendations and also draw upon the GHG Protocol. In addition, many in the US view the SEC's proposed climate disclosure rules as deviating significantly from the SEC's principles-based approach to disclosures.

The SEC climate rule (which has not been finalised at time of writing), likely will have some key substantive and conceptual differences to the CSRD, including having a more limited focus on climate issues as opposed to the broader extent of ESG matters, and also being tied to financial materiality, as opposed to the double materiality concept that the CSRD will adopt.

The SEC has also proposed a number of additional ESG-related rules since 2022, including rules regarding ESG disclosure requirements for investment advisers and investment companies, and has announced rulemaking priorities on other ESG topics, such as human capital management disclosure and board diversity.

Other US regulators have also been considering requiring climate-related disclosures. For example, in November 2022, the Federal Acquisition Regulation (FAR) Council proposed rules that would require certain federal contractors to disclose climate-related information, including greenhouse gas (GHG) emissions and financial risks, and to establish science-based emissions reduction targets.[6]

---

5   Securities and Exchange Commission, The Enhancement and Standardization of Climate-Related Disclosures for Investors, www.sec.gov/rules/proposed/2022/33-11042.pdf.

6   Federal Register, "Federal Acquisition Regulation: Disclosure of Greenhouse Gas Emissions and Climate-Related Financial Risk" (14 November 2022), www.federalregister.gov/documents/2022/11/14/2022-24569/federal-acquisition-regulation-disclosure-of-greenhouse-gas-emissions-and-climate-related-financial.

In October 2023, California enacted major mandatory climate disclosure legislation through the Climate Corporate Data Accountability Act (SB 253), the Climate-Related Financial Risk Act (SB 261) and the Voluntary Carbon Market Disclosures Business Regulation Act (AB 1305). SB 253 creates new greenhouse gas emissions reporting requirements for public and private entities incorporated in a US state, in the District of Columbia or by an act of the US Congress that are doing business in California with more than $1 billion in revenue. Companies are required to report Scope 1 and Scope 2 greenhouse gas emissions starting in 2026 (for 2025 data), and Scope 3 greenhouse gas emissions beginning in 2027 (for 2026 data). In several respects, SB 253 goes further than the SEC's proposal, for instance regarding the scope of covered entities, requirements on Scope 3 emissions reporting and methodology, and the requirement for verification of emissions. SB 261 sets out reporting requirements in line with TCFD recommendations (or alternatively, the ISSB's climate standard), for public or private entities incorporated in a US state, in the District of Columbia or by an act of the US Congress that are doing business in California with revenue over $500 million. AB 1305 establishes three distinct disclosure requirements for businesses: (i) marketing or selling voluntary carbon offsets within California; (ii) purchasing or using voluntary carbon offsets and making claims regarding carbon neutrality, net zero or significant greenhouse gas emissions reductions regarding the entity's operations or products; or (iii) making claims about carbon neutrality, net zero or significant greenhouse gas emissions reductions with respect to the entity's operations or products, regardless of any voluntary carbon offsets. Similar bills have been or may be introduced in other US states, such as New York's S897A, which is largely in line with California's SB 253, as well as Washington State's State Bill 6092 which, when initially introduced, was also in line with SB253.

Potentially diverging approaches of federal and state authorities regarding corporate climate disclosure further exemplify challenges with regards to standardisation. Furthermore, the US has witnessed a growing politicisation of and backlash to ESG that exacerbates standardisation challenges. For example, Republican lawmakers in a number of states have promulgated legislation, alongside actions by state executive bodies and state attorneys-general, seeking to curtail or have a chilling effect on ESG efforts. Such actions implicate both companies and financial institutions, as well as private funds seeking capital from these states, as well as from states and other jurisdictions that require the consideration of ESG factors, and add yet another layer of complexity and uncertainty for those subject to reporting requirements across jurisdictions.

4. United Kingdom

In 2019, the UK adopted a Green Finance Strategy[7] which sought to set the framework for the UK becoming the world's first "net zero-aligned financial centre". This strategy was updated in March 2023 providing, amongst other things, updates on the development of ESG disclosure proposals and requirements in the UK.

As of 1 January 2022, standard and premium listed companies in the UK have been required to publish TCFD-aligned disclosures, or explain why they have not done so. In January 2022, the Financial Conduct Authority (FCA) introduced rules for listed companies and large regulated asset owners and asset managers to disclose transition plans as part of their TCFD-aligned disclosures, initially on a comply or explain basis. The first disclosures under these rules will be made in 2023. The UK government has also launched a Transition Plan Taskforce, tasked with providing guidance as to what a best practice transition plan should contain.

In January 2022, the UK adopted legislation requiring UK companies and LLPs that have over 500 employees and: (i) have an annual turnover of £500+ million; or (ii) are listed, to publish additional information in their non-financial reporting statement (which is, a public statement given in the annual strategic report required under the Companies Act 2006). The additional disclosure requirements are based on the recommendations of the TCFD, although they contain certain differences. Furthermore, pursuant to the Streamlined Energy and Carbon Reporting Scheme (SECR),[8] quoted companies, large unquoted companies and large LLPs are required to disclose certain GHG emissions and under the Energy Savings Opportunity Scheme[9] companies are required to undergo energy savings assessments, energy audits and detect opportunities for further energy savings.

In relation to non-climate related reporting requirements, the Equality Act 2010[10] and the Modern Slavery Act,[11] respectively, require in-scope companies to conduct gender pay gap reporting and public disclosures about safeguards taken for a slavery-free business and supply chain.

4.1 Sustainability Disclosure Requirements

As part of its Green Finance Strategy, the UK Government has indicated its

---

7   HM Government, "Green Finance Strategy: Transforming Finance for a Greener Future" (July 2019).
8   Companies (Directors' Report) and Limited Liability Partnerships (Energy and Carbon Report) Regulation 2018 (SQ 2018/1155), available at www.legislation.gov.uk/uksi/2018/1155/pdfs/uksi _20181155_en.pdf.
9   Department for Energy Security and Net Zero, Environment Agency and Department for Business, Energy & Industrial Strategy, "Energy Savings Opportunity Scheme (ESOS)" (26 June 2014), www.gov.uk/guidance/energy-savings-opportunity-scheme-esos.
10   Equality Act 2010, Chapter 3 (Equality of terms), Section 78 (Gender pay gap information), available at www.legislation.gov.uk/ukpga/2010/15/contents.
11   Modern Slavery Act 2015, available at www.legislation.gov.uk/ukpga/2015/30/contents/enacted.

intention to adopt so-called Sustainability Disclosure Requirements (SDR), which would contain disclosure requirements for both financial and non-financial entities (in effect combining the scopes of the SFDR and CSRD in Europe).

From a corporate reporting perspective, the UK Government announced in August 2023 that it would consult on the development of Sustainability Disclosure Standards ('UK SDS'), which would form the basis of any future requirements in UK legislation or regulation for ESG reporting. The government announced that the UK SDS will be published by July 2024, and will be based on the ISSB Standards (see below), departing from the ISSB Standards only "if absolutely necessary for UK-specific matters".

In October 2022, the Financial Conduct Authority (FCA) consulted on certain of the financial services-related aspects of the SDR, which included proposals on the use of sustainable investment labels, disclosure requirements and restrictions on the use of sustainability-related terms in product naming. In November 2023, the FCA published its Policy Statement setting out the final rules on UK SDR and investment labels.

Likewise, similar to the EU's regulatory framework, the UK is currently in the process of developing a UK Green Taxonomy. The UK Green Finance Institute, which is chairing the Green Technical Advisory Group (GTAG) that has been established by the UK Government for the purpose of developing the UK Green Taxonomy, has indicated that a public consultation will take place although specific timelines are to be confirmed. In advance of such announcement, in September 2023 GTAG published two reports on operational considerations for taxonomy reporting and the treatment of green financial products under the UK Green Taxonomy.

5.   Key voluntary standards

While mandatory ESG reporting requirements proliferate globally, voluntary standards continue to remain a key part of many companies' ESG reporting strategies. These voluntary frameworks exist to enable companies to report information in a consistent manner, such that investors and other stakeholders can gain valuable information when assessing the ESG credentials of a company.

In addition, when voluntary frameworks have become widely accepted, respected and used, they can often provide the underlying basis of mandatory disclosure requirements that get introduced in jurisdictions. In this way, the introduction of voluntary reporting under specific frameworks can provide a good method of 'testing' the ability of those frameworks to deliver the high quality and decision-useful ESG information that investors require. This can take the form of a direct requirement from legislators or regulators that companies comply with a voluntary framework or can involve legislators or regulators developing their own standard, or set of standards, based on the overarching principles and structures of a pre-existing voluntary standard.

A good example of both of these possibilities is the recommendations of the TCFD. The TCFD recommendations have been directly applied as mandatory reporting requirements (eg, the requirement for UK listed companies to disclose against the TCFD recommendations on a comply or explain basis) and have also been adapted by legislators and regulators in the creation of a new standard (eg, the UK Mandatory Climate Disclosures, the SEC climate disclosure regime, and California rules SB 253, SB 261 and AB 1305). In each of these instances, the success and widespread application of the TCFD as a voluntary ESG (in this case climate-only) reporting framework has meant that many companies will be in a position to report at least some of the required information under the mandatory standards without being required to implement entirely new internal data collection and verification processes.

While the number of voluntary ESG reporting frameworks (including sector-specific initiatives such as the ESG Data Convergence Initiative for the private equity industry) in existence makes it impossible to cover them all in this chapter, below we discuss two of the key frameworks that companies and investors alike should be particularly aware of, given their widespread recognition as key disclosure standards among a number of stakeholders, and relevance to existing and proposed mandatory reporting requirements.

5.1   TCFD

The TCFD was created in December 2015 by the Financial Stability Board (FSB), an international body primarily tasked with monitoring and making recommendations about the global financial system. The task of the TCFD was to develop a voluntary disclosure framework that corporates and investors could use to bring more standardisation and clarity into reporting on climate-related issues.

In 2017, the TCFD issued its initial set of climate-related financial disclosure recommendations, structured around four thematic areas that, in the view of the TCFD, represent the core elements of how companies operate – governance, strategy, risk management, and metrics and targets. Given the financial focus of the FSB, it is unsurprising that the TCFD recommendations are focused on the disclosure of information that may be financially material to the disclosing company.

Since issuing its recommendations, the TCFD has published a number of other guidance documents and annual status reports opining on the state of TCFD-aligned disclosures. The TCFD recommendations have, since their publication in 2017, received widespread adoption from companies globally, as well as recognition and public approval from a number of international bodies and countries. This has played out in many cases, as discussed above, in the form of national legislative requirements either adapting or fully utilising the TCFD recommendations to form the basis of mandatory obligations placed on certain companies. In addition, the success of the TCFD has led to the creation of a similar body in relation to nature-based disclosures (the Taskforce on Nature-Related Disclosures (TNFD)), which published its own initial recommendations in August 2023.

5.2 ISSB

While the TCFD has gained significant traction in the climate-related reporting sphere, it is inherently limited in that it is focused only on climate issues, and not the broader ESG universe. On 3 November 2021, at COP26 in Glasgow, following strong market demand for the introduction of a global baseline ESG reporting framework, the IFRS Foundation announced the launch of the ISSB, a body set up in order to develop standards that are intended to lead to a high-quality, comprehensive ESG disclosure framework, focused (as in the case of the TCFD) on the needs of investors and the financial markets.

The ISSB will consolidate and build on existing frameworks, standards and guidance. For instance, the industry-based SASB Standards provide the starting point for the ISSB's industry-specific requirements. As of August 2022, the ISSB assumed responsibility for the SASB Standards and has committed to maintain, enhance and evolve them. The GRI's voluntary sustainability reporting framework will also be considered in relation to the ISSB standards. A Memorandum of Understanding between the GRI and the IFRS Foundation committed the organisations to work together to ensure complementary and interoperable standards.

The ISSB has received international support with its work to develop sustainability disclosure standards backed by the G7, the G20, the International Organization of Securities Commissions, the Financial Stability Board, African Finance Ministers and Finance Ministers and Central Bank Governors from more than 40 jurisdictions.

The ISSB published its first standards in June 2023, ready to be reported against from 1 January 2024, with one standard focused on climate-related reporting and the other on general sustainability disclosures. However, due to what the ISSB has termed a 'transitional relief', companies looking to report to these ISSB standards will, for the first year of reporting, be required to focus on the climate-related reporting aspects only, and also be exempted from reporting certain information under the climate-standard itself (including Scope 3 emissions).

The ISSB has also had consolidated into it a number of existing organisations that provided ESG reporting frameworks, and also has leveraged the work of other standard setters (including the TCFD) in developing its standards. In July 2023 it was announced that the IFRS Foundation would take over monitoring of the progress on companies' climate-related disclosures relating to the TCFD. It is hoped this broad approach to the development of the ISSB standards will reduce the market fragmentation in ESG reporting, and lead to the ISSB standards becoming the global benchmark voluntary standard moving forwards.

6. Global outlook

While the jurisdictions noted above are in many ways leading the global charge toward mandatory ESG reporting, countries globally are increasingly looking to implement mandatory reporting standards to ensure that investors in their jurisdiction have access to high quality and comparable ESG information.

Although the EU and other western jurisdictions are often at the forefront of developing ESG reporting requirements, there is important nuance required in considering the implications of an increased focus on ESG disclosures in emerging jurisdictions. Developing reporting frameworks often seek to reflect this, taking into account local contexts and unique developmental challenges.

In many cases, such requirements are focused on listed companies only, and often come in the form of stock exchange requirements and rules as opposed to primary legislation adopted as applicable to all companies. In addition, we see a number of these jurisdictions look to incorporate existing international voluntary standards into their domestic requirements, to avoid the need to set up a brand new reporting framework.

In Asia-Pacific, the recommendations of the TCFD in particular have gained widespread recognition, with companies listed on the Tokyo Stock Exchange being required to report in alignment with TCFD and similar requirements in place in relation to Singapore among other countries. India has also published mandatory ESG reporting requirements for the top 1,000 listed companies, which need to prepare Business Responsibility and Sustainability Reports, which build upon a number of international frameworks.

In addition, it is not just the EU and UK that are working on the development of green taxonomies, with jurisdictions including Singapore, China, Canada, Mexico, Colombia and regional groups such as ASEAN all looking to develop taxonomies that provide investors with certainty and credibility in the context of labelling investments as sustainable, and may also introduce specific reporting requirements for corporate entities as well as financial institutions.

As discussed elsewhere in this book, ESG requirements are also developing in a number of other jurisdictions globally, including Latin America, Africa and the Middle East, and we expect this trend to continue to emerge in the coming years.

7. Moving forward

As has been demonstrated by the foregoing, ESG reporting is a fast developing area which is currently undergoing significant change across the globe. While frameworks continue to be developed and adjusted in order to try and encourage the provision of more decision-useful and comparable ESG data, the risk remains that the proliferation of more frameworks across different jurisdictions will exacerbate the problem that it initially sought to fix, and lead to global investors being faced with a situation where ESG-related disclosures between companies in different jurisdictions have a completely different focus.

Companies, especially those with significant operations in multiple jurisdictions, will also be faced with challenges as different stakeholders, including investors, increasingly expect disclosures aligned with whatever framework is most relevant to their country/operations. Companies and financial product providers may therefore be faced with costly disclosure obligations across jurisdictions, both from government- or regulator-mandated disclosures but also stakeholder requests, and ensuring alignment between the information provided under these different frameworks will be resource intensive but critical.

As the landscape continues to evolve, it is hoped that the global regulatory framework will become increasingly aligned, maximising the efficiency of ESG disclosures without sacrificing the importance of acknowledging the bespoke position that each disclosing entity is in.

ESG corporate issues: shareholder activism

Carmen XW Lu
Elina Tetelbaum
Wachtell, Lipton, Rosen & Katz

1.   Overview

Shareholder activism, which encompasses a range of actions taken by shareholders to apply pressure to boards and management teams to align corporate actions and company priorities with those of activist shareholders, has become a major feature of the corporate landscape in recent years. Whereas investors previously voted with their feet by selling a company's stock, many more are now leveraging the rights associated with the ownership of company securities, particularly proxy voting rights, rights to nominate directors and the right to bring business before shareholder meetings, to engage privately and publicly with boards and management.

After a brief lull in activist activity during the COVID-19 pandemic, global activism activity soared to record levels in 2022, a trend that has persisted into the first half of the 2023.[1] While market volatility, regulatory changes, rising interest rates and sector weaknesses have all helped to drive the recent resurgence in shareholder activism, ESG issues have also increasingly become a key piece of the activist thesis. The growth of ESG activism reflects the growing recognition that such issues can at times have material financial impacts on businesses. ESG issues can be a powerful coalition building tool that can unite the interests of a range of stakeholders, from institutional investors who are focused on protecting and enhancing the long-term value of their portfolios to proxy advisers who increasingly consider ESG issues when making voting recommendations and retail investors, a growing number of whom expect businesses in which they invest to align with their broader values.

This chapter provides an overview of the key players within the ESG activism landscape, the issues that have driven ESG activism, the range of tactics and strategies deployed by activists, and considerations for boards and management in dealing specifically with ESG concerns within their stakeholder base. Following this chapter are in-depth case studies of two recent activism campaigns (McDonald's Corporation/Carl C Icahn and Activision Blizzard, Inc/SOC Investment Group) where ESG issues formed a key part of the activist agenda.

---

1   FactSet, as of 16 July 2023.

2.   Key players and the supporting cast

ESG activism has attracted interest from traditional hedge fund activists as well as smaller impact-oriented investors. These shareholders have been supported in their efforts by investor coalitions, non-profits and, in certain cases, institutional investors and proxy advisers.

Several large activist hedge funds have entered ESG activism in recent years, with some going as far as establishing funds or bringing in senior personnel specifically to examine opportunities in the area. One of the earliest movers was ValueAct which established the ValueAct Spring Fund in 2018 with a focus on ensuring that there is "excess return to be captured in identifying and investing in businesses that are emphasising and addressing environmental and societal problems".[2] That same year, JANA Partners launched an Impact Investing Fund, which subsequently teamed up with CalSTRS to issue a letter to the board of Apple Inc, asking the company to examine the adverse health consequences of its devices on children and teenage users.[3] More recently, funds such as Inclusive Capital Partners, Engine No.1 and Impactive Capital have come to focus exclusively on creating value from investing in companies based on ESG-related metrics and considerations. Traditional economic hedge fund activists such as Elliott, Third Point, Carl Icahn, Legion and Bluebell Capital have also led ESG-oriented campaigns from time to time.

Changes to the US Securities and Exchange Commission's guidance on Rule 14a-8 shareholder proposals in 2021[4] that made it more challenging for companies to exclude certain proposals have also empowered a new wave of smaller, often impact-oriented, shareholder activists in the United States, including As You Sow, Mercy Investment Services, New York State Common Retirement Fund, Arjuna Capital and Green Century Capital Management. Many of these shareholders include state and city pension funds, religious groups, labour unions, private foundations and advocacy organisations, often working as part of, or supported by, broader investor coalitions such as the Interfaith Center on Corporate Responsibility, the Ceres Investor Network and Climate Action 100+. During the 2023 proxy season, over 700 shareholder proposals were submitted concerning ESG issues, including close to 500 shareholder proposals on environmental and social matters, setting a new record.[5]

Institutional investors and proxy advisers also play an important role in determining the outcomes of ESG activism. Neither traditional hedge fund activists nor proponents of shareholder proposals typically command sizeable voting positions and their success will often depend on whether institutional

---

2   CNBC, "Jeff Ubben's ValueAct launching fund with social goals, following similar moves by Jana, BlackRock", 19 January 2018, www.cnbc.com/2018/01/19/jeff-ubbens-valueact-launching-fund-with-social-goal.html.

3   Letter from JANA Partners & CalSTRS to Apple Inc, 19 January 2018.

4   US Securities and Exchange Commission, Shareholder Proposals: Staff Legal Bulletin No 14L (CF).

5   Deal Point Data as of 16 July 2023.

investors and/or proxy advisers align with the dissidents. In particular, among US companies with dispersed ownership, activists will often need the support of key institutional investors and/or Institutional Shareholder Services (ISS) and Glass Lewis, with the latter two able to swing as much as 20% of the overall vote.

3. ESG issues giving rise to shareholder activism

While a wide range of issues and circumstances can give rise to ESG activism, there are a few key issues that draw activist attention time and again. These issues include: climate and sustainability risk management; greenhouse gas emissions targets; matters relating to diversity, equity and inclusion at the board level and in the workplace; political contributions and lobbying; and worker rights and safety. Economic hedge fund activists have sought to leverage ESG-related crises to demand changes to the board and management. Market opportunities created by the influx of capital into sustainable investments have also prompted economic activists to seek the separation of green and brown assets. And when companies are perceived as having gone too far in their pursuit of ESG targets and strategies and underperformed as a result, activists have also sought to lay blame on management.

Among hedge fund activists, ESG-related issues continued to weave their way into economic campaigns throughout 2022 and 2023. In particular, activists looked to capitalise on emerging market opportunities created by regulatory changes and continued investor demand in green investments. For example, in early 2022, Sachem Head acquired a position in Denbury, a company specialising in carbon capture and storage. Following the passage of the Inflation Reduction Act of 2022, Sachem Head deemed the company to be an attractive takeover target for a larger legacy energy company looking to capitalise on the new tax incentives to build out Denbury's capabilities. Third Point, meanwhile, called on Shell to separate its refining and renewables operations to allow for more aggressive investment in decarbonisation and to optimise the company's ability to address the different strategic priorities of its various stakeholders. Similarly, Bluebell urged Glencore to reassess its climate transition plan, separate its thermal coal business and reposition its business as a leading provider of metals required for the energy transition. Bluebell argued that Glencore's exposure to coal was adversely impacting the company's overall valuation and pressure on financial institutions to curb financing of the fossil fuels sectors could threaten the company's long-term access to capital and threaten shareholder value. Meanwhile, Engine No.1 – the once little known activist fund that successfully took on ExxonMobil in 2021 – called on Coca-Cola to commit to a partnership with Republic Services, a plastics recycler and in which Engine No.1 owns a stake, as part of the company's efforts to phase out single-use plastics. Engine No.1 also conducted outreach and engagement with several oil and gas giants including ConocoPhillips, Pioneer Natural

Resources and Devon Energy, urging them to commit to OGMP 2.0, the flagship oil and gas reporting and mitigation programme of the United Nations Environment Programme (UNEP).

Other economic activists capitalised on crises to drive a wedge between the company and its shareholders. Legion, for example, ran a high-profile campaign against Guess, calling for the removal of the company's co-founders in the wake of sexual misconduct allegations. While Legion's "vote no" campaign did not succeed in unseating any Guess directors (in part due to the sizeable stakes held by Guess's co-founders), the campaign attacted significant press attention.[6] Not all ESG-oriented campaigns have an economic thesis: Carl Icahn's campaigns at Kroger and McDonald's focused on the companies' treatment of pigs (a matter of interest to his daughter).[7] Icahn's campaign was not an isolated instance where ESG issues were not leveraged solely to drive near-term returns. While neither proxy contest campaign resulted in Icahn gaining any board seats, they drew significant public attention to the issue at hand. Bluebell purchased one share of chemicals maker Solvay and partnered with the World Wildlife Fund to draw opposition to the company's release of waste water onto beaches near Rosignano Solvay in Italy.

Among activists that have relied on shareholder proposals to draw attention to ESG issues, both 2022 and 2023 saw new records being set in the volume of such proposals. Climate and sustainability issues remain the top priority among proposal proponents and have led to a range of proposals that target emissions directly as well as the policies and third-party participants that have continued to support the fossil fuels industry.[8] Notably, the latest proxy season saw several proposals targeted at financial institutions calling for banks and insurers to align their financing and underwriting activities with emissions reduction targets aligned with a science-based net zero pathway – a proposal which would effectively require these institutions to address value chain emissions arising from their business activities that comprise the bulk of their aggregate carbon footprint. Shareholder proponents have also looked to political lobbying as another avenue to limit the influence of the heaviest GHG emitters and hold companies fully accountable for their commitments to reduce GHG emissions. Proposals focused on disclosure of trade association activities and alignment of lobbying activities with emissions reduction goals aim to catalyse powerful business interests against the influence of the fossil fuels sector. Social issues, including those relating to workers' rights to freedom of association and

6   PR Newswire, "Legion Partners Launches 'Vote No' Campaign Against Guess?, Inc. Directors Paul and Maurice Marciano", 16 March 2022, www.prnewswire.com/news-releases/legion-partners-launches-vote-no-campaign-against-guess-inc-directors-paul-and-maurice-marciano-301503725.html.
7   CNBC, "Carl Icahn launches proxy fight with McDonald's over treatment of pigs", 21 February 2022, www.cnbc.com/2022/02/20/carl-icahn-launches-proxy-fight-with-mcdonalds-over-treatment-of-pigs.html.
8   Deal Point Data as of 16 July 2023.

collective bargaining, diversity, equity and inclusion, and reproductive rights, have also drawn increasing attention from shareholder proponents who are looking to businesses to fill the legislative and regulatory gap created by a polarised and frequently paralysed political system in the US.

4. The ESG activist playbook

Hedge fund activists frequently deploy similar tactics when engaging on ESG issues as compared to traditional economic campaigns. Such tactics may include sending private and public letters to the board and management setting forth their thesis and demands, leaking information on sensitive matters to the media and/or sell-side analysts, making public filings regarding the activist's holdings, contacting former employees and other shareholders and stakeholders, nominating director candidates and opportunistically criticising company strategy and performance. Given that ESG issues often draw outsized attention from the media, many ESG-oriented campaigns tend be played out in the public forum early on, particularly where an activist is leveraging a corporate crisis to undermine shareholder confidence in the board and management, or more simply to draw attention and enhance the positioning of the activist fund *vis-à-vis* other funds. For example, Legion Partners launched a highly publicised "vote no" campaign against Guess following allegations of sexual harassment against one of the company's co-founders. The campaign was launched notwithstanding the fact that Guess's co-founders collectively owned 42% of outstanding shares.[9] Similarly, Carl Icahn only held 200 shares in McDonald's before publicly nominating two director candidates over concerns regarding the company's animal welfare policies.[10] McDonald's, on the other hand, spent US$16 million in its proxy contest with Icahn.[11]

Among proponents of shareholder proposals, an increasingly popular tactic is the use of exempt solicitations and proxy memos to draw attention and broader shareholder support. US securities law permits shareholders to freely communicate to other shareholders without having to comply with the proxy rules associated with the solicitation of shareholder votes as long as the shareholder is not seeking proxy voting authority (ie, the power to act as proxy for another stockholders). Because exempt solicitations are publicly filed, cost-effective and generally taken into consideration by proxy advisers, they have become a powerful tool for lobbying fellow shareholders beyond the 500-word limit imposed on shareholder proposals included in a company's proxy statement. Many exempt solicitations take the form of letters to other

---

9   FactSect, as of 2 May 2022.
10   CNBC, "Carl Icahn launches proxy fight with McDonald's over treatment of pigs", 21 February 2022, www.cnbc.com/2022/02/20/carl-icahn-launches-proxy-fight-with-mcdonalds-over-treatment-of-pigs.html.
11   McDonald's Corporation, DEFC14A dated 8 April 2022.

shareholders and may be filed by the shareholder proponent or other shareholders in the weeks and days leading up to a shareholder meeting. Other shareholder groups have also leveraged proxy memos, which are shared throughout investor networks, such as Climate Action 100+ to help draw attention to and disclose the rationale for shareholder proposals being brought before shareholder meetings. Similarly, vote pre-declarations, where investors signal their voting intent, have been another coalition-building strategy among ESG-oriented activist shareholders.

Ongoing engagement is another key tactic among ESG activists, particularly institutional investors. In 2023, Climate Action 100+, the world's largest investor-led engagement initiative on climate change, launched a new phase in its engagement efforts following consultation with its membership. Phase 2,[12] which runs until 2030, will ask focus list companies to implement climate transition plans in line with the final recommendations of the Task Force on Climate-related Financial Disclosures (TCFD) and other relevant sector and regional guidance. Companies will also be asked to take action to reduce greenhouse gas emissions "across the value chain, including engagement with stakeholders such as policymakers and other actors to address the sectoral barriers to transition", with a guiding goal of halving greenhouse gas emissions by 2030 and achieving net zero emissions by 2050. Notably, the latest phase of Climate Action 100+'s engagement strategy is focused on providing investors with new avenues to engage with companies. Whereas prior engagement efforts relied on a lead investor spearheading the discussions, Climate Action 100+ will, going forward, expand avenues for different investors to lead thematic and sectoral engagements at the same target company.

Activists also continue to use publicity to draw attention to ESG issues. As You Sow, for example, maintains public scorecards on corporate performance on racial justice and workplace equity which have become the basis for ongoing engagement with various companies.[13] The Changing Markets Foundation supports the work of non-profits through campaigns and reports drawing awareness to environmental and social issues ranging from plastics pollution to food fortification to greenwashing.[14] The Ellen MacArthur Foundation has also advanced work on the circular economy by publicly working in partnership with companies to advance the reuse and recycling of plastics.[15]

5. Anti-ESG activism

The success of ESG activism in placing issues such as climate, sustainability and

---

12   Climate Action 100+, "Climate Action 100+ Announces its Second Phase", 8 June 2023, www.climateaction100.org/news/climate-action-100-announces-its-second-phase/.
13   As You Sow Reports, www.asyousow.org/reports.
14   The Changing Markets Foundation, https://changingmarkets.org/campaigns/.
15   Ellen MacArthur Foundation, The Global Commitment, https://ellenmacarthurfoundation.org/global-commitment-2022/overview.

diversity, equity and inclusion atop the priorities of companies and investors has led to growing opposition, particularly within the US to such efforts. Broadly, opposition to ESG has taken three forms: (i) state-level legislation that has sought to prohibit the consideration of non-pecuniary factors in pension investments and to boycott financial institutions that utilise ESG investment strategies; (ii) shareholder proposals focused on unwinding ESG initiatives adopted by companies; and (iii) the emergence of anti-ESG investment vehicles, such as Strive Asset Management, which claim to use their proxy voting power for the sole purpose of maximising shareholder returns without giving consideration to ESG factors.

In recent months, opposition to ESG has gained traction within the Republican primaries with various candidates vying to criticise companies that have adopted ESG initiatives as "woke". In July 2023, the House Committee on Financial Services commenced a series of hearings focused on efforts to reign in ESG-related efforts by the US Securities and Exchange Commission, including curbing the scope of shareholder proposals and curbing the power of proxy advisers. The consequence of growing political pressure on investors and companies has been a gradual 'chilling' or 'green-hushing' of ESG-oriented initiatives. Most noticeably, in late 2022 and 2023, Vanguard and several insurers withdrew from the Glasgow Financial Alliance for Net Zero (GFANZ),[16] even though many continued to pursue ESG-aligned strategies. State attorneys general have also leveraged books and record demands and threats of antitrust violations to target asset managers, companies and even service providers who have engaged in ESG-related activities.

6. Preparing for ESG activism

While ESG activism is substantively different from economic activism, there are some key steps that boards and management can deploy to be ready when an activist comes knocking on the door. These steps include:

- assessing one's business from the lens of a potential activist, paying close attention to material ESG issues that present risks or opportunities to the company;
- ensuring the board is fully informed, empowered and equipped to oversee ESG matters, including having the right level of subject matter knowledge and oversight experience to ask the necessary questions of management;
- recognising that ESG activism can catalyse a range of stakeholders beyond traditional hedge fund activists and casting a wide net in terms

---

16   Bloomberg, "Munich Re Exits Insurance Climate Group Due to Legal Risks", 31 March 2023, www.bloomberg.com/news/articles/2023-03-31/munich-re-quits-climate-finance-alliance-due-to-legal-risks.

of monitoring stakeholder sentiment, seeking feedback and demonstrating responsiveness;

- remaining alert to trending issues and early warning signs, particularly activism within the sector or the emergence of ESG issues that may implicate either the business directly or indirectly through its value chain;

- building and maintaining credibility with the company's stakeholders, including taking care that the company's ESG disclosures and initiatives are aligned and integrated into the company's broader strategy and operations; and

- recognising and preparing for the fact that ESG activism is likely to develop in multiyear events as shareholders seek to address issues that often require fundamental systemic change within organisations and sectors. Moreover, incremental changes that may constitute a "win" for one shareholder may not satisfy other shareholders who may be drawn into pushing for further action.

7. Where next?

ESG activism is likely still in its nascent stages as activists, companies, investors and other stakeholders continue to grapple with the scope of risks and opportunities created by ESG issues. The arrival of the EU Corporate Sustainability Reporting Directive and the Corporate Sustainability Due Diligence Directive, which covers companies with operations in the EU, along with the disclosure frameworks being developed by the International Sustainability Standards Board may prove to be pivotal in eliciting the information that stakeholders need to identify company-specific issues that need to be addressed through activism. The growing body of sustainability regulations, particularly those that take aim at greenwashing, may also prove fertile grounds for future ESG activism. While it may be difficult to pinpoint the next hotbed of ESG activism activity, ESG activism is almost surely here to stay, propelled by deepening geopolitical divisions, growing societal polarisation fuelled by gaping inequality, and the significant scale (and growing evidence) of the risks and challenges that may arise from failure to address issues such as climate change, nature loss and the rise of artificial intelligence.

Shareholder activism: case studies

Desi Baca
Lawrence Elbaum
Patrick Gadson
Vinson & Elkins

1. McDonald's Corporation/Carl C Icahn

ESG, ESG, ESG. For the better part of a decade, these three letters have been (depending upon which side of the aisle you happen to be standing) the 21st century's greatest form of corporate governance progress or a resource-wasteful, management-distracting movement by progressives. Regardless of anyone's personal views about the increasing focus by management and boards on ESG issues, it should be clear that ESG as an ideology and the debate around its worthiness is going nowhere.

However, as part of this debate, we must remember to be intellectually honest about where the real tension around ESG lies. In the 'E'? No. Although, in the not too distant past, the existence of civilisation's (and, particularly, industrialisation's) effects on Earth's habitability was viewed by some to be an open question, eventually sense and reason prevailed. We sophisticated primates are causing it. And, the international community, including public corporations, is going to have to change in order to manage it.

So, if it isn't the 'E' in which the tension around ESG resides, does the friction lie on the other bookend of the acronym? The 'G'? Nope. The idea of 'shareholder-friendly corporate governance' is so engrained into the idea of corporate democracy and capital markets that at some point the phrase 'shareholder-friendly corporate governance' was replaced by 'proper/best corporate governance' and no one even seemed to notice.

That leaves us with one letter, 'S', and here is where the ideological battlefield rests. 'Social' includes cultural, and cultural includes political, and political inherently means there will be strong disagreement. This disagreement in shareholder activism can be particularly acute in campaigns focusing on the 'S', where the nexus between the social issue and the related financial impact may be less apparent to shareholders.

Such was the case with the proxy fight brought by legendary activist Carl C Icahn against fast-food giant McDonald's Corporation (McDonald's). As opposed to getting more people to eat more burgers and more fries, Mr Icahn focused on the promotion of humane animal-welfare practices. In 2012, Mr

Icahn had reached out to McDonald's after learning that it sourced pork from suppliers that kept pigs in gestation crates (small crates in which pregnant or breeding pigs are often held with little room to move) and that the Humane Society of the United States (where Mr Icahn's daughter worked at the time) had been unsuccessful in its attempts to have McDonald's agree to end the use of gestation crates by its pork suppliers.[1] On the heels of these discussions and Mr Icahn's request that McDonald's announce a plan, McDonald's made a public commitment in 2012 to phase out, over a ten-year period, the sourcing of pork from suppliers that housed pregnant pigs in gestation crates.[2] Safe to say that in making this commitment in 2012 about the square-footage future sausage McMuffins are entitled to, McDonald's probably did not expect that failing to meet this voluntary undertaking would result in a proxy fight from Mr Icahn nearly a decade later.

But Mr Icahn held McDonald's to its word. In August 2021, McDonald's disclosed that due to the COVID-19 pandemic and the African swine fever outbreak, it would have to extend the timeline for achieving its commitment to 2024. Following additional discussion, Mr Icahn, despite only holding 200 shares of McDonald's stock worth less than $50,000,[3] launched a campaign against the fast food chain in February 2022, alleging that the company had failed to keep its promise.[4] Mr Icahn nominated two director candidates for election at the company's 2022 Annual Meeting in opposition to the two McDonald's directors who were the longest tenured members on McDonald's Sustainability and Corporate Responsibility Committee, including the chair, and sought to raise social awareness to change McDonald's pig practices. McDonald's claimed that it was a leader in promoting animal welfare, and pointed to the progress it had made to date on its commitment, stating that realising Mr Icahn's "crate-free" demand would place great financial strain on the business and its customer base, which values accessible food, and that there was an insufficient supply of crate-free pork needed to meet the company's demands.[5]

Although Mr Icahn called on large asset managers who appeared concerned with ESG issues, but whom he believed were cherry picking which issues to support based on financial benefit, to take a stand on animal welfare, including the mistreatment of pigs,[6] he failed to garner the support needed from the proxy

1   Definitive Proxy Statement filed with the SEC by Carl C Icahn *et al* on 21 April 2022, www.sec.gov/Archives/edgar/data/63908/000119312522112029/d292171ddefc14a.htm.
2   Globe Newswire, "McDonald's USA Outlines 10-Year Plan for Ending Gestation Stall Use", 31 May 2012, www.globenewswire.com/news-release/2012/05/31/1103959/0/en/McDonald-s-USA-Outlines-10-Year-Plan-for-Ending-Gestation-Stall-Use.html?msclkid=f1f4fcb3b43f11ecb980a858c3a6b08e.
3   ISS Report for McDonald's (2022).
4   Definitive Proxy Statement filed with the SEC by Carl C Icahn *et al* with the SEC on 21 April 2022.
5   See DEFA14A filed with the SEC by McDonald's on 25 April 2022; see also Definitive Proxy Statement filed with the SEC by McDonald's on 8 April 2022; see also DEFA14A filed by McDonald's with the SEC on 5 May 2022.
6   DFAN14A filed with the SEC by Mr Icahn *et al* on 21 April 2022.

advisory firms. ISS and Glass Lewis supported all of McDonald's nominees at the Annual Meeting. While Mr Icahn emphasised the social concern arising from inhumane pig practices, he failed to provide a strong economic argument on how phasing out gestation crates could benefit shareholders' bottom line, and his small ownership stake meant that he would face very little negative impact from the adoption of the policies he was promoting should they be unsuccessful. ISS was "hesitant to support a proxy contest predicated on ESG issues in instances where the dissident is economically divorced from the potential impact of its proposals on the company's financial performance" and noted that McDonald's had seen strong performance since the COVID-19 pandemic and in light of 800 restaurants closing in Russia due to the ongoing Russia–Ukraine war.[7] Glass Lewis echoed this sentiment, stating that Mr Icahn's campaign took a "decidedly simplistic and myopic view of ESG concerns, with no substantive regard given to the economics of [McDonald's] business nor to the creation of shareholder value".[8]

This sentiment was evident among shareholders, too, with each of Icahn's nominees receiving less than 2% of the votes at the Annual Meeting.[9] In a statement to McDonald's shareholders, Mr Icahn reflected on the voting results, stating that "it [was] clear that shareholders, even if they are concerned about the issues … are not willing to change the board configuration if a company is performing well financially". Believing that the outcome would be the same at the upcoming annual meeting of shareholders of Kroger, where he had launched a similar campaign focusing on the treatment of pigs, Mr Icahn withdrew his Kroger campaign.

The Icahn/McDonald's campaign underscores the fact that even for 'S' issues which seem uncontroversial (if such an 'S' issue exists), getting to "win" is still more stormy weather than clear skies. The debate over ESG may be far from over, but what is clear is that unless activist investors are able to successfully appeal to shareholders on how addressing these ESG concerns can result in shareholders realising real, tangible returns, they are less likely to gain the broad support of shareholders and proxy advisory firms. Either way, somewhere there is an adorable piglet whose life will likely be a little bit easier because of one of the wealthiest men in the history of Wall Street, and that's not nothing.

2. Activision Blizzard, Inc/SOC Investment Group

In the wake of the #MeToo movement, the connection between stakeholder value and allegations of sexual harassment by those in power at public

---

7   ISS Report on McDonald's (2022). Permission to quote ISS in these case studies was neither sought nor obtained.
8   Glass Lewis Report on McDonald's (2022). Permission to quote Glass Lewis in these case studies was neither sought nor obtained.
9   Form 8-K filed with the SEC by McDonald's on 2 June 2022.

companies has tightened. Over the past few years, shareholder activists began to focus fully fledged campaign themes nearly exclusively within the 'S' domain of ESG, holding companies accountable over allegations of hostile work environments.

Among the handful of recent examples is SOC Investment Group's (SOC) campaign at gaming giant, Activision Blizzard, Inc (Activision), which spanned from 2020 to 2022. Over time, this multi-year proxy contest transformed from being centred on governance ('G') to social ('S'). But despite SOC's shift in focus, the history of SOC's engagement with Activision evidences a consistent, overarching goal of targeting and removing Activision's CEO, Robert Kotick, first as a result of what SOC deemed excessive compensation, then in connection with the culture SOC argued Mr Kotick permitted during his tenure.

SOC kicked off its initial campaign in June 2020, urging shareholders to vote against Activision's "Say-On-Pay" proposal to approve executive compensation at the 2020 annual meeting of shareholders.[10] SOC voiced concern with Mr Kotick's compensation, specifically, his equity grants that SOC alleged had "consistently been larger than the total pay ... of CEO peers at similar companies".[11] Notably, SOC did not critique Mr Kotick's compensation when he first entered into his employment agreement four years earlier,[12] but instead used the announcement that Activision would be laying off nearly 800 employees as a springboard for SOC's campaign.[13] Like many tenets of 'S', shareholder perceptions of fairness related to an executive's compensation is highly dependent on circumstances, and circumstances change. Activision opted not to engage with SOC. At the 2020 annual meeting, the Company's "Say-On-Pay" proposal passed, receiving 56.8% of the vote,[14] compared to the 82% and 92% approvals that the "Say-On-Pay" proposal had received at Activision's 2019 and 2018 annual meetings, respectively.[15] It would appear that the views of SOC were in harmony with those of shareholders generally.

Shareholders spoke, and the company listened – Activision amended Mr Kotick's employment agreement on 28 April 2021,[16] removing certain awards and incentives for future equity grants for which SOC had taken issue in the 2020 campaign. Mr Kotick also agreed to reduce his base salary by 50%.[17] Rarely does a public company CEO agree to accept $0.50 cents on the dollar of his previous salary. However, these changes did not satisfy SOC: it again launched

10   PX14A6G filed with the SEC by SOC on 3 June 2020.
11   *Ibid.*
12   Current Report on Form 8-K filed with the SEC by Activision on 25 November 2016.
13   Matt Perez, "Activision Blizzard To Lay Off Nearly 800 People As Its 2019 Looks Bleak", *Forbes*, 12 February 2019, www.forbes.com/sites/mattperez/2019/02/12/activision-blizzard-to-layoff-nearly-800-employees/?sh=629c9d7376f5.
14   PX14A6G filed with the SEC by SOC on 16 June 2021.
15   *Ibid.*
16   Current Report on Form 8-K filed with the SEC by Activision on 29 April 2021.
17   *Ibid.*

an exempt solicitation at Activision, urging shareholders to vote against the "Say-On-Pay" proposal at the 2021 annual meeting and against the re-election of Compensation Committee Chair Robert Morgado.[18] Despite fairly significant changes made by the company, SOC argued that the changes made to Mr Kotick's employment agreement resulted in no meaningful change and accordingly, Mr Morgado should be held responsible for failing to adequately address the compensation issues.[19]

This time, Activision decided that this would be the last time the company did not defend itself. Activision addressed SOC's criticisms in an open letter to shareholders, defending its rationale for Mr Kotick's compensation and pointing to its significant shareholder outreach.[20] And while there was a moment of uncertainty as to whether Activision would garner sufficient votes to pass "Say-on-Pay" (the company adjourned its 2021 annual meeting for a week with respect to "Say-on-Pay",[21] which SOC characterised as a "desperate attempt to avoid a loss"),[22] ultimately, Mr Morgado was re-elected and the "Say-on-Pay" proposal passed with 55.6% of the vote.[23]

After two consecutive campaigns focused on Mr Kotick's compensation, campaigns that likely required countless hours of attention from the board and management of the company, SOC notified Activision that the fund was not done. Now, SOC was focused on an entirely new issue after reports surfaced questioning whether Mr Kotick knew for years about certain sexual misconduct allegations at Activision.[24] The timing of SOC's focus pivot likely could not have been worse for Activision, as SOC made the hostile workplace allegations a central aspect of its "Vote No" campaign in opposition to Microsoft Corporation's (Microsoft) acquisition of Activision. SOC criticised the board for failing to address widespread sexual harassment claims, even though the lawsuit related to the claims was investigated by multiple federal agencies.[25] In response, Activision announced, in connection with its approval of Glass Lewis's recommendation in support of the merger, that the board had taken steps within the past three years to improve workplace culture, centralise certain

---

18   PX14A6G filed with the SEC by SOC on 8 June 2021.
19   *Ibid.*
20   DEFA14A filed with the SEC by Activision on 11 June 2021.
21   DEFA14A filed with the SEC by Activision on 14 June 2021.
22   PX14A6G filed with the SEC by SOC on 16 June 2021.
23   Current Report on Form 8-K filed with the SEC by Activision on 21 June 2021.
24   Compare SOC's letter sent to the Activision board on 5 August 2021, https://static1.squarespace.com/static/5d374de8aae9940001c8ed59/t/6112affe2aea584297c35a92/1628614654961/SOC+IG+to+Activision+8-10-21.pdf, with SOC's letter sent to the Activision board on 27 November 2021, https://static1.squarespace.com/static/5d374de8aae9940001c8ed59/t/61951ca2ae62940ca8c22c28/1637162146586/Activision_Blizzard_sign_on_FINAL+11-17-21.pdf; see also Michael McWhertor, "Activision shareholder group calls for Bobby Kotick and board members' resignation", *Polygon*, 17 November 2021, www.polygon.com/22787226/activision-blizzard-shareholder-bobby-kotick-resignation.
25   See SOC's letter sent to the Activision board on 27 November 2021, https://static1.squarespace.com/static/5d374de8aae9940001c8ed59/t/61951ca2ae62940ca8c22c28/1637162146586/Activision_Blizzard_sign_on_FINAL+11-17-21.pdf; see also PX14A6G filed with the SEC by SOC on 14 April, 2022.

human resources functions to promote accountability, and increase resources for reporting and responding to complaints of harassment and retaliation.[26] Shareholders voted for the merger with nearly a 98% approval rate at the special meeting.[27]

Likely to very little, if any, surprise on the part of the board and company management, SOC was seemingly unmoved by the approval of the Microsoft merger. On 27 May 2022, SOC launched another exempt solicitation campaign – this time in connection with Activision's 2022 annual meeting.[28] In a repeat of previous SOC themes, it focused its thesis on the hostile workplace claims and its allegations of a "frat house" culture at Activision.[29] SOC called for shareholders to vote against the re-election of Mr Kotick and five other incumbent directors, including Mr Morgado, because of their alleged "inadequate response to the sexual harassment crisis" and an inability to hold management accountable[30] (SOC also abandoned its calls for the resignation of Mr Kotick, who still serves as CEO of Activision). Activision responded with a point-by-point breakdown of purported misrepresentations in SOC's latest missive and listed out 12 actions it had taken to address the hostile work place allegations.[31] Ultimately, all six incumbent directors were re-elected at the 2022 annual meeting.[32]

Following the 2022 annual meeting, SOC did not pursue further campaigns at the company and instead left that Call of Duty to be answered by other shareholders. For years, SOC was unrelenting in its activism at Activision. Its several campaigns illustrate how an activist's thesis can morph over time from a more traditional platform to increasingly focus on ESG-centric objectives, and more broadly suggests that as the ESG activism landscape continues to develop, recent campaigns, like SOC's, may indicate that activists will increasingly attempt to include social themes in activism situations. While activists' focus on ESG is by no means novel, SOC's campaign at Activision suggests that the activist playbook continues to evolve and illustrates how the reputational risk of controversies can be used by activists to challenge board composition.

---

26   DEFA14A filed with the SEC by Activision on 20 April 2022.
27   Current Report on Form 8-K filed with the SEC by Activision on 28 April 2022.
28   PX14A6G filed with the SEC by SOC on 27 May 2022.
29   Ibid.
30   Ibid.
31   DEFA14A filed with the SEC by Activision on 31 May 2022.
32   Current Report on Form 8-K filed with the SEC by Activision on 21 June 2022.

ESG corporate issues: M&A

Rachel Barrett
Dearbhla Cantwell
Vanessa Havard-Williams
Linklaters

1.   Introduction

In recent years, ESG has garnered recognition for creating both risks and opportunities for businesses. The rise in ESG-related regulation, litigation, investor scrutiny, shareholder and NGO activism, corporate commitments and counterparty expectations has placed a spotlight onto specific ESG-related issues. Looking at transactions through an ESG lens is increasingly necessary even if it is not yet common practice or the subject of a consistent approach.

For a purchaser in any corporate transaction, identification of financially or reputationally material issues is key and traditional due diligence processes are slowly adapting to capture ESG-related issues with the potential for significant liability or adverse impacts on brand value and reputation. Early consideration of these issues is advisable particularly where they are critical to the target or the purchaser's corporate strategy, involve potentially material expenditure or liability, or significant reputational risk. Red flag issues could potentially lead to more difficult or protracted negotiations, reduction in value or at worst, no transaction at all.

This requires a clear-eyed approach by sellers and their advisers who now need to anticipate, explain and, to the extent possible, de-risk those ESG issues associated with the target business that have the potential to deter potential purchasers. Not all purchasers will have the same risk appetite or ESG issue sensitivity – this may depend, for example, on the nature of a private equity (PE) fund and the regulatory regime to which it and its major investors are subject, or on the strategy and climate or sustainability commitments of the potential acquirer. For purchasers, it means ensuring their due diligence process takes account of both their own strategic sustainability parameters and the ESG issues salient in the target business, and that they have enough information and understanding of the uncertainties to make reasonable judgements within the transaction process. Given that ESG issues have the potential to significantly impact a deal and, in some cases, the entire acquirer group, the juice is certainly worth the squeeze when it comes to this process.

This chapter will explore how ESG issues are identified through the due diligence process, including the approach to ESG due diligence and how it can be scoped, the impact of identified ESG issues and how to manage these in the transaction documents and in post-closing integration.

2.   Issue spotting through due diligence

Due diligence is the main tool through which ESG-related issues are typically identified in a private acquisition before a deal is signed. It is a critical process for understanding the sustainability risk profile of the target business. While it has long been commonplace to consider environmental and health and safety, employment and anti-bribery and corruption issues as part of this process, due diligence is starting now to be undertaken through a broader and more holistic ESG lens.

A rapidly shifting ESG policy and regulatory landscape, major impacts on corporate strategy and capital allocation, growing litigation risk and the extension of corporate responsibility into the value chain mean that it is more necessary than ever to properly understand and characterise ESG issues. Failure to do so can lead to significant financial liabilities and/or adverse reputational impacts.

This should drive more blended diligence exercises involving technical, strategy, legal and financial diligence inputs, so that the implications of each strand of work can be considered in the round. In practice this is currently the exception rather than the rule.

3.   Scoping due diligence

There is no one-size-fits-all when it comes to scoping ESG due diligence but, as in all things, careful preparation at the beginning of the process is likely to save time and reduce risk.

ESG as a concept covers a wide range of topic areas and these need to be refined to those issues material to the target, and relevant ESG targets, commitments or exclusions applied by the acquirer or its finance providers. The types of ESG issues affecting the target will vary depending on the sector, industry and jurisdiction(s) in which the target business operates, as well as its history and current relationships. A first step therefore involves identifying relevant ESG topics and ensuring that these are covered by the due diligence scope. Lawyers with significant ESG experience and/or deep sector expertise will often have a good sense of what thematic areas should be prioritised for consideration. This should also be informed and cross-checked by review of publicly available materials (eg, any sustainability report published by the target, relevant industry reports on sustainability opportunities and challenges for that sector, searches on controversy indices or special interest group campaign databases) and the use of risk screening tools now increasingly offered by ESG data providers.

The purchaser's own ESG strategy should be considered as part of this exercise. For example, if there are specific targets it has set, commitments it has made or areas in which it has set policy requirements, the acquisition must be assessed to see whether it creates material risk. These issues may also be relevant if debt finance is required: this is most likely to be an important consideration if the acquisition relates to assets that are particularly high risk in climate, human rights or biodiversity terms.

A sample range of topics might include:

- *Traditional topics:* land contamination, emissions to air, discharges to water, environmental or health and safety-related permitting and regulatory capex, handling or storage of hazardous substances and waste, employee health and safety incidents, worker and community human rights, ESG-related litigation or investigations.
- *Newer topics:* greenhouse gas (GHG) emission data including Scope 3, transition plan and related capex, climate resilience assessment, extent/robustness of value chain mapping, human rights assessment and its boundaries (ie, own operations or broader), certification schemes, carbon allowances/offsets/removals and renewable energy certificate schemes, target group exposure to material sustainability reporting or due diligence obligations and preparedness, relevant sustainability-related trade regulation (eg, CBAM, conflict minerals, etc), sustainability-related product claims and governance maturity, entity/product-related complaints, including any relating to its advocacy approach (direct and through trade bodies).

The scoping of any due diligence exercise involves the setting of a materiality threshold to guide the selection of issues sufficiently important to impact transaction value. This threshold has always been largely financial in nature and has never lent itself particularly well to environmental and social due diligence where issues can be complex and contingent, making them challenging to quantify precisely as a near-term cost. In addition, persistent minor or systemic issues can be indicative of poor corporate culture and housekeeping that can together create material risk. The increased scrutiny on all ESG matters means that lawyers can expect more focus and complexity in applying materiality judgements. They should therefore try to frame observations on these types of issue precisely and carefully (including flagging areas of uncertainty).

The practical realities of transaction timelines, budgetary parameters and access to specialist advisers limit what can be done. Even if the pre-acquisition phase is very short and due diligence correspondingly constrained, it is prudent to consider building in other options, such as greater contractual protections and/or post signing or post completion diligence, possibly with retention or indemnity arrangements for defined areas of risk.

4.   Multi-stakeholder approach to due diligence

Within any law firm, coverage of the broad spectrum of ESG topic areas is likely to involve specialists from a range of practices, for example, environmental lawyers, employment lawyers, data protection or supply chain lawyers and others (including a small but increasing number of lawyers specialising in ESG issues). Many will already be involved in the relevant due diligence process, likely conveying their findings into a corporate transaction team with overall responsibility for delivering legal support on the transaction, and who will also be compiling corporate focused due diligence findings.

To present coherent legal commentary on ESG matters reflective of the way clients are now thinking about this area, specialists are increasingly likely to need to speak to each other and their corporate colleagues to coordinate at least some joined-up ESG commentary in any due diligence report. Market practice on this is still at a very early stage, and evolving, and will of course also depend to some degree on individual client preference. A critical area for law firm development is the training of non-specialist ESG lawyers to ensure they have a good current understanding of how the business environment has already changed in this regard and of the policy direction on these issues, recognising this will have significant regional variation.

The scope of legal due diligence on most ESG topic areas will typically focus on compliance with applicable current or future law and required capital expenditure or major operational or product change, as well as clearly identifiable liability risks such as ongoing or threatened litigation. ESG risks can be highly technical in nature, requiring a synthesis of legal, financial or technical input to ensure that analysis is robust. For example, technical and legal support may be required to assess the target's carbon footprint, waste management, air emissions management, etc and planned approaches to improve or remediate consistent with incoming requirements or stated strategy, and robustness of internal ESG-related systems and controls. In particular cases, financial and accounting issues may arise as major technology changes are driven by the global energy transition or other changes require investment to improve the resilience of the operation or critical supply chains.

Given the importance of ESG to investors and counterparties, purchasers are increasingly interested in understanding the appropriateness and maturity level of a target's ESG strategy and the extent to which it is adapting to the shifting expectations (eg, action it is taking in anticipation of significant new ESG regulation, its engagement with its value chain, etc), and the way in which its ESG profile is perceived by key stakeholders.

Lawyers can play an important role at the outset of any transaction in being a trusted adviser to their clients, thinking strategically and mapping areas where other specialist advisers may be required. They may help coordinate work, and open communication between adviser teams is essential to ensure that the collection of work products the client ultimately receives is coherent and complementary. Where blended advice is required, consideration of privilege issues may also be very relevant. Lawyers will be expected to review the findings of other advisers and advise on any associated legal risks arising from the issues identified. Traditionally, these will likely have been compliance focused, but increasingly lawyers are expected to consider a broader set of legal risks (eg, 'greenwash' risk, shareholder activism, potential legal risks associated with a particularly ambitious strategy or, conversely, perceived gaps in approach, etc).

Finally, as organisations begin to establish ESG legal functions or centres of excellence, a portion of the due diligence process may well be managed in-house. Equally, operational specialists or subject matter experts within a client organisation should be involved in more strategic and technical aspects of due diligence. Bringing expert members of the client team into relevant conversations and ensuring they have access to the information they need at the right time is a key role for lawyers on many transactions.

5. Locating ESG-related information

A due diligence exercise generally begins with the launch of a virtual data room containing a wide range of documentation in a more or less orderly format. Any seller and its advisers should be incentivised to reveal sufficient information to make a fair assessment of material ESG risks possible, particularly where this offers protection in relation to warranties the seller will be giving. That said, data room quality varies significantly, and can also be impacted by the transaction timeline, budgets and commercial sensitivities which impede or delay access to information on parts of the target business.

Lawyers must work quickly to establish material gaps in information provided and request this from counterparties. To be effective, requests need to be carefully curated and precise in nature, and overlaps between advisers should be removed to maintain goodwill and ensure an efficient process.

Typically, information relevant to ESG matters will not be neatly displayed under a folder in the data room marked 'ESG', or even 'environment'. In fact, generally, a thorough review of any data room index is required to establish where relevant information may be located. This may not always be in obvious places. For example, while environmental audit reports, permitting-related documentation, correspondence with environmental regulators and social and governance policies may immediately stand out, minutes of board and other committee meetings can provide useful insights into material ESG-related issues that have been escalated. Similarly, litigation trackers and grievance logs can be fertile ground for information on ESG issues.

That said, it is rare that a comprehensive picture of all relevant ESG-related issues can be established through documentary review alone. Increasingly, where their scope permits or requires this, lawyers are searching for information in less conventional places – for example, by undertaking press searches (including on social media), reviewing non-governmental organisation commentary and controversy reports prepared by ESG rating agencies. There has also been an increase in the use of tech solutions such as artificial intelligence-powered analysis and evaluation (the role of technology tools is explored in detail in the chapter "How technology is transforming ESG reporting". These non-traditional resources can shed light on important ESG-related issues and trends, including brewing litigation risk, which may not otherwise be apparent from data room documents (particularly where financial materiality thresholds have been applied). However, it is important to note that external sources, particularly ESG ratings, should only be viewed as an indirect indicator of issues that may require further investigation, and reviewers should focus on the underlying data and information as part of the due diligence process.

Many target businesses will also be generating significant volumes of ESG-related data in coming years in response to incoming sustainability disclosure requirements. Where these are disclosed publicly in a sustainability report (or in the target's annual report and accounts) or as part of a report prepared by the target's ultimate parent company, lawyers will increasingly wish to review these materials for information that reveals potential legal risks.

Several rounds of follow-up questions may be needed to plug information gaps and explore issues to better understand their materiality. Indeed, often ESG topic areas may be more productively addressed through discussions with the seller subject matter experts where this is possible. Human rights and social issues often fall into this category, where documents and policy commitments or public statements of intent tend not to reveal much. A reasonable understanding of the target's approach to implementing risk and impact management systems and controls on social matters can be difficult to assess without dialogue between subject matter experts.

6.   Identifying material ESG-related issues

ESG lawyers need to have a broad understanding of the types of ESG issues that can arise to ensure they have a good sense of what to look for and can accurately isolate and characterise significant ESG matters. A matter that has been a material issue on one transaction may be relatively inconsequential on others. It often pays dividends for lawyers to familiarise themselves with key sector, regional and jurisdictional issues and trends before embarking on the relevant due diligence process, to provide useful context for their work.

It would not be possible to develop a comprehensive list of issues that can arise under each of the three ESG pillars, but some commonly observed issues include:

- *Environment:* Contribution to greenhouse gases (GHG) and other air emissions and operational compliance with emission limits or benchmarks, contamination of soil or water, current and future compliance with and implications of permitting arrangements and regulation, including relating to the use, storage, handling or disposal of hazardous substances, chemicals, waste, usage of persistent pollutants, etc. Alignment with stated net zero targets and robustness of transition planning, any commercial obligations with regard to environmental performance. Emissions allowances, offsetting and certification arrangements (including for raw materials and products). Product and supply-related regulation and regulation of product claims.

- *Social:* Regulatory due diligence compliance, defective products, human rights in supply chains, unsafe working conditions, employee incidents and accidents, claims in relation to industrial disease, issues with corporate culture including issues relating to discrimination, bullying, unequal pay, lack of diversity in senior roles, whistleblowing. Other potential issues include problematic community relations in areas of operation, which may undermine the social 'licence to operate' and lead to future disruptions. Alignment with just transition components of transition planning, any commercial obligations with regard to social performance.

- *Governance:* ESG governance maturity level, gaps in the policies, systems and processes needed to assess, monitor, mitigate and manage ESG-related risks, including employee training, failures to apply internal controls, instances of corruption and bribery in an environmental and social context, relevance of and compliance with ESG-focused trade requirements.

Once particular ESG-related issues have been identified, it is essential to consider the legal risks that arise from them, and to contextualise these for clients. Potential reputational and commercial risks may also be highlighted.

7. Understanding the implications of identified ESG issues

Properly characterising the legal risks associated with ESG issues can be challenging. Often a range of inputs are needed to understand the full implications and a simple answer is not possible: in these circumstances it may be possible to provide indications by reference to ranges and probabilities. For example, complex human rights issues may need investigation by specialist advisers with local support to ensure jurisdictional or area-specific operating environments are accounted for. Lawyers need to be open to developing creative solutions and suggesting the involvement of other subject matter experts where this is appropriate and possible.

Effective characterisation can be rendered even trickier by the fast-paced development of the regulatory and litigation landscape, and rapidly evolving stakeholder expectations. A plethora of new and incoming ESG regulations are set to materially change the legal risk profile attached to certain ESG issues. At the time of writing, corporate accountability for ESG harms (including in supply chains) is growing as is the liability risk attached to unsubstantiated sustainability claims and disclosures. Stakeholder activism is on the rise, and an understanding of 'hot button' issues of the moment and ideally having some sense as to how they may develop is part of an assessment as to what may be material to the target's business (or indeed, to the purchaser).

Each identified ESG issue will need to be assessed to develop strategies for determining potential impact on the value of the target business, whether this is a roadblock to the transaction, and for allocating risks as between the purchaser and seller. While it will always ultimately be for the client to decide how they would prefer to address issues, lawyers can play a valuable role in explaining their potential significance and possible ways of addressing them in a transactional context.

8.   Managing and mitigating ESG-related risks in transaction documents

There are a number of different ways in which material ESG issues that have been identified during due diligence can be addressed on any given transaction. What approach is taken will depend on the nature and the severity of the issues, the extent of information known about them, the length of time it might take to address them, the risk appetite of the purchaser and of course the overall bargaining position of the parties as a whole.

9.   Decision not to proceed

While it is rare that an issue is identified of such a magnitude, and so irremediable in nature, that a deal cannot go ahead in its entirety, this does now sometimes happen in relation to ESG matters. This is particularly so if they are systemic or if the change required is too significant for the potential buyer to be willing to commit. Some businesses may be in run-off mode; and in these circumstances a smaller subset of purchasers may engage.

10.   Price chips

Purchase price reductions may be the simplest route when a purchaser feels it can properly quantify the financial risk associated with a particular ESG issue and assuming the competitive environment allows.

11.   Contractual mechanisms

Other options may also be available to purchasers to ensure risks are appropriately allocated. Some tools can also help support completion of the due diligence process in parallel with the negotiation of the transaction documents, as explained below.

12. Warranties

Warranties are contractual statements of fact about the business given at the point in time they are given by a seller, which will typically be upon signing and possibly also on completion of the deal. If the statement proves to be untrue, the purchaser may be able to claim damages for the loss it has suffered (subject to any agreed limitations in the transaction documents). Loss is usually measured as the difference between the value of the business as warranted and the business as is.

Standard warranties still tend to be limited to legal non-compliances (eg, with environment, health and safety laws) or other legal risks (eg, the existence of litigation or threatened claims) and grouped by ESG topic area (eg, environment, anti-bribery and corruption, etc) rather than grouped together under an ESG heading. Other than in relation to employment matters (and to a lesser degree, value chain matters), social topics are still rarely addressed through warranty packages.

Where the purchaser feels that information provided to it during the due diligence process did not enable a fulsome consideration of the ESG risk profile of the target business, or if there are issues that have been identified, but which could not be properly characterised through lack of information, then the purchaser may seek to include additional, more specific warranties within the transaction documentation.

Because matters fairly disclosed by the seller typically qualify the warranties, the inclusion of a specific warranty in a draft sale and purchase agreement can be enough to prompt further disclosure in relation to the issue at hand, thereby facilitating further due diligence.

Where there is no further information to be had, or the transaction timeline does not permit this, then of course the warranty becomes a risk allocation tool as between the parties in relation to the relevant ESG issue – with the seller bearing the risk that, for example, a relevant non-compliance has occurred which ultimately lessens the value of the target.

The role of insurance in relation to warranty claims is explored in the chapter "ESG in the insurance sector". It should be noted from a practical perspective that the extensive use of warranty and indemnity insurance has eroded the commercial focus on and value of warranties. This is particularly problematic in the case of ESG where exclusions may apply to the coverage, which are still not well understood by non-specialist advisers; additionally, the forward-looking nature of many ESG issues means that the practical value of warranties is limited.

While ESG warranties may be a useful tool in the context of any due diligence process, they cannot be viewed as a substitute for fulsome due diligence where the business has innate risk. It is preferable to understand as many of the issues as possible in advance of entering into the deal, to maximise optionality in relation to the way in which they are addressed and to minimise the risk of disputes after the deal is done.

13. Indemnities

In some instances, the parties may seek to agree an indemnity arrangement in relation to a particular ESG issue. Indemnities are a useful tool under which purchasers can seek quick reimbursement of their losses in relation to a particular issue subject to agreed triggers, processes and limitations. In an ESG context they are most deployed in relation to potential liability for historic soil and groundwater contamination or specific compliance-related upgrades pre-dating the transaction for which the purchaser does not wish to assume liability, but in respect of which precise quantification of loss can be a challenge at the time of the transaction. They can be detailed 'deals within the deal' on major transactions and the subject of lengthy negotiations in their own right. Indemnities are, of course, sometimes used in relation to other issues, including asbestos-related exposure or other industrial disease claims, and are used in some regions more than others.

14. Material adverse change

In exceptional circumstances, a transaction document may need to include 'walk away' rights in respect of the period between signing and closing if a particular event arises. Occasional use of this type of clause occurred in the immediate aftermath of the Deepwater Horizon/Macondo incident in 2010 in a few extractive sector transactions, but they have never gained traction because they are highly unattractive to sellers.

15. Accounting for ESG-related allowances, credits and certifications, and transfer of certifications, permits and permit variations

Depending on the nature of the business and the interest being sold (if the environmental asset is held by the target group and equity is sold, contractual requirements will be much reduced), provisions may be required to provide for recording of emissions at completion and provision for transfer of allowances, certificates or offsets to the buyer, and for the transfer of permits. Where permits must be split or are in the process of being varied, additional provisions may be required. In all these circumstances information and cooperation provisions are important.

16. Conduct of claims and collaboration between signing and closing

Given the potential reputational impacts of ESG issues in general and ESG litigation and quasi litigation in particular, it is likely that conduct of claims clauses and information and cooperation provisions in respect of ESG matters in the period after signing and before completion will come under much greater scrutiny. This is likely to be most relevant where there are known issues in play, but general provisions may ultimately be required to reflect the increased sensitivity to these topics.

17. Post-closing investigation and improvement plans

There can be ESG issues the burden of which will be assumed by the purchaser (directly in an asset sale, or indirectly in a share sale where it is retained in the target group) once the deal is done. Increasingly, purchasers are implementing specific post-close diligence to flush out issues, and where these are foreshadowed pre-sale, they may be contractually addressed by providing for investigation, remediation and payment or cost sharing arrangements in the agreement. These can address very specific issues but are sometimes broader programmes designed to upgrade the target's compliance and risk management systems. While these mechanisms have always had a role in relation to environmental and wider regulatory concerns, they are likely to play a bigger role as ESG issues become more prominent. It is crucial to ensure that there are sufficient financial and human resources retained in the target business and it retains relevant information and records to implement post-completion programmes and that these workstreams are completed after the deal has closed.

Examples of post-completion remediation might include those:

- *in relation to community complaints about emissions, vibration, noise, etc of an industrial operation:* stakeholder engagement, assessment of any grievance mechanism, liaising with the relevant regulator, developing an investigation and remediation strategy, engaging an environmental consultant to further assess the extent and severity of impacts and make recommendations, and taking steps to actually mitigate or remediate the issue or otherwise propose compensatory measures;
- *where there are ongoing investigations by a regulator:* the purchaser should make contact and liaise with the regulator as soon as possible post-close to establish a relationship and to demonstrate that management of the issue is in hand, despite a change in ownership of the business; or
- *where minor, persistent ESG-related issues have occurred across the target business:* the purchaser may wish to take steps to implement enhanced risk management procedures, updated policies, or employee training.

18. The evolving nature of ESG due diligence

The market is slowly broadening its approach to ESG in transactions. Considering ESG at the outset of a deal will slowly become the default option and it is already often an important area for purchasers when conceptualising a target's value and managing any risk.

A wide range of factors drive ESG due diligence, and these will continue to develop over time given the rapidly evolving ESG policy landscape. The recent introduction of mandatory supply chain due diligence regimes, for example, particularly in the European Union, is one such factor. Mandatory due diligence regimes such as these will drive transparency over time in relation to specific ESG topics, solidifying what were previously often viewed as 'nice to have' information into hard requirements.

These regimes will elicit more granular information from companies on specific topics such as deforestation, forced labour or human rights violations because of the reporting and disclosure obligations under the regimes. Such disclosures will be a useful resource for purchasers and will increasingly form part of a purchaser's ESG due diligence toolkit.

While there will always be a need for customisation when it comes to scoping ESG due diligence and developing contractual provisions in response, it remains to be seen how the approach to ESG issues will develop and standardise as time goes on and as the market gains more experience of engaging with these topics and their positive and negative implications.

ESG in private equity

Paul Davies
Michael D Green
Latham & Watkins

1.   Introduction

ESG criteria have increasingly driven investment decisions for private equity investors. However, private equity firms face unique challenges incorporating ESG into their decision-making processes. Those challenges include increasing expectations from Limited Partners (LPs); limited data transparency and ESG regulation for private companies (to date); and fluctuating ESG measurement standards.

Notwithstanding these challenges and external criticism received, private equity has made significant advancements in ESG – on acquisition of companies, on the hold of portfolio companies, and on exit. This is driven by both the requirements imposed by LPs, and the understanding that ESG can not only lower risk, but also create value and provide attractive investment opportunities. Many private equity firms stated that ESG was an essential part of their investment proposition long before 'ESG' was even a recognised term. Growing collaboration and peer pressure within the sector is further accelerating ESG integration, as stakeholders demand a more purpose-driven approach.

Over time, the private equity sector has emerged as a major global player. Globally, approximately 10,000 private equity firms oversee over 20 million employees at around 40,000 portfolio companies. Projections indicate that industry assets could surpass $11 trillion by 2026.[1] Through private equity's emergence as a market force, significant opportunity has arisen for ESG to support the industry's value creation proposition. Notably, several major private equity firms are now publicly listed, and therefore subject to the same regulatory pressures as all public companies. Moreover, as the private equity industry has expanded, so too has the scope of its responsible investing. Heightened scrutiny, together with increasing internal interest in ESG, means that broadly (although not universally) ESG considerations have shifted from the strategic periphery to the critical centre.

---

1   Robert G Eccles, Vinay Shandal, David Young and Benedicte Montgomery, "Private Equity Should Take the Lead in Sustainability", *Harvard Business Review*, July–August 2022, https://hbr.org/2022/07/private-equity-should-take-the-lead-in-sustainability.

Comparable foundations form the core of strong ESG structures for both LPs and General Partners (GPs). LPs mainly invest in funds and specific opportunities (which they then continue to monitor and assess) whereas GPs oversee and manage their investments. Despite these differences, prevailing ESG approaches share key traits: endorsement from top-level stakeholders, assigned accountability, resource availability, comprehensive monitoring and engagement, and a commitment to internal ESG standards. Within such a competitive industry, private equity is still able to foster discussions around ESG and exhibits a willingness among peers to collaborate and exchange insights (for example, the ESG Data Convergence Project led in part by the Institutional Limited Partners Association). This collaborative impetus plays an important role in helping to advance individual organisations and propel the industry forward.

Private equity now finds itself at the centre of ESG regulatory developments. These developments range from ESG fund labelling regimes and associated taxonomies (see the chapter "Global obstacles and opportunities for regulated financial institutions" for further details), impacts on portfolio companies through ESG disclosure obligations (see the chapter "ESG reporting" for further details), value chain due diligence requirements, through to regulations applying to private equity firms themselves (particularly those who are subject to public company obligations). These regulatory demands also represent an opportunity for many private equity firms to integrate ESG into their fundraising, transaction and portofolio development ecosystem. While this will give rise to complex decision-making considerations, as ESG drives material macroeconomic developments, such approaches could also facilitate productive relationships between LPs and GPs and provide value-creation opportunities.

This chapter explores the comprehensive integration of ESG in transactions, first examining the acquisition stage's amplified ESG due diligence and transaction document nuances, before looking at the challenges faced during the holding phase and the need for prioritisation in critical areas. Finally, it assesses how escalating demand for ESG reporting impacts the PE sector, considering regulatory aspects such as the Corporate Sustainability Reporting Directive (CSRD) and the Sustainable Finance Disclosure Regulation (SFDR), alongside stakeholder pressures and popular voluntary frameworks like the UN Principles for Responsible Development (UN PRI).

2. ESG in transactions

Basic ESG integration in private equity is a question of good hygiene, while advanced ESG integration offers a competitive edge – Anna Follér, Head of Sustainability, Sixth Swedish National Pension Fund.[2]

---

2   UN PRI, "The mainstreaming of ESG in private equity" (2022), www.unpri.org/pri-blog/the-mainstreaming-of-esg-in-private-equity/9451.article.

Private equity firms are increasing their scrutiny of ESG factors in transaction due diligence as they navigate the evolving investment landscape. As highlighted by Follér,[3] one powerful incentive (particularly for LPs) is the growing consideration of the potential value generated by ESG practices. ESG integration is not merely a compliance exercise, rather, it can be central to a company's long-term viability. In addition, companies are increasingly motivated by reputational concerns, compliance with regulations and meeting reporting obligations. This evolution has seen a shift from a basic 'risk and compliance' checklist provided during due diligence, to a comprehensive evaluation of how well a target company understands and manages ESG issues that materially impact its operations. The extent of this increased due diligence varies during the acquisition process; depending on the private equity firm's philosophy and approach, investors adopt different strategies when it comes to incorporating ESG considerations into their investment process.[4] Nonetheless, the process fundamentally involves a focus on industry-specific risks, an assessment of company-level risks and potential mitigation strategies if deemed necessary.

2.1 ESG in the due diligence process

As outlined in the chapter "ESG corporate issues: M&A", ESG due diligence encompasses a comprehensive evaluation of material risks in an organisation's systems, procedures and performance metrics in these specific domains. In the context of private equity, ESG due diligence often necessitates more manual steps. Instead of relying on publicly available data increasingly provided by listed companies, private equity investors typically have to solicit information and data directly from the target's management. This process generates a significant workload in gathering diverse information from various sources, consolidating it, and then analysing it (which requires considerable resource and effort). This may change as ESG disclosure obligations increasingly include requirements on private companies, but for now represents a potentially onerous addition to the obligations of tightly managed competition auction processes. This is one of the reasons we see private equity firms driving the development of technology solutions in the ESG space – see the chapter "How technology is transforming ESG reporting" for further details.

As a broad overview, we see private equity houses take the following approaches.

- Certain private equity firms prefer to target companies with pre-existing ESG processes and structures in place and a robust ESG track-record.

---

3   *Ibid.*
4   PitchBook, "ESG, Impact, and Greenwashing in PE and VC" (2022), https://pitchbook.com/news/reports/q1-2022-pitchbook-analyst-note-esg-impact-and-greenwashing-in-pe-and-vc.

These target companies are typically more mature in their organisational structure, larger, and have more complex operations. Consequently, private equity investors seek to ensure they possess a deep understanding of the ESG risks associated with the industry in which the target company operates and conduct thorough due diligence to assess the company's ability to manage ESG risks and their mitigation. Private equity investors who subscribe to this approach leverage the availability and ESG scores or ratings for private companies. These scores can assist in early-stage due diligence by helping to identify and eliminate unsuitable entities from consideration.

- A middle-of-the-road strategy is where private equity investors seek to understand ESG risks primarily based on the industry in which the target company operates, rather than solely focusing on the company's specific operations. They may conduct a comprehensive ESG gap analysis, offering recommendations for implementation to address significant risks. This assessment can take place either before making the investment, or after acquisition. As this chapter later examines, during the holding period, regular monitoring becomes crucial under this approach, and typically occurs quarterly or biannually. This is when private equity firms work with portfolio companies to help those companies establish, or significantly develop, comprehensive ESG programmes addressing various issue areas.

- Alternatively, some investors take a minimal pre-investment due diligence approach (or do not specifically consider ESG matters at all). They are more open to accepting companies with both manageable and unmanageable ESG risks. Advocates of this philosophy may still use pre-investment or post-acquisition ESG risk assessments to identify potential areas for improvement or opportunities, particularly for companies with high levels of risk. Similar to the middle-ground approach (discussed above), private equity houses adopting this minimal pre-investment approach may still monitor progress, document ESG-related enhancements and employ exit assessments, and this can all be valuable in demonstrating value addition in the ESG domain. The extent to which these activities are conducted often depends on the level of risk associated with the investment and the private equity firm's desire (or obligations or resources) to consider ESG matters.

2.2 ESG considerations in transaction documents

Beyond the due diligence phase, the acquisition stage offers additional mechanisms to bolster investor confidence and assurance regarding the target company's ESG performance. One such mechanism is the use of ratchets. Private equity firms seek new investment opportunities which will foster growth and profitability, but these firms also desire full commitment, particularly from the company's management team. The inclusion of ratcheting provisions in transaction documents when acquiring a company can provide this incentive and economic alignment.

Ratchets manifest as specific performance targets or indicators that the company must achieve to unlock additional rewards for its management and key employees, functioning much like performance-based bonuses. These metrics can encompass a wide spectrum and, in recent years, there have been increasing instances of ratcheting clauses coming to encompass ESG considerations.[5] This incentivises the management team to commit to the company's long-term ESG agenda, often extending until a successful exit event such as an acquisition or IPO. These ESG targets may be isolated and entity-specific or – through the increasing shift to more streamlined data collection – by peer benchmarking. In doing so, ratchets ensure alignment of interests and a steadfast focus on sustainable growth. This approach also provides an additional layer of security for private equity firms in relation to the target's ESG performance during the holding period.

While ratchets (and associated shareholder and management arrangements) are proving increasingly popular, the traditional warranties and indemnities in transactional documents currently represent a less promising source of contractual protection. Although specific and bespoke ESG-related warranties and indemnities can provide protection against specific identified historical ESG issues, the forward-looking nature of ESG matters does not lend itself to the warranty and indemnity structure. Further, to date, the lack of ESG regulations presents a challenge to defining the scope of any such ESG warranties and indemnities, particularly when many private equity transactions are limited to an ability to claim under a warranty and indemnity policy (where coverage of ESG matters is either excluded or very limited). The position may change in the near term with increased ESG regulations – particularly regarding disclosure obligations and value chain due diligence requirements. However, this remains an area that is under development.

Against this background of limited transactional coverage for ESG matters, it underscores the importance of robust ESG due diligence processes, with tailored strategies enabling effective risk management and value creation across varying investment profiles.

Private equity firms may also consider the role of finance in creating economic investments for portfolio companies in improving ESG performance (see the chapter "The basics of ESG finance" for further details).

---

5   New Private Markets, "In brief: Inflexion's ESG linked management ratchet" (2022), www.newprivatemarkets.com/in-brief-inflexions-esg-linked-management-ratchet/.

3. ESG integration into portfolio companies

The private equity sector is well-positioned to take a leading role in sustainable investing and the integration of ESG principles. Particularly for GPs, managing a diverse portfolio with varying regulatory frameworks, levels of sophistication and engagement is a formidable task, but it presents an opportunity for private equity firms to discover value.

One of the foremost challenges facing private equity firms is navigating the intricate web of ESG regulations and standards, which differ from one region to another. Companies within the portfolio may operate in various jurisdictions, each with its own set of ESG compliance requirements and guidelines. Adding to the complexity, portfolio companies vary widely in their ESG maturity and understanding. Some may have well-established ESG strategies in place, while others may be newcomers to the field. This disparity in sophistication necessitates a tailored approach to ESG integration, as a uniform strategy may not produce optimal results. Moreover, private equity firms encounter varying degrees of engagement towards ESG issues among portfolio companies. While some portfolio companies proactively embrace ESG principles, others may exhibit reluctance or limited interest. Bridging these engagement gaps is pivotal for developing ESG integration across the portfolio.

Providing adequate support for a diverse portfolio, particularly concerning ESG matters, is logistically challenging. To ensure that portfolio companies exert control over decision making, private equity firms need to balance their expectations as a shareholder with the importance of not overreaching. This can be resource-intensive and is one of the reasons for increased investment in ESG personnel within private equity firms. The sheer breadth of a private portfolio can strain resources, both financial and human – prioritisation, and the effective allocation of resources, has become essential to avoid spreading resources too thin.

To address these multifaceted challenges, we are seeing private equity firms adopt a strategic approach to ESG integration. Rather than establishing uniform ESG expectations across the entire portfolio, they are focusing on material areas. Employing governance methods, and providing the appropriate support and expertise to portfolio companies to develop their own strategy, can lead to more effective ESG outcomes. The methods by which private equity firms can achieve this are examined below.

3.1 Tailored ESG integration

First, private equity's distinctive business model confers significant advantages; in particular, it allows for a customised approach to ESG for portfolio companies. These tailored strategies acknowledge individual company circumstances, and can range from modest improvements to comprehensive ESG overhauls.

A private equity firm can have significant influence over its portfolio companies. Even when it does not have full ownership, it typically appoints one or more representatives to the board and wields substantial influence over other board appointments. Additionally, private equity firms have access to information regarding both financial and sustainability performance. This stands in contrast to investors in publicly traded companies, who rely solely on the information provided by the company. In addition, private equity firms may have influence over executive compensation of portfolio companies and any decision to replace underperforming CEOs. This level of involvement empowers private equity firms to assist their portfolio companies in advancing their ESG journeys.

Traditionally, distinctions existed between those responsible for investment decisions, asset oversight and sustainability within private equity firms. However, some firms are now acknowledging the need to broaden the level of expertise as deal and operational management teams undergo training in ESG. This is expedited by the industry's increasing appetite to engage ESG experts and establish advisory boards to guide portfolio companies. These experts possess specialised knowledge in ESG matters and can assist portfolio companies in the design and execution of effective ESG strategies.

Notwithstanding the above, it is important for private equity firms to consider the need for the necessary and appropriate degree of separation between private equity firms and the portfolio companies that they have invested in. Private equity firms are important stakeholders for their portfolio companies, but private equity firms should not control and manage the operations of those portoflio companies. Litigation risks arising from exercising control are flagged in the chapter "Global trends in ESG litigation", and it is therefore important for private equity firms to have in place appropriate governance arrangements managing the relationship with portfolio companies.

3.2 Monitoring and reporting mechanisms

Secondly, implementing a measurable and standardised set of ESG key performance indicators (KPIs) and reporting mechanisms has proven essential for tracking ESG progress across private equity portfolios. For instance, certain European KPIs cover both general and sector-specific principles – including greenhouse gas emissions, staff turnover and litigation.[6] KPIs seek to provide transparency and accountability, allowing portfolio companies to monitor their ESG performance and make improvements where necessary. GPs are adopting a disciplined approach to gathering KPIs from portfolio companies, with some

---

6   European Federation of Financial Analysts Societies, "KPIs for ESG: A Guideline for the Integration of ESG into Financial Analysis and Corporate Valuation" (2009), https://effas.com/wp-content/uploads/2021/09/KPIs_for_ESG_3_0_Final.pdf.

reporting as many as 50 to 100 KPIs annually or quarterly.[7] KPI reporting is tailored to include ESG issues relevant to a company's financial performance, aligning with materiality. Additionally, transparency between GPs and LPs regarding ESG performance is on the rise, with some GPs publicly sharing annual ESG reports. ESG integration is an ongoing process that requires continuous monitoring. These regular reporting mechanisms and audits ensure portfolio companies remain aligned with ESG objectives.

Notably, several private equity firms have recently announced their commitment to science-based climate targets.[8] In conjunction with the newly introduced Science Based Targets initiative's private equity sector guidance,[9] these commitments reflect not only a growing pressure, but also a growing readiness in the private equity sector to make changes tailored to the industry's unique characteristics. Two additional areas of ESG reporting metrics have emerged as priorities. Both GPs and LPs consider diversity, equity and inclusion (DEI) and climate change as crucial areas to address, not only internally within their organisations, but also in the context of their portfolios.[10] The private equity model positions GPs to assist portfolio companies in elevating their ESG integration and reporting practices through various means. This includes sharing best practices, providing measurement and reporting tools, benchmarking against peer portfolio companies, granting access to internal and external ESG experts and staying abreast of regulatory developments.

3.3 Legal risk mitigation and knowledge sharing

Finally, in an environment where various standards, frameworks and reporting methodologies exist, private equity firms recognise the need for a cohesive approach. Projects such as the Data Convergence Project (discussed later in this chapter) serve as a response to the increasingly complex landscape of ESG reporting. By aligning around common metrics, private equity firms aim to streamline the reporting process, reduce fragmentation and enhance comparability among portfolio companies.

This alignment contributes to the overall credibility of ESG reporting in the private equity industry and efficacy in reporting arrangements between portfolio companies, GPs and LPs. It demonstrates a commitment to rigour and accountability, which can bolster investor confidence and attract capital from those seeking sustainable and responsible investment opportunities. Such

---

7   Robert G Eccles, Vinay Shandal, David Young and Benedicte Montgomery, "Private Equity Should Take the Lead in Sustainability", *Harvard Business Review* (2022), https://hbr.org/2022/07/private-equity-should-take-the-lead-in-sustainability.
8   *Ibid.*
9   Science Based Targets, "Private Equity Sector Science-Based Target Guidance" (2021), https://sciencebasedtargets.org/resources/files/SBTi-Private-Equity-Sector-Guidance.pdf.
10 UN PRI, "A GP's guide to integrating ESG factors in private equity" (2014), www.unpri.org/private-equity/integrating-esg-factors-into-the-investment-process-due-diligence/94.article.

collaboration and discussion can enhance efficiency within private equity firms. By reducing the burden of navigating multiple ESG reporting frameworks, firms can allocate resources more effectively and focus on value-adding activities rather than grappling with reporting intricacies.

ESG integration in diverse private equity portfolios is a complex endeavour. By strategically prioritising material ESG areas, customising approaches, conducting thorough due diligence and leveraging governance methods, private equity firms can effectively navigate the challenges while enhancing portfolio-wide ESG performance. Balancing ESG integration with legal risk mitigation ensures a sustainable and responsible approach to managing private equity portfolios.

4.   Reporting considerations

LPs and Investment Managers can't see standardized, comparable ESG data across their portfolios; GPs are struggling under a mounting volume of bespoke ESG data requests; portfolio companies are sorting through an increasingly complex set of ESG frameworks; and broad-based data about ESG performance in the private investment markets don't exist.[11]

This is the start of the description of the Data Convergence Project: an alliance within the private equity sector under the auspices of the Institutional Limited Partners Association and dedicated to simplifying the previously disjointed process of gathering ESG data by generating a performance-oriented, and standardised, pool of ESG data from private enterprises. This movement, and others like it, demonstrates how the emphasis on ESG reporting is gaining considerable traction within the private equity industry. This is being driven by a combination of regulatory shifts, evolving investor expectations, and growing pressures from various stakeholders.

Regulatory bodies worldwide are increasingly adopting ESG mandates for both companies and investors. Europe, in particular, leads in this regard, with regulations such as the SFDR,[12] the CSRD[13] and the EU Taxonomy.[14] As outlined in the chapters "Global obstacles and opportunities for regulated financial institutions" and "ESG reporting", the SFDR obliges fund managers to integrate sustainability risks into investment decisions and align remuneration policies accordingly, the CSRD requires captured companies to produce annual reports detailing their sustainability information, and the EU Taxonomy establishes the criteria by which fund managers and/or companies describe the extent to which

---

11   ESG Data Convergence Initiative, www.esgdc.org/.
12   Regulation (EU) 2019/2088 of the European Parliament, EUR-Lex (2020), https://eur-lex.europa.eu/legal-content/EN/TXT/?uri=CELEX%3A02019R2088-20200712.
13   Regulation (EU) Directive 2013/34/EU of the European Parliament, EUR-Lex (2023) https://eur-lex.europa.eu/legal-content/EN/TXT/?uri=CELEX%3A02013L0034-20230105.
14   Regulation (EU) 2020/852 of the European Parliament and of the Council, EUR-Lex (2020), https://eur-lex.europa.eu/legal-content/EN/TXT/?uri=CELEX:32020R0852.

their economic activites are considered 'sustainable'. As a result, private equity firms are being increasingly compelled to proactively engage with their portfolio companies to ensure compliance and accurate ESG reporting.

Even beyond regulatory requirements, stakeholders are exerting pressure on private equity firms to embrace voluntary ESG reporting. End investors, including institutional investors and individual shareholders, are increasingly scrutinising the ESG impact of their investments. They are seeking greater transparency and assurance that their investments align with ESG principles. This heightened investor demand is compelling private equity firms to issue ESG reports, demonstrating their commitment to responsible and sustainable investment practices. In response to these forces, many private equity firms are actively incorporating ESG reporting into their strategies. They are collaborating closely with portfolio companies to enhance ESG performance and disclosure in addition to considering their own reporting obligations and navigating the impact of regulations such as CSRD and SFDR.

4.1   The Data Convergence Project

The consideration of knowledge and data-sharing projects is a notable development in the private equity sphere. These initiatives are driven by the desire of private equity firms to align on common metrics and standards, and establish a unified framework for reporting and assessment. This is exemplified by the popularity of projects such as the Data Convergence Project. Such projects seek to provide comparable data to guide firms as a response to the increasingly complex landscape of ESG reporting. The Data Convergence Project now includes over 350 GPs and LPs, representing roughly $28 trillion in assets under management (AUM).[15] In an environment where various standards, frameworks and reporting methodologies exist, private equity firms recognise the need for a cohesive approach.

The rationale for these efforts is multifaceted. First and foremost, common metrics facilitate consistency and transparency in ESG reporting. Additionally, private equity firms, along with their portfolio companies, can use standardised metrics to assess performance, identify areas for improvement and benchmark against industry peers. This not only simplifies decision making but also provides investors with reliable data for informed investment choices.

4.2   The UN PRI

Another pivotal player in private equity's adoption of ESG principles to drive sustainable investments is the UN PRI.

During the beginning of 2005, the then-United Nations Secretary-General, Kofi Annan, urged a consortium of major global institutional investors to

---

15   ESG Data Convergence Initiative website, www.esgdc.org/.

collaborate in creating the Principles for Responsible Investment.[16] This effort entailed a 20-person investor team from institutions in 12 countries, backed by a 70-person group of experts from the investment sector, intergovernmental organisations and civil society.[17] In the succeeding 18 years, the group has grown exponentially – as of December 2023, the UN PRI now has 5,372 signatories, representing $121 trillion of AUM.[18] It has gained traction among private equity firms by advocating and providing a global framework for the incorporation of environmental, social and corporate governance factors into investment decision making.

The UN PRI looks to synchronise its members' capital with critical sustainability objectives, such as net zero emissions and the UN's Sustainable Development Goals. This is achieved through the enforcement of their six sustainable investment principles for all signatories:

- incorporate ESG issues into decision making;
- active ownership and ESG integration;
- advocate for ESG disclosure;
- promote ESG principles industry-wide;
- enhance effectiveness through collaboration; and
- transparent reporting.[19]

Its core aim is to promote responsible investing by integrating ESG factors into investment strategies.

The UN PRI has influenced the private equity sector significantly. It encourages a more structured approach to ESG integration, leading to improved risk management, better governance and alignment with investor expectations. Private equity firms embracing the UN PRI principles often benefit from improved access to capital, enhanced appeal to institutional investors and operational efficiencies within portfolio companies. Particularly in light of growing stakeholder demand, it is expected that the UN PRI's role in shaping private equity practices will continue to grow in importance as ESG considerations become increasingly integral to the industry's future success.

5. Conclusion

The intensified focus on ESG factors within private equity reflects the industry's adaptive response to a changing investment landscape, prompted by growing recognition of the value generated by ESG practices, compliance requirements and evolving reporting obligations. This evolution signifies a shift towards more

---

16 UN PRI, "About the PRI" (2021), www.unpri.org/about-us.
17 *Ibid.*
18 UN PRI, "Signatory Update", October–December 2023, www.unpri.org/download?ac=20150.
19 UN PRI, "What are the Principles for Responsible Investment?", www.unpri.org/about-us/what-are-the-principles-for-responsible-investment.

comprehensive evaluations, integrating industry-specific and company-level risk assessments and mitigation strategies. Both LPs and GPs are incorporating ESG elements throughout the entire process, from due diligence and integration to the hold phase and exit strategies. Investors' diverse attitudes towards incorporating ESG considerations are dependent upon their underlying philosophies, ultimately shaping their approach to risk management and value creation within the ESG framework.

Meanwhile, ESG integration in portfolio companies involves navigating diverse regulatory frameworks, ensuring comprehensive oversight and prioritising material areas for effective governance. Customised ESG strategies, performance monitoring and reporting mechanisms contribute to successful integration, while efforts such as the Data Convergence Project and the UN PRI promote standardised ESG reporting and responsible investment practices. By aligning around common metrics, private equity firms aim to streamline the reporting process, reduce fragmentation and enhance comparability among portfolio companies.

Fundamentally, there remains a great deal required from both GPs and LPs in order to succeed in any efforts to incorporate ESG factors into their investment procedures and operations. In particular, horizon-scanning for legislative developments and restructuring internal organisations and investment strategies. The private equity sector and its advisers have significant room to further develop and explore the route to effective implementation of ESG principles within their field. Nevertheless, the precipitation of initiatives to help adapt to these changes reflects much of the industry's commitment to aligning investments with sustainable and responsible objectives.

The basics of ESG finance

Helene R Banks
Gregory J Battista
Patrick Gordon
Meghan McDermott
Cahill Gordon & Reindel LLP

1. Introduction

Since 2018, ESG investment has been exploding. As the corporate and legal sectors have increased focus on ESG values and developed more sophisticated policies and standards, ESG investing has become increasingly popular. As a result, a significant number of borrowers/issuers have taken advantage of such investments in recent years.

As of 2013, there were just shy of US$29 billion in ESG investments, primarily comprised of green loans and green bonds.[1] That number increased dramatically year over year, with the market seeing almost US$763 billion in ESG investments in 2020. In addition to green loans and green bonds, 2020 saw significant investment in sustainability-linked financings and social bonds. By 2021, ESG investments exploded to over US$1,643 billion. This increase more than doubled the market from the previous year while maintaining a roughly equal proportion of investment in the above mentioned ESG products.

In this chapter, we provide an overview of the most common financial vehicles to advance ESG objectives: (i) the so-called 'green' bonds; and (ii) the newer alternative, 'sustainability-linked' instruments. We explain key terms, detail the main differences between 'green' and 'sustainability-linked' financings, explore best practices and highlight certain benefits and challenges of ESG financing.

2. Getting started

The first step for a borrower/issuer pursuing an ESG financing is to create a suitable framework – a green bond framework for green bonds or a sustainability framework for sustainability-linked instruments. In preparing its framework, a company should conduct a thorough assessment of its ESG goals in collaboration with its stakeholders and outside advisers. In either case, the framework should define ESG goals, outline the company's strategy and demonstrate alignment with applicable standards, as further detailed below.

---

1 www.bloomberg.com/news/articles/2022-02-03/esg-by-the-numbers-sustainable-investing-set-records-in-2021.

2.1   Green bonds

Prior to marketing a green bond, an issuer will create either: (i) a green bond framework for the issuance of one green bond in a single offering; or (ii) a broader framework for multiple sustainable finance transactions. This framework should be reviewed by an independent, external reviewer, the most popular type being a second-party opinion (SPO) provider.[2] The SPO provider should be independent from any advisers used in the development of its bond framework, and the SPO should affirm that the bond is in compliance with market principles, assess the credibility of the environmental and/or social features of the eligible projects, and highlight any benefits or risks of the projects.[3] The issuer will then post the framework and the SPO on its website to demonstrate to potential investors that the financing qualifies as a green bond in accordance with the Green Bond Principles (discussed under section 4 below). Potential investors will use this information to evaluate the basis of the framework and determine whether the bond will meet the investors' ESG investing requirements.

2.2   Sustainability-linked loans or bonds

Prior to marketing a sustainability-linked loan or bond, a borrower/issuer will create a sustainability framework. This process involves selecting one or more key performance indicators (KPIs), setting sustainability performance targets (SPTs) and formulating specific loan/bond characteristics (discussed under section 7.3 below). Here, borrowers/issuers will also obtain an SPO from an independent, external reviewer who will assess the relevance of the KPIs, the rationale and level of ambition of the proposed SPTs, the relevance and reliability of the selected benchmarks, and the credibility of the selected strategy to achieve each such benchmark.[4]

Sometimes when a company is not yet ready to create a sustainability framework or commit to a sustainability feature in its financing but is working toward that goal, it will enter into what has become known as a 'sleeping' sustainability-linked loan which incorporates the flexibility to add sustainability-linked terms within a pre-determined range through an amendment that generally requires approval only of the agent and sustainability coordinator (discussed under section 8 below).[5]

---

2   While the Green Bond Principles (discussed under section 4 below) do not make an external review mandatory, a recent Climate Bonds Initiative survey of Group Treasurers from 2020 found that 85% of respondents commissioned an SPO for their bond offering: "2020 Green Bond Treasurer Survey", www.climatebonds.net/files/reports/climate-bonds-gb-treasurer-survey-2020-14042020final.pdf.

3   International Capital Markets Association, "Guidelines for Green, Social, Sustainability and Sustainability-Linked Bonds External Reviews" (June 2022), www.icmagroup.org/assets/documents/Sustainable-finance/2022-updates/External-Review-Guidelines_June-2022-280622.pdf.

4   Ibid.

5   Loan Syndications and Trading Association, "Summer Series 2022: Key Considerations In Sustainability Linked Lending Recap" (20 July 2022), www.lsta.org/news-resources/summer-series-2022-key-considerations-in-sustainability-linked-lending-recap/, noting that in some SLLs, the ESG amendment must be agreed to by a majority of lenders.

3.   Green, social and sustainability bonds

Green, social and sustainability bonds (collectively referred to as 'green bonds') are fixed-income securities that are used to finance projects offering environmental or social benefits. The European Investment Bank and the World Bank issued the first green bond in 2007. Since then, the World Bank has issued approximately US$18 billion equivalent in green bonds,[6] and the market has expanded rapidly. In the past several years, the green bond market has been fuelled by the broader trend of ESG investing. Issuers are increasingly looking for ways to highlight their commitment to ESG, while investors are seeking opportunities that align with their own ESG targets. The Climate Bonds Initiative has calculated the average annual growth rate of the green bond market at approximately 95%, observing that, between 2007 and 2020, the annual market for such bonds grew from US$807.2 million to US$1 trillion.[7]

Green bonds are the largest category of sustainable debt as measured by aggregate principal amount issued, and they are the most common type of ESG debt issued by sovereigns.[8] While there are various structures, such as green revenue bonds, green project bonds, and green securitised bonds,[9] this section discusses the most common form, ie, so-called 'use of proceeds' bonds, or asset-linked bonds. The main feature of these bonds is that they are used exclusively to finance eligible projects. Largely similar to green bonds, green loans have a use of proceeds covenant tying the loan proceeds to designated eligible projects. Green loans comprise a much smaller (though growing) share of the sustainable finance market, and as such are not discussed further in this chapter.

There are three general categories of these use of proceeds bonds: traditional green bonds, social bonds, and sustainability bonds.[10] The documents and

---

6   World Bank, "IBRD Funding Program: Green Bonds", https://treasury.worldbank.org/en/about/unit/treasury/ibrd/ibrd-green-bonds#:~:text=Since%202008%2C%20the%20World%20Bank,quality%20credit%20fixed%20income%20product.

7   Climate Bonds Initiative, "Explaining Green Bonds" (19 October 2023), www.climatebonds.net/market/explaining-green-bonds.

8   Caleb Mutea, "Green Bonds Post Record Quarter as Issuers Pounced Before Banking Turmoil", Bloomberg (6 April 2023) www.bloomberg.com/news/articles/2023-04-06/green-bonds-post-record-quarter-as-issuers-pounced-before-tumult#xj4y7vzkg; (2020 statistics can be found in Jochen Schmittmann and Chua Han Teng, "How Green are Green Debt Issuers?", IMF Working Paper: WP/20/194 (July 2020), www.imf.org/-/media/Files/Publications/WP/2021/English/wpiea2021194-print-pdf.ashx); Peter Lindner and Kay Chung, "Sovereign ESG Bond Issuance: A Guidance Note for Sovereign Debt Managers", IMF Working Paper No 2023/058 (10 March 2023), www.imf.org/en/Publications/WP/Issues/2023/03/11/Sovereign-ESG-Bond-Issuance-A-Guidance-Note-for-Sovereign-Debt-Managers-530638.

9   International Capital Market Association, "Green Bond Principles (GBP)", www.icmagroup.org/sustainable-finance/the-principles-guidelines-and-handbooks/green-bond-principles-gbp/.

10   Traditional green bonds finance projects that focus on environmental conservation or climate change mitigation, such as renewable energy, energy efficiency and green buildings. There are many other terms used to define specific types of green bonds, including blue bonds, which finance projects focused on conservation of marine ecosystems, and transition bonds, which finance projects that assist a company progress toward decarbonisation goals aligned with the Paris Climate Agreement. Social bonds finance projects that address issues such as housing, unemployment, education or sustainable food systems: International Capital Market Association, "Social Bond Principles (SBP)", www.icmagroup.org/sustainable-finance/the-principles-guidelines-and-handbooks/social-bond-principles-sbp/. Social bonds have been gaining traction recently as investors are increasingly interested in investing in projects that extend beyond the 'E' in ESG: Rebecca Isjwara, "The 'S' in ESG here to stay after pandemic-induced surge

process are largely the same for green bonds as for conventional bonds, but with features to demonstrate the link between an issuer's sustainability goals and the use of proceeds. While issuers may incur additional transaction costs for at least the first issuance of green bonds due to the resources required to establish the necessary framework and reporting mechanisms, green bonds remain attractive to potential issuers as the benefits of appealing to new investors and promoting green initiatives outweigh these increased expenses.

4.   Green bond structure

There are currently no mandatory, enforceable standards for green bonds, though some governments are beginning to develop standards. In November 2023, the European Parliament and the Council of the European Union adopted the voluntary European Green Bonds (EuGB) Standard, which will allow labelling for bonds that fund environmentally sustainable objectives so long as the uniform requirements of the EuGB Standard have been met.[11]

Given the lack of government standards to date, the market has converged around the International Capital Market Association's (ICMA) Green Bond Principles, Social Bond Principles and Sustainability Bond Guidelines (collectively, the GBP).[12] These voluntary guidelines have become the generally accepted framework to evaluate the ESG principles of these bonds and have been used by nearly all green bond issuers.[13] To qualify as a green bond under the GBP, a bond must align with four core components: (i) use of proceeds; (ii) process for project evaluation and selection; (iii) management of proceeds; and (iv) reporting.

4.1   Use of proceeds

The net proceeds of a green bond must be applied to fund 'eligible projects' that advance the issuer's defined sustainability goals as set forth in the underlying

---

in social bond sales" S&P Global Market Intelligence (29 July 2021), www.spglobal.com/marketintelligence/en/news-insights/latest-news-headlines/the-s-in-esg-here-to-stay-after-pandemic-induced-surge-in-social-bond-sales-65663064. Sustainability bonds fund a combination of both green and social projects: International Capital Market Association, "Sustainability Bond Guidelines (SBG)", www.icmagroup.org/sustainable-finance/the-principles-guidelines-and-handbooks/sustainability-bond-guidelines-sbg/.

11   "Regulation (EU) 2023/2631 of the European Parliament and of the Council of 22 November 2023 on European Green Bonds and optional disclosures for bonds marketed as environmentally sustainable and for sustainability-linked bonds", https://eur-lex.europa.eu/legal-content/EN/TXT/?uri=celex:32023R2631. Projects will be evaluated against the EU Taxonomy Regulation. The Council will publish standardised templates that can be used regardless of adherence to the EuGB Standard, and create a registration system for external reviewers: "European Green Bonds: Council adopts new regulation to promote sustainable finance", www.consilium.europa.eu/ en/press/press-releases/2023/10/24/european-green-bonds-council-adopts-new-regulation-to-promote-sustainable-finance/.

12   International Capital Market Association, "Green Bond Principles (GBP)", www.icmagroup.org/sustainable-finance/the-principles-guidelines-and-handbooks/green-bond-principles-gbp/. For green loans, the Green Loan Principles substantially mirror the GBP: Loan Syndications and Trading Association, "Green Loan Principles (GLP)", www.lsta.org/content/green-loan-principles/.

13   International Capital Market Association, "Sustainable bonds based on GBP, SBP, SBG and SLBP in 2020" www.icmagroup.org/assets/documents/Sustainable-finance/GBP-Infographic-040521.pdf.

framework. What constitutes an eligible project will vary for each issuer and each bond issuance and must be clearly disclosed to potential investors in the offering document. While the GBP does not favour specific project types or technologies, it includes a list of eligible project categories, such as renewable energy, energy efficiency, pollution control and climate change adaptation. The eligible projects do not have to be selected at the time of the bond issuance and can be selected on an ongoing basis during the life of the bond based on described criteria and goals. Additionally, the proceeds of green bonds can be applied to projects already underway or completed within a lookback period. Although there is no rule on the maximum length of the lookback period, market preference is between three and five years, with two years being a common preference.[14]

4.2 Project evaluation and selection

The GBP requires that issuers clearly communicate to investors the process of evaluating and selecting eligible projects. Project selection should conform to the issuer's sustainability goals as outlined in its green bond framework and should show how the green bonds strengthen the issuer's corporate strategy or goals. As a best practice, the issuer should form a committee to manage this effort,[15] and disclose to investors the decision-making process for selecting the respective green projects or assets. Also, the green bond framework should demonstrate alignment with the four core GBP components, indicate any reference standards adopted by the issuer and explain the issuer's broader sustainability goals and strategy. Additionally, the issuer, with assistance from external consultants if necessary, should establish a process for identifying and mitigating risks and negative impacts of the projects.

4.3 Management of proceeds

To satisfy the GBP, the net proceeds of a green bond must be tracked, whether through moving it to a sub-portfolio, crediting it to a sub-account, or by other means, and then be formally certified by the issuer.[16] Tracking efforts should include placing the proceeds in a segregated account, earmarking such funds for the identified green projects and estimates, and managing any unallocated proceeds.

---

14   International Finance Corporation, "Green Bond Handbook: A Step-by-Step Guide to Issuing a Green Bond" (2020), www.ifc.org/content/dam/ifc/doc/mgrt/202203-ifc-green-bond-handbook.pdf noting that for some investors, the "lookback period" cannot exceed two years.

15   International Finance Corporation, "Green Bond Handbook: A Step-by-Step Guide to Issuing a Green Bond" (2020), www.ifc.org/content/dam/ifc/doc/mgrt/202203-ifc-green-bond-handbook.pdf.

16   An issuer can have its green bond or associated green bond framework or use of proceeds certified against a recognised external green standard or label. A standard or label defines specific criteria, and alignment with such criteria is normally tested by qualified, accredited third parties, which may verify consistency with the certification criteria. An example is through the Climate Bonds Initiative which is based on the Paris Climate Agreement: www.climatebonds.net/certification.

The issuer can manage proceeds using a bond-by-bond approach (where the proceeds are managed for each bond issuance separately) or a portfolio approach (where the proceeds for multiple green bonds are managed on an aggregate basis). If a bond has multiple tranches with only one or some used for green purposes, separate accounting for each is vital. The ICMA strongly recommends that the issuer employ an external auditor or other independent, third party to verify the issuer's tracking and allocation processes.[17] The remaining balance of the tracked proceeds should be periodically adjusted to account for allocations made to eligible projects. Investors will want clear proof that their investments have been used to fund only eligible projects. The disclosure in the offering documents will generally detail how any proceeds will be tracked and allocated as well as the treatment of any unallocated proceeds and the anticipated timeline for full allocation of the green bond proceeds. Many issuers choose to hold the unallocated proceeds in short-term, liquid assets to reassure investors that the funds will not be deployed in non-green projects.[18]

4.4 Reporting

The GBP provides that issuers should prepare an annual report to be posted on the issuer's website detailing how the proceeds have been allocated, along with a description of each project and the expected impact, until all proceeds are allocated. If an issuer is using a portfolio approach, the issuer may report the allocation of proceeds on an aggregate basis.[19] Performance against relevant parameters, such as qualitative and quantitative performance indicators of the expected and/or achieved impact, as well as the underlying methodology and assumptions used by the issuer, should be disclosed in this annual report.[20] It is also recommended that the issuer reports if there is a material change in the framework, such as a change in the targeted projects or a shift in the scope or scale of the eligible projects or assets.

5. Green project examples

The chart below illustrates the wide variety of projects that green bond offerings are used to finance.

---

17 International Capital Market Association, "Green Bond Principles (GBP)", www.icmagroup.org/sustainable-finance/the-principles-guidelines-and-handbooks/green-bond-principles-gbp/.
18 International Finance Corporation, "Green Bond Handbook: A Step-by-Step Guide to Issuing a Green Bond" (2020), www.ifc.org/content/dam/ifc/doc/mgrt/202203-ifc-green-bond-handbook.pdf.
19 This might be necessary if confidentiality considerations restrict the detail that can be disclosed, or if a large number of small-sized projects are financed by a green bond (eg, green bonds financing a loan programme).
20 International Capital Market Association, "Handbook: Harmonised Framework for Impact Reporting" (June 2022), www.icmagroup.org/assets/documents/Sustainable-finance/2023-updates/Handbook-Harmonised-framework-for-impact-reporting-June-2023-220623.pdf.

Table 1. Green project examples

Green project	Category	Example
Renewable energy	Production, transmission, appliances and products	Goldman Sachs Renewable Power, US$500 million Refinance acquisition of solar assets in the US[21]
Energy efficiency	New or refurbished buildings, energy storage, appliances and products	PNC Financial Services Group, US$650 million Renewable energy, energy efficiency, green buildings[22]
Pollution prevention and control	Reduction of air emissions, greenhouse gas control, remediation, waste reduction/recycling and waste to energy	Coca Cola, US$705 million 1. Equipment, operational improvements to reduce energy consumption 2. Pollution prevention 3. Eco-efficiency, production technologies and processes 4. Preservation and reforestation 5. Renewable energy facilities[23]
Clean transportation	Electric, hybrid, public, rail, infrastructure for clean energy vehicles	Red Electrica, €700 million/US$775 million Renewable energy and clean transportation[24]

continued on next page

---

21 Climate Bonds Initiative, "Green Bonds Factsheet: Goldman Sachs Renewable Power" (4 March 2020), www.climatebonds.net/files/files/2020-02_US_Goldman_Sachs_Renewable_Power%281%29.pdf.
22 Climate Bonds Initiative, "Green Bonds Factsheet: PNC Financial Services Group" (14 November 2019), www.climatebonds.net/files/files/2019-11_US_PNC_Financial_Services_Group.pdf.
23 Climate Bonds Initiative, "Green Bonds Factsheet: Coca Cola FEMSA" (1 October 2020), www.climatebonds.net/files/files/2020-09_MX_Coca_Cola_FEMSA.pdf.
24 Climate Bonds Initiative, "Green Bonds Factsheet: Red Eléctrica" (11 February 2020), www.climatebonds.net/files/files/2020-01_ES_Red_El%C3%A9ctrica.pdf.

Green project	Category	Example
Sustainable water and wastewater management	Sustainable infrastructure for clean water, wastewater treatment, drainage systems and flood mitigation	Verizon Communications Inc, US$1 billion Renewable energy, energy efficiency, green buildings, sustainable water management and biodiversity and conservation[25]
Green buildings, sustainable water and wastewater management	Buildings that meet recognised standards or certifications for environmental performance	M&G Real Estate Asia, KRW11.5 billion/US$98.5 million Refinancing investment in Northgate, a high-rise office building with LEED Gold in Seoul[26]
Social bond	Address issues that impact low-to-moderate income neighbourhoods in the United States	Bank of America, US$500 million Refinance the company's investments in affordable housing and community development financial institutions[27]
Sustainability bond	Support various environmental and social initiatives	Alphabet Inc, US$5.75 billion 1. Energy efficiency 2. Clean energy 3. Green buildings 4. Clean transportation 5. Circular economy and design 6. Affordable housing 7. Commitment to racial equity 8. Support for small businesses 9. COVID-19 crisis response[28]

25   Climate Bonds Initiative, "Green Bonds Factsheet: Verizon Communications Inc" (20 February 2019), www.climatebonds.net/files/files/2019-02%20US%20Verizon%20Communications%20Inc.pdf.
26   Climate Bonds Initiative, "Green Bonds Factsheet: M&G Real Estate Asia" (3 September 2020), www.climatebonds.net/files/files/2020-08_KR_M%26G_Real_Estate_Asia.pdf.
27   Euromoney, "Bank of America issues first US bank social bond" (22 February 2019), www.euromoney.com/article/b1d7q0jdqkmm47/bank-of-america-issues-first-us-bank-social-bond.
28   Ruth Porat, "Alphabet issues sustainability bonds to support environmental and social initiatives:, Google: The Keyword (3 August 2020) https://blog.google/alphabet/alphabet-issues-sustainability-bonds-support-environmental-and-social-initiatives/; www.smartenergydecisions.com/energy-management/2022/08/31/alphabets-sustainability-bond-impact-report-2022#:~:text=Alphabet's%20Sustainability%20Bond%20Impact%20Report%202022&text=Alphabet%20%2D%20the%20parent%20company%20of,are%20environmentally%20or%20socially%20responsible.

6.   Sustainability-linked financing

Sustainability-linked loans (SLLs) and sustainability-linked bonds (SLBs) tie a company's sustainability performance to its cost of borrowing. Unlike green bonds, which are used to fund specified projects, SLLs and SLBs are more flexible, as the proceeds can generally be used for any purpose so long as the borrower/issuer commits to pursuing SPTs. Also in contrast to green bonds, sustainability features are built into the terms of the contractual documents governing SLLs and SLBs, with SPTs that, upon achievement, could result in decreases to the applicable interest rate or other favorable terms.

Generally, most SLLs and SLBs have focused on targets that relate to the 'E' in ESG. For example, SPTs can include carbon emission reductions, and this market has grown as companies face increased pressure to reduce their carbon footprint and embrace ESG-related goals. More recently, however, there have been more SLLs and SLBs focused on the 'S' and/or 'G' targets of social and/or governance (eg, increased workplace diversity).

Sustainability-linked financing has significantly widened the market for potential ESG investments as it provides issuers and borrowers who are not in typical 'green' industries the opportunity to participate in such investments so long as a company has a sustainability strategy. SLLs first appeared in 2017, and their growth was accelerated by the development in 2019 of the Sustainability Linked Loan Principles (the SLLP)[29] by the Loan Market Association (LMA), the Asia Pacific Loan Market Association (APLMA), and the Loan Syndications and Trading Association (LSTA). The SLL market has grown to US$747 billion, making it the second-largest sustainable debt asset class after green bonds.[30] SLBs have a much smaller, but rapidly growing, share of the sustainable finance market, as issuances have increased more than seven-fold since 2020 with the total number of issuances reaching US$178 billion.[31]

7.   Sustainability-linked structures

As with green bonds, there are no mandatory, enforceable standards for SLLs and SLBs. The most widely accepted guidelines are the SLLP for SLLs and the ICMA's Sustainability-Linked Bond Principles (SLBP), issued in June 2023, for SLBs.[32] These principles help bring transparency and consistency to

29   Loan Syndications and Trading Association, "Sustainability Linked Loan Principles (SLLP)", www.lsta.org/content/sustainability-linked-loan-principles-sllp/.

30   Standard Chartered and Bloomberg Media Studies, "Incentivizing Change With Sustainability-Linked Loans" https://sponsored.bloomberg.com/article/scb/incentivizing-change-with-sustainability-linked-loans. Despite difficult economic conditions, the global SLL market saw a 7% increase in 2022, rising to volumes of US$240 billion and reaching a quarterly record high in the fourth quarter of the year: Moody's Investor Services, "Sustainable bond issuance to rebound 10% in 2023 to $950 billion, short of record high" (31 January 2023), www.asifma.org/wp-content/uploads/2023/03/sustainable-finance-global-31jan2023-pbc_1356648.pdf.

31   Denis Sugrue and Bryan Popoola, "Sustainable Bond Issuance Will Return To Growth In 2023" S&P Global Ratings (7 February 2023), www.spglobal.com/_assets/documents/ratings/research/101572346.pdf.

32   ICMA, "Sustainability-Linked Bond Principles" (June 2023), www.icmagroup.org/assets/documents/

sustainability-linked instruments by focusing on five core components: (i) selection of KPIs; (ii) setting (calibration) of SPTs; (iii) loan and bond characteristics; (iv) reporting requirements; and (v) verification. For SLLs, the SLLP mirrors the five core components of the SLBP.

7.1 Selection of KPIs

The selection of KPIs is vital because the credibility of the offering will depend on the suitability of the KPIs to the particular company and industry. The SLLP and SLBP each stress that KPIs must be 'relevant, core and material' to the company's current and/or future business and operations.[33] KPIs should reflect the ESG values of the company, and the company's operations should be able to exert a measurable influence on those KPIs.

When selecting KPIs, the loan/bond parties need to ensure the KPIs are clearly defined and based on a credible methodology that can be consistently quantifiable. KPIs must be established through careful research and analysis and have a clear connection to the company's business strategy and sustainability framework. They should include the applicable scope/parameters, calculation methodology, a definition of a baseline for each KPI, and be benchmarked against an industry standard and/or industry peers where feasible.[34] This enables lenders and investors to assess the company's progress against performance targets. The ability to benchmark the KPIs using external references or industry standards should demonstrate the level of ambition of the SPTs.

7.2 Setting (calibration) of SPTs

After the KPIs have been selected, SPTs must be chosen and calibrated carefully to fit each of the selected KPIs. Well-calibrated SPTs should be ambitious but realistically achievable. SPTs should take into account the following factors while being calibrated:

- represent a material improvement in the KPIs;
- go beyond a 'business as usual' trajectory and required regulatory targets;
- be compared to a verified benchmark or an external reference, where possible;

Sustainable-finance/2023-updates/Sustainability-Linked-Bond-Principles-June-2023-220623.pdf. ICMA reports that in 2020 the Principles were referenced by an estimated 97% of sustainable bonds issued globally: ICMA, "Sustainable bonds based on GBP, SBP, SBG and SLBP in 2020", www.icmagroup.org/assets/documents/Sustainable-bonds-finance/GBP-Infographic-040521.pdf.

33   Loan Syndications and Trading Association, "Sustainability Linked Loan Principles (SLLP)", www.lsta.org/content/sustainability-linked-loan-principles-sllp/; ICMA, "Sustainability-Linked Bond Principles" (June 2023), www.icmagroup.org/assets/documents/Sustainable-finance/2023-updates/Sustainability-Linked-Bond-Principles-June-2023-220623.pdf.

34   The ICMA has provided additional guidance on the selection of KPIs in its June 2022 SLB Q&A: ICMA, "Sustainability-Linked Bond Principles Related Questions" (June 2022), www.icmagroup.org/assets/documents/Sustainable-finance/2022-updates/SLB-QA-CLEAN-and-FINAL-for-publication-2022-06-24-280622.pdf and illustrative KPIs registry: ICMA, "Notes to Users"www.icmagroup.org/assets/documents/Sustainable-finance/2022-updates/Registry-SLB-KPIs_Final_2022-06-24-280622.xlsx).

- be consistent with the company's overall ESG strategy; and
- follow a predefined timeline, set before (or concurrently with) the origination of the loan or issuance of the bond.

SPT targets can be set against the issuer's baseline (typically involving a three-year lookback), industry standards or peers, or a science-based or governmental target.

The company should clearly communicate to arrangers, underwriters, lenders and investors the motivation for the SPTs, any relevant benchmarking and the strategy to achieve such SPTs, with appropriate disclosure included in the offering documents with respect to SLBs. Companies typically engage one or more 'sustainability coordinators' to assist with providing market context regarding the KPIs and SPTs and facilitate answering questions from prospective investors. The sustainability coordinator is often selected from among the lenders or the underwriting group.

KPIs and SPTs are sometimes recalibrated pursuant to so-called 'rendezvous clauses' in SLLs that allow for amending the loan agreement when the SPTs are no longer relevant or ambitious. Instances that may require recalibration include (but are not limited to): certain SPTs cannot be set at loan origination; the SPTs are achieved well in advance of the target date; acquisitions or divestitures significantly change the issuer's assets or operations; substantive changes in methodologies (eg, evolving science) require adjustments to SPTs and KPIs; and the need to maintain the alignment of targets set in the loan documentation with the borrower's sustainability obligations over the life of the loan.[35,36]

It is recommended by the SLBP and SLLP that issuers and borrowers seek an independent review and secure a SPO from an external, independent reviewer, assessing KPI relevance and ambitiousness, SPT rationale, benchmarks reliability and the KPI implementation strategy.[37] Alternatively, if an external review is not performed, then it is at least recommended that the issuer or borrower document its own internal expertise to verify the KPIs and evaluate the methodology.

---

35   In Clean Energy's 2022 Senior Secured First Lien Term Loan Credit Agreement, the rendezvous clause was used to amend the KPI metric implicated by any significant or structural changes in Parent, changes in methodology in respect of the KPI Metric, or changes in data reported due to improved calculation methodologies or better data accessibility, www.sec.gov/Archives/edgar/data/1368265/0001104659 22130319/=tm2233499d1_ex10-1.htm.

36   What's Market: 2022 Year-End Trends in Large Cap and Middle Market Loan Terms, Practical Law Practice Note w-038-0539; ICMA, "Guidance Handbook" (November 2023), www.icmagroup.org/assets/documents/Sustainable-finance/2023-updates/The-Principles-Guidance-Handbook-November-2023-291123.pdf.

37   The ICMA highlights that second party opinions are "especially recommended where benchmarks are absent or lack clear performance thresholds pertinent to the company", www.icmagroup.org/assets/documents/Sustainable-finance/2023-updates/Sustainability-Linked-Bond-Principles-June-2023-220623.pdf

7.3   Loan and bond characteristics

The key feature of sustainability-linked instruments is the adjustment to the economic terms of the loan/bond upon achievement, or failure to achieve, the SPTs. The SLLP and SLBP do not define the structural or financial characteristics of an SLL or SLB that may be tied to the achievement of the SPTs. Typically, these characteristics include a decrease/increase of the interest rate, a change in the maturity date or, if applicable, the optional redemption premiums.[38] SLLs sometimes also include an adjustment to the commitment fee on the undrawn portion of a revolving facility.

The most common characteristic in SLLs and SLBs is a change in the applicable interest rate (generally by 25 basis points (0.25%)) based on whether or not the company achieves their selected SPTs.[39] In SLLs, the applicable loan margin may be reduced where the borrower has satisfied the predetermined SPTs as measured by the KPIs, or increased if they have not satisfied such SPTs; in some cases, a neutral bracket may exist in which no adjustment applies.

Like SLLs, SLBs encourage the achievement of SPTs by providing for interest rate adjustments depending on whether or not the selected KPIs reach the predefined SPTs or interim milestones. SLBs typically include a one-time step-up in coupon if the SPT is not satisfied as of a certain date, for example, three to five years after issuance. If the SPT is met as of such date, then the coupon remains unchanged. Some SLBs include a two-tiered increase or 'step up' that refers to an initial 'Threshold' component and a more ambitious 'Target'. SPTs structured in this way are typically adjusted as illustrated in Table 2.

Table 2. Thresholds and Targets

If neither the Target nor the Threshold level is achieved, then ...	Pricing is increased
If the Threshold level is achieved (but not the Target), then ...	No change in pricing
If the Target level is achieved (in addition to the Threshold), then ...	Pricing is reduced

---

38   Rita Mangalick, "Sustainability-Linked Loans: What They Are, How They Work and Why They Matter", Blackrock (15 September 2023), www.blackstone.com/insights/article/sustainability-linked-loans-why-they-matter/#:~:text=Sustainability%2Dlinked%20loans%20are%20loans,secure%20a%20lower%20interest%20rate.

39   S&P Global Market Intelligence, "Higher costs loom for sustainability-linked bond issuers as deadlines approach" (16 May 2023), www.spglobal.com/marketintelligence/en/news-insights/latest-news-headlines/cpil-2709806-article_news_title-textbox-higher-costs-loom-for-sustainability-linked-bond-issuers-as-deadlines-appro-75516523.

An SLB may also have an additional step-up in the redemption price to be paid in an optional redemption if certain SPTs are not met by the respective certification dates.[40]

7.4   Reporting requirements

Because SLLs and SLBs link sustainability performance to economic terms, it is important for the documentation to require regular, robust reporting regarding the borrower/issuer's ongoing sustainability performance, particularly with respect to the selected KPIs. Under the SLLP and SLBP reporting requirements, companies must provide current information so that investors can monitor the performance of the SPTs and verify that the SPTs remain ambitious and relevant to the company's business. It is recommended that companies: (i) report at least annually; and (ii) maintain a regularly updated verification assurance report highlighting the company's performance and any strategic changes relative to its SPTs. Robust reporting may include other key factors contributing to KPI performance, positive sustainability impacts of company's strategy and any considered or implemented shifts in baseline or KPI scope. In addition to an annual report posted to the company's website, disclosures may be included in bond offering documents, investor presentations, sustainability reports and financial reports.

In the context of SLLs, reporting will often involve the delivery of a certification by the borrower to the administrative agent of their achievement or failure to achieve SPTs or KPI thresholds. This certificate allows the agent to easily determine what the pricing adjustment for the applicable reporting period should be. Along with the delivery of the pricing certificate, the reporting requirements should also require a more fulsome report of the borrower's sustainability performance. Unlike more traditional financial-related reporting covenants, failure to deliver the pricing certificate or the annual sustainability report does not typically result in an event of default under the credit agreement, but instead results in the interest rate margin (and commitment fees, as applicable) automatically adjusting to the highest possible rate.[41]

Similarly to SLLs, it is customary for SLBs to require delivery by the issuer of a sustainability report by posting it to the issuer's website and/or providing it to the trustee. SLBs typically do not include a separate reporting covenant with respect to the sustainability report, and the trustee has no obligation or duty to monitor any such compliance itself. Instead, in order for the issuer to reap the

---

40   ESG Monitor "2022 European Sustainability-Linked Bonds Wrap: Sustainability-Linked Bonds Show Resilience in 2022 and Increase Information Flow to Fight Greenwashing" (26 January 2023), https://reorg.com/2022-european-sustainability-linked-bonds-wrap/.

41   Understanding Sustainability-Linked Loans, Practical Law Practice Note w-023-1549; ICMA, "Guidance Handbook" (November 2023), www.icmagroup.org/assets/documents/Sustainable-finance/2023-updates/The-Principles-Guidance-Handbook-November-2023-291123.pdf.

benefits of the interest rate adjustment, the issuer must: (i) achieve the applicable SPTs; and (ii) deliver to the trustee a sustainability compliance certificate from an executive officer prior to the applicable certification date. If the issuer fails to deliver a sustainability compliance certificate in relation to a specific fiscal year by the relevant certification date, then the issuer will be deemed to not have achieved the relevant SPT for that fiscal year (regardless of whether the SPT is in fact achieved).

7.5   Verification

The third-party verification of progress toward achieving SPTs is an essential requirement for SLLs and SLBs. Companies are required to obtain independent, external verification of their performance levels for each relevant KPI. This verification is required for any period leading up to a potential adjustment of the SLL/SLB economic terms. Verification of performance must continue for the duration of the loan or bond or until the last adjustment period is reached. The typical credit agreement for an SLL will require verification to be provided in conjunction with each sustainability report delivered under the credit agreement. Under the indenture for an SLB, a review should be conducted at least once a year, and in any case for any period relevant for assessing the SPT performance leading to a potential adjustment of the SLB characteristics, until after the bond's last SPT trigger event has been reached. The verification of the performance against the SPTs should be publicly available.

The verification process typically involves the use of a qualified independent third-party adviser, which may be an accounting firm, a sustainability consultant or another type of expert with relevant expertise.[42] The ICMA has prepared voluntary Guidelines for External Reviews.[43]

The verification of the performance against the SPTs must be shared with the lenders/investors in a timely manner. Where there is a lag between the time required to deliver the annual sustainability report and the related third-party verification, consideration needs to be given to the impact for the interim period. For instance, if a sustainability report shows achievement of an SPT and results in a decrease to pricing, but the verification later shows that the SPT has not been met, parties should consider whether any difference in margin in the intervening period should be repaid to lenders.

8.   Sustainability coordinators

In order to properly maintain the sustainability-linked framework and monitor the progress toward achieving the respective SPTs, companies often engage a

---

42   For example, in Jacobs Solutions' 2023 First Supplemental Indenture, the external verifier definition includes any one or more qualified independent public accountants, assurance providers, or environmental consultants: www.sec.gov/Archives/edgar/data/52988/000119312523041184/d418190d8k.htm.

43   ICMA, "External Reviews", www.icmagroup.org/sustainable-finance/external-reviews/.

sustainability coordinator to assist with SLLs and SLBs. The sustainability coordinator (also known as a sustainability structuring agent for SLLs) is an evolving role in ESG financing and, to date, is typically filled by one of the lead arrangers/underwriters or one of their affiliates. The sustainability coordinator's responsibilities may vary between SLLs and SLBs and different transactions, but generally include facilitating dialogue between the company and financial institutions regarding the SPTs and KPIs, assisting the company with developing KPIs and SPTs, preparing materials to present the SLL/SLB structure and assisting the company in responding to investor questions.[44] The coordinator may work with various company departments like sustainability, finance, and internal legal to aid in developing a comprehensive sustainability framework that meets market expectations. Sustainability coordinators are primarily involved at the beginning of the SLL/SLB process where their role is to discuss sustainability targets, help the company identify KPIs and SPTs, provide insight to the potential consequences of not meeting these metrics and what may be expected by the target market. They also act generally as a liaison between borrowers/issuers and lenders/investors in discussions regarding the structure of the SLL/SLB, as applicable.

The scope of the sustainability coordinator's engagement is carefully defined in order to avoid exposing the coordinator to inappropriate liability or duties to the borrower/issuer and/or the lenders/investors. To date, market practice remains unsettled on whether the sustainability coordinator requires a separate engagement letter with its own indemnification provision. For SLLs, the sustainability coordinator's indemnity can be incorporated into the indemnification section of the credit agreement, and, in our experience, SLLs generally follow that approach. For SLBs, on the other hand, an indemnity would not typically be included in the indenture, so the bond parties should consider including applicable protections in the indemnification provisions in the purchase/underwriting agreement or having a separate indemnity letter. The LSTA has developed a template for indemnification for the sustainability structuring agent that may be helpful to practitioners.[45]

9. Benefits and challenges of ESG financings

While green and sustainability-linked instruments offer several benefits over traditional debt financings, they also come with challenges that should be carefully considered.

---

44 Betty Huber, Edward Kempson, Karmpreet Grewal, "Experts' View: Developments in ESG/Sustainable Finance", Practical Law (24 March 2023), https://1.next.westlaw.com/w-038-0539?isplcus=true&transitionType=Default&contextData=(sc.Default)&firstPage=true#co_anchor_a994331.

45 LSTA, "Sustainability Structuring Agent Engagement Agreement Inserts" (17 February 2023), www.lsta.org/content/sustainability-structuring-agent-engagement-agreement-inserts-feb-17-2023/.

9.1 Benefits

(a) Access to capital and sustainable investing

With ESG considerations increasingly being a significant factor for investors, these instruments provide a mechanism for deploying capital in sustainability-focused investments while at the same time providing access to a large and growing pool of capital. SLLs/SLBs have the added benefit of expanding investment options by providing borrowers/issuers who are not in typical 'green' industries the opportunity to issue instruments linked to their sustainable goals without obligating them to a specific use of proceeds.

(b) Potential to lower cost of capital

The structure of green bonds and SLLs/SLBs is intended to provide borrowers/issuers with a financial incentive for progress on sustainable projects or goals. A strong and growing demand for ESG bonds at a time of inadequate supply could also lead to lower interest rates compared to conventional bonds. In a climate of rising interest rates, and a heavy emphasis on increasing sustainability bona fides, borrowers/issuers may find ESG financing instruments an even more compelling option.

(c) Principles provide guidance

The principles under which green bonds and SLL/SLBs are issued, while voluntary, serve as a roadmap in an area that is not yet very well-defined. They provide a general structure for issuers and borrowers, and bring transparency, consistency and credibility to the market. By adhering to the principles, both lenders/investors and borrowers/issuers are able to participate in the sustainable financing market without the uncertainty that might otherwise make it too risky to take advantage of this new pool of capital.

9.2 Challenges

(a) Lack of enforceable standards and market maturity

The lack of enforceable standards for these instruments, both in their structure and what qualifies as an eligible project, also means that investors are exposed to risk as market norms evolve. As part of this evolution, it will be important to continue to consider whether codified, enforceable standards are warranted. For example, while the use of green bond proceeds for eligible projects is detailed in the offering document, typically the indenture governing the bond will not include any specific covenants regarding the use of proceeds. Therefore, if an issuer does not use the proceeds as disclosed, there may be no recourse for breach of contract, and failure to allocate proceeds to eligible projects will not result in an event of default by the company. In order to contain potential securities liability risk, issuers typically do not include in the offering document any supporting materials, such as their green bond framework, SPOs or sustainability reports. This practice could make it more difficult to successfully pursue a claim for material misstatements under the securities laws.

With respect to SLL/SLBs, the main risk for lenders/investors surrounds the step-up. For example, many SLB offerings are structured with a one-time step-up penalty. Often this step-up occurs several years after the issuance, with no intervening penalties for non-compliance, even if it becomes clear that the SPT will not be met. The ICMA advises setting an appropriate step-up penalty date well before the end of the financing term to avoid this.[46] Until the market convention for financings with a longer tenor moves to include one or more intermediate target observation dates, the potential exists for the borrower/issuer to be benefitting from paying a lower interest rate than its ESG bona fides warrant.

Another structuring issue relates to the timing of the step up for SLL/SLBs. If the SLL/SLBs are prepayable/callable at a date before the SPT observation date, the company could pay off the debt and avoid any step-up penalties and higher coupon rates resulting from missing SPTs. To avoid this possibility, the ICMA advises that an issuer's optional call rights should not be effective before the SPT observation date or, if it is, then the call price should assume that the SPT has not been met.[47] As problems with the SLL/SLB structure are identified, solutions need wide market adoption if SLL/SLBs are to continue to be a desirable product for investors.

(b) Reporting

The complexity of monitoring and reporting sustainability performance can be particularly challenging to implement and monitor effectively, especially for companies operating in complex supply chains or for those that lack clear sustainability goals. Reporting challenges may lead to inaccuracies or misleading information. Borrowers/issuers must have or engage the necessary resources to manage the associated complexity and evaluate and report on sustainability performance, and investors must have the necessary resources to monitor this additional feature of their ESG investments.

(c) Greenwashing

The lack of a mandatory regulatory standard leaves open the possibility that some borrowers/issuers may use a green or sustainable label on their debt despite not adhering to any of the established principles and could exaggerate

---

46   ICMA, "Guidance Handbook" (November 2023), www.icmagroup.org/assets/documents/Sustainable-finance/2023-updates/The-Principles-Guidance-Handbook-November-2023-291123.pdf.
47   *Ibid.*

the environmental benefit of their project to try to reap the benefits of an ESG label. Misleading or untrue disclosure of sustainability benefits, known as greenwashing, can create scepticism or distrust of the overall market and can result in reputational damage in addition to litigation and regulatory enforcement.[48] For example, in a recent, novel claim filed by non-profit Mighty Earth with the US Securities and Exchange Commission, Mighty Earth alleges that disclosure by JBS Foods in connection with its recently issued SLBs amounts to greenwashing because JBS failed to incorporate Scope 3 emissions (ie, emissions from its supply chain) into its SPTs and that JBS has contributed to or ignored deforestation carried out by its suppliers.[49] While this claim is only at the early stages and the outcome cannot be predicted, it illustrates the need for issuers and their counsel to focus on drafting balanced disclosure and appropriate SPTs, and the importance of thorough due diligence.[50]

10. Conclusion

Government regulation, lender/investor pressure and the general trend toward sustainable operations are compelling companies to incorporate ESG factors into their business models. ESG financial instruments offer an attractive opportunity for companies to raise capital in support of their ESG strategies. Companies are looking for access to capital at the scale needed for a transition to a lower carbon, more sustainable economy. The competition among financial institutions to deliver these products is fierce and growing. Banks and investors recognise a potentially vast market and are eager to enhance their ESG credentials and build their ESG portfolios or risk missing these opportunities.

As not all ESG financial products are created equal, companies will have to determine which products best serve their needs. Table 3 opposite provides a quick summary of the key features of the various ESG products discussed in this chapter.

---

48   Enforcement of ESG-related disclosure is on the rise. See "2023 Examination Priorities", SEC Division of Examinations (2023), www.sec.gov/files/2023-exam-priorities.pdf, for more detail.

49   Steven Mufson, "Brazilian meat giant under fire for allegedly misleading investors" *Washington Post* (18 January 2023), www.washingtonpost.com/climate-environment/2023/01/18/jbs-food-giant-brazil-bonds/.

50   Various tools exist for lenders/investors to conduct diligence, including the LSTA's ESG Integrated Disclosure Project Template, a questionnaire intended to promote greater harmonisation and consistency of ESG disclosure: see www.esgidp.org/.

Table 3. Key features of ESG products

	Green bonds	Sustainability-linked loans (SLLs)	Sustainability-linked bonds (SLBs)
KPIs/SPTs	N/A	Mutually agreed upon 'relevant, core and material' metrics and targets; clearly defined and based on a credible methodology.	Similar to SLLs
Use of proceeds	Net proceeds earmarked for specific eligible green projects.	Net proceeds can be used for any purpose, including general corporate purposes.	Similar to SLLs
Agent	Same as conventional bonds.	Same as conventional loans; also, in some instances, a sustainability coordinator.	Same as conventional bonds; also, in some instances, a sustainability coordinator.

continued on next page

	Green bonds	Sustainability-linked loans (SLLs)	Sustainability-linked bonds (SLBs)
Interest rate provision	Typically lower than conventional bonds.	Linked to borrower's satisfaction of predefined SPTs; depending on the borrower's achievement of the specified KPIs, rates may: • decrease if the metric is achieved; • stay the same (loss of pricing benefit) if the metric is not achieved; or • increase, in some instances, if the metrics decline, as a penalty.	Similar to SLLs
Reporting	Qualitative and, where possible, quantitative performance indicators should be provided annually to investor.	Borrowers typically provide information about mutually agreed SPTs annually.	Similar to SLLs

continued on next page

	Green bonds	Sustainability-linked loans (SLLs)	Sustainability-linked bonds (SLBs)
Verification	Internal tracking and certification of bond proceeds required. External auditor strongly recommended, but not required, to verify tracking and allocation of proceeds.	Typically involves the use of a qualified, independent third-party adviser, which may be an accounting firm, a sustainability consultant or another type of expert with relevant experience.	Similar to SLLs
Liability	Issuers are not subject to any contractual provision regarding use of proceeds in their indentures. Bondholders rely on the sanctions related to misrepresentation, reputational harm, and other potential claims applicable to typical bonds.	Loan agreement contractually binds the borrower; can cause an event of default or trigger other loan agreement penalties (eg, loss of discount or interest rate premium).	Financial and/or structural characteristics can vary depending on whether the selected KPIs reach or don't reach the predefined SPTs.

The authors would like to thank Lynn R Schmidt, senior attorney, and David Fuchs, Joseph W Messina II and Emma Sykes, associates, for their significant contributions to and assistance with the preparation of this chapter.

Global obstacles and opportunities for regulated financial institutions

Nicola Higgs
Anne Mainwaring
Gary Whitehead
Latham & Watkins

1. Introduction

Environment, social and governance (or 'sustainability')-related matters have come under an increasing level of focus from investors, companies, ratings agencies, regulators and politicians alike. Regulated financial institutions are now subject to a considerable number of sustainability-related frameworks and requirements, some mandatory and others voluntary. The political imperative behind the ESG transition has led to a very rapid pace of change in this area, which shows no signs of abating. Topics such as climate change and the transition to net zero consistently feature prominently in regulatory publications and pronouncements, but more recently there has been an expansion in focus to include the 'social' and 'governance' elements of ESG.

This constant flux arguably creates as many obstacles as it does opportunities for regulated firms navigating the space and determining their ESG positioning across the different jurisdictions in which they operate.

This chapter explores the drivers underpinning the ESG landscape, including the developing regulatory regimes applicable to regulated firms. It is important to have an awareness of the developments that have already taken place and as such, the chapter will also look at the current legislative frameworks that have been devised in several key global jurisdictions (the European Union, the United Kingdom, the United States, Hong Kong and Singapore), highlighting how the rapid pace of regulatory development has led to a number of challenges for global firms, including international divergence on ESG and the absence of a multi-jurisdictional commonly applied ESG framework.

2. International regulatory regimes

2.1 The European Union

The central foundations of the positioning and subsequent regulation of ESG by the EU can be found in the commitment to the Paris Agreement and the UN

2030 Agenda for Sustainable Development in 2015. These landmark agreements underpinned the EU's development of various policies targeting change and broader ESG issues. In accordance with these initiatives, a high-level expert group was established to determine the EU's roadmap to sustainability and following the conclusion of their work, a 2018 final report titled 'Financing a Sustainable European Economy'[1] was published, detailing the following key measures (please note other measures were recommended (including 'cross-cutting recommendations') but for the purposes of this chapter, we have focused on the following):

- establishing and maintaining a common sustainability taxonomy at the EU level;
- clarifying investor duties to better embrace long-term horizon and sustainability preferences;
- upgrading disclosure rules to make sustainability risks fully transparent;
- developing official EU sustainability standards; and
- reforming governance and leadership with respect to sustainability.

These recommendations formed the fundamental basis upon which the European Commission (EC) developed and implemented the EU Action Plan on Sustainable Finance (the 'Action Plan')[2] which had three key aims:

- to reorient capital flows towards sustainable investment in order to achieve sustainable and inclusive growth;
- to manage financial risks stemming from climate change, resource depletion and inclusive growth; and
- to foster transparency and long-termism in financial and economic activity.

The EU identified that the financial system would need to play an essential role in helping the continent achieve its obligations and targets, including the overarching aim of achieving net zero emissions by 2050 and the European Green Deal (the 'EGD'), which was approved in 2020 and represented a broader recalibration of the EU's environmental policy. The EGD contains a set of policy initiatives by the European Council with the overarching objective of making Europe climate neutral in 2050, supplying clean, affordable and secure energy, a zero pollution and toxic-free environment and a push to halt bio-diversity loss. The EU also determined that investment decisions were not adequately taking into account environmental and social considerations, largely because such risks tend to materialise over a longer period than often catered for.

---

1   EU High-Level Expert Group on Sustainable Finance, "Financing a Sustainable European Economy", https://finance.ec.europa.eu/system/files/2018-01/180131-sustainable-finance-final-report_en.pdf.
2   European Commission, "Action Plan: Financing Sustainable Growth", 8 March 2018, https://eur-lex.europa.eu/legal-content/EN/TXT/?uri=CELEX:52018DC0097.

Further uplifts to Europe's strategy came in the form of the Sustainable Finance Strategy,[3] which was published in July 2021 which built upon the Action Plan and reiterated the European focus on sustainable finance and the Sustainable Finance Roadmap 2022–2024,[4] published by the European Securities and Markets Authority (ESMA) with the stated priorities of tackling greenwashing and promoting transparency, building out ESMA and national competent authorities understanding and experiences of sustainable finance and to monitor, assess and analyse ESG-related markets and risks.

With the EU's increased focus on sustainability and achieving carbon neutrality by 2050 as a stated goal, it should be no surprise that these strategic initiatives have paved the way for the development of an EU-wide sustainability legislative framework, which will continue to develop and undergo further amendments and refinement over the coming years.

The Sustainable Finance Disclosure Regulation (SFDR),[5] enacted first in 2019 forms part of the package of measures by the EC arising directly as a result of the work done under the Action Plan. SFDR is intended to 'level the playing field' for financial market participants and to improve transparency for sustainable investments. It introduces disclosure and reporting requirements applicable to fund and asset managers in an attempt to harmonise the information that asset managers and other in-scope participants provide to end investors. In order to embed sustainability considerations into the existing regulatory framework, a number of measures were published in August 2021 to amend the Markets in Financial Instruments Directive 2014 (MiFID II), Alternative Investment Fund Managers Directive 2011 (AIFMD) and Undertakings for Collective Investment in Transferable Securities (UCITS) to integrate sustainability risks and factors. The EC has previously sought to clarify the SFDR including through the 'conventional' Q&A process and in April 2023, the European supervisory authorities issued a consultation, focusing on potential amendments to the regulatory technical standards complementing the SFDR. The consultation is structured such that there is a targeted consultation paper, aimed at financial market participants, public authorities, national regulators amongst other bodies who are subject directly and indirectly to the SFDR provisions and there is also a public consultation aimed at individuals and organisations that have general knowledge and awareness of SFDR. The consultation closed in December 2023 and the EC is now reviewing and collating responses to assess whether the SFDR is meeting investor needs and expectations and whether it is fit for purpose.

---

3   European Commission, "Strategy for Financing the Transition to a Sustainable Economy", 6 July 2021, https://eur-lex.europa.eu/resource.html?uri=cellar:9f5e7e95-df06-11eb-895a-01aa75ed71a1.0001.02/DOC_1&format=PDF.

4   European Securities and Markets Authority, "Sustainable Finance Roadmap 2022–2024", 10 February 2022, www.esma.europa.eu/sites/default/files/library/esma30-379-1051_sustainable_finance_roadmap.pdf.

5   Regulation (EU) 2019/2088, https://eur-lex.europa.eu/legal-content/EN/TXT/?uri=CELEX:32019R2088.

It is worth noting that the proposed amendments to SFDR are potentially far-reaching and include proposals to revoke the existing Article 6, Article 8 and Article 9 classifications. As such, it is expected that the SFDR regime will undergo significant reform in the near future.

The Taxonomy Regulation[6] first entered into force in July 2020 and established an EU-wide framework for defining a 'sustainable investment', in conjunction with numerous delegated acts and secondary legislation that have been and continue to be published in relation to it. In addition to providing the underlying classification system, the Taxonomy Regulation further introduced certain specific requirements for funds in the EU. The Taxonomy Regulation is a 'cornerstone' of the EU's sustainable finance framework and is designed to act to support the goals of the EGD, specifically addressing the issue of greenwashing. The Taxonomy Regulation dovetails with the Corporate Sustainability Reporting Directive (CSRD), which addresses data availability and quality issues (please see the chapter "ESG reporting" for more details on CSRD). The EU is further considering the development of a separate taxonomy to consider social objectives to support socially sustainable investments.[7]

Complementary to SFDR and the Taxonomy Regulation is the Low Carbon Benchmark Regulation which entered into force in December 2019 with the aim of reducing carbon emissions in line with commitments made under the Paris Agreement. It introduces a regulatory framework for EU benchmark labels and provides for sustainability-related disclosures related to benchmarks.

In June 2023, the EC published its proposal in relation to ESG ratings activities.[8] The proposals require that ESG ratings providers will need to acquire authorisation from ESMA (transitional arrangements will be implemented) so that there is a certain level of harmony in relation to classification of providers, ratings methodologies and the use of sustainability-related products and services. The proposals also include certain organisational requirements for ESG ratings providers including that they are subject to general principles concerning their governance requirements in respect of individuals involved in the provision of ESG ratings.

From a prudential perspective, the EU has worked on the Banking Package[9] for the last number of years. The primary aim of the Banking Package is to implement amendments to the Basel framework which will include a number

---

6   Regulation EU 2020/852, https://eur-lex.europa.eu/legal-content/EN/TXT/?uri=CELEX:32020R0852.
7   Platform on Sustainable Finance, "Final Report on Social Taxonomy", February 2022, https://commission.europa.eu/system/files/2022-03/280222-sustainable-finance-platform-finance-report-social-taxonomy.pdf.
8   European Commission, "Sustainable finance – environmental, social and governance ratings and sustainable risks in credit ratings", https://ec.europa.eu/info/law/better-regulation/have-your-say/initiatives/13330-Sustainable-finance-environmental-social-and-governance-ratings-and-sustainability-risks-in-credit-ratings_en.
9   European Commission, "Banking Package", 26 October 2021, https://finance.ec.europa.eu/publications/banking-package_en.

of ESG provisions including disclosure by firms of the degree to which they are exposed to ESG risks.

2.2 The United Kingdom

While in some respects the EU has led the way in developing and implementing sustainability regulation, the UK has made several ambitious commitments to sustainability including being the first country to commit to making the Task Force on Climate-related Financial Disclosures (TCFD) aligned disclosures mandatory.

The Green Finance Strategy[10] is the latest iteration of the UK Government's goals in relation to sustainability and ESG. It sets out the five primary objectives that UK stakeholders are working towards, namely:

- UK financial services growth and competitiveness;
- investment in the green economy;
- financial stability;
- incorporation of nature and adaptation; and
- alignment of global financial flows with climate and nature objectives.

With the above 'aspirations' in mind, it is helpful to examine how the UK has developed its sustainability agenda and the foundation of this is the Roadmap to Sustainable Investing (the 'Roadmap'),[11] published by the UK Government in October 2021. The Roadmap set out the UK Government's strategy to ensure that decision-useful, comparable and reliable sustainability information is available to financial market participants in the UK. The Roadmap envisaged three distinct phases of 'informing', 'acting' and 'shifting', and includes plans to develop sustainability disclosures and a green taxonomy. A cornerstone initiative of the Roadmap is the Sustainability Disclosure Requirements (SDR). The SDR will function as a consolidated sustainability reporting regime, applicable both in relation to corporate sustainability reporting and also financial market participant/product level sustainability reporting.

In November 2023, the FCA published its Policy Statement (PS23/16)[12] containing final rules on SDR which introduces:

- an anti-greenwashing rule for all FCA-authorised firms to reinforce that sustainability-related claims must be fair, clear and not misleading. The

---

10   HM Government, "Mobilising Green Investment: 2023 Green Finance Strategy", March 2023, https://assets.publishing.service.gov.uk/government/uploads/system/uploads/attachment_data/file/1149690/mobilising-green-investment-2023-green-finance-strategy.pdf

11   HM Government, "Greening Finance: A Roadmap to Sustainable Investing", October 2021, https://assets.publishing.service.gov.uk/government/uploads/system/uploads/attachment_data/file/1031805/CCS0821102722-006_Green_Finance_Paper_2021_v6_Web_Accessible.pdf.

12   Financial Conduct Authority, Policy Statement PS23/16 "Sustainability Disclosure Requirements (SDR) and investment labels", November 2023, www.fca.org.uk/publication/policy/ps23-16.pdf.

FCA highlights that sustainability-related references can be present in, but are not limited to, statements, assertions, strategies, targets, policies, information and images;

- naming and marketing rules for investment products to ensure the use of sustainability-related terms are accurate. The FCA had originally proposed to restrict such products from using any sustainability-related terms in their product names and marketing. However, most of the feedback the FCA received suggested that its proposed approach was too restrictive. Therefore, the FCA has tried to strike a balance by allowing products that do not use a label to use sustainability-related terms (such as 'green', 'climate', 'social') in product names and marketing if they meet the FCA's product name, disclosure and statement conditions, as set out in the Policy Statement;

- four labels to help consumers navigate the sustainable investment product landscape; and

- enhanced disclosure requirements, falling into three distinct buckets of consumer-facing disclosures, detailed product-level disclosures and entity-level disclosures, which will provide consumers and investors with better and more accessible information to help them understand the key sustainability features of a product.

SDR will be introduced on a phased basis, with the majority of requirements taking effect in 2024. In relation to the anti-greenwashing rule, the FCA is also consulting on new guidance on the expectations for FCA-authorised firms making claims about the sustainability of a product or service and this guidance will also take effect in 2024. The SDR regime will apply to UK funds, and overseas funds are not currently in scope.

HM Treasury will determine the approach to overseas funds, including whether and how the SDR regime should be extended to overseas funds. It is also worth noting that the FCA emphasises that these rules are a starting point and they intend to further develop SDR in due course, including by consulting on extensions to the regime to cover portfolio management services in 2024. The FCA have also indicated that they will conduct a post-implementation review of the regime after three years. Also derived from the Roadmap is the UK Government's implementation of a UK Green Taxonomy. The implementation of this initiative is a direct acknowledgment that there is a distinct lack of a harmonised framework in the context of sustainability, and it is an attempt at devising common definitions so that businesses and investors alike are not only cognisant of, but understand the environmental impact of their investment-making decisions. The Green Taxonomy remains under consideration and HM Treasury expects to consult on this in 2024.

At a more focused level, the FCA has identified that it has a vital role to play in shaping the sustainability agenda and as such, it too has launched several initiatives to support sustainability into the future. The FCA's strategy was published in November 2021,[13] identifying its core principles and the outcomes that the FCA want to achieve. The FCA has stated that they want the UK to be at the 'forefront' of sustainability thinking on a global level and in order to achieve this they have enhanced their rulebook around sustainability, particularly relating to transparency, and closely aligned to the TCFD recommendations. The FCA has required that UK firms managing funds and portfolios with more than £5 billion of assets under management must produce entity-level reports by 30 June 2023 if they have more than £50 billion in assets under management, or 30 June 2024 if they have less than £50 billion in assets under management. Such firms must also produce public product-level reports and on-demand product-level reports, either on the firm website or through appropriate cross-referencing in existing client reporting.

The FCA has also updated its handbook to reflect the strategic commitment to ESG. They have amended the Listing Rules for premium companies to mandate climate-related financial disclosures and have also adopted an ESG sourcebook,[14] set-up an ESG advisory committee in December 2022, hosted specific sustainability digital sandboxes and established a group to consider and develop a code of conduct for ESG data and ratings providers.[15] The UK Government, as part of the Edinburgh Reforms,[16] have included the development of a regime for ESG data and ratings providers as a stated aim of the overall regulatory reform agenda. HM Treasury published a consultation paper[17] to help inform the government's next steps in terms of shaping the regime and in December 2024, following a three-month consultation period, the International Regulatory Strategy Group published a code of conduct for ESG ratings and data product providers,[18] grounded in the International Organization of Securities Commission (IOSCO) recommendations for ESG data and ratings.

Supplemental to the FCA work from a regulatory perspective, the Bank of England (BoE) and the Prudential Regulation Authority (PRA) have made it clear that sustainability is a key issue, particularly the areas of governance and

13   Financial Conduct Authority, "A strategy for positive change: our ESG priorities", 3 November 2021, www.fca.org.uk/publications/corporate-documents/strategy-positive-change-our-esg-priorities.

14   Financial Conduct Authority, *FCA Handbook*, www.handbook.fca.org.uk/handbook/ESG/1/?view=chapter.

15   Financial Conduct Authority, "Code of conduct for ESG data and ratings providers", 22 November 2022, www.fca.org.uk/news/news-stories/code-conduct-esg-data-and-ratings-providers.

16   Gov.uk, "Financial Services: The Edinburgh Reforms", www.gov.uk/government/collections/financial-services-the-edinburgh-reforms.

17   HM Treasury Consultation, "Future regulatory regime for Environmental, Social and Governance (ESG) ratings providers", https://assets.publishing.service.gov.uk/government/uploads/system/uploads/attachment_data/file/1147458/ESG_Ratings_Consultation_.pdf.

18   ESG Data and Ratings Working Group, "Code of Conduct for ESG Ratings and Data Products Providers", December 2023, www.irsg.co.uk/assets/DRWG/DRWG-Code-of-Conduct-for-ESG-Ratings-and-Data-Products-Providers.pdf.

managing financial risks from climate change. In 2019, the PRA published both a policy statement[19] and a supervisory statement,[20] setting out expectations on how banks and insurers should manage climate-related financial risks. In March 2023, the BoE published a report[21] on climate-related risks and the regulatory capital frameworks. Significantly, this requires firms to identify an appropriate senior management function with specific responsibility for identifying and managing climate risk. The report does not set out policy changes but does set out the BoE's thinking and identifies future areas for work including what an effective risk-management control framework would look like from an ESG perspective and also examining 'regime gaps' in relation to climate risks.

Finally, at a macro-level and sitting alongside the strategy as set out in the Roadmap and the associated legislative initiatives, the UK also became the first major economy to commit in legislation to achieve a net zero economy by 2050. In 2021, and just as the UK was preparing to host the COP 26 summit, the then-Chancellor Rishi Sunak announced a number of UK climate finance projects to help the UK become the world's first net zero-aligned financial centre and in one of the first steps towards this goal, the Financial Services and Markets Act 2023 includes a provision introducing a new regulatory principle that regulators must have regard to the UK's net zero emissions target.[22]

2.3 The United States

Contributors: Laura Ferrell, Betty M Huber, Karmpreet Prewal, Isabelle Russo and Yvette Valdez (Latham & Watkins)

In May 2022, the US Securities and Exchange Commission (SEC) proposed rules that would require registered investment advisers, certain unregistered advisers and registered investment and business development companies to provide standardised ESG disclosures as well as proposed amendments to Rule 35d-1 that have since been finalised and are discussed below.[23] If adopted as proposed, the disclosure requirements would vary based on the centrality of ESG factors in investment strategies. Advisers and registered funds that treat ESG factors in a manner similar to other investment considerations would be subject to

---

19 Bank of England, Policy Statement PS11/19 "Enhancing banks' and insurers' approaches to managing the financial risks from climate change", April 2019, www.bankofengland.co.uk/-/media/boe/files/prudential-regulation/policy-statement/2019/ps1119.

20 Bank of England, Supervisory Statement SS3/19, "Enhancing banks' and insurers' approaches to managing the financial risks from climate change", April 2019, www.bankofengland.co.uk/-/media/boe/files/prudential-regulation/supervisory-statement/2019/ss319.

21 Bank of England, "Report on climate-related risks and the regulatory capital frameworks", 13 March 2023, www.bankofengland.co.uk/prudential-regulation/publication/2023/report-on-climate-related-risks-and-the-regulatory-capital-frameworks.

22 Financial Services and Markets Act 2023, www.legislation.gov.uk/ukpga/2023/29/section/27/enacted.

23 Securities and Exchange Commission, "Enhanced Disclosures by Certain Investment Advisers and Investment Companies about ESG Investment Practices", www.sec.gov/files/rules/proposed/2022/ia-6034.pdf.

comparatively brief requirements. However, registered funds that focus on ESG or particular impacts would be required to make more extensive prospectus disclosures and, in some cases, annual report disclosures.[24]

In September 2023, the SEC adopted amendments to Rule 35d-1 under the Investment Company Act, also known as the Names Rule, which governs naming conventions and prohibits the use of 'materially deceptive or misleading' names for registered funds.[25] The Names Rule requires registered investment companies or business development companies whose names suggest that they focus on a particular type of investment, or investments in a particular country, geography, or industry, or that suggest certain tax treatment, to invest at least 80% of assets in a manner implied by the name. Acknowledging the potential for investor confusion and greenwashing in fund names, the SEC broadened the scope of the 80% requirement to registered funds whose names suggest particular characteristics or a thematic investment focus, including terms relating to ESG. Notably, however, the final rule departed from the proposal in that ESG terms in the names of 'integration funds', where ESG factors are considered alongside other factors but generally carry no greater significance, would not automatically be considered materially deceptive or misleading. Finally, funds seeking to attract investors in multiple jurisdictions will need to be mindful where there may be friction between these new rules and rules with different definitions or requirements in other jurisdictions.[26]

The SEC also proposed rules in March 2022 that, broadly speaking, are intended to elicit more comparable and consistent climate-related information from registrants, including the impact of and governance of climate-related risks, greenhouse gas emission metrics and related attestations, climate-related targets and goals, and climate-related financial metrics and supporting notes. If adopted as proposed, the rules may present both unique challenges and opportunities for financial institutions. See further information on the proposal in the chapter "ESG reporting". Other US financial regulators have also been focused on climate-related risk. For example, in June 2022, the US Commodity Futures Trading Commission, which regulates derivatives market participants submitted a request to the public for information on climate-related risk[27] and has since met to discuss and inform the Climate Risk Unit's recommendations for any new or amended guidance. As another example, federal bank regulatory agencies, the Board of Governors of the Federal Reserve System, the Federal Deposit Insurance Corporation and the Office of the Comptroller of the

---

24   See Latham & Watkins Client Alert Commentary, 27 May 2022, www.lw.com/admin/upload/ SiteAttachments/Alert%202965.v2.pdf.
25   17 CFR § 270.35d-1.
26   See Latham & Watkins Client Alert Commentary, 19 October 2023, www.lw.com/admin/upload/ SiteAttachments/SEC-Adopts-Changes-to-Names-Rule-for-Registered-Funds.pdf.
27   Commodity Futures Trading Commission, 2 June 2022, www.cftc.gov/PressRoom/PressReleases/8541-22.

Currency jointly finalised in October 2023 principles for large financial institutions on climate-related financial risk management.[28]

Additionally, some states have proposed or adopted ESG-related requirements. In California, for example, several pieces of landmark climate disclosure legislation were signed into law in October 2023 which will apply to in scope financial institutions. The Climate Corporate Data Accountability Act (SB 253) and the Climate-Related Financial Risk Act (SB 261) establish climate-related disclosure requirements (including emissions metrics) for public and private US entities that are doing business in California over certain revenue thresholds. The Voluntary Carbon Market Disclosures Business Regulation Act (AB 1305) creates disclosure requirements for businesses engaged in certain types of activities in California relating to voluntary carbon offsets and claims around carbon neutrality, net zero or significant greenhouse gas emissions reductions. These developments are discussed in further detail in the chapter "ESG reporting". At the same time, the US has seen the rise of anti-ESG sentiment along partisan lines that has resulted in fragmentation, particularly at the state level. This ESG backlash implicates numerous types of financial market participants from asset managers to insurers.

While there are differences from state to state, several themes have emerged in anti-ESG legislation across the country to date. These themes include prohibiting industry 'boycotting', whereby a financial institution judged to 'boycott', for example, the fossil fuel industry may be barred from receiving investments by state funds or state contracts, more explicitly narrowing the definition of fiduciary duty for managing state funds to limit consideration of ESG factors, or designating the use of certain environmental and social standards or scores as an unfair or unsound trade practice. Anti-ESG efforts also expand beyond legislatures such as allegations by state attorneys general that ESG initiatives may present antitrust violations. Anti-ESG efforts such as these create risks for financial market participants, especially where they clash with requirements in other jurisdictions both domestically and globally.

2.4   Hong Kong

Contributor: Simon Hawkins (Latham & Watkins)

The current sustainability landscape in Hong Kong is underpinned by the work of the territory's regulatory authorities, particularly the Hong Kong Monetary Authority (HKMA), the Securities and Futures Commission (SFC) and the Stock Exchange of Hong Kong (SEHK). Both the HKMA and the SFC have taken collective and separate steps towards shaping strategy relating to sustainability,

---

28   See Latham & Watkins LLP, Global Financial Regulatory blog, 8 November 2023, www.globalfinregblog.com/
2023/11/occ-frb-and-fdic-finalize-joint-principles-for-climate-related-financial-risk-management/.

including the co-chairing of the Green and Sustainable Finance Cross-Agency Steering Group (the 'Steering Group'), which was set-up to ensure that there is a coordinated approach to addressing sustainability issues in Hong Kong and following the Hong Kong Government's climate-related strategies and objectives. The Steering Group announced as two of its key action points that it would seek to develop: (i) climate-related disclosures aligned with the TCFD recommendations by 2025; and (ii) a classification framework aligned with the Common Ground Taxonomy[29] prepared by the International Platform on Sustainable Finance (IPSF). The regulators are also active in working with international bodies such as the IPSF, IOSCO and the Central Banks and Supervisors Network for Greening the Financial System (NGFS) to exchange best practices and promote international cooperation around the sustainable economy.

Alongside the work of the Steering Group, the SFC has adopted a range of measures relating to sustainability. In June 2021, the SFC published a circular[30] setting out its expectations with respect to authorised unit trusts and mutual funds with green or ESG investment as their objectives, including the naming of the fund, disclosure requirements in offering documents, periodic assessment and reporting. The circular took effect in January 2022 and, importantly, it provides alignment with the EU SFDR by stating that UCITS funds that comply with either Article 8 or Article 9 of SFDR will be deemed to have complied with certain requirements of the circular. The SFC has also introduced obligations on collective investment scheme fund managers to consider climate-related risks in their investment and risk management processes and to make appropriate disclosures to investors; a tiered approach has been taken to require larger fund managers to comply with enhanced standards.

The HKMA has also published a supervisory policy manual[31] on climate-risk management which provides guidance to banks on how to build a level of climate resilience by embedding climate risk considerations into their risk management and disclosure framework. Recently, in April 2023, the HKMA also published a circular and guidelines[32] as part of their second round of climate risk stress testing. First launched in 2021 to assess climate resilience of the Hong Kong banking sector, the HKMA has made a number of enhancements to the

---

29   International Platform on Sustainable Finance, "Common Ground Taxonomy – Climate Change Mitigation", https://finance.ec.europa.eu/system/files/2021-12/211104-ipsf-common-ground-taxonomy-instruction-report-2021_en.pdf.

30   Securities and Futures Commission, "Circular to management companies of SFC-authorised unit trusts and mutual funds – ESG funds", 29 June 2021, https://apps.sfc.hk/edistributionWeb/gateway/EN/circular/products/product-authorization/doc?refNo=21EC27.

31   Hong Kong Monetary Authority, Supervisory Policy Manual, "Climate Risk Management", 30 December 2021, www.hkma.gov.hk/media/eng/doc/key-functions/banking-stability/supervisory-policy-manual/GS-1.pdf.

32   Hong Kong Monetary Authority, "Climate risk stress test", 21 April 2023, www.hkma.gov.hk/media/eng/doc/key-information/guidelines-and-circular/2023/20230421e1.pdf.

framework in anticipation of a second round of testing commencing in June 2023, running for a 12-month period, and including the participation of more than 30 financial institutions. Noting the risks around greenwashing, the HKMA has also conducted a thematic review of the sale of green and sustainable products and provided guidance to banks around setting up a robust product governance framework and conducting appropriate due diligence to reduce potential exposure to greenwashing risks.[33]

Companies listed on the SEHK are also required, under the SEHK Listing Rules, to make certain mandatory and other disclosures in their annual ESG reporting around matters such as emissions, employment, health and safety and supply chain management.[34] At the time of writing, proposals are being considered to enhance climate-related disclosures made by the listed companies and align these with the International Sustainability Standards Board (ISSB) Climate Standard.[35]

2.5 Singapore

Contributors: Jeffy Katio, Farhana Sharmeen and Chong Shi Cheng (Latham & Watkins)

In 2017, the Monetary Authority of Singapore (MAS) established a taskforce to consider green finance and this work eventually led to the launch of the Green Finance Action Plan,[36] setting out the four pillars upon which MAS sustainability is based. The plan seeks to develop financial sector resilience, develop markets and solutions, particularly around green and sustainable bonds and green investment mandates by asset managers, the harnessing of technologies to enable efficient and trusted sustainable finance flows and finally to build regional knowledge and capabilities. MAS has also worked on the development of its taxonomy – the Green Finance Industry Taskforce (GFIT), convened by MAS, launched its third public consultation paper in February 2023[37] on a green and transition taxonomy for Singapore-based financial institutions. The third consultation seeks views on the detailed thresholds and criteria for classification of green and transition activities in

---

33   Hong Kong Monetary Authority, "Due diligence processes for green and sustainable products", 9 December 2022, www.hkma.gov.hk/media/eng/doc/key-information/guidelines-and-circular/2022/20221209e3.pdf.

34   HKEX, Rules and Guidance, Appendix C2 Environmental Social and Governance Reporting Guide, https://en-rules.hkex.com.hk/rulebook/environmental-social-and-governance-reporting-guide-0.

35   HKEX, Consultation paper, "Enhancement of climate-related disclosures under the ESG framework", www.hkex.com.hk/-/media/HKEX-Market/News/Market-Consultations/2016-Present/April-2023-Climate-related-Disclosures/Consultation-Paper/cp202304.pdf.

36   Monetary Authority of Singapore, "Green Finance Action Plan", www.mas.gov.sg/-/media/MAS/News/Media-Releases/2020/MAS-Green-Finance-Action-Plan.pdf.

37   Monetary Authority of Singapore, "Industry Taskforce launches third consultation on green and transition taxonomy", 15 February 2023, www.mas.gov.sg/news/media-releases/2023/industry-taskforce-launches-third-consultation-on-green-and-transition-taxonomy.

various key sectors. A fourth and final consultation paper was released by MAS in June 2023 which seeks views on the detailed thresholds and criteria for the early phase-out of coal-fired power plants under the Singapore-Asia Taxonomy.[38] In December 2023, after taking into account the feedback received from the previous four rounds of public consultation, MAS launched the Singapore-Asia Taxonomy, which sets out detailed thresholds and criteria for defining green and transition activities that contribute to climate change mitigation across eight focus sectors.

Other initiatives in Singapore include:

- the publication of a circular[39] on disclosure and reporting guidelines for retail ESG funds. The circular sets out expectations on how existing requirements applicable to collective investment schemes apply to retail ESG funds, and the disclosure and reporting guidelines applicable to these funds. The circular took effect from 1 January 2023 for funds that sell investments to retail investors in Singapore under an ESG label;

- the launch of ESGenome, a digital ESG disclosure platform, by MAS and the Singapore Exchange (SGX) in September 2022.[40] ESGenome facilitates sustainability reporting by SGX-listed companies and enhance investor access to ESG performance data through structured reporting of ESG data in a comparable format. The disclosure platform is operated by World Wide Generation, a UK-based sustainability fintech firm, and provides access to SGX's 27 core ESG metrics[41] that are mapped to global standards and frameworks. ESGenome also offers a wide range of other metrics mapped across international ESG reporting global standards including the Global Reporting Initiative, TCFD and Sustainable Development Goals;

- the launch of the ESG Impact Hub (the 'Hub') by MAS in October 2022 with the objectives of:[42] (i) facilitating the development and growth of ESG fintechs to power innovation and address the ESG needs of companies and financial institutions, in particular in the area of ESG data solutions; (ii) anchoring ESG enablers such as investors, financial

---

38 Monetary Authority of Singapore, "MAS Launches World's First Multi-Sector Transition Taxonomy", 3 December 2023, www.mas.gov.sg/news/media-releases/2023/mas-launches-worlds-first-multi-sector-transition-taxonomy.

39 Monetary Authority of Singapore, "CFC 02/2022 Disclosure and Reporting Guidelines for Retail ESG Funds", 28 July 2022, www.mas.gov.sg/regulation/circulars/cfc-02-2022—-disclosure-and-reporting-guidelines-for-retail-esg-funds.

40 SGX, ESGenome, www.sgx.com/sustainable-finance/esgenome.

41 SGX, "Starting with a Common Set of Core ESG Metrics", April 2023, https://api2.sgx.com/sites/default/files/2023-05/SGX%20Core%20ESG%20Metrics_for%20website%20%28updated%20Apr2023%29.pdf.

42 Monetary Authority of Singapore, "MAS launches ESG Impact Hub to spur growth of ESG ecosystem", 5 October 2022, www.mas.gov.sg/news/media-releases/2022/mas-launches-esg-impact-hub-to-spur-growth-of-esg-ecosystem.

institutions and knowledge partners to organise training and capacity building workshops, thought leadership events and other accelerator programmes at the Hub; and (iii) supporting ESG stakeholders through engagement with the Hub community to deploy MAS's programmes and solutions to drive transition with a particular emphasis on the focus sectors identified by the GFIT;

- the publication of the Information Papers on Environmental Risk Management ('EnRM Information Papers') by MAS on 31 May 2022,[43] which highlight best practices by banks, insurers and asset managers, and identifies areas that require further work. Under the EnRM Information Papers, financial institutions must also set tangible targets to address environmental risk such as calculated portfolio exposures to geographical areas and sectors with higher environmental risk and carbon intensity of customers in high-risk sectors;

- the publication of the Singapore Green Bond Framework (the 'Framework'),[44] a governance framework for sovereign green bond issuances under the Significant Infrastructure Government Loan Act 2021[45] (SINGA), by the Singapore Government in June 2022. The Framework sets out guidelines for public sector green bond issuances under the SINGA, emphasising its alignment with international standards, market principles and best practices. The Framework is intended to serve as a benchmark for the corporate green market, attract capital, green issuers and investors, paving ways for more private sector green finance activity;

- the publication of the Guidelines on Environmental Risk Management (the 'Guidelines') for banks, insurers and asset managers, by MAS in December 2020.[46] The Guidelines aim to enhance the resilience and management of environmental risk by the banking and insurance sectors, as well as by funds and segregated mandates, by setting out sound environmental risk management practices. Although the Guidelines are not issued on a 'comply or explain' basis, these financial institutions are expected to implement the Guidelines in a risk proportionate manner and while they may implement the Guidelines in phases, they are expected to showcase their implementation progress over the 18-month transition period outlined by MAS; and

43   Monetary Authority of Singapore, "Information papers on environmental risk management", 31 May 2022, www.mas.gov.sg/publications/monographs-or-information-paper/2022/information-papers-on-environmental-risk-management.

44   Ministry of Finance, "Singapore Green Bond Framework", June 2022, www.mof.gov.sg/docs/default-source/policies/fiscal/singapore-green-bond-framework.pdf.

45   Singapore Statutes Online, Government Gazette, https://sso.agc.gov.sg/Acts-Supp/15-2021/Published/20210628?DocDate=20210628.

46   Monetary Authority of Singapore, "Guidelines on Environmental Risk Management for Banks", 8 December 2020, www.mas.gov.sg/regulation/guidelines/guidelines-on-environmental-risk-management.

- the launch of a public consultation on proposals to elevate standards and disclosures of ESG ratings and data products in Singapore via a phased and proportionate regulatory approach, starting with a voluntary industry code of conduct for ESG rating and data product providers.[47] The industry code will cover best practices on governance, management of conflicts of interest and transparency of methodologies and data sources, including disclosure on how forward-looking elements are taken into account in the products. The intent is to enable users to better consider transition risks and opportunities when making decisions on capital allocation.[48]

Finally, in April 2023, MAS and the People's Bank of China announced the establishment of the China-Singapore Green Finance taskforce, which will deepen bilateral cooperation in green and transition finance between Singapore and China, facilitate greater public-private sector collaboration to better meet Asia's needs as it transitions to a low-carbon future and work towards improving the interoperability of taxonomies.

3.   Issues

3.1   Fragmentation, the rate of change and institutional level compliance
As we have seen above, governments and regulators have put ESG at the heart of their regulatory agenda and appear determined to see a positive impact for their efforts. However, the journey towards a collective understanding across global jurisdictions of ESG concepts and issues is ongoing. Whilst regulators do acknowledge that there needs to be a level of 'jurisdictional interoperability'[49] the current landscape of key ESG regulatory provisions applying across the globe is possibly best described as a 'patchwork' of rules and obligations. The lack of consistency between jurisdictions presents a challenge, particularly for multi-jurisdictional financial institutions who must map the differing standards globally and seek to align with a cohesive corporate purpose and strategy. This is made all the more challenging considering the constant flux of regulation. It is important that financial institutions ensure their internal teams are adequately resourced and supported in this challenge.

Depending on the jurisdiction in question, integration at a company level or a fund level can be a challenge. Financial institutions primarily based in

---

47   Monetary Authority of Singapore, "Consultation Paper on Proposed Code of Conduct for ESG Rating and Data Product Providers", 28 June 2023, www.mas.gov.sg/publications/consultations/2023/consultation-paper-on-proposed-code-of-conduct-for-esg-rating-and-data-product-providers#.
48   *Ibid.*
49   Speech by Mr Ashley Alder, Chief Executive Officer of the Securities and Futures Commission, "Sustainable investment: regulatory priorities", PRI China Conference: Investing for Net Zero and SDGs, 27 May 2022, www.sfc.hk/-/media/files/ER/PDF/Speeches/Speech-27-May-2022.pdf.

Europe and the UK will note a very pro-ESG agenda compared with the US, where there is a highly active anti-ESG lobbyist movement. Notwithstanding the varying levels of sentiment, ESG is a *de facto* mainstream consideration in the industry, and it is often perceived that financial institutions and funds who have integrated ESG into their operations, particularly in a European and UK context, have derived a competitive advantage. Integration of ESG is a central topic on the minds of regulators across the globe and the expectation is that a proactive approach is taken in incorporating ESG into business strategies. This necessitates uplifts to policies, procedures, frameworks and processes to embed ESG in the end-to-end investment process. The difficulty that financial institutions and funds face is the different approaches taken by global regulators in achieving full ESG integration. For example, in the EU there is a significant focus on demonstrable integration of sustainability into the investment process and this is closely aligned to disclosures to verify compliance, as seen with the implementation of SFDR. Contrast this with the approach in the US, where the dominant scrutiny is on the investment process and is driven by the need to avoid potentially misleading statements. It is therefore important that the ESG strategies are aligned to business visions, values and corporate ideals. Some practical considerations for financial institutions and funds when implementing and developing an ESG strategy are to:

- define which businesses are in scope;
- identify and articulate the impact and roles on each of the three lines of defence;
- exercise enterprise wise awareness including appropriate training and messaging from senior management on the importance of ESG;
- understand the basis for evaluation of an ESG integration strategy; and
- monitor – evidence alignment and where applicable, any deviations.

3.2 Disclosure and transparency and the rise of greenwashing

A core area of regulatory focus and enforcement is disclosure and transparency. Ensuring that investors are provided with the necessary information to make informed investment decisions is pervasive across the global regulatory agenda.

While not defined uniformly in legislation, greenwashing broadly refers to the practice of providing misleading information about how 'green' a firm is or its products are. Greenwashing is a key focus, not just for regulators but also climate activists, journalists and non-governmental organisations so there is an expectation that there is an increased level of scrutiny of any public statements or corporate pronouncements from a sustainability perspective. Regulators are undoubtedly scrutinising the way financial institutions and funds are operating and we have seen recent examples of greenwashing actions in the

UK[50] and the US, which have subsequently led to increased levels of enforcement activity.[51] In the EU, there is a focus on ensuring that financial institutions and funds have an integrated investment process in relation to ESG and regulators will look to verify this through external disclosures being made. The European Supervisory Authorities have recently published a report[52] on greenwashing in the financial sector and attempted to create a common high-level understanding of greenwashing across the EU. In the US, the SEC has launched its own Climate and ESG Task Force, aligned to its enforcement division, with the specific aim of 'proactively identifying ESG-related misconduct consistent with increased investor reliance on climate and ESG-related disclosure'.[53] So, while each jurisdiction has identified greenwashing as an issue and they have taken proactive steps to address the issue, the actual approach and focus by regulators on certain ESG areas differs from country to country.

It is therefore advisable to be cognisant of both the fragmentation highlighted above and also the risks of greenwashing inherent in the attempts of firms to comply with the plethora of ESG disclosure rules. For example, the first mover intent of the European regulators has led to ambitious regulatory reform. However, a lack of clarity in the legislation is leading to a number of unintended consequences. Specifically in the context of SFDR, confusion around what is classified as an Article 8 or Article 9 product is leading to inconsistent disclosures amongst market participants and increasingly, allegations of greenwashing.

3.3 Double materiality

Materiality assessments can serve as a useful tool in identifying areas of priority from a stakeholder perspective and in understanding ESG-related risks. However, jurisdictional divergence occurs in relation to the scope of materiality. In the US, the focus is on the concept of single materiality, whereas the EU has incorporated the concept of 'double materiality' in a prescriptive manner across a range of disclosure regulations such as SFDR, CSRD and the EU Taxonomy. In the context of funds, they are required to consider their funds, under the concept of double materiality through two prisms: (i) how do climate and broader ESG considerations affect the value of the asset; and (ii) what is the

---

50   Advertising Standards Authority, "ASA Ruling on HSBC UK Bank plc", 19 October 2022, www.asa.org.uk/rulings/hsbc-uk-bank-plc-g21-1127656-hsbc-uk-bank-plc.html.

51   Securities and Exchange Commission, "SEC Charges BNY Mellon Investment Adviser for Misstatements and Omissions Concerning ESG Considerations", 23 May 2022, www.sec.gov/news/press-release/2022-86.

52   European Banking Authority, "ESAs present common understanding of greenwashing and warn on related risks", 1 June 2023, www.eba.europa.eu/esas-present-common-understanding-greenwashing-and-warn-related-risks.

53   Securities and Exchange Commission, "Enforcement Task Force focused on climate and ESG issues", www.sec.gov/securities-topics/enforcement-task-force-focused-climate-esg-issues.

environmental impact of the activities being conducted? SFDR further mandates the disclosure of principal adverse impacts which requires the assessment of AUM against a wide range of ESG factors in order to determine the overall outward ESG impact.

3.4 Stewardship

ESG legislation in the EU and the UK is driving an increased focus on stewardship which did not exist previously. There has been an influx of both product and entity level drivers in this regard such as commitments made under the Stewardship Code and voluntary commitments such as TCFD. Europe is seemingly embracing engagement from stakeholders as a positive and as demonstrable progress of the ESG agenda. Contrast this with the US, which is pulling in the opposite direction with a focus on prohibiting index fund managers from voting on shareholder proposals and director elections unless they have approval from larger institutional investors.

3.5 Data availability and credibility

It must be noted that one of the fundamental problems with ESG outside of regulatory and legislative considerations is that ESG involves matters that are profoundly difficult to evaluate. There is a distinct lack of reliable and timely data for a range of company activities which will be required by the anticipated evolution of global ESG regulations.

We are seeing now that companies are required to disclose particularly granular ESG data in their annual financial reports and in many instances, this 'pool of data' does not exist or is not easily produced to placate regulatory requirements.

Consequently, there remains significant reliance on third party data sources to establish the proxy data needed for reporting. Regulators are conscious of the substantial reliance on third party ESG data sources, including raw data, ratings, scores and indices by financial institutions making large scale capital allocation decisions. The ability to ensure the integrity of that data is therefore of paramount concern.

Accordingly, IOSCO has issued a call to action to global regulatory supervisors to embed a voluntary code of conduct for the producers of ESG data, score and ratings to enhance the integrity of the data being relied on by regulated firms (the 'IOSCO Code'). The IOSCO Code has been adopted by the Japan Financial Services Agency (JFSA) and the FCA, with certain jurisdictions such as the UK, India and the EU seeking to create a formal licensing regime for ESG ratings providers.

4. Conclusion

Whilst there have been significant steps taken from a sustainability perspective to foster global convergence, noting in particular TCFD and ISSB as core global frameworks, significant fragmentation remains as a result of jurisdictions considering sustainability on a local-jurisdictional basis. As a result, fragmentation is likely to remain a key and on-going theme in the sustainability space, with the burden remaining on financial institutions to navigate the regulatory disparities, absorb the associated costs and to manage the resulting risk that this generates.

Global trends in ESG litigation

Robin M Hulshizer
Sophie Lamb KC
Latham & Watkins

1. Introduction

As companies, consumers and the media have continued to increase their focus on ESG matters, there has been an attendant rise in ESG-related litigation. The scope and scale of ESG litigation has the potential to profoundly impact a company and its ongoing viability. Large-scale ESG litigation matters go to the heart of a company's business purpose, reputation, corporate values and approach to risk management, and relationships with investors, suppliers, customers, employees and other stakeholders.

In prior decades, ESG litigation largely focused on the inadequacy of government climate policy or claims for damages following catastrophic environmental events. However, as this chapter highlights, the breadth of ESG litigation is now wide-ranging. In recent years, there has been an increase in cases brought against corporate actors, focusing on environmental and social issues arising from their operations, including the environmental or human rights diligence of group companies or supply-chain partners. Increasingly, these claims are directed at the level of parent companies or brought against individual directors. Additionally, corporate actors have been targeted for statements made about their ESG credentials in disclosures, and industries that had historically avoided greenwashing litigation have now found themselves in plaintiffs' crosshairs.

This chapter does not seek to provide an all-encompassing survey of ESG litigation (if such a survey were even possible). Rather, it highlights the various forms ESG litigation has taken to date, explores recent developments in those areas, and identifies trends in the field. Given the fast-moving developments in the ESG space broadly and within ESG litigation specifically, this chapter represents but a snapshot in time, and these categories and trends may morph as public and private actors continue to grapple with ESG issues.

2. Government ESG litigation

As observed by the Intergovernmental Panel on Climate Change (IPCC), litigation has "influenced the outcome and ambition of climate governance."[1]

Historically, the bulk of ESG litigation has been precisely that: challenges to government climate policy which seek to alter the design and overall ambition of policy or the adequacy of its implementation. These challenges are typically coupled with requests for a court order to compel governments to revise their climate policy or even adopt specific national emissions targets. To date, there have been over 70 of these challenges globally, spearheaded by a diverse range of plaintiffs, including non-governmental organisations (NGOs), municipal governments and trade associations.[2]

This category of ESG litigation also includes cases which target the operations of governments, particularly those that are seen to contribute to GHG emissions or otherwise hinder the goals of the Paris Agreement.[3] For example, in *La Rose v Her Majesty the Queen*, the plaintiffs' claim, which was ultimately dismissed, was that Canada had violated constitutional rights by providing subsidies for fossil fuel exploration and acquiring pipeline projects.[4] More recently, an NGO filed a claim against BNDES, Brazil's national development bank, for failing to assess the impact of its investments on the climate crisis, in violation of Brazil's commitments under the Paris Agreement and its national climate policy.[5]

Challenges to the scope of governmental regulatory powers with respect to climate and other policies also fall under this category. A recent example is *West Virginia v EPA*,[6] in which the US Supreme Court held that the Environmental Protection Agency (EPA) had exceeded its statutory authorisation by interpreting the Clean Air Act to allow it to force coal-fired power plants to shift to natural gas or renewable energy-based production.[7] In contrast, Brazil's Federal Supreme Court recently held that the government's failure to maintain the National Fund on Climate Change was a violation of the Brazilian constitution. In the court's view, the Paris Agreement should be treated as a

---

1   IPCC Sixth Assessment Report (AR6), "Climate Change 2023: Synthesis Report", p18.
2   In the US, the majority of these challenges are filed by municipal or state governments, companies and trade associations. Outside of the US, they have been filed primarily by non-governmental organisations (NGOs) and individuals.
3   *La Rose v Her Majesty the Queen* 2020 FC 1008. See also *ClientEarth v Belgian National Bank* (filed 13 April 2021) (Brussels Tribunal of First Instance rejected ClientEarth's claim that the Belgian National Bank had violated certain provisions of the Treaty on the Functioning of the EU and Article 37 of the EU Charter of Fundamental Rights on procedural grounds).
4   NGOs have pursued similar constitution-based litigation at the state level in the US. See, eg, *Held v State*, No CDV-2020-307 (Mont Dist Ct) (action comprised of youth plaintiffs (supported by non-profit Our Children's Trust) where the court held the state of Montana violated its constitutional provision that "[a]ll persons ... have ... the right to a clean and healthful environment" by supporting the fossil fuel industry and prohibiting the state from considering how its projects impact climate change).
5   *Conectas Direitos Humanos v BNDES and BNDESPAR* 2022 1038657-42.2022.4.01.3400.
6   142 S Ct 2587 (2022).
7   In yet another example, the State of Louisiana filed suit against EPA for actions taken against two companies as part of EPA's environmental justice polices. *Louisiana v EPA*, No 23-cv-00692 (WD La 2023). The court limited EPA's ability to bring environmental justice cases, ruling that EPA cannot impose disparate impact-based requirements on states or state agencies. See *ibid*, Mem. Ruling (Dkt 48) (23 January 2024).

human rights treaty with 'supranational' status, and any act or omission by the Brazilian Government that contradicted the Paris Agreement may be invalid.[8]

These challenges to government climate policy or operations are usually based on well-known legal principles, from tort law, human rights and constitutional law, and international law. For example, in *VZW Klimaatsaak v Belgium*, the challenge to Belgium's climate policy was based on a duty of care under its Civil Code, as well as Belgium's human rights obligations, including the right to life (Article 2) and the right to home and private life (Article 8) of the European Convention on Human Rights (ECHR), with reference to Belgium's obligations under the United Nations Framework Convention on Climate Change (UNFCCC) and the Paris Agreement.[9]

A common feature of these cases is the use of human rights law. As part of their case theories, plaintiffs place emphasis on how inadequate climate policy or insufficient national emissions targets may have impacted the enjoyment of human rights. This approach has been successful in some jurisdictions, but not others. In *Urgenda*, the Dutch Supreme Court agreed with the plaintiff that the Netherlands had direct obligations under Articles 2 and 8 of the ECHR to ensure that greenhouse gas (GHG) emissions were reduced in line with acceptable limits, which it had breached by setting an insufficient national emissions target.[10] However, this broad view of ECHR rights has been rejected in other jurisdictions. For example, in a recent challenge to the United Kingdom's Climate Change Act 2008 and Net Zero Strategy, the High Court found there had been no violation of Articles 2 and 8 of the ECHR because, among other things, the ECHR could not be interpreted in such a way to require a government to minimise climate impacts.[11]

Even in circumstances where government climate policy is found to be lacking, some courts have considered their hands tied by the separation of powers doctrine or its equivalent. For example, in *Family Farmers and Greenpeace Germany v Germany*, the claimants sought an order to compel the German federal government to meet its stated goal of reducing national greenhouse gas emissions by 40% of 1990 levels by 2020.[12] The Administrative Court of Berlin recognised that the government must undertake measures to provide adequate protection of the fundamental rights affected by climate change, but refused to order the government to make specific changes to the national Climate Protection Programme, on the basis that the separation of powers principle

---

8   *PSB et al v Brazil (on Climate Fund)* 2022 ADPF 708.
9   *VZW Klimaatsaak v Kingdom of Belgium, et al* 2021/AR/1589 (Brussels Court of Appeal).
10   *Urgenda Foundation v State of the Netherlands* ECLI:NL:HR:2019:2007.
11   *R (on the application of Friends of the Earth Ltd) v Secretary of State for Business, Energy and Industrial Strategy* 2022 EWHC 1841, paras 264–267. The Court refused to adopt a broad interpretation of the ECHR, noting that it was obliged to interpret the ECHR consistently with the jurisprudence of the European Court of Human Rights, which had not yet interpreted Articles 2 and 8 in the context of climate change.
12   *Family Farmers and Greenpeace Germany v Germany* (2019) 00271/17/R/SP.

granted the government wide discretion in selecting what measures to use to achieve emissions goals.

Despite their varied success, these challenges to government climate policy continue to be filed at pace. They are often used as "framework" cases that form part of wider litigation strategies for plaintiffs, with further cases being brought based on the same case theories and evidence (see section 4 below). For example, the decision of *Neubauer et al v Germany*,[13] in which Germany was found to have violated certain constitutional rights by failing to implement precautionary measures to mitigate emissions, has since been relied on by plaintiffs in a further challenge to Germany's amendments to the Act,[14] as well as in several actions brought against German automobile manufacturers (see section 4 below).[15]

Some clarity on the scope of a government's international obligations with respect to climate change may be provided in the foreseeable future. In March 2023, the United Nations General Assembly adopted a resolution requesting an advisory opinion from the International Court of Justice on states' obligations under international law with respect to climate change. The ICJ may interpret the obligations under both the Paris Agreement and the UNFCCC, as well as international human rights instruments such as the Universal Declaration of Human Rights. Additionally, there are several cases pending before the European Court of Human Rights (ECtHR) which address the human rights impacts of climate change.[16] Any future decision by the ICJ or the ECtHR on these matters will have important implications for this area of ESG litigation going forward.

3. Infrastructure ESG litigation

A second category of ESG litigation relates to the various challenges to government approval of, or financial support for, significant infrastructure projects. By way of example, plaintiffs are currently challenging Mexico's decision to increase transmission rates that affect renewable energy projects, South Africa's plans to procure new coal-fired power electricity capacity and Argentina's approval of offshore exploration activities.[17] This type of challenge has only increased in number in recent years, particularly with respect to projects for the development of fossil fuels, but they have had limited success.

---

13   *Neubauer et al v Germany* (Federal Constitutional Court, 2021).
14   *Steinmetz et al v Germany* (Federal Constitutional Court, 2022).
15   See, for example, *Kaiser et al v Volkswagen AG* (Regional Court of Braunschweig, 2021); *Deutsche Umwelthilfe v Mercedes-Benz AG* (Regional Court of Stuttgart, 2021).
16   See, for example, *Duarte Agostinho and Others v Portugal and Other States* (no 39371/20), *Union of Swiss Senior Women for Climate Protection v Swiss Federal Council and Others* (no 53600/20) and *Carême v France* (no 7189/21).
17   *CEMDA v Comisión Reguladora de Energía* Amparo 232/2021; *Africa Climate Alliance et al v Minister of Mineral Resources & Energy et al* 2021 Case No 56907/21; *Fundación Greenpeace Argentina y Ots v Estado Nacional y Ots* 2022 FMP 105/202.

As discussed below, national courts will typically refrain from intervening in this type of government decision-making unless there is clear evidence that the decision maker has acted outside its authority.

As a starting point, these challenges involve an assessment of whether the government entity in question was acting within the scope of its authority when granting the relevant project approval. Plaintiffs rely on well-established public law principles, with arguments often based on whether the government had taken into account the environmental impact of the project or acted in accordance with its commitments under the UNFCCC and Paris Agreement. For example, in *Friends of the Earth v Secretary of State for Transport*, the plaintiff alleged that the UK Secretary of State for Transport had breached various duties under the UK's Planning Act 2008 by failing to take into account the Paris Agreement in its policy statement providing support for the Heathrow Airport expansion.[18] The UK Supreme Court rejected this argument, finding instead that the Secretary of State had a broad discretion under the Planning Act 2008 as to what should be considered in terms of mitigating climate change, and in fact had considered the implications of the Paris Agreement in its policy statement, even though there was no obligation to do so.[19]

A similar result was reached by the UK Court of Appeal, in response to an application for judicial review of the Secretary of State's decision to provide export finance and support to an LNG gas project in Mozambique. The Court of Appeal upheld the decision, finding that it was not inconsistent with the UK's obligations under the Paris Agreement and, in any event, the judiciary "cannot and should not second-guess the executive's decision-making in the international law arena".[20]

This approach is in line with that taken by other jurisdictions. National courts are, on the whole, reluctant to intervene in government decision making and instead afford governments a wide scope of discretion when reviewing approvals for infrastructure projects or finance (see section 2 above). For example, in *Greenpeace Nordic and others v Norway*, the Norwegian Supreme Court rejected a claim that Norway's decision to issue oil and gas licences for deep-sea extraction had violated Articles 2 and 8 of the ECHR, finding instead the judiciary's role was limited to ensuring that the government had "struck a fair balance of interests" and taken into account all mandatory considerations.[21]

---

18 *R (on the application of Friends of the Earth Ltd and others) v Heathrow Airport Ltd* [2020] UKSC 52.
19 *Ibid*, para 125.
20 In summary, the Court of Appeal held that, while in principle the issue was justiciable, the Secretary of State's conclusion that the LNG project in Mozambique aligned with the UK's obligations under the Paris Agreement was tenable given the role of gas in a wide range of scenarios compatible with the temperature goals of the Paris Agreement. The claimant's application for permission to appeal to the Supreme Court was denied as the Supreme Court found that it did not raise an arguable point of law: *R (Friends of the Earth Ltd) v Secretary of State for International Trade/Export Credits Guarantee Department (UK Export Finance)* 2023 EWHC Civ 14.
21 *Greenpeace Nordic and others v Norway* HR-2020-2472-P, para 182.

However, where there is clear evidence that a government has overstepped its authority, courts will step in and set aside government approvals. For example, in *EarthLife Africa Johannesburg v Minister of Environmental Affairs and others*, the Minister was found to have breached its duties under the South African National Environmental Management Act 1998 when it failed to undertake its own environmental assessment of plans for a new coal-fired power project, which was expressly required under the Act.[22] Similarly, in the United States, plaintiffs have also had some success targeting infrastructure projects for failure to adequately address environmental justice concerns.[23] In *Friends of Buckingham v State Air Pollution Control Board*,[24] the Court of Appeal held that the environmental justice evaluation conducted by the state of Virginia's air pollution control board before project approval was insufficient for failure to fully analyse various environmental justice concerns.[25] In so ruling, the court observed "environmental justice is not merely a box to be checked".[26]

4.   ESG litigation relating to company operations

The private sector has been a target of ESG litigation for some time, however, in recent years, there has been a flood of claims which seek to impose legal responsibility on companies for environmental or social governance issues that arise out of their business activities or that of their subsidiaries or supply chain. Defendants to this type of claim are from a wide range of sectors, such as transport, food and agriculture, energy and finance.[27]

The significant majority of these cases have been filed in the US,[28] with cases brought by governments and private actors alike seeking compensatory damages for past harm and injunctive relief to prevent future damage. Perhaps most famously, the wave of litigation that followed the Deepwater Horizon oil explosion in the Gulf of Mexico involved a variety of plaintiffs – including the

---

22   The Minister of Environmental Affairs had not completed its own environmental impact assessment as required, but made it a condition of the environmental authorisation that the applicant do so. Following this decision by the High Court of South Africa, the Minister again approved the permit application for the plant, but issued a new environmental impact assessment in conjunction. This approval was later challenged by the claimant NGO and, following an agreement between all parties, the court issued an order setting aside all government approvals for the plant. *EarthLife Africa Johannesburg v Minister of Environmental Affairs and Others* (case no 21559/2018).

23   See, for example, *Vecinos v FERC*, No 20-1045 (DC Cir 2021) (remanding approvals given by the Federal Energy Regulatory Commission on two proposed natural gas export projects holding that the commission had failed to properly review and consider the climate change and environmental justice impacts).

24   947 F3d 68 (4th Cir 2020).

25   *Ibid,* at 87–93.

26   *Ibid,* at 92.

27   Catherine Higham, "Taking companies to court over climate change: who is being targeted?" Grantham Research Institute (2021), www.lse.ac.uk/granthaminstitute/news/taking-companies-to-court-over-climate-change-who-is-being-targeted/.

28   See, for example, *Ohio v Norfolk Southern Corp*, No 4:23-cv-00517 (ND Ohio 2023) (seeking civil penalties, damages, and injunctive relief related to a train derailment in East Palatine, Ohio); *Illinois v 3M Co*, No 2023L000996 (Ill Cir Ct 2023) (alleging that several companies knowingly polluted Illinois' natural resources by manufacturing and selling chemicals containing PFAS and seeking damages and injunctive relief).

five Gulf states (Florida, Alabama, Mississippi, Louisiana and Texas), the US Federal Government and local business owners – and led to the largest environmental damage settlement in US history of US$20.8 billion. However, there has now been a flurry of cases brought in other jurisdictions. Recent examples, which are discussed further below, include the claims filed against Shell in the Netherlands,[29] TotalEnergies and BNP Paribas in France,[30] and Volkswagen and Mercedes-Benz in Germany.[31] These cases differ from those brought in the US as they do not necessarily involve claims for compensation, but instead call for changes in corporate governance and decision-making.

The legal basis for this type of claim will vary depending on jurisdiction, but have included tort law, consumer protection law and company law, as well as human rights law and corporate due diligence standards. It is not unusual to see the same case theories advanced in challenges against government climate policy refashioned to support cases brought against companies (see sections 2 and 3 above). One clear example of this is *Milieudefensie v Royal Dutch Shell plc*. In its application, the plaintiff relied on the earlier decision by the Dutch Supreme Court in *Urgenda* as evidence in support of its case against Shell.[32] According to the plaintiff, Shell had a corporate duty of care and due diligence obligations under Dutch tort law to take action to reduce its GHG emissions. The first instance court in The Hague agreed with the plaintiff and issued a groundbreaking judgment, ordering Shell to reduce its net carbon dioxide emissions by 45% by 2030. Shell is appealing, and the outcome of that appeal and of similar cases in other jurisdictions[33] will undoubtedly inform future ESG litigation against companies going forward.

In parallel, there have been a number of actions filed recently against German automobile manufacturers, in which it is alleged that the manufacturers' failure to commit to the phase out of the sale of passenger cars and light commercial vehicles with internal combustion engines by 2030 violates a duty of care owed under tort law, as well as the plaintiffs'

---

29 *Milieudefensie v Royal Dutch Shell plc* ECLI:NL:RBDHA:2021:5339.

30 *Notre Affaire à Tous and Others v Total* (Nanterre Court, 2019); *Notre Affaire à Tous Les Amis de la Terre, and Oxfam France v BNP Paribas* (Judicial Court of Paris, 2023); *Friends of the Earth et al v Total* (Nanterre Judicial Court, 2019); *Comissão Pastoral da Terra and Notre Affaire À Tous v BNP Parnibas* (Judicial Court of Paris, 2023).

31 *Kaiser et al v Volkswagen AG* (Regional Court of Braunschweig, 2021); *Deutsche Umwelthilfe v Mercedes-Benz AG* (Regional Court of Stuttgart, 2021).

32 *Milieudefensie v Royal Dutch Shell plc* ECLI:NL:RBDHA:2021:5339, para 4.4.10. See also section 2 above.

33 The case against Shell is only one of an increasing number of cases. Similar claims have been filed against ENI S.p.A. in Italy, Holcim in Switzerland, RWE in Germany, Polska Grupa in Poland and a group of companies in New Zealand, which seek to impose civil liability for climate change-related damages suffered in the relevant jurisdiction and, in some cases, globally. In these cases, all of which were pending at the time of publication, the plaintiffs allege that the company's operations causes or contributes to climate change and seek injunctive relief for the reduction of emissions by specified levels. See *Smith v Fonterra Co-Operative Group Limited* [2024] NZSC 5; *Greenpeace Italy et al v ENI SpA, the Italian Ministry of Economy and Finance and Cassa Depositi e Prestiti SpA* (2023 Civil Court of Rome); *Asmania et al v Holcim* (2022 Zug); *Luciano Lliuya v RWE AG* (Case No 2 O 285/15 Essen Regional Court); *ClientEarth v Polska Grupa Energetyczna* (2019 Łódź Regional Court).

constitutional rights under the German Civil Code.[34] Claims have also been brought against several French companies for alleged failure to identify human rights violations and environmental harms arising from their operations, based on the 2017 French Duty of Vigilance Law.[35] In the claims against TotalEnergies and BNP Paribas, the plaintiff NGOs allege that both companies have failed to adequately assess in their *'plan de vigilance'* the threats to human rights and the environment presented by certain fossil fuel projects.[36]

There are a number of legal hurdles that a claim of this nature must overcome. One such hurdle is the separation of powers doctrine. As with ESG litigation against governments (see sections 2 and 3 above), this doctrine has played a significant role in restricting the success of ESG litigation concerning company operations. For example, in *Smith v Fonterra*, the plaintiff alleged that the business activities of several companies based in New Zealand amounted to a public nuisance and breached the companies' duty of care in tort law to take reasonable care not to operate their business in a way that would contribute to climate change. This was rejected by the New Zealand Court of Appeal, which held that tort law was not an appropriate vehicle for dealing with climate change,[37] as climate change was a "polycentric issue that is not amenable to judicial resolution" and better addressed by regulation at the national level.[38] The same approach has also been adopted in other jurisdictions.[39]

These claims may also face significant jurisdictional obstacles, particularly where the claim is made against a parent company for the activities of its subsidiary. This issue of 'parental responsibility' has been addressed in two decisions of the UK Supreme Court, which provide guidance on the limited

---

34 *Kaiser et al v Volkswagen AG* (Regional Court of Braunschweig, 2021); *Deutsche Umwelthilfe v Mercedes-Benz AG* (Regional Court of Stuttgart, 2021); *Deutsche Umwelthilfe (DUH) v Bayerische Motoren Werke AG (BMW)* (Regional Court of Munich, 2021).

35 This legislation requires companies to identify and prevent, through a *'plan de vigilance'*, any serious violations of human rights and environmental risks that may occur as a result of their business practices or by their foreign subsidiaries, suppliers or contractors.

36 See, for example, *Notre Affaire à Tous and Others v Total* (Nanterre Court, 2019); *Notre Affaire à Tous Les Amis de la Terre and Oxfam France v BNP Paribas* (Judicial Court of Paris, 2023); *Friends of the Earth et al v Total* (Nanterre Judicial Court, 2019); *Comissão Pastoral da Terra and Notre Affaire À Tous v BNP Paribas* (Judicial Court of Paris, 2023). In a similar action against Casino, a major French supermarket chain, the plaintiffs argue that the operations of Casino's suppliers in the cattle industry in Brazil and Colombia has resulted in serious environmental harm, which was not properly identified in Casino's *'plan de vigilance'*. See *Envol Vert et al v Casino* (Saint-Étienne Judicial Court, 2021).

37 On appeal, the Court of Appeal struck out all three causes of action, with an overarching conclusion that "the magnitude of the crisis which is climate change simply cannot be appropriately or adequately addressed by common law tort claims pursued through the courts", which is "quintessentially a matter that calls for a sophisticated regulatory response at a national level supported by international co-ordination". The Supreme Court has recently disagreed, allowing all three causes of action to proceed to trial: *Smith v Fonterra Co-Operative Group Limited* [2024] NZSC 5. See also Sophie Lamb KC and Stephanie Forrest, "New Zealand Supreme Court Paves Way for Novel Climate Change Claim" (2024) Latham & Watkins Environment Land & Resources Blog, www.globalelr.com/2024/02/new-zealand-supreme-court-paves-way-for-novel-climate-change-claim.

38 *Ibid*, paras 26–28.

39 See, for example, *Deutsche Umwelthilfe v Mercedes-Benz AG* (Regional Court of Stuttgart, 2021) (claim requesting court order for Mercedes-Benz to, among other things, refrain from placing ICE passenger cars on the market was dismissed on the basis that it was for the legislator, not the judiciary, to decide the appropriate measures to protect the climate).

circumstances in which English courts will assume jurisdiction over both the parent company and its subsidiary.[40] The Supreme Court also set out the test under English law for when a duty of care in tort would be owed by a parent company in respect of the activities of its subsidiaries, which includes circumstances where the parent has taken over management of the relevant activity of its subsidiary or has promulgated defective group-wide safety or environmental policies.[41]

This issue of 'parental responsibility' was also considered recently by the Hague Court of Appeals, where a parent company was found to be liable for breach of duty of care regarding environmental harm committed abroad by its foreign subsidiary company.[42] The District Court of Rotterdam also recently accepted jurisdiction over a claim against a Brazilian holding company and its three Dutch subsidiaries for damages for the environmental harm allegedly caused by the operations of the Brazilian entity.[43]

Companies may be targets of ESG litigation for other governance issues that may arise out of their business activities, including concerns over systemic discrimination, slavery or working conditions or other violations of human rights or corporate due diligence standards. For example, in the case of *National Center for Public Policy Research v Schultz*,[44] an interest group filed what is often termed as an anti-ESG lawsuit against Starbucks alleging that its diversity policies, including those touching on hiring, compensation and contracting, require Starbucks to discriminate based on race in violation of state and federal civil rights laws.

Potential liability in this regard may also extend to the conduct of a company's subsidiary or supply chain. In the Canadian case of *Nevsun v Araya*, the plaintiffs alleged that the foreign subsidiary of the defendant mining company had hired sub-contractors that operated a system of forced labour in Eritrea, in breach of customary international law prohibitions (including those against slavery and forced labour) and domestic tort law. These claims were

---

40 *Vedanta v Lungowe & Ors* [2019] UKSC 20 and *Okpabi and others v Royal Dutch Shell Plc and another* [2021] UKSC 3. See also *Municipo de Mariana v BHP Group (UK) Ltd and BHP Group LTD* [2022] EWCA Civ 951 (Court of Appeal assumed jurisdiction over tort claims where the relevant environmental damage had occurred in Brazil).

41 *Okpabi and others v Royal Dutch Shell Plc and another* [2021] UKSC 3, paras 141–151.

42 In summary, the Hague Court of Appeal found that Shell Nigeria was liable under Nigerian law for damage caused by an oil leak, and its parent company Royal Dutch Shell plc was also liable as it had a common law duty of care to ensure particular safety measures were installed in pipelines operated by its Nigerian subsidiary. *Four Nigerian Farmers and Stichting Milieudefensie v Shell*, The Hague Court of Appeal, 29 January 2021, ECLI:NL:GHDHA:2021:132, ECLI:NL:GHDHA:2021:133 and ECLI:NL:GHDHA:2021:134.

43 *Persons v Braskem SA and others* ECLI:NL:RBROT:2022:7549.

44 *National Center for Public Policy Research v Schultz* No 22-cv-00267 (ED Wash 2022). Though the court dismissed the case on the grounds that plaintiffs were pursuing their own interests above those of the Starbucks board of directors, which they cannot do in a derivative lawsuit, plaintiffs continue to bring anti-ESG lawsuits. Following the US Supreme Court's ruling that struck down affirmative action in college admissions (*Students for Fair Admissions v Harvard*, 600 US 181 (2023)), plaintiffs have targeted DEI practices at other entities such as corporations and law firms. See, for example, *Am Alliance for Equal Rights v Perkins Coie*, No 3:23-cv-01877 (ND Tex); *Do No Harm v Pfizer Inc*, 1:22-cv-07908 (SDNY), appeal docketed No 23-15 (2d Cir).

withdrawn following a settlement between the parties, but the Canadian Supreme Court accepted in principle that a company could be liable for its foreign sub-contractor's use of forced labour or other human rights abuses abroad.[45] Similarly, in a more recent case brought against British American Tobacco and Imperial Tobacco, the claimants argued that the defendants "facilitated, assisted and/or encouraged such unlawful, exploitative and dangerous conditions in order to acquire tobacco leaves at the lowest possible costs and to maximize their profits from the sale of cigarettes", and so owed a duty of care to the claimant Malawian tobacco workers. The UK High Court refused to strike out the claim, which is expected to proceed to trial.[46]

Alongside the increase in this type of ESG litigation, some jurisdictions are introducing stricter rules in order to regulate international business conduct. For example, the European Commission is working on adopting the Corporate Sustainability Due Diligence Directive (CSDDD), which aims to enhance compliance with the voluntary OECD Guidelines for Multinational Enterprises. As discussed in the chapter "The S in ESG", the CSDDD introduces best-effort due diligence obligations for companies, for their own activities and that of their suppliers, which will require them to identify and prevent any actual or potential adverse impact of their operations on human rights and on the environment. Once adopted, companies will face civil liability for any damages caused by breaches of obligations under the CSDDD, and these obligations may be enforced by the national supervisory authority in each European Union member state or by private litigants. Naturally, these types of regulatory developments will mean that scrutiny of companies' operations abroad and their supply chains will only continue to increase going forward.

5. ESG litigation relating to corporate governance and directors' duties

Corporate directors in virtually all jurisdictions owe certain legal duties and responsibilities, and plaintiffs are increasingly targeting directors for allegedly failing to exercise these duties when considering ESG issues. For example, in the US, the duty of care requires directors to act with a reasonable level of care consistent with the care that would be applied by a reasonable director similarly situated.[47] The duty of loyalty requires directors to refrain from self-dealing.[48] It also requires directors to make good-faith efforts to implement an oversight programme over the company's operations, and to monitor that oversight

---

45   *Nevsun Resources Ltd v Araya and others* [2020] 1 SCR 166.
46   *Milasi Josiya and others v British American Tobacco Plc and others* [2021] EWHC 1743 (QB).
47   *United Food & Com Workers Union & Participating Food Indus Emp Tri-State Pension Fund v Zuckerberg*, 262 A 3d 1034, 1050 (Del 2021).
48   *Ibid* at 1049–1050; see also *In re Caremark Intern Inc Derivative Litig*, 698 A 2d 959 (Del Ch 1996).

programme.[49] Similar iterations of these directors' duties are owed in other jurisdictions.

Companies face risk from both sides when they incorporate ESG considerations into their decision making. A failure to adequately address ESG-related risks could foster allegations of a breach of fiduciary duty, as the future impact of environmental issues like climate change can impair the value of a company or investment.[50] In the UK, two claims of this nature have recently been dismissed by the Court of Appeal, but may be subject to further appeal. The first is against the directors of the University Superannuation Scheme Limited (USSL), a pension scheme for university staff, alleging that they had breached various statutory and fiduciary duties by failing to form an adequate plan to divest their investments in fossil fuels.[51] A similar action has also been filed by ClientEarth against Shell plc and its board of directors, claiming its failure to adopt an energy transition plan that aligns with the Paris Agreement constitutes a violation of their directors' duties.[52]

On the other hand, boards face risk from overemphasising ESG – for example, in 2022, 19 US attorneys general wrote to the CEO of BlackRock, raising concerns that its support for green initiatives at the expense of shareholder returns for their state employee pension funds could be in violation of its directors' duties and multiple state laws.[53] A putative class of plaintiffs recently brought a challenge under that very premise, alleging that American Airlines and its pension investors breached their fiduciary duties by improperly investing in funds that emphasise ESG goals at the expense of financial returns.[54] A similar question was recently considered by the English High Court, where the trustees of two charities sought the court's approval for the adoption of their proposed new investment policies, which were drafted to ensure their investments were aligned with the Paris Agreement even if the financial returns may not be maximised as a result.[55] The court held that, under certain provisions of the Trustees Act 2000, charity trustees were entitled to exclude

---

49 *In re McDonald's Corp S'holder Deriv Litig*, 289 A 3d 343 (Del 2023) (holding that plaintiffs adequately alleged facts suggesting the head of human resources breached his fiduciary duty of loyalty by allowing a corporate culture to develop that condoned sexual harassment and misconduct); see also *Stone ex rel AmSouth Bancorporation v Ritter*, 911 A 2d 362 (Del 2006) (explaining that *Caremark's* duty of oversight is subsumed under the duty of loyalty).

50 See, for discussion, Maria Antonia Tigre and Cynthia Hanawalt, "The Fiduciary Duty of Directors to Manage Climate Risk: An Expansion of Corporate Liability Through Litigation?", Sabin Center for Climate Change Law (15 February 2023), https://blogs.law.columbia.edu/climatechange/2023/02/15/the-fiduciary-duty-of-directors-to-manage-climate-risk-an-expansion-of-corporate-liability-through-litigation/#:~:text=As%20climate%2Drelated%20financial%20risk,material%20risks%20to%20the%20company.

51 *McGaughey v Universities Superannuation Scheme Limited and others* [2022] EWHC 1233 (Ch); [2023] EWCA Civ 873.

52 *ClientEarth v Shell plc and others* [2023] EWHC 1137 (Ch); [2023] EWHC 1897 (Ch).

53 Letter from Mark Brnovich (Arizona Attorney General) *et al*, to Laurence D Fink, CEO, BlackRock Inc (4 August 2022), www.texasattorneygeneral.gov/sites/default/files/images/executive-management/BlackRock%20Letter.pdf.

54 *Spence v Am Airlines, Inc*, No 4:23-cv-00552-O (ND Tex 2023).

55 *Butler-Sloss v Charity Commission* [2022] EWHC 974 (Ch).

investments that they considered would conflict with a charity's purpose, so long as they had reasonably balanced all relevant factors, including the likelihood and seriousness of any potential financial effect of the exclusion of such investments.[56]

Directors have also faced risk when addressing social issues. An example of this can be found in the US, where the directors of at least 10 companies (such as Qualcomm and Monster Beverage) were the target of shareholder derivative lawsuits asserting breaches of the duties of care and loyalty based on alleged insufficient commitment to diversity at the board level and within the company, as well as alleged misleading disclosures regarding these companies' commitment to diversity and compliance with anti-discrimination laws.[57] For various reasons, most of these cases did not survive the early pleading stage, but this remains a growing area of risk for companies and their directors.

6.   ESG litigation relating to corporate disclosures

Financial regulators across the world are broadening the scope of ESG-related metrics that reporting companies must disclose to shareholders and investors. For example, as discussed in the chapter "ESG reporting", the EU has introduced new rules on corporate sustainability reporting, which requires companies which meet a certain size threshold to report on climate change and other sustainability issues.[58] There are also specific sustainability disclosure obligations in place for investment funds and financial advisers, aimed at making the sustainability impacts of certain investments better understood by investors.[59] The EU has also recently proposed a new Directive to establish a corporate due diligence duty to prevent and account for negative human rights and environmental impacts, as well as directors' duties to oversee the due diligence process and take into account human rights and environmental considerations in their decision making.[60] This would require companies to conduct due diligence not only on their own operations, but that of their subsidiaries and those in their value chains. They would need to develop 'prevention action' plans to identify, prevent and bring an end to any human

---

56   The court also observed that charity trustees, when considering the financial effect of making or excluding certain investments, could take into account the risk of losing support from donors and damage to the charity's reputation generally and in particular among its beneficiaries. The court also noted that trustees had to be careful in relation to making investment decisions on purely moral grounds, recognising that among the charity's supporters and beneficiaries there might be differing legitimate moral views on certain issues. See *Butler-Sloss v Charity Commission* [2022] EWHC 974 (Ch).
57   See, for example, *Kiger v Mollenkopf*, No 1-21-cv-00409 (D Del); *Falat v Sacks*, No 8:20-cv-01782 (CD Cal).
58   Corporate Sustainability Reporting Directive (CSRD) 2022/2464/EU. See, for discussion, Latham & Watkins, Client Alert: "The EU Corporate Sustainability Reporting Directive – How Companies Need to Prepare", 27 January 2023, www.lw.com/admin/upload/SiteAttachments/Alert%203059.pdf.
59   Sustainable Finance Disclosures Regulation (SFDR) 2020/852/EU [2020] OJ L198/13. See, for discussion, the chapter "ESG reporting".
60   See Directorate-General for Justice and Consumers, Proposal for a Directive on corporate sustainability due diligence, 23 February 2022, https://commission.europa.eu/publications/proposal-directive-corporate-sustainability-due-diligence-and-annex_en.

rights abuses or negative environmental impact and, for certain large companies, draft a plan to ensure their business strategy is in line with the goals of the Paris Agreement. While companies are not yet subject to these specific requirements, they will have significant impact when they come into force.

Similarly, the US Securities and Exchange Commission's (SEC) proposed Climate Risk Disclosure Risk Rule, for example, would compel disclosure of material 'climate-related risks'.[61] Under the proposed rule, an SEC registrant would be required to identify and describe any climate-related risks reasonably likely to have a material impact on the registrant's business or consolidated financial statements over the short, medium and long term.[62] As corporations are increasingly required to disclose their management of ESG risk, there will be more opportunities to contend that they have misrepresented such risks, which necessarily increases litigation risk stemming from such disclosures.

In parallel to these regulatory developments, there has been a significant increase in ESG-related enforcement by regulators in connection with corporate disclosures. For example, in the US, the SEC created the Climate and ESG Task Force within the Division of Enforcement to identify ESG-related misconduct under the existing legal framework.[63] The Task Force pursued its first enforcement action in 2022, charging Vale SA, a publicly traded Brazilian mining company, with securities fraud.[64] Specifically, the SEC alleged that Vale knew its Brumadinho dam, which collapsed in 2019 and killed 270 people, was unsafe before its collapse and made false disclosures about the safety of the dam to deceive authorities and investors.[65] Notably, the SEC complaint cited not only Vale's securities filings but also public statements and disclosures featured in Vale's sustainability reports, presentations and ESG webinars provided to investors.[66]

---

61   See The Enhancement and Standardization of Climate-Related Disclosures for Investors, 87 Fed Reg 21334 (11 April 2022) (to be codified at 7 CFR §210; 7 CFR §229; 7 CFR §232; 7 CF. §239; 7 CFR §249).

62   The SEC has not specified the year ranges for these proposed time periods. Instead, a registrant would be required to describe how it defines short, medium and long term, as well as how it takes into account or reassesses the expected useful life of its assets and the time horizons for its climate-related planning processes and goals. *Ibid*, at 21353–54. There will likely be challenges to the EPA's authority to promulgate the rule under, among other reasons, the major questions doctrine, especially considering the US Supreme Court's decision in *West Virginia v EPA*, 142 S Ct 2587 (2022) (see section 2 above).

63   See "SEC Announces Enforcement Task Force Focused on Climate and ESG Issues", Securities and Exchange Commission (4 March 2021), www.sec.gov/news/press-release/2021-42.

64   See *Sec & Exch Commission v Vale SA*, No 22-cv-2405 (EDNY 2022), www.sec.gov/litigation/complaints/2022/comp-pr2022-72.pdf.

65   *Ibid* at 52.

66   For example, *ibid*, at 10 ("Vale's public statements, including through SEC periodic filings on Forms 20-F and 6-K in 2017 and 2019, sustainability reports issued in 2017 and 2018, and a 2018 ESG webinar, touted the stability declarations and reassured investors that its dams were stable and safe. In its 2017 Sustainability Report issued in 2018, for example, Vale affirmed that '100% of the audited structures were certified to be in stable condition' with stability declarations issued 'by the responsible auditors', and that all of their dams 'are completely normal'"). Vale ultimately settled the SEC's claims in 2023 by agreeing to pay US$25 million in civil penalties and US$30.9 million in disgorgement and prejudgment interest, for a total of nearly US$56 million. See "Brazilian Mining Company to Pay $55.9 Million to Settle Charges Related to Misleading Disclosures Prior to Deadly Dam Collapse", Securities and Exchange Commission (29 March 2023), www.sec.gov/news/press-release/2023-63.

The SEC Climate and ESG Task Force has also pursued non-environmental ESG claims, demonstrating a willingness to investigate and charge alleged violations of all ESG elements. In early 2023, for example, the SEC announced a settled enforcement action involving Activision Blizzard, the maker of popular video games *Call of Duty*, *World of Warcraft* and *Candy Crush*, relating to allegations that it failed to maintain disclosure controls related to tracking workplace complaints regarding sexual harassment and discrimination.[67]

Shareholder derivative suits stemming from inadequate corporate disclosures have also increased in number in recent years. In *In re Danimer Scientific, Inc Securities Litigation*, for example, investors filed a class action suit against Danimer Scientific, Inc, a bioplastics company whose primary proprietary product was a plastic substitute called Nodax that the company alleged was 100% biodegradable.[68] The plaintiff investors alleged that Danimer misled them by claiming that its Nodax plastic replacement product was 100% biodegradable, renewable and sustainable, when in reality it does not fare better than fossil fuel-based plastics.[69] Similarly, in *Fagen v Enviva, Inc*, a putative class of plaintiffs alleged that Enviva misrepresented the environmental sustainability of its wood pellet production and procurement and misled investors by touting itself as a "growth-oriented" ESG company, when in reality Enviva is not profitable.[70] The plaintiffs in *Fagen* cite statements made on earnings calls where company directors discussed Enviva's commitment to sustainability and statements in the company's 10-K, including statements related to the company's Health, Safety, Sustainability and Environmental Committee.[71]

In the UK, similar claims have not been brought, although commentators have suggested that shareholders of UK companies may rely on Sections 90 and 90A of the Financial Services and Markets Act (FSMA) 2000 for loss they have suffered as a result of inaccurate statements published by the company in prospectuses (Section 90) or in other published information (Section 90A) with respect to their ESG-related risks. There are, however, a number of legal hurdles to such claims, such as the need to show recklessness or dishonesty on the part of directors or the requirement that the shareholder relied on the misleading statement or omission and suffered a financial loss as a result.

Litigants have also targeted regulators for failing to properly assess corporate disclosures. For example, a judicial review challenge has been filed against the Financial Conduct Authority (FCA) over its decision to approve the IPO

---

67   See Activision Blizzard, Inc, Exchange Act Release No 34-96796 (3 February 2023), www.sec.gov/litigation/admin/2023/34-96796.pdf.
68   *In re Danimer Scientific, Inc Securities Litigation*, No 1:21-cv-02708 (EDNY 2021).
69   *Ibid*, Compl, ECF No 1, at ¶ 6.
70   *Fagen v Enviva, Inc*, No 8:22-cv-02844-DKC (D Md 2022).
71   *Ibid*, Compl, ECF No 1, at ¶ 32.

prospectus of Ithaca Energy plc.[72] As part of its case, ClientEarth alleged that the prospectus failed to adequately describe the climate-related risks of the company's activities in certain oil and gas fields in the North Sea, which should have been required under the UK Prospectus Regulation. The High Court refused ClientEarth's application for judicial review, finding that it was not arguable that the prospectus failed to properly disclose the climate-related financial risks.

7. Marketing ESG litigation

With growing employee and customer engagement on all things ESG, companies are increasingly focused on green communications, whether in the form of marketing for a particular product or labelling the corporation in some 'green' manner, such as having a commitment to sustainability, waste reduction, recycling, or net zero or low-carbon initiatives. Litigation in this space historically targeted industries with reputations for being heavy polluters (notably the fossil fuel industry), but as more companies have taken to green marketing, more industries – from restaurants and fashion to airlines and banks – have been targeted by these so-called 'greenwashing' claims.[73]

Since marketing oftentimes transcends political boundaries, defendants can find themselves facing parallel proceedings from a variety, and multitude, of plaintiffs. Journalists and special interest groups frequently spur greenwashing litigation – especially involving specific product claims – by publishing exposés and reports that plaintiffs (and plaintiffs' attorneys) use as the bases for their claims.[74] In the US the primary plaintiffs are consumers, usually in the form of class actions,[75] and government entities, either the Federal Trade Commission (FTC) enforcing federal consumer protection laws,[76] or state Attorneys General enforcing the consumer protection laws of their respective states.[77]

---

72   *R (on the application of ClientEarth) v Financial Conduct Authority* [2023] EWHC 3301 (Admin).
73   See, for example, Zahra Hirji, "Report Suggests 'Rampant' Greenwashing in Food Sector", Bloomberg (20 March 2023), www.bloomberg.com/news/articles/2023-03-20/report-suggests-rampant-greenwashing-in-food-sector#xj4y7vzkg; "Companies Accused of Greenwashing", Truth in Advertising (updated 5 January 2024), https://truthinadvertising.org/articles/companies-accused-greenwashing/.
74   For example, two separate putative classes sued H&M, one in Missouri (*Lizama v H&M Hennes & Mauritz LP*, No 4:22-cv-01170 (ED Mo 2022)) and one in New York (*Commodore v H&M Hennes & Mauritz LP*, No 7:22-cv-06247 (SDNY 2022)) after a Quartz report indicated the environmental impact metrics on H&M's website may be incorrect.
75   See, for example, *Marshall v Red Lobster Mgmt LLC*, No 2:21-cv-04786 (CD Cal 2021) (alleging the company misled consumers when it marketed its seafood products as "Seafood with Standards" and "Traceable. Sustainable. Responsible." despite the seafood purportedly being sourced from suppliers that use environmentally destructive practices).
76   See, for example, *United States v Kohl's Inc*, No 1:22-cv-00964 (DDC 2022) (alleging that Kohl marketed products as bamboo, and accordingly, the products were environmentally friendly (tagging them with phrases like "Cleaner Solutions," and "MADE IN GREEN") despite being chemically reformulated to be rayon, a process which releases hazardous air pollutants).
77   See, for example, *Vermont v Exxon Mobil Corp*, No 2:21-cv-00260 (D Vt 2021) (alleging that several fossil fuel companies violated the Vermont Consumer Protection Act by failing to disclose the climate impact of their products to consumers).

Whether the plaintiff is the government or a consumer, in the US greenwashing claims are often premised as being unfair and deceptive business practices under federal and/or state law. The FTC's Guides for the Use of Environmental Marketing Claims (the 'Green Guides') play an outsized role in greenwashing claims in the US.[78] The Green Guides do not have the force of law under federal law, but rather are used to guide marketers, consumers and governments alike as to what may or may not constitute 'unfair and deceptive' marketing. However, several states have codified the Green Guides into state law, imbuing them with the force of law under their consumer protection acts and regulations.[79] Additionally, courts can look to the Green Guides as instructive, even if not binding.[80]

The Green Guides cover a wide span of 'green' marketing claims. Among other things, they instruct companies how to substantiate their 'green' claims,[81] what is needed for a product to earn the label 'recyclable',[82] and how to avoid deceiving consumers with third-party certifications.[83] Litigants invoke the Green Guides in their lawsuits, pointing to deviations from the Guides as evidence of deception and adherence to the Guides as evidence of honesty. For example, in a case filed in 2020 in the District of Massachusetts, the putative class of plaintiffs alleged the manufacturer improperly labelled its coffee pods as "recyclable" because the pod design, with their foil tops and tendency to get crushed, made it unlikely a facility would actually recycle them.[84] In finding that the allegations plausibly alleged the products were not 'recyclable' under the Green Guide definition, the court denied the company's motion to dismiss.[85]

As part of its decennial review of the Green Guides, the FTC is looking into updating both the scope of the Green Guides (potentially pursuing rulemaking to imbue them with the force of law) and the substance (giving guidance on use of the word 'sustainable' for the first time). These updates will have a significant impact on how companies position themselves and their products and will shed light on how the modern consumer interprets 'green' marketing. Finally, it is worth noting that greenwashing claims need not, and indeed do not always rely on the Green Guides to show marketing is unfair or deceptive. Litigants have challenged companies who use PFAS, or 'forever chemicals', in their products

---

78   16 CF §260.
79   Some states reference FTC regulations in general (eg, Illinois, Massachusetts and New York), while others explicitly incorporate the Green Guides in part (eg, Alabama, Indiana, Maryland and Michigan), or in whole (eg, Maine, Minnesota and Rhode Island). Some states both incorporate and impose restrictions beyond the Green Guides (eg, California).
80   See, for example, *Curtis v 7-Eleven, Inc*, No 21-cv-6079, 2022 WL 4182384, at *16 (ND Ill 2022).
81   16 CFR §260.3.
82   *Ibid*, at §260.12.
83   *Ibid*, at §260.6.
84   *Downing v Keurig Green Mountain, Inc*, No 1:20-cv-11673-IT (D Mass 2020).
85   *Ibid*.

and market themselves as sustainable, challenging the companies without referencing the Green Guides.[86]

The FTC's pending update to the Green Guides will also inform how companies report their use of voluntary carbon credits, providing much-needed clarity concerning the use of such credits to meet 'net zero' or 'carbon neutral' commitments.[87] Two recent cases illustrate some of the greenwashing risks associated with relying on carbon credits to meet advertised "net zero" targets. In 2023, plaintiffs in California filed a class action lawsuit against Delta Airlines, alleging that "foundational issues" in the voluntary carbon market mean that Delta cannot be "the world's first carbon neutral airline".[88] Significantly, the lawsuit reads as an indictment of the entire voluntary carbon market, rather than specifying particular carbon credits that fail to meet certain quality criteria. A similar claim was filed against Air France-KLM SA for violations of the Netherland's Unfair Commercial Practices directive, alleging that various communications parts of its "Fly Responsibly" campaign and its "CO2ZERO" programme, which allows a customer to offset or reduce their carbon impact online, mislead consumers into believing that flying is sustainable.[89]

These types of claims are not limited to airlines, and regulators now scrutinise companies from all industries to assess whether their net zero or low-carbon claims stack up. A good example of this is the series of claims brought in multiple European jurisdictions, claiming that the advertising of the 2022 World Cup in Qatar was "fully carbon-neutral", had misled consumers and that the carbon credits bought as an offset failed to meet market standards for offsetting.[90]

---

86   *Dickens v Thinx, Inc*, No 1:22-cv-04286 (SDNY 2022).
87   Both the UK and the EU are also developing and implementing further rules concerning the use of carbon credits and other carbon-based claims. The UK's Committee of Advertising Practices (CAP) and its broadcasting counterpart (BCAP) recently updated their guidance on carbon neutral and net zero claims in advertising. See "Updated Environment Guidance: Carbon Neutral and Net Zero Claims in Advertising", CAP News (10 February 2023), https://practicalesg.com/wp-content/uploads/2023/02/Updated-environment-guidance-carbon-neutral-and-net-zero-claims-in-advertising-ASA-CAP.pdf. The regulators have already applied these rules, barring a Repsol advert which stated "At Repsol, we are developing biofuels and synthetic fuels to achieve net zero emissions" because it did not provide enough details or qualifications to support the claim; ASA Ruling on Repsol SA, (7 June 2023), www.asa.org.uk/rulings/repsol-sa-a23-1185942-repsol-sa.html. The European Commission in March 2023 published a Proposal for a Directive on Green Claims that, among other things, require "climate-related claims that include the use of offsets … to be substantiated by methodologies that ensure the integrity and correct accounting of these offsets". European Commission, "Proposal for a Directive of The European Parliament and of the Council on substantiation and communication of explicit environmental claims (Green Claims Directive)", at p31. Additionally, the Council of the European Union has approved a Directive on Empowering Consumers for the Green Transition, which amends the EU's existing Unfair Commercial Practices Directive and the Consumer Rights Directive. The amendments to the Green Transition Directive prohibit claims "based on the offsetting of greenhouse gas emissions, where a product has a neutral, reduced or positive impact on the environment in terms of greenhouse gas emissions". *Ibid*.
88   *Berrin v Delta Air Lines, Inc*, No 2:34-cv-04150 (CD Cal 2023) (Compl ¶ 6).
89   *FossielVrij NL v Air France-KLM SA* (Amsterdam District Court, 2022).
90   *New Weather Institute v FIFA* (UK), *Notre Affaire à tous v FIFA* (France), *Carbon Market Watch v FIFA* (Belgium), *KlimaAllianz v FIFA* (Switzerland). The Swiss Fair Advertising Commission upheld all the complaints (which were joined into one proceeding).

More generally, regulators have now turned to the ever-growing number of complaints made about the way products are being marketed to customers as sustainable or eco-friendly. For example, the UK's Advertising Standards Authority (ASA), its independent marketing regulator, has increased its efforts in recent years to review environmental claims in advertising. Advertisements for a wide range of industries and products, from aviation, fashion and automotive, to washing liquid and oat milk, have been found by the ASA to be misleading and in breach of the UK's Code of Non-broadcast Advertising and Direct & Promotional Marketing ('CAP Code').[91] At the same time, the UK's Competition Markets Authority (CMA) has launched enforcement action against well-known fashion brands for failing to comply with the Green Claims Code, and announced it will also examine the accuracy of 'green' claims in the travel, transport and 'fast-moving consumer goods' sectors (particularly food and drink, cosmetics and household cleaning products).[92] This uptick in enforcement action has resulted in companies worldwide carefully reviewing how they advertise their green credentials, to ensure they are clear, substantiated and comply with national guidelines.

8. Soft law and other mechanisms

A discussion of ESG litigation would not be complete without mention of soft law forums, where an increasing number of ESG disputes are playing out. The non-judicial grievance mechanisms at National Contact Points (NCPs) established under the Organisation for Economic Cooperation and Development (OECD) now frequently handle cases dealing with allegations of greenwashing,[93] environmental harm caused by a company's operations or that of their supply chain,[94] or failures to conduct appropriate due diligence[95] or set adequate emissions targets.[96] Other mechanisms include voluntary reporting

---

91   The ASA released new guidelines for environmental claims in advertising, to assist companies in understanding how to communicate their green credentials and avoid complaints of misleading advertising. See ASA, "The environment: misleading claims and social responsibility in advertising" (6 June 2022), www.asa.org.uk/resource/advertising-guidance-misleading-environmental-claims-and-social-responsibility.html.

92   See Competition Markets Authority, Press release: "CMA to scrutinise 'green' claims in sales of household essentials" (26 January 2023), www.gov.uk/government/news/cma-to-scrutinise-green-claims-in-sales-of-household-essentials; Press release: "Greenwashing: CMA puts businesses on notice" (20 September 2021), www.gov.uk/government/news/greenwashing-cma-puts-businesses-on-notice; Press release: "ASOS, Boohoo and Asda investigated over fashion 'green' claims" (29 July 2022).

93   See ClientEarth v BP (UK NCP, 2020) (complaint concerning the marketing of BP's low-carbon energy activities; BP later withdrew the ad campaign and the UK NCP declined to accept the complaint). See also The Lifescape Project et al v Drax Group PLC (UK NCP, 2022) (complaint involving allegations of various misleading or inaccurate statements about the Group's carbon emissions).

94   See Focus et al v Ascent Resources plc (Slovenia NCP, 2019).

95   See AJTZP, RAID, PILC v Glencore UK Ltd (UK NCP, 2021) (complaint concerning alleged failure to conduct appropriate environmental and human rights due diligence in relation to wastewater leaks and an alleged oil spill in Chad).

96   See BankTrack, Greenpeace Nederland, Milieudefensie et al v ING Bank (Dutch NCP, 2017) (NGOs collectively filed a complaint against ING Bank for failure to set targets to reduce the GHG emissions of its financial products in line with the Paris Agreement).

under internationally recognised frameworks such as UN Guiding Principles on Business and Human Rights, which expose corporate actors to an increased risk of litigation when their disclosures do not align with practice.

Given that the soft law forums are often more accessible to plaintiffs, due to the decreased costs compared to litigation and the absence of the usual legal obstacles that may prevent the bringing of a court claim such as standing, it is expected that the number of these cases will only continue to rise in number. While bodies such as the NCP lack the enforcement mechanisms that courts have, with no power to order monetary fines or similar remedies, the risk of reputational harm has the potential to make these forums equally as effective.

9. Role of NGOs in ESG litigation

In conclusion, it would be remiss not to note how increasingly common it has become for NGOs to engage in strategic ESG litigation, with the NGO now the usual claimant in many recent cases. Most NGO claimants are typically driven by the objective of ultimately changing corporate behaviour or bringing public attention to certain ESG issues. Companies and sectors are targeted due to the nature of their business, their general reputation or for their 'green' marketing. It may also be the case that a particular respondent is targeted following a specific incident, such as an environmental disaster, which has received significant public attention.

Given this, cases brought by NGOs present their own unique challenges. Because NGOs are motivated by raising the profile of certain issues and altering public opinion, they typically seek declarations of wrongdoing or injunctive relief (as opposed to financial damages). NGOs are often backed by funding and receive specific input from backers or litigation funders, and may be less likely to settle. Indeed, the objective for most NGOs is less about receiving a favourable court decision; it is more about driving public debate and bringing attention to a particular ESG issue.

The authors would like to thank and acknowledge Stephanie Forrest, Brett Frazer, Danny Dvorak and Aleksandra Dulska, for their contributions to this chapter.

Africa

Edward Kempson
Chidi Onyeche
Kathleen Teo
David J Ziyambi
Latham & Watkins

1. Introduction

With a predicted population of 2.4 billion by 2050 and continuing economic development, the African continent is a region that will experience significant growth and change in the coming decades which presents both challenges and opportunities. A number of ESG issues are intrinsically linked to this development, including the impact of climate change, to which Africa is especially vulnerable, and the constantly evolving global environmental agenda with its associated economic challenges. Several African nations are beginning to embrace ESG as an important theme in their on-going development. This takes a variety of forms, including the introduction of sustainability-focused financial policies and the introduction of ESG disclosure frameworks in countries including South Africa, Namibia, Uganda and Egypt. In addition, all African nations, with the exception of Eritrea and Libya, have ratified the Paris Agreement and set net zero targets between 2030 and 2050 to achieve alignment with the United Nations Sustainable Development Goals (UNSDGs),[1] indicating a level of engagement with global sustainability initiatives.

The future of ESG in Africa will undoubtedly be important to the continent's macroeconomic development. This was underscored by the African Development Bank (AfDB) launching a pan-African framework to encourage the deployment of green finance across the continent in 2022.[2] Indeed, a notable area of development is in relation to ESG finance initiatives which this chapter will review in detail, given the range of initiatives and corresponding challenges the continent is facing.

2. An introduction to ESG finance in Africa

In data provided by Bloomberg, in 2022 there were US$1.2 trillion investments

---

1   Ben Smith, "ESG and Energy on the African Continent", Fenwick Elliott, *International Quarterly*, Issue 33, www.fenwickelliott.com/research-insight/newsletters/international-quarterly/esg-energy-africa.
2   African Development Bank, "African Development Bank launches model for deploying green financing across the continent", 29 November 2022, www.afdb.org/en/news-and-events/african-development-bank-launches-model-deploying-green-financing-across-continent-56903.

in energy transition products globally, as well as in ESG-related financing more generally, spanning renewable energy, electrification and low-carbon technologies.[3] Recently, it has been estimated that 1,000 climate technology companies will become unicorns (ie, companies with a valuation of more than US$1 billion), with investors pledging over US$120 trillion to align with the principles of ESG-related finance as investor appetite in the sector increases.[4] Additionally, many different forms of ESG-related finance have developed over time, including sustainable finance (the process of factoring ESG considerations into investment decision-making processes), green finance (the financing of projects that will have a positive impact on the environment) and climate finance (financing drawn from public sources to support climate change initiatives). For the purposes of this chapter, references to 'ESG finance' include sustainable finance, green finance, climate finance and financings that involve the use of financial products to develop ESG initiatives.

The African continent is no stranger to ESG finance. The continent is home to 60% of the world's solar resources and 39% of the world's renewable energy potential.[5] However, according to the AfDB, a multilateral development finance institution that provides financing to African governments and private companies investing in the continent, Africa requires approximately US$1.3 trillion to reach its UNSDGs by 2030.[6] Yet, the continent is far away from achieving its goals – current levels of foreign investment are low and the AfDB estimates that private investment must increase by 36% each year until 2030 for such goals to be met.[7] This can be attributed to the nascency of ESG finance in many African countries, a disconnect between the actual and perceived risk of investing in ESG-related initiatives and poor global macroeconomic conditions since 2022.[8]

Additionally, market participants have focused on three main challenges with raising ESG finance. First, while certain countries in Africa have successfully established ESG finance regulation and taxonomies (as we will explore further in this chapter), there is no standardised regulatory framework across the continent. Accordingly, to fill any perceived gaps, European and American regulatory frameworks and taxonomies are increasingly being applied to African borrowers and issuers, without appropriate adaptation to the

3   Nathaniel Bullard, "Clean Energy Sets $1.1 Trillion Record That's Bound to Be Broken", Bloomberg, 26 January 2023, www.bloomberg.com/news/articles/2023-01-26/clean-energy-fossil-fuel-investment-tied-for-first-time-in-2022?leadSource=uverify%20wall.
4   Matt Hattam, "Climate unicorns: the myth becoming a reality", *Illuminem*, 22 June 2023, https://illuminem.com/illuminemvoices/climate-unicorns-the-myth-becoming-a-reality.
5   IEA, "Africa Energy Outlook 2022", www.iea.org/reports/africa-energy-outlook-2022/key-findings.
6   AFDB, "Private Sector Financing for Climate Action and Green Growth in Africa", 2023, www.afdb.org/sites/default/files/aeo_2023-chap2-en.pdf.
7   *Ibid.*
8   Burges Salmon LLP, "Sustainable Finance: a spotlight on Africa", 11 October 2023, www.lexology.com/library/detail.aspx?g=15e77216-0d6e-482d-8951-d465680e98f1.

idiosyncrasies of the African continent. As a result, both African companies and potential investors are required to keep abreast of rapidly changing and evolving regulation in multiple jurisdictions, creating a lack of clarity and an uncertain investing landscape, particularly where the application of such regulation or taxonomies are not nuanced or localised for the African borrower or issuer. Secondly, the pace of change is slower than is needed for most African countries to meet their 2030 and 2050 UNSDGs. At least 71% of companies in the world are not aligned with a transition pathway or net zero targets and are not allocating capital for this purpose at the right pace. Lastly, investors are still working with inadequate data for both emerging markets and private markets, making it harder for investors to commit to long-term investments in this space.

Despite this challenging landscape and context, African countries have recognised the need for ESG finance. Although the continent has contributed the least to global greenhouse gas emissions, it bears the brunt of its effects, as rising global temperatures have caused devastating floods, prolonged drought and forest fires.[9] Additionally, a recent study by McKinsey & Company estimates that rapid urbanisation and widespread population growth mean that Africa's energy demand could double by 2050.[10] Over the course of 2023, various institutions in South Africa, Nigeria, Kenya, Egypt and Rwanda have introduced novel ESG-related financial products and policies to secure long-term ESG finance. This chapter explores key developments in ESG finance in these countries, and how such developments will contribute to these countries reaching their UNSDGs and ESG goals.

3. South Africa

As the largest carbon emitter in Africa and the 11th highest polluter in the world,[11] South Africa is in need of ESG finance to fund renewable power projects and infrastructure to transport clean energy. The 'Big Four' banks in South Africa – Absa Bank, FirstRand Bank, Nedbank and Standard Bank – have actively developed their ESG finance businesses in 2023. ESG finance now comprises 8% of all of the Big Four Banks' loans in H1 2023 alone, which is a significant increase from 4% in FY 2022.[12] In particular, Nedbank financed a significant

---

9   "Africa Climate Summit: Nairobi Declaration makes strong push for accelerated climate action and financing mechanisms", United Nations *Africa Renewal*, 8 September 2023, www.un.org/africarenewal/ magazine/september-2023/africa-climate-summit-nairobi-declaration-makes-strong-push-accelerated.

10   César Augier, Hauke Engel, François Jurd de Girancourt and Oliver Onyekweli, "Green energy in Africa presents significant investment opportunities", McKinsey Sustainability, 17 October 2023, www.mckinsey.com/capabilities/sustainability/our-insights/green-energy-in-africa-presents-significant-investment-opportunities.

11   Promit Mukherjee, "Exclusive: South Africa to miss 2030 emissions goal as it keeps coal plants burning", Reuters, 9 November 2023, www.reuters.com/sustainability/south-africa-miss-2030-emissions-goal-it-keeps-coal-plants-burning-2023-11-09/.

12   UBS, "South African Banks: ESG Company Radars", 25 October 2023, (Figure 36: Sustainable finance provided to date and targets (Rbn)).

number of renewable projects, totalling US$7.2 billion and equating to 15% of its loan book.[13] Nedbank also raised US$112 million to invest in local renewable energy projects across South Africa.[14]

South African companies have also proven to be active in ESG finance. The country now dominates the green, social, sustainability and sustainability-linked (GSS+) bond market, and 58% of issuances in the African GSS+ bond market are made by borrowers and/or issuers based in South Africa.[15] Additionally, the South African government announced plans to enter the ESG bond market with an extremely rare sovereign sustainability-linked bond in 2024, which would make it the third sovereign to issue an instrument linked to key performance indicators (KPIs) following Chile and Uruguay.[16] Investors can expect information on the KPIs to be released in Q1 2024.[17]

The uptake in ESG finance in South Africa is also complemented by initiatives to facilitate South Africa's "just energy transition" – focusing on an energy transition which not only has a positive environmental impact, but also ensures a positive impact on society, social groups and communities – and to reduce its reliance on coal.[18] In November 2023, the South African cabinet approved the Just Energy Transition Implementation Plan (JET-IP). The JET-IP, worth US$713 million, outlines South Africa's plan to decarbonise the economy from 2023 to 2027, and in particular the development of new energy vehicles, clean electricity and the green hydrogen industry.[19] Additionally, in 2023, Denmark and the Netherlands agreed to join the International Partners Group (IPG) already consisting of the United States, the United Kingdom, Germany, France and other European Union countries, to help South Africa's "just energy transition".[20] Consequently, the level of commitment the IPG has pledged over the next three to five years has increased from US$8.5 billion to US$9.3 billion.[21]

Despite these efforts, officials are concerned that South Africa may not be able to meet its 2030 greenhouse gas emission targets, and that the "just energy transition" will still have a negative social impact. The South African

13   *Ibid.*
14   UBS, "South African Banks: ESG Company Radars" 25 October 2023, (Figure 15: Key ESG Factors Analysis).
15   Jack Grogan-Fenn, "Africa's GSS+ Bond Market Ripe for Growth", ESG Investor, 13 March 2023, www.esginvestor.net/africas-gss-bond-market-ripe-for-growth/.
16   Julian Lewis, "South Africa set to lift sovereign SLBs", IFR, 4 November 2023, www.ifre.com/story/4213314/south-africa-set-to-lift-sovereign-slbs-lnwp6j1cth.
17   *Ibid.*
18   UNDP, "What is a just transition? And why is it important?', 3 November 2022, https://climatepromise.undp.org/news-and-stories/what-just-transition-and-why-it-important.
19   Lameez Omarjee, "COP28: Ramaphosa invites more countries to back SA's Just Energy Transition", News 24, 3 December 2023, www.news24.com/fin24/climate_future/cop28-ramaphosa-invites-more-countries-to-back-sas-just-energy-transition-20231203#:~:text=The%20implementation%20plan%20builds%20on,hydrogen%20and%20new%20energy%20vehicles.
20   British High Commission Pretoria and British Consulate-General Cape Town, "South Africa's Just Energy Transition is progressing", UK Government, 30 November 2023, www.gov.uk/government/news/south-africas-just-energy-transition-is-progressing.
21   *Ibid.*

government had pledged to cut emissions to between 350 and 420 million tonnes by 2030 to comply with its obligations under the Paris Agreement, but officials have suggested that this is unlikely to be achieved.[22] The country had planned to decommission eight coal-fired power plants to meet targets, but those plans were impacted by bureaucratic delays and insufficient developments in renewable projects.[23] Moreover, there is significant trade union resistance to the implementation of the JET-IP, because the "just energy transition" would result in widespread job losses for those working in the coal industry.[24] The National Union of Mineworkers in South Africa has requested additional consultations on the JET-IP, claiming that the decommissioning of coal-fired power plants will put 51,000 jobs at risk.[25] However, it is hoped that various initiatives will facilitate the transition without harming the livelihoods of those working in the coal industry. For example, the IPG has committed a large portion of its funds to: (i) the training and upskilling of people living in the Mpumalanga province, where 85% of South Africa's coal-related jobs are located; and (ii) research on the impact of the JET-IP on vulnerable communities.[26]

In addition to its energy transition and carbon reduction goals, South Africa also faces a greater issue regarding sufficient energy production for energy demand. Current levels of energy production do not meet energy demands in the country and, consequently, South Africa's coal plants are being overworked. However, these plants are ageing, and efforts have not been taken to improve their efficiency, causing a progressive increase in load shedding since 2022.[27]

Nonetheless, in 2023, the South African Department of Trade, Industry and Competition launched an energy one-stop shop (EOSS) to speed up approval processes for the development of all energy projects. The EOSS will be implemented in four phases and, as of 2023, the first of four phases has been completed.[28] The second phase is expected to be completed by 2025 and will involve making the EOSS operational at both a provincial and municipal level.[29]

---

22 Promit Mukherjee, "Exclusive: South Africa to miss 2030 emissions goal as it keeps coal plants burning", Reuters, 9 November 2023, www.reuters.com/sustainability/south-africa-miss-2030-emissions-goal-it-keeps-coal-plants-burning-2023-11-09/.
23 *Ibid.*
24 Mandisa Nyathi, "Unions unhappy as cabinet gives nod to energy transition plan", *Mail & Guardian*, 28 November 2023, https://mg.co.za/the-green-guardian/2023-11-28-unions-unhappy-as-cabinet-gives-nod-to-energy-transition-plan/.
25 *Ibid.*
26 British High Commission Pretoria and British Consulate-General Cape Town, "South Africa's Just Energy Transition is progressing", UK Government, 30 November 2023, www.gov.uk/government/news/south-africas-just-energy-transition-is-progressing.
27 Promit Mukherjee, "Exclusive: South African utility Eskom pollutes more in bid to keep lights on", Reuters, 27 September 2023, www.reuters.com/business/energy/south-african-utility-eskom-pollutes-more-bid-keep-lights-2023-09-27/#:~:text=Africa%27s%20most%20developed%20economy%20is,for%20the%20past%2018%20months.
28 Emma Roberts, Jurg van Dyk, "South Africa's energy 'one-stop shop' to tackle its energy crisis", *Out-Law*, Pinsent Masons, 15 August 2023, www.pinsentmasons.com/out-law/analysis/south-africa-s-energy-one-stop-shop-to-tackle-its-energy-crisis.
29 *Ibid.*

Additionally, South Africa recently introduced its own Green Finance Taxonomy designed to provide a common framework on sustainable economic activities in South Africa,[30] and simultaneously providing investors with greater clarity and certainty in selecting ESG-related investments in line with international and local practices in South Africa.

4. Nigeria

Nigeria's ESG regulatory framework is generally more advanced than the frameworks in most African nations. According to the Nigerian Code of Corporate Governance 2018 and the Nigerian Stock Exchange Sustainability Disclosure Guidelines 2019, companies must report ESG-related issues that are material and relevant to their businesses and disclose how those issues are to be managed.[31] The Nigerian Companies Act 2020 was also introduced to ensure that the scope of a director's duty to act in the best interests of the company includes consideration of the impact of the company's operations on the environment.[32]

Additionally, Nigeria has tapped into the ESG-related financing market on numerous occasions. In 2017, Nigeria issued its first ever five-year sovereign green bond for over US$26 million and, subsequently, a second tranche of a seven-year bond for US$44 million, which was heavily oversubscribed.[33] The year 2023 saw widespread investment in financial products that have had positive environmental and social impact in Nigeria. For instance, it has been reported that 7% of issuances in the African GSS+ bond market came from Nigerian companies.[34] Additionally, BURN Manufacturing, a world-leading Kenyan manufacturer and distributer of cookstoves, is issuing a landmark US$10 million green bond to support clean cooking.[35] The proceeds will be used to open a new plant in Lagos, Nigeria, which will increase production by 200,000 units per month and cover life-saving biomass, electric and liquefied petroleum gas stoves.[36]

Nigeria's banking sector has also witnessed the introduction of various facilities to encourage ESG finance. Wema Bank, a commercial bank in Nigeria, launched the "Green Energy Finance Facility" to enable small and medium-

---

30 Paula-Ann Novotny, "South Africa launches green taxonomy", Linklaters, 11 May 2022, https://sustainablefutures.linklaters.com/post/102hm4p/south-africa-launches-green-taxonomy.

31 Ben Smith, "ESG and Energy on the African Continent", Fenwick Elliott, *International Quarterly*, Issue 33, www.fenwickelliott.com/research-insight/newsletters/international-quarterly/esg-energy-africa.

32 *Ibid.*

33 Banwo & Ighodalo, "Spotlight: Sustainable finance instruments in Nigeria", *Lexology*, 6 January 2023, www.lexology.com/library/detail.aspx?g=91192d9c-a921-43f9-a2d1-e70c859b3e0a#:~:text=The%20first%20series%20of%20the,(approximately%20US%2444%20million).

34 Jack Grogan-Fenn, "Africa's GSS+ Bond Market Ripe for Growth", *ESG Investor*, 13 March 2023, www.esginvestor.net/africas-gss-bond-market-ripe-for-growth/.

35 Lolade Akinmurele, "World's Largest Cookstove Manufacturer To Open Nigerian Plant After Record Green Bond", *Business Day*, 27 October 2023, https://businessday.ng/business-economy/article/worlds-largest-cookstove-manufacturer-to-open-nigerian-plant-after-record-green-bond/.

36 *Ibid.*

sized enterprises and individuals to access up to US$12,412 to purchase renewable energy sources to power their businesses.[37] These sources include solar panels, inverters, batteries and more.[38] Other facilities have also been introduced by overseas financiers. In August 2023, FSD Africa Investments, the investing arm of FSD Africa (a specialist development agency funded by UK aid from the UK Government),[39] partnered with InfraCredit, a provider of local currency guarantees for debt instruments used to finance infrastructure assets in Nigeria,[40] to invest £10 million into the development of its Risk Sharing Backstop Facility (RSBF).[41] The RSBF is the first-of-its-kind and seeks to increase the accessibility of finance for climate-related infrastructure projects and incentivise investment from local institutions using bonds.[42]

There have also been notable developments in Nigeria's development of a carbon market. Nigeria, in recent months, has looked to establish and scale its carbon market with an aim of shortly introducing a carbon tax policy.[43] The tax policy is not a direct mechanism to cut emissions, but it will, at the very least, raise revenues for the Nigerian Government to invest in other sustainable initiatives and encourage businesses to reduce their carbon emissions. In April 2023, the Nigerian Sovereign Investment Authority signed an agreement with Vitol, an oil and commodities trader based in Switzerland, to invest in US$50 million worth of carbon credit projects in Nigeria, and set up a joint venture that will invest in projects involving carbon avoidance and removal.[44]

5.　　Kenya

Kenya also has a comprehensive ESG regulatory framework and stands out for its commitment to produce clean energy from renewable energy sources. According to the Kenya Investment Authority, as of 2022, 86.98% of the country's electricity is generated from renewable sources.[45] It is the eighth largest global geothermal power user and, after ongoing projects have been completed, it will be the fourth-highest user of geothermal power, following the US, Indonesia and

---

37   *Ibid.*
38   WEMA Bank, "Other SME Loans", https://wemabank.com/smes/sme-loans/otherloans/.
39   FSD Africa, "FSD Africa Investments commits £8m to finance a new class of asset allocators in Africa", 9 June 2022, https://fsdafrica.org/press-release/fsd-africa-investments-commits-8m-to-finance-a-new-class-of-asset-allocators-in-africa/.
40   InfraCredit, "About Us", https://infracredit.ng/about-us/.
41   Foreign, Commonwealth & Development Office and The Rt Hon James Cleverly MP, "FSD Africa invests £10m in Nigeria's climate infrastructure", UK Government, 2 August 2023, www.gov.uk/government/news/fsd-africa-invests-10m-in-nigerias-climate-infrastructure#:~:text=The%20Risk%20Sharing%20Backstop%20Facility,field%20climate%2Daligned%20infrastructure%20projects.
42   *Ibid.*
43   Eklavya Gupte, "Nigeria sets sights on developing carbon markets, government working on carbon tax", S&P Global, 5 April 2023, www.spglobal.com/commodityinsights/en/market-insights/latest-news/electric-power/040523-nigeria-sets-sights-on-developing-carbon-markets-government-working-on-carbon-tax.
44   *Ibid.*
45   Sylvia Mwago, "Kenya's Renewable Power Generation Hits 86pct Of Total Output", KenInvest, 11 January 2023, www.invest.go.ke/kenyas-renewable-power-generation-hits-86pct-total-output/.

the Philippines.[46] In the solar energy scene, as of 2023, the Kenyan Government has received expressions of interest for investments in 35 solar projects and there are more than six projects under construction.[47] Additionally, GivePower – a solar-powered desalination plant – received a three-year commitment worth US$3 million from American technology firm ServiceNow to provide its water technology to four counties in Kenya.[48]

Additionally, Kenya's financial markets have seen a number of ESG finance instruments in 2023. Safaricom, Kenya's largest telecommunications provider, secured a first-of-its-kind US$137 million sustainability-linked loan deal in September 2023.[49] Safaricom will use the proceeds to reduce its carbon emissions, monitor social equality and track diversity and inclusion.[50] It is hoped that this will serve as a catalyst for more ESG finance in Kenya from the private sector. There has also been notable activity in social and governance financing. In February 2023, Absa Bank's Kenyan branch and Acorn Holdings Limited, the largest institutional rental housing developer in East Africa, concluded a US$43.9 million financing agreement to develop student accommodation in Nairobi, and add 12,000 beds to the Acorn Student Accommodation over three years.[51] The purpose of the agreement is to reduce Kenya's housing deficit and provide decent and affordable housing.[52]

6. Egypt

Egypt is arguably at the centre of cutting-edge ESG finance in Africa as of 2023. It became the first African country to issue sustainable Panda bonds on the Chinese financial markets worth US$478 million.[53] Panda bonds are renminbi-denominated bonds sold by a non-Chinese issuer within mainland China, and provide foreign issuers (ie, Egypt, in this case) the opportunity to receive financing from Chinese investors without exposure to foreign exchange risks.[54] AfDB and the Asian Infrastructure Investment Bank have provided credit

46   Gavin Maguire, "Kenya steps up as global geothermal powerhouse", Reuters, 5 October 2023, www.reuters.com/markets/commodities/kenya-steps-up-global-geothermal-powerhouse-2023-10-05/#:~:text=In%20Kenya%2C%20the%20Great%20Rift,access%20to%20subterranean%20heat%20pockets.
47   EPRA, "Solar Energy", https://renewableenergy.go.ke/technologies/solar-energy/#:~:text=The%20estimated%20solar%20potential%20in,Solar%20with%2055MW%20installed%20capacity.
48   Edna Mwenda, "Solar-powered desalination firm to get Sh410m funding", *Business Daily Africa*, 11 May 2023, www.businessdailyafrica.com/bd/corporate/companies/solar-powered-desalination-firm-to-get-sh410m-funding—4229954.
49   Manny Pham, "Safaricom secures ESG-linked $137m loan", Developing Telecoms, 5 September 2023, https://developingtelecoms.com/telecom-business/operator-news/15445-safaricom-secures-esg-linked-137m-loan.html.
50   *Ibid.*
51   Absa Bank, "Acorn, Absa Announce KES 6.7 Billion Financing Deal For Students' Affordable Housing", 8 February 2023, www.absabank.co.ke/media-centre/press-releases/absa-africa-financial-markets-index1/.
52   *Ibid.*
53   *Arab News*, "Egypt sells region's first yuan-denominated 'panda bonds' in $479m issue", 17 October 2023, www.arabnews.com/node/2392786/business-economy.
54   Lee Irvine, "Explaining Panda Bonds: it's black and white", Simmons & Simmons, 22 February 2021, www.simmons-simmons.com/en/publications/cklgnc85j1bwy0917it92jhmd/explaining-panda-bonds-it-s-black-and-white.

guarantees, increasing the attractiveness and competitiveness of the bonds.[55] Egypt will use the bond proceeds to achieve its Sovereign Sustainable Financing Framework, which aims to support sustainable development, as well as investments into Egypt's renewable power generation, water and waste management, health services and financing for small-to-medium enterprises. This issuance also paves the way for African countries to access China's fast-growing debt capital market, and provides an alternative way for foreign and Chinese investors to invest in African countries.

The Central Bank of Egypt (CBE) has also established a regulatory framework with the goal of ensuring long-term ESG finance. As of April 2023, all banks must establish an independent department for sustainability and sustainable finance, and incorporate sustainable finance policies into credit and investment policies.[56] Additionally, from 2024 onwards, all banks are required to prepare an annual sustainability report each year.[57] The report must document the banks' activities related to sustainability and their efforts to achieve their sustainability goals.[58] The CBE has also confirmed that green banks will be licensed as banks operating under Egypt's Central Bank Law,[59] defining 'green banks' as banks that provide low-cost financing specifically for renewable energy projects and other initiatives to improve the quality of the environment. This gives investors and lenders the regulatory certainty required to engage in ESG finance in Europe.

The Egyptian Government also announced, in August 2023, that investors will be permitted to invest in green hydrogen projects (the process of creating fuel from the electrolysis of water where such electrolysis is powered by renewable energy sources (ie, solar, wind and geothermal energy)) in Egypt. Consequently, more than 20 memoranda of understanding have been signed between Egypt and major companies.[60] Egypt plans to designate an area around the Suez Canal as a free-trade zone for the export of green hydrogen and its derivatives to Europe.[61] It is understood that this is the driver for the large-scale investment into Egypt's green hydrogen industry. As such, Egypt is well positioned to be a global leader in the production and exporter of green

55   *Arab News*, "Egypt sells region's first yuan-denominated 'panda bonds' in $479m issue", 17 October 2023, www.arabnews.com/node/2392786/business-economy.

56   Enterprise, "CBE issues binding regulations for sustainable finance for banks", 6 November 2022, https://enterprise.press/stories/2022/11/06/cbe-issues-binding-regulations-for-sustainable-finance-for-banks-86194/.

57   SBF Network, "Central Bank of Egypt's Sustainable Finance Binding Regulations", November 2022, www.sbfnetwork.org/wp-content/assets/policy-library/688_Sustainable_Finance_Binding_Regulations_Egypt.pdf.

58   *Ibid.*

59   Hossam Mounir, "CBE opens door for establishment of green banks in Egypt", *Daily News Egypt,* 4 September 2023, www.dailynewsegypt.com/2023/09/03/cbe-opens-door-for-establishment-of-green-banks-in-egypt/.

60   Rachel Parkes, "Egypt has an $83bn pipeline of green hydrogen projects that could produce millions of tonnes of green ammonia", *Hydrogen Insight*, 3 August 2023, www.hydrogeninsight.com/production/egypt-has-an-83bn-pipeline-of-green-hydrogen-projects-that-could-produce-millions-of-tonnes-of-green-ammonia/2-1-1495879.

61   *Ibid.*

hydrogen. Although it is unclear if all of Egypt's planned projects will come to fruition, the hope is that Egypt will continue to be a pioneer in the development of green hydrogen projects in the Global South and globally.

7.   Rwanda

The Rwandan government has been committed to low-carbon growth for more than a decade and Rwanda was selected as an initial launch location for Africa's carbon market because of political support from the government, its environmental protection policies, their quality of trees and special measures to protect forests.[62] Moreover, Rwanda is considering offsetting carbon credits on blockchains instead of traditional methods such as paper documentation, which would make the credits more accessible to investors globally.[63] Although details of the framework remain to be seen, investors and government in Rwanda alike are aware of the urgency of funding sustainable and green projects through ESG finance.[64]

Additionally, in 2023, the Development Bank of Rwanda (BRD), a leading provider of long-term investment loans for projects in Rwanda, launched its very first seven-year sustainability-linked bond targeting US$25 million.[65] The offer is also part of a US$124 million Medium Term Note Programme, making BRD the world's first national development bank globally and in East Africa to issue a sustainability-linked bond.[66] The KPIs linked to this bond focus on a wide range of social initiatives, such as financing businesses led by women and affordable housing.[67] It is hoped that the bond will also encourage private sector investment in ESG finance.[68]

Rwanda has also seen efforts to develop and diversify its renewable energy capabilities in 2023. Arc Power, a UK-based electricity access provider, has secured a US$10 million financing to continue installing off-grid solar panels in rural communities in Rwanda.[69] The financing will be provided by Triodos Investment Management, a Dutch-incorporated subsidiary of Triodos Bank which has offered sustainable investment funds for over 25 years,[70] as well as

---

62   Climate Analytics, NewClimate Institute, "Climate Action Tracker Climate Governance – An assessment of the government's ability and readiness to transform Rwanda into a zero emissions society", August 2022, https://climateactiontracker.org/documents/1066/2022_08_CAT_Governance_Report_ Rwanda.pdf.
63   Michel Nkurunziza, "Rwanda: Carbon Market – A Look At Rwanda's Probable Prices", All Africa, 9 October 2023, https://allafrica.com/stories/202310090042.html#:~:text=Rwanda%27s%20minister %20for%20environment%20recently,to%20achieve%20global%20emission%20targets.
64   Ibid.
65   The World Bank, "Rwanda Development Bank Launches First Sustainability-Linked Bond to Promote Inclusive Sustainable Development", September 2023, www.worldbank.org/en/news/press-release/2023/ 09/29/rwanda-afe-development-bank-launches-first-sustainability-linked-bond-to-promote-inclusive-sustainable-development.
66   Ibid.
67   Ibid.
68   Ibid.
69   Philbert Girinema, George Obuluts, "Rwanda signs agreement to build test nuclear power reactor", Reuters, 12 September 2023, www.reuters.com/business/energy/rwanda-signs-agreement-build-test-nuclear-power-reactor-2023-09-12/.
70   Triodos Investment Management, "About Us", www.triodos-im.com/about-us.

Oikocredit, a global social impact investor and one of the world's largest sources of private financiers of microfinance for low-income earners and countries.[71] In September 2023, the Rwandan Government also signed an agreement with Dual Fluid Energy Inc – a Canadian-German company specialising in nuclear reactors – to build a test nuclear power reactor.[72] If the testing is successful and a nuclear power plant is successfully built, Rwanda will be the second country in the continent to have an operational nuclear power plant, thereby encouraging the production and usage of nuclear power in the region.[73]

However, it should be noted that Rwanda's regulatory framework is not as comprehensive as the frameworks in other African nations. The National Bank of Rwanda, Rwanda's sole regulator and supervisor of Rwanda's financial sector, currently has no regulation on climate-related risks and there are currently no standards, nor a taxonomy related to ESG finance.[74] It is clear that, despite the encouraging developments noted above, there are more opportunities for development in ESG finance in Rwanda.

8.   Conclusion

Overall, significant developments have been made in the ESG space in Africa in 2023, particularly in ESG finance. The regulatory framework for ESG finance has also seen widespread change and it is clear that a number of nations in Africa have taken steps towards building a carbon-neutral future. However, the regulatory framework is yet to be standardised across the continent, which makes it difficult for investors to assess risks and commit to long-term investment. As such, while there is some private investment activity on the continent, there is inadequate investment for the continent to achieve its UNSDGs. Additionally, while most ESG finance activity on the continent is focused on producing positive environmental impact, there appear to be relatively fewer initiatives encouraging social and governance impact, with such initiatives being driven primarily by non-government players. Nonetheless, it is clear that African nations such as South Africa, Nigeria, Kenya, Egypt and Rwanda are committed to achieving a sustainable future through different forms of ESG finance. However, more effort is needed to standardise the regulatory framework applicable to African borrowers and issuers in order to increase the pace of the energy transition and establish reliable data sets to encourage the investment needed to reach the continent's goals and UNSDGs by 2030.

---

71   Oikocredit, "About Us", www.oikocredit.coop/en/about-us.
72   Philbert Girinema, George Obuluts, "Rwanda signs agreement to build test nuclear power reactor", Reuters, 12 September 2023, www.reuters.com/business/energy/rwanda-signs-agreement-build-test-nuclear-power-reactor-2023-09-12/.
73   Ibid.
74   United Nations, "Climate risk regulation in Africa's financial sector and related private sector initiatives", November 2021, https://gca.org/wp-content/uploads/2022/06/climate_risk_regulation_in_africas_financial_sector_and_related_private_sector_initiatives_report.pdf.

Asia

Farhana Sharmeen
Latham & Watkins

1. Introduction

Today, ESG needs no introduction, and it is here to stay. In Asia in particular, while ESG has gained significant momentum, it is still in a developing stage.

The year 2023 was a headline year for Asia, with regulators around the region pushing through frameworks and collaborative efforts with stakeholders. However, the road ahead is long – while countries are actively moving towards a sustainable investment landscape, the turning point has not yet arrived in establishing a fully integrated global roadmap.

In this chapter, we highlight the ESG initiatives in Asia, looking at the regulatory framework to date, the rise of greenwashing and future expected trends.

2. The regulatory framework

In developing the ESG guidance in Asia, it is the authorities across Asia who are playing a leading role in developing and fine-tuning ESG reporting requirements and standards. Hong Kong's Securities and Futures Commission (SFC) in January 2022 introduced enhanced disclosure requirements for ESG funds, while the Monetary Authority of Singapore (MAS) is moving towards a more detailed and prescriptive approach to ESG issues, including issuing guidelines for portfolio construction and risk management. Furthermore, exchanges in Hong Kong, Malaysia, Thailand, Indonesia, Japan, India and Vietnam have made ESG reporting a listing rule for listed companies.[1]

2.1 Overview of Asia's regulatory initiatives

The Association of Southeast Asian Nations (ASEAN) has also set up the ASEAN Taxonomy of Sustainable Finance to promote the adoption of green finance and encourage sustainable development.

In Thailand, the Securities and Exchange Commission (SEC) has mandated sustainability reporting in annual public filings for listed companies which are

---

1   In India, this applies to certain companies listed on the National Stock Exchange and the Bombay Stock Exchange.

binding. Key areas of coverage include identifying and clarifying factors that may cause material risks in the business, operation and financial condition and operating results or going concern of a company and its group, including risks in environmental and social areas, for example, bio-hygiene risks, safety issues, disputes with communities, corruption and environmental risks. The Stock Exchange of Thailand (SET) has also established non-binding sustainability-themed indices (the SETTHSI index) whereby the SET annually announces a list of companies on the SET with outstanding sustainability performance. In August 2021, the Working Group on Sustainable Finance in Thailand (which consists of the Fiscal Policy Office, the Bank of Thailand, the SEC, the SET and the Office of Insurance Commission) jointly published the Sustainable Finance Initiatives for Thailand to set the direction and framework for driving sustainable finance across the financial sector. Initiatives proposed include: (i) developing a practical taxonomy; (ii) improving data collection and disclosures which meet international standards; (iii) implementing effective incentives to encourage creation of sustainable financial products; (iv) the creation of demand-led products which follow the real underlying demand for sustainable products and services; and (v) building trained human capital in sustainability.

In Hong Kong, in addition to the binding ESG reporting obligations on listed companies which have been in effect since July 2020, the Hong Kong Exchanges and Clearing Limited (HKEx) published a guide to net zero for business[2] to introduce practical steps for businesses to develop a net zero pathway in line with Hong Kong's national targets and global commitments. While the measures are not mandatory, they encourage companies to follow essential steps to calculate and establish a carbon emissions baseline, setting short- and long-term carbon emission reduction targets. HKEx has also introduced a new equities section on Sustainable and Green Exchange displaying the ESG metrics of Hong Kong listed companies published by leading ESG data providers which provide a consolidated view of ESG ratings from different providers enabling a comparison basis of companies across sectors and sources to better inform investors. The SFC's Green and Sustainable Finance Cross-Agency Steering Group announced its ambition[3] to have mandatory climate-related disclosure requirements aligned with the Task Force on Climate-Related Financial Disclosures (TCFD) framework by 2025 across all relevant sectors for financial investors, although no further details have been released. Similar to the MAS in Singapore although binding in Hong Kong, the SFC made

---

2   HKEx, "Practical Net-Zero Guide for Businesses", www.hkex.com.hk/-/media/HKEX_Common/Market/Stage/Resources-Library/Guidance-Materials/HKEX-Net-Zero-Guide_E.pdf.
3   Press Release, HKMA, "Cross-Agency Steering Group Launches its Strategic Plan to Strengthen Hong Kong's Financial Ecosystem to Support a Greener and More Sustainable Future", 17 December 2020, www.hkma.gov.hk/eng/news-and-media/press-releases/2020/12/20201217-4/.

amendments to the Fund Manager Code of Conduct in August 2021 introducing obligations to take a climate-related risks into consideration in their investment and risk management processes and make appropriate disclosures. The expected standards are set out in the SFC's circular dated 20 August 2021.[4] The Hong Kong Monetary Authority issued a module[5] in its Supervisory Policy Manual requiring banks to implement certain requirements by 30 December 2022 including establishing governance frameworks for climate risk management regularly assessing vulnerability under different climate scenarios, aligning climate disclosures with TCFD recommendations to name a few.

In Singapore, the Accounting and Corporate Regulatory Authority (ACRA) and Singapore Exchange Regulation (SGX RegCo) have also launched a public consultation in July 2023 on the recommendations by the Sustainability Reporting Advisory Committee (SRAC) that certain companies should report International Sustainability Standards Board (ISSB)-aligned climate-related disclosures. In particular, the SRAC recommendations require issuers of equity securities listed on Singapore Exchange ('Listed Issuers') to report ISSB-aligned climate-related disclosures starting from financial year 2025, with large non-listed companies with annual revenue of at least S$1 billion to follow in financial year 2027.[6] Additionally, a review will be conducted in 2027 with the view to mandate climate reporting on large non-listed companies with revenue of at least S$100 million by around financial year 2030. If the SRAC recommendations are made into law, this would mark a big step towards enhancing the ESG regulatory regime in Singapore.

In Japan, apart from the mandatory disclosures for top listed companies on the Tokyo Stock Exchange, the Financial Services Agency finalised in December 2022 a new code of conduct for ESG ratings and data providers with a hope that organisations will support the same and either comply or explain non-compliance. There is also the Green Growth Strategy[7] announced by the Japanese government to reduce greenhouse gas emissions to net zero by 2050 which has been entrenched by law in May 2021 through an amendment to the Act on Promotion of Global Warming Countermeasures.

While South Korea has announced mandatory ESG disclosure for all listed companies by 2030, from 2025 the requirement for sustainability reporting

---

4   SFC, "Circular To Licensed Corporations: Management And Disclosure Of Climate-Related Risks By Fund Managers", https://apps.sfc.hk/edistributionWeb/gateway/EN/circular/intermediaries/supervision/doc?refNo=21EC31.

5   Supervisory Policy Manual, HKMA, "Module IC-7 'The Sharing and Use of Commercial Credit Data through a Credit Reference Agency'", 16 November 2022, www.hkma.gov.hk/media/eng/doc/key-information/guidelines-and-circular/2022/20221116e1.pdf.

6   Accounting and Corporate Regulatory Authority, "Public consultation on turning climate change ambition into action in Singapore", www.acra.gov.sg/legislation/legislative-reform/listing-of-consultation-papers/public-consultation-on-turning-climate-ambition-into-action-in-singapore—recommendations-by-the-sustainability-reporting-advisory-committee.

7   METI, "Green Growth Strategy Through Achieving Carbon Neutrality in 2050", www.meti.go.jp/english/policy/energy_environment/global_warming/ggs2050/index.html.

applies to all listed companies with net assets of 2 trillion won (US$1.8 billion). Until such time, listed companies are expected to undertake voluntary reporting in preparation of 2025 and 2030 requirements.

2.2 Taxonomies and frameworks

While countries around Asia are setting out rules and regulations dealing with ESG, there remain uneven attitudes toward ESG in Asia, which has resulted in a current climate of regulators working closely together, including developing the ASEAN Taxonomy, Version 2 of which was released on 27 March 2023.[8]

The ASEAN Taxonomy has adopted a different approach to the EU Taxonomy in adopting a multi-tiered approach in classifying activities as opposed to using the binary approach adopted by the EU Taxonomy. Hence, the ASEAN Taxonomy has used a 'traffic light' system of classifying activities into red, amber and green depending on whether the activity contributes to climate change mitigation: this recognises that there are different starting points across ASEAN and that a singular definition would not be realistic for ASEAN.

On 15 February 2023, Singapore's Green Finance Industry Taskforce (GFIT) published the final public consultation paper on its proposed taxonomy ('Singapore Asia Taxonomy') seeking views on the detailed thresholds for classification and transition activities in the following sectors:

- agriculture and forestry/land use;
- industrial;
- waste and water;
- information and communications technology; and
- carbon capture and sequestration.

The aim of the Singapore Asia Taxonomy is to provide a common framework for the classification of economic activities on which financial institutions can build products and services and which can combat greenwashing claims. A key focus is to encourage flow of capital to support low-carbon transition. A key proposal of the final consultation paper is the adoption of a 'measures based approach' for the industrial sector which requires the adoption of a range of emissions reduction measures in the production process of the industrial raw materials.

On 31 May 2023, it was reported[9] that the Singapore Asia Taxonomy would include specific criteria on the managed phase-out of coal-fired power plants and that a consultation will be launched soon on its draft proposals.

---

8   ASEAN Taxonomy Board, "ASEAN taxonomy for sustainable finance", 9 June 2023 https://asean.org/wp-content/uploads/2023/03/ASEAN-Taxonomy-Version-2.pdf.

9   Monetary Authority of Singapore, "MAS Launches Consultation on Coal Phase-Out Criteria under the Singapore-Asia Taxonomy", 28 June 2023, www.mas.gov.sg/news/media-releases/2023/mas-launches-consultation-on—coal-phase-out-criteria-under-the-singapore-asia-taxonomy.

On 11 April 2023, the Malaysian government announced[10] it would introduce a framework on ESG standards by the end of 2023 to assist small and medium-sized enterprises in raising funding and capacity building in the transition to renewable energy.

Thailand, which launched Phase 1[11] of its draft taxonomy in December 2022, officially adopted the Green Taxonomy on 5 July 2023. While the current version covers energy and transportation sectors (and which is responsible for two-thirds of the country's emissions), it is expected to expand to other key sectors covering up to 95% of the country's emission-related activities. The Thailand Green Taxonomy is threshold and traffic light-based and can be used to issue green bonds, green loans, label investment funds, calculate insurance ratios, collect statistics and implement special support measures.

In South Korea, the K-Taxonomy is the reference point, based on the Environmental Technology and Industry Support Act (amended in 2021),[12] providing the principles and standards on what types of economic activities are considered green activities. While not legally binding, it serves as a basis for assisting in the allocation of funds to proper green projects and technologies by categorising green economic activities into the 'green sector', that is, truly green activities which are essential for improvement in the environment and achieving carbon neutrality, and the 'transition sector' which focuses on intermediary steps towards carbon neutrality.

2.3 Guidelines for financial institutions

In addition to the Singapore Asia Taxonomy, the MAS issued several guidelines[13] on financial institutions' obligations in relation to environmental risk management. The key takeaway from the guidelines is that financial institutions are expected to embed governance protocols and strategies to be able to assess environmental risk considerations in a risk-proportionate manner. While this is on a non-binding basis, the expectations remain that these guidelines will be implemented over the 18-month period MAS had outlined.

2.4 ESG reporting platform

The Singapore regulators launched Project Greenprint with a view to developing a vibrant green fintech ecosystem that would facilitate the flow of ESG data, which would be reliable, clear and consistent.

---

10 Azanis Shahila Aman, "Govt to launch ESG framework by year end", *Business Times*, 11 April 2023, www.nst.com.my/business/2023/04/898591/govt-launch-esg-framework-year-end.

11 Bank of Thailand, "Thailand Taxonomy A Reference Tool for Sustainable Economy", www.bot.or.th/en/financial-innovation/sustainable-finance/green/Thailand-Taxonomy.html.

12 Shin & Kim, "The Korean Green Taxonomy (K-Taxonomy) Guideline and Its Implications", Lexology, 25 January 2022, www.lexology.com/library/detail.aspx?g=861eba8d-0fdd-44d8-af20-2dc26ce55fbc.

13 Monetary Authority of Singapore, "Guidelines on Environmental Risk Management", 8 December 2020, www.mas.gov.sg/regulation/guidelines/guidelines-on-environmental-risk-management.

On 12 September 2022, as part of Project Greenprint, the MAS and SGX announced the joint launch of ESGenome, a digital disclosure portal for companies to report ESG data.[14] ESGenome is a SaaS solution operated by World Wide Generation to help ESG-listed companies to have a simplified disclosure process aligned with recognised standards and frameworks according to varying materiality and business needs, including:

- the Task Force on Climate-Related Financial Disclosures (TCFD);
- the Global Reporting Initiative (GRI); and
- the UN's Sustainable Development Goals (SDGs).

Other initiatives under the umbrella of Project Greenprint include:

- ESGpedia – a registry of green certifications;
- Greenprint Marketplace – a forum for green technology providers to network and connect with corporations, financial institutions and potential investors; and
- Greenprint Data Orchestrator – a group of data platforms that provide access to trustworthy ESG and sectoral sources.

Another recent development is the launch of the MAS ESG Impact Hub,[15] or simply 'the Hub'. The Hub is community-established to facilitate collaboration and cooperation between financial technology companies, financial institutions and other stakeholders. The ultimate aim of the Hub is to further the integration of ESG standards and metrics throughout Singapore's financial sector and the economy as a whole.

Bursa Malaysia, the Malaysian stock exchange, announced that it would launch a sustainability reporting platform in conjunction with the London Stock Exchange which would enable companies to calculate their carbon emission impact and disclose common ESG datasets in compliance with established global standards, including the Task Force on Climate-Related Financial Disclosures. Companies listed on Bursa Malaysia are also encouraged to reference the Sustainability Reporting Guide in reporting on sustainability which is required under the listing requirements.

2.5   Net Zero Action Plan

The MAS announced the launch of its Finance for Net Zero (FiNZ) Action Plan

---

14   Monetary Authority of Singapore, "MAS and SGX Group Launch ESGenome Disclosure Portal to Streamline Sustainability Reporting and Enhance Investor Access to ESG Data", 12 September 2022, www.mas.gov.sg/news/media-releases/2022/mas-and-sgx-group-launch-esgenome-disclosure-portal-to-streamline-sustainability-reporting-and-enhance-investor-access-to-esg-data.

15   Monetary Authority of Singapore, "MAS launches ESG Impact Hub to spur growth of ESG ecosystem", 5 October 2022, www.mas.gov.sg/news/media-releases/2022/mas-launches-esg-impact-hub-to-spur-growth-of-esg-ecosystem/.

on 20 April 2023. The FiNZ Action Plan aims to achieve four strategic outcomes, namely:

- *data disclosures* – consistent, comparable and reliable disclosures including interoperable taxonomies across Asia;
- *a climate-resilient financial sector* – continued engagement with financial institutions to develop international best practices for environmental risk management;
- *credible transition plans* – the development of science-based transition plans for decarbonisation pathways which can be referenced by financial institutions when setting emissions reduction targets; and
- *green and transition solutions and markets* – the promotion of innovative and credible green and transition financing solutions and markets with a focus on scaling blended finance. Existing sustainable bond and loan grant schemes will be expanded to include transition bonds and loans as well as extending the Insurance-Linked Securities (ILS) Grant Scheme until the end of 2025 to support the continued growth of catastrophe bonds and additional climate risk financing instruments such as sidecars[16] and collateralised reinsurance arrangements. Plans are also underway for the support of carbon services and a carbon credits market in Singapore to facilitate the flow of financing towards decarbonisation projects in Asia.

3. Greenwashing and increasing risk of litigation

Claims against greenwashing are, and will continue to be, on the rise. This is something regulators are particularly concerned with in respect of financial institutions being privy to any structuring which can give rise to claims of greenwashing. For example, a landmark case involving legal proceedings in South Korea against greenwashing is set out below.

3.1 South Korea

Summary: The country's largest private LNG provider SK E&S (the 'Company') was accused[17] of greenwashing its gas development project off the northern coast of Australia as "CO_2-free" LNG.

Legal action: The legal action commenced by environmental group Solutions for Our Climate centred around the Company's false advertising of "CO_2-free"

---

16 Monetary Authority of Singapore, "MAS launches finance for net-zero action plan", 20 April 2023, www.mas.gov.sg/news/media-releases/2023/mas-launches-finance-for-net-zero-action-plan. As noted in the media release, catastrophe bonds, sidecars and collateralised reinsurance are forms of insurance-linked securities. Sidecars are financial structures that enable third-party investors to take on risk and returns from a specified book of re/insurance. Collateralised reinsurance are reinsurance contracts which are fully collateralised by investors or third-party capital.

17 Heesu Lee/Bloomberg, "A South Korean Company Said a Natural Gas Project Was 'CO_2-Free.' It's Being Accused of 'Greenwashing'", TIME, 23 December 2021, https://time.com/6131226/sk-natural-gas-greenwashing-lawsuit/.

LNG from the $5.6 billion Barossa gas project under development through carbon capture and storage technologies and "eco-friendly" blue hydrogen. The Barossa gas project is expected to produce a total of 13.5 million tons in annual greenhouse gas emissions, including final consumption of natural gas. However, the project will only partially remove emissions (ie, capture up to 2.1 million tons of greenhouse gas emissions from its upstream production stage, which is only 16% of the total annual emissions estimate), not including carbon dioxide released when the gas is burned.

Result: Accordingly, the Company edited previous press releases and promotional videos to remove its assertion that LNG from the Barossa project would be "CO_2-free" and amended its claim to "low-carbon" gas.

The main risks of greenwashing include:
- loss of consumer trust and/or investor confidence;
- increased scrutiny and potential penalties by regulatory bodies;
- damage to company reputation arising from perceived dishonesty;
- competitive disadvantage associated with non-sustainable practices; and
- legal consequences (ie, fines, litigation, false advertising claims, etc).

Some of the areas which introduce the risks for corporates listed above are as follows.

3.2 Energy policy and energy transition

The concept of 'net zero' refers to the reduction of greenhouse gases produced to as close to zero as possible, removing them from the atmosphere. The net zero target was introduced by the Paris Agreement, which aims to limit global warming through net zero greenhouse gas emissions by 2050. Several Asian countries have committed to this target including, but not limited to, Japan, South Korea, Singapore and the Maldives. For example, Japan's Prime Minister, Yoshihide Suga, announced in October 2020 that the country aims to cut greenhouse gases to zero by 2050 and become a carbon-neutral society through a greater reliance on renewable energy.[18] Likewise, the Maldives has pledged to become carbon neutral by 2030, a more ambitious target than most other countries.[19] In addition, while China has not committed to the 2050 timeline, it aims to peak carbon dioxide emissions by 2030 and, subsequently, achieve

---

[18]   Tasuku Kuwabara, Detlev Mohr, Benjamin Sauer and Yuito Yamada, "How Japan could reach carbon neutrality by 2050", *McKinsey Sustainability*, 4 August 2021, www.mckinsey.com/capabilities/sustainability/our-insights/how-japan-could-reach-carbon-neutrality-by-2050.

[19]   The World Bank, "Maldives: Towards a Sustainable Net-Zero Future", 13 July 2021, www.worldbank.org/en/news/feature/2021/07/12/towards-a-sustainable-net-zero-future-in-maldives.

carbon neutrality by 2060.[20] Greenwashing by corporates can undermine international efforts in transitioning towards a net zero target, inviting greater scrutiny from both national and international regulatory bodies.

3.3 Proliferation of sustainability-related public statements and reports, as well as advertising and branding

Generally, Asia has less rigorous mandatory laws, rules and regulations related to sustainability reporting. For example, both Singapore and Thailand merely mandate sustainability reporting on a 'comply or explain' basis. Similarly, South Korea plans to maintain ESG disclosure voluntarily until at least 2025. However, the proliferation of sustainability-related public statements and reports in Asia reflects the region's growing commitment to sustainable development and environmental protection. This development can be attributed to voluntary leadership within the business community, seeking competitive advantage, the demands of civil society, market opportunities and consumer preferences, as well as regulation and politics. For example, there has been a rise in sustainability reporting disclosures identifying climate-related risks and/or opportunities, from 77% in 2021 to 88% in 2022, amongst the top 50 listed companies by market capitalisation across 14 Asia Pacific jurisdictions.[21]

3.4 Rapidly evolving rules and standards

There has been a rise in the emergence of interconnected rules and guidelines and taxonomies as well as a myriad of soft laws, reporting frameworks and best practices. The rise of varying rules across jurisdictions creates an uneven playing field, increasing the risk of different exposures to ESG litigation. For example, in China, the China Securities Regulatory Commission has made it mandatory for listed companies and bond issuers to disclose ESG risks associated with their operations. In addition, the Financial Services Agency (FSA) in Japan has revised its corporate governance code, encouraging companies to enhance disclosures on ESG issues. Similarly, the Securities and Exchange Board of India has introduced new sustainability disclosure requirements for the top 1,000 listed companies by market capitalisation.

3.5 Rise in activism

Recent years have seen an increase in well-organised and financed activism in Asia which involves stakeholders taking action to procure corporate

---

20 The World Bank, "China's Transition to a Low-Carbon Economy and Climate Resilience Needs Shifts in Resources and Technologies", 12 October 2022, www.worldbank.org/en/news/press-release/2022/10/12/china-s-transition-to-a-low-carbon-economy-and-climate-resilience-needs-shifts-in-resources-and-technologies.

21 A study by PwC Singapore and the Centre for Governance and Sustainability at the National University of Singapore Business School, https://bizbeat.nus.edu.sg/press-release/article/new-asia-pacific-study-reveals-overall-progress-in-sustainability-reporting-but-critical-gaps-remain-pwc-and-nus-business-school.

accountability on ESG compliance. For example, Greenpeace East Asia has staged protests and lobbied the South Korean Government to phase out coal power. Similarly, Japan has seen a rise in shareholder activism pushing for systemic shifts in capital allocation, climate policy and transparency, and mandating companies to account for board diversity and ESG.[22]

4. Looking forward

Crystal ball gazing is always difficult, but looking at the increase in regulatory activity from 2021 to the present it would not be too presumptuous to say that we can expect the following developments.

4.1 Increased regulatory enforcement

Regulators are progressively refining and revising the standards for ESG practices and compliance requirements, introducing more stringent climate-related disclosures aligned with the ISSB standards. For example, the Sustainability Standards Board of Japan (SSBJ) was established in July 2022, after the formation of the ISSB, to develop sustainability disclosure standards based on the ISSB standards. This was followed by the implementation of new rules designed by the FSA on mandatory sustainability disclosure, which apply to all listed companies in Japan. In addition, with effect from 1 January 2025, the HKEx intends to adopt climate-related disclosure requirements in its upcoming Listing Rule amendments to align with ISSB standards.

4.2 Increased greenwashing legal proceedings

There have been an increasing number of legal proceedings arising from greenwashing claims, giving rise to novel ways of looking at concepts of misrepresentations, reliance and loss. It is likely that more cases will find their way to court given how well-funded organisations are, and we will see a legal evolution in well-established principles in tort and contract law.

4.3 Trends in sustainable finance

According to data published by the Climate Bonds Initiative in 2022, the volume of green bond issuances has grown 50% each year since 2007 to US$1.9 trillion. This number is expected to increase, with a growing number of green debts being issued under local currency denominations.[23] In addition, from July through September 2023, 20 new sustainable funds were launched across the Asia region. These represent a robust demand for sustainable financing methods, despite macroeconomic headwinds such as inflationary pressure.

---

22 Leo Lewis, "Activist shareholders threaten Japan's AGM season", *Financial Times*, 31 May 2023, www.ft.com/content/1e05e8f2-83c6-4a7f-a28c-a9ca055604cf.

23 Association of Southeast Nations, "Asean Sustainable Finance State of the Market 2022", www.climatebonds.net/files/reports/cbi_asean_sotm_2022_02f.pdf.

4.4 Increased ESG focus on credit rating for corporates

An increasing number of global credit rating agencies and regional credit rating agencies (eg, the Japan Credit Rating Agency) have started to incorporate ESG risks into their credit rating methodologies. These rating methodologies evaluate how ESG factors could affect a company's financial performance and creditworthiness.

4.5 Evolution of blended and transition financing products and services

There have been an increasing number of novel financing products and services to address practical ways of reaching net zero. According to BloombergNEF, transition bonds, which finance the shift of high-carbon industries towards lower-carbon technologies, more than doubled in value in 2022 compared with 2021, in Asia. In China, transition finance is expected to surpass its US$3.6 trillion green debt market,[24] exemplified by Yankuang Group, China's largest coal miner, issuing a US$500 million transition bond in 2020. Similarly, a Hong Kong-based power company, Castle Peak, issued transition bonds in July 2017 and in June 2020, respectively.[25] In addition, Japan is expected to raise as much as US$154 billion in sovereign transition bonds over the next decade.[26] Accordingly, there will be a sustained proliferation of transition financing products and services as governments in Asia explore sustainable funding to decarbonise.[27]

4.6 Evolution of directors' duties in ESG reporting and formulating corporate policies

With the emergence of ESG risks, directors have to contend with formulating policies and strategies to manage any challenges in defining concepts such as 'green', 'sustainable' or 'net zero'. Directors are also responsible for considering any ESG impacts that may arise from their respective companies. Generally, any ESG or regulatory oversight by a director can potentially lead to financial and reputational damage to its company.

According to the Asian Corporate Governance Association, the percentage of investors in Asia that considered ESG issues in their investment decisions increased to 92% in 2020 from 85% in 2016.[28] It is this author's view that ESG

24 Sheryl Tian Tong Lee and Lisa Du, "China's Green Debt Pioneer Says Transition Market Is Bigger", Bloomberg, 30 March 2023, www.bloomberg.com/news/articles/2023-03-30/china-s-green-debt-pioneer-says-transition-market-is-even-bigger.
25 TPEx, "Introduction of Transition Bond", 7 April 2021, www.tpex.org.tw/storage/bond/2021/12/1639614639_7120_en_news.pdf.
26 "China's green debt pioneer says transition market is bigger", Business Times, 31 March 2023, www.businesstimes.com.sg/esg/chinas-green-debt-pioneer-says-transition-market-is-bigger.
27 Elizabeth Beattie, "AS Asia sees and ESG push, regulators need to play a bigger role", Asean Legal Business, 28 June 2021, www.legalbusinessonline.com/features/asia-sees-esg-push-regulators-need-play-bigger-role.
28 R Boffo and R Palatino, "ESG Investing: Practices, Progress and Challenges", OECD Paris, 2020, www.oecd.org/finance/ESG-Investing-Practices-Progress-Challenges.pdf.

compliance will become similar to compliance requirements for anti-bribery and anti-corruption in time to come, and such compliance will become fundamental in corporate transactions. It remains an exciting road ahead.

Australia and New Zealand

Christine Covington
Kate Gill-Herdman
Corrs Chambers Westgarth

1. Introduction

In June 2023 Australia and New Zealand entered into the inaugural Australia-New Zealand 2+2 Climate and Finance Dialogue ('the Dialogue'), agreeing a number of initiatives directed to increased cooperation and coordination in order to realise the transition to low-emissions and climate-resilient economies.[1] Initiatives include establishing a Net Zero Government Working Group to support decarbonising public services, climate-related disclosures and sustainable procurement, as well as aligning sustainable finance frameworks to enhance interoperability and working together to develop adaptation indicators and monitoring frameworks.[2]

The Dialogue is symbolic of the ongoing partnership between the two nations. Through consideration of the following themes – transitioning to a low-carbon economy; protection and restoration of the environment; regulatory responses to climate risk and sustainability disclosures; the rights of indigenous peoples; respect for human rights in the workplace, supply chains and beyond; governance of cyber risk, data protection and privacy law reform; directors' duties; and litigation trends – this chapter will show that Australia and New Zealand are on parallel paths to transitioning to a low-carbon economy and face similar risks and opportunities.

2. Transitioning to low-emissions and climate-resilient economies

2.1 Emissions reduction targets

Legislating emissions reduction targets has provided certainty for market participants in Australia and New Zealand in the transition to net zero.

---

1   Jim Chalmers *et al*, "Inaugural Australia-New Zealand 2+2 Climate and Finance Dialogue joint statement" (Media Release, Treasury Portfolio (Cth), 8 June 2023), https://ministers.treasury.gov.au/ministers/jim-chalmers-2022/media-releases/inaugural-australia-new-zealand-22-climate-and-finance.
2   *Ibid.*

(a) *Australia*

Australia's legislated target for 2030 is 43% below 2005 levels and net zero greenhouse gas (GHG) emissions by 2050.[3] The Climate Change Act 2022 (Cth) ('Climate Change Act') establishes an accountability framework for tracking progress against the targets, including the annual preparation and tabling of a climate-change statement addressing matters such as progress towards targets, the effectiveness of policies to achieve the targets and risks to Australia from climate-change impacts.[4] It requires Australia's Climate Change Authority to advise the relevant Federal Minister on the targets to include in any Nationally Determined Contribution, as well as the social, employment and economic benefits of those targets and physical climate-change risks to Australia.[5]

Although not bound by the Climate Change Act, most Australian states and territories have their own targets and tools for achieving emissions reduction targets. The State of Victoria's commitment is to achieve emissions reduction of 75% to 80% by 2035 with the goal of net zero by 2045. New South Wales's Net Zero Plan 2020–2030 aims to reduce emissions by 70% by 2035 and reach net zero by 2050. Both are supported by policy frameworks.[6]

Federally legislated targets mean that government policy is now aligned with the net zero commitments made by many of Australia's largest businesses, many of which had considered the lack of coherent Federal policy a barrier to investment, innovation and economic progress.

(b) *New Zealand*

New Zealand has legislated a domestic target of net zero GHG emissions by 2050, excluding biogenic methane which has a separate target[7] supported by a system of emissions budgets[8] and an emissions reduction plan.[9]

2.2 Sustainable finance strategies

At the Australia–New Zealand 2+2 Climate and Finance Dialogue the governments of both countries agreed to work to align sustainable finance frameworks and tools to enhance interoperability, support businesses operating across the economic region and to establish a Net Zero Government Working

---

3   Climate Change Act 2022 (Cth), Section 10(1).
4   Climate Change Act 2022 (Cth), Pt 3.
5   Climate Change Act 2022 (Cth), Pt 4.
6   Climate Change Act 2017 (Vic); State of NSW and Office of Environment and Heritage, "NSW Climate Change Policy Framework" (Report, 2016).
7   Climate Change Response Act 2002, Section 5Q. New Zealand's biogenic methane target is 24% to 47% reduction below 2017 biogenic methane emissions by 2050, including a 10% reduction below 2017 biogenic methane emissions by 2030.
8   The New Zealand Government's emissions budgets are found at: https://environment.govt.nz/what-government-is-doing/areas-of-work/climate-change/emissions-budgets-and-the-emissions-reduction-plan/.
9   Climate Change Response Act 2002, Sections 5V-5Z; 5ZG-5ZI.

Group to support climate-related disclosures.[10] Initiatives included in the sustainable finance strategies of both countries are broadly aligned.

(a)   *Australia*

Australia's proposed sustainable finance strategy is at the centre of policy reform and directed to transitioning Australia to a financially secure, low-carbon economy. The Federal Treasury consulted on the sustainable finance strategy in the latter part of 2023 and has foreshadowed the release of a sustainable finance roadmap in 2024.

Key pillars of Australia's proposed sustainable finance strategy include:

Sustainable finance taxonomy: Government and industry collaboration has resulted in agreement to develop an Australian sustainable finance taxonomy[11] to assist investors to target sustainability objectives when allocating capital. A key design feature of the taxonomy will be interoperability with sustainable finance taxonomies in other jurisdictions and include principles such as 'do no significant harm' and 'minimum social safeguards' which were identified by the Australian Sustainable Finance Institute in its taxonomy project.[12]

Sovereign green bonds: Commencing in 2024, a sovereign green bonds programme will be introduced to enable investors to back public projects contributing to decarbonising Australia's economy.[13]

Mandatory climate disclosures: The introduction of mandatory climate risk disclosures is a key element of Australia's sustainable finance strategy. The government has committed to introducing mandatory climate risk reporting for financial year 2024–2025. The reporting framework will be aligned to the International Sustainability Standard Board's climate risk disclosure standard and will adopt a phased approach to implementation commencing with large, listed businesses and financial institutions. The framework will be designed to enable it to be expanded to other sustainability topics over time.[14]

---

10   Jim Chalmers *et al*, "Inaugural Australia-New Zealand 2+2 Climate and Finance Dialogue joint statement" (Media Release, Treasury Portfolio (Cth), 8 June 2023), https://ministers.treasury. gov.au/ministers/jim-chalmers-2022/media-releases/inaugural-australia-new-zealand-22-climate-and-finance.

11   Jim Chalmers, Chris Bowen and Jenny McAllister, "Investor Roundtable aligns efforts to deliver cleaner, cheaper energy" (Media Release, Treasury Portfolio (Cth), 21 April 2023), https://ministers.treasury. gov.au/ministers/jim-chalmers-2022/media-releases/investor-roundtable-aligns-efforts-deliver-cleaner.

12   Australian Sustainable Finance Institute, "Taxonomy Project", www.asfi.org.au/taxonomy.

13   Jim Chalmers, Chris Bowen and Jenny McAllister, "Investor Roundtable aligns efforts to deliver cleaner, cheaper energy" (Media Release, Treasury Portfolio (Cth), 21 April 2023), https://ministers.treasury. gov.au/ministers/jim-chalmers-2022/media-releases/investor-roundtable-aligns-efforts-deliver-cleaner.

14   Australian Government, "Climate-related financial disclosure" (Consultation Paper, December 2022).

(b)   New Zealand

New Zealand's sustainable finance *Roadmap for Action*[15] was developed by the Aotearoa Circle's Sustainable Finance Forum through collaboration between public and private actors in New Zealand's financial system. The Centre for Sustainable Finance is tasked with coordinating the implementation of the Roadmap.[16] New Zealand has already implemented a number of initiatives identified in the Roadmap, similar to those proposed in Australia's sustainable finance strategy. These include:

Green Investment Finance: New Zealand Green Investment Finance (state-owned investment bank) provides finance on a commercial basis to accelerate investment in scalable companies, technologies and projects that are commercial-ready and offer low-carbon benefits for New Zealand.[17]

Sovereign green bonds: Governed by the Sovereign Green Bond Framework, the government will finance or refinance expenditure through the issuance of green bonds across eight categories including clean transport, improving energy efficiency and reducing reliance on fossil fuels, transitioning to lower-emissions land uses and systems, and restoring and protecting New Zealand's natural environment.[18] Approximately NZ$5.6 billion of government expenditure was approved for inclusion in the Green Bond Programme for financial year 2023–2024.[19]

Mandatory climate risk disclosures: In 2021, New Zealand became the first country globally to introduce mandatory climate risk disclosures for banks, insurers and debt and equity issuers. The reporting period commenced on 1 January 2023, with first disclosures to be made against the Task Force for Climate-Related Financial Disclosures (TFCD) in April 2024.[20]

3.   Protection and restoration of the natural environment

Target 14 of the Global Biodiversity Framework calls for the full integration of biodiversity across policy, regulation, development process and environmental assessment and impacts statements. Both Australia and New Zealand are undergoing environmental law reform to better respond to the challenges of climate change and biodiversity loss.

---

15   "Sustainable Finance Forum Roadmap for Action", *The Aotearoa Circle* (Final Report, November 2020), https://static1.squarespace.com/static/637d83c964e50e3125f983aa/t/637d88f7bb81cc1f51a2dc32/1670 385195639/Sustainable%2BFinance%2BForum%2BRoadmap%2Bfor%2BAction.

16   New Zealand Government, "*Te hau mārohi ki anamata* towards a productive, sustainable and inclusive economy: Aotearoa New Zealand's first emissions reduction plan" (Report, May 2022), p122.

17   New Zealand Green Investment Finance, "About us", https://nzgif.co.nz/about-us/who-we-are/.

18   The Treasury, New Zealand Sovereign Green Bond Framework (Report, August 2022),

19   The Treasury, New Zealand Sovereign Green Bond Programme, https://debtmanagement.treasury. govt.nz/investor-resources/green-bonds.

20   Financial Sector (Climate-related Disclosures and Other Matters) Amendment Act 2021.

3.1 Australia

Central to Australian environmental policy is both the economic value of nature and its importance to human wellbeing. It is estimated that Australia could lose up to US$20 billion annually from nature loss to 2050.[21]

The Federal Government's December 2022 Nature Positive Plan responds to the decline of Australia's natural environment and its lack of resilience to withstand current or emerging threats.[22] Once implemented, it will result in extensive reform of Australia's environmental protection regime directed to achieving faster and more efficient decision making while at the same time ensuring better protection of Australia's natural environment and indigenous cultural heritage in order to repair and regenerate Australian species and ecosystems.[23]

3.2 New Zealand

Like Australia, New Zealand's economy depends on its natural resources. Thirteen of New Zealand's top 30 export commodities depend on natural resources, equating to more than 70% of its export earnings.[24]

(a) Biodiversity strategy

New Zealand's biodiversity strategy, *Te Mana o te Taiao*, was released in 2020 and provides a national strategy for the protection, restoration and sustainable use of biodiversity, including indigenous biodiversity in New Zealand. The principles of the Treaty of Waitangi are an essential part of *Te Mana o te Taiao*, including working in partnership towards a shared vision for nature and actively protecting Māori knowledge and other customs.[25]

(b) Indigenous biodiversity

The government is also developing a National Policy Statement for Indigenous Biodiversity with the objective of protecting, restoring and maintaining indigenous biodiversity that recognises both Māori culture and people and communities as stewards, as well as providing for the social, cultural and economic wellbeing of people.[26]

---

21 Australian Council of Superannuation Investors, "Biodiversity: unlocking natural capital value for Australian Investors" (Research Report, November 2021).

22 Department of Climate Change, Energy, the Environment and Water (DCCEEW), "Nature Positive Plan: better for the environment, better for business" (Report, December 2022); ID Cresswell, T Janke and EL Johnston (2021) "Australia state of the environment 2021", independent report to the Australian Government Minister for the Environment, Commonwealth of Australia, Canberra.

23 Department of Climate Change, Energy, the Environment and Water (DCCEEW), "Nature Positive Plan: better for the environment, better for business" (Report, December 2022).

24 Abbie Reynolds, "Putting a Value on Natural Resources" (Media Release, Sustainable Business Council, 15 July 2016), https://sbc.org.nz/putting-a-value-on-natural-resources.

25 New Zealand Government, "*Te Mana o te Taiao* – Aotearoa New Zealand Biodiversity Strategy" (Report, August 2020), www.doc.govt.nz/nature/biodiversity/aotearoa-new-zealand-biodiversity-strategy/te-mana-o-te-taiao-summary/.

26 New Zealand Government, National Policy Statement for Indigenous Biodiversity, Exposure Draft June 2022.

(c)   *Biodiversity credit market*

A government-commissioned panel into Cyclone Gabrielle in February was released in May 2023. Alongside producing findings related to several factors that contributed to the environmental disaster, the panel also urged the New Zealand Government to set up a voluntary biodiversity credit market.[27]

4.   Regulatory responses to climate risk and sustainability disclosures

With both jurisdictions implementing mandatory climate risk disclosure regimes, regulatory scrutiny of sustainability claims and enforcement action in relation to greenwashing are likely to increase.

4.1   Australia

(a)   *Prudential oversight*

Since 2021 the Australian Prudential Regulatory Authority (APRA) has indicated that entities with material exposure to climate risk should make disclosures in line with the TCFD.[28]

In June 2023 the Federal Government communicated its expectation to APRA that it would promote prudent practices and transparency of climate-related financial risks and the adoption of climate reporting standards by regulated entities – banks, insurers and superannuation entities.[29]

(b)   *Greenwashing*

Australia's financial markets regulator, the Australian Securities and Investments Commission (ASIC) has encouraged Australian listed companies to make voluntary climate related disclosures since 2018[30] and in 2021 encouraged listed companies to disclose climate-related risk in line with the TCFD framework.[31]

Also on the rise in Australia is regulatory scrutiny of sustainability claims. While Australia does not expressly prohibit 'greenwashing', laws exist against

---

27   "Outrage to Optimism", Report of the Ministerial Inquiry into land uses associated with the mobilisation of woody debris (including forestry slash) and sediment in Tairawhiti/Gisborne District and Wairoa District, pp29, 31.

28   Australian Prudential Regulation Authority (APRA), *CPG 229 Climate Change Financial Risks* (Practice Guide, November 2021) 19 [50]; Sean Hughes, "Corporate governance update: climate change risk and disclosure" (Speech, Governance Institute of Australia Fellows Roundtable, 14 October 2021), https://asic.gov.au/about-asic/news-centre/speeches/corporate-governance-update-climate-change-risk-and-disclosure/.

29   APRA, "Statement of Expectations", June 2023, www.apra.gov.au/statement-of-expectations.

30   Karen Chester, "ASIC and Greenwashing Antidotes" (Speech, Responsible Investment Australia 2023 Annual Conference, 10 May 2023), https://asic.gov.au/about-asic/news-centre/speeches/asic-and-greenwashing-antidotes; see also ASIC, "Climate Risk Disclosure by Australia's listed companies" (Report No 593, September 2018).

31   Sean Hughes, "Corporate governance update: climate change risk and disclosure" (Speech, Governance Institute of Australia Fellows Roundtable, 14 October 2021); Sean Hughes, "ASIC's current focus: What are the regulator's expectations on sustainability-related disclosures?", ASIC, 7 December 2022), https://asic.gov.au/about-asic/news-centre/articles/asic-s-current-focus-what-are-the-regulator-s-expectations-on-sustainability-related-disclosures/.

making false or misleading representations or engaging in misleading or deceptive conduct.[32]

Given that 70% or A$1.6 trillion of the ASX 200 market cap is subject to a net zero commitment,[33] it is no surprise that both ASIC and the Australian Competition and Consumer Commission (ACCC) have greenwashing as an enforcement priority.

ASIC's enforcement activity is broader than just environmental claims and has included issuing corrective disclosure notices for the use of vague phrases such as 'social diversity' and 'robust sustainable practices'. In early 2023 it commenced civil penalty proceedings against a large retail superannuation fund for holding shares in companies whose activities were inconsistent with representations the fund had made about its sustainable investment option.[34]

Businesses in Australia also face the risk of private litigation for misleading or deceptive conduct because of greenwashing. For example, in 2021, the Australasian Centre for Corporate Responsibility commenced proceedings in the Federal Court of Australia against Santos Limited, alleging Santos had breached the Corporations Act 2001 (Cth) and the Australian Consumer Law by engaging in misleading or deceptive conduct in relation to its "clean energy" claims and net zero plans.[35] Those proceedings remain on foot.

4.2 New Zealand

The Reserve Bank of New Zealand has also issued guidance to its supervised entities on the governance, risk management, scenario analysis and disclosure of climate risks.[36]

New Zealand's Financial Markets Authority (FMA) is actively pursuing regulatory action in response to greenwashing consistent with its mandate of ensuring fair dealing.[37] It conducted a sweep of managed funds and concluded that the managed fund sector overall had an immature approach to sustainability disclosures, using vague and inconsistent language, and overall

---

32 ASIC Act 2001 (Cth), ss 12DA-12DC and 12DF; Corporations Act 2001 (Cth), Sections 1041E and 1041H.
33 Karen Chester, 'ASIC and Greenwashing Antidotes' (Speech, Responsible Investment Australia 2023 Annual Conference, 10 May 2023); ASIC, "Climate Risk Disclosure by Australia's listed companies" (Report No 593, September 2018).
34 *Australian Securities and Investments Commission v Mercer Superannuation (Australia) Limited ACN 004 717 533*, Proceedings No VID117/2023, Concise Statement dated 27 February 2023.
35 Australasian Centre for Corporate Responsibility, "Australasian Centre for Corporate Responsibility expands landmark Federal Court case against Santos" (Media release, 25 August 2022). www.accr.org.au/news/australasian-centre-for-corporate-responsibility-expands-landmark-federal-court-case-against-santos.
36 Reserve Bank of New Zealand, "Managing climate-related risks: guidance for regulated entities" (Guidance document, 29 March 2023).
37 Paul Gregory, "Sustainable? Ethical? The substance must back up the claims", Financial Markets Authority, 25 May 2023, www.fma.govt.nz/library/opinion/sustainable-ethical-the-substance-must-back-up-the-claims/.

was inconsistent with the FMA's guidance on greenwashing.[38] It has issued two warnings in relation to these issues.[39]

The FMA has also released a disclosure framework for integrated financial products, which are products that incorporate non-financial factors.[40] This involves the FMA leveraging the provisions of the Financial Markets Conduct Act 2013 in relation to fair dealing to address 'greenwashing' and deceptive conduct in relation to the incorporation of non-financial factors into products and claims.[41] While the FMA has not taken any enforcement action on greenwashing to date, it warned integrated financial product funds in mid-July 2022 that it now "expected them to take the necessary care not to mislead or confuse investors with greenwashing". To that end, it recently issued Vanguard Group with a warning for failing to disclose details to FMA within the required time of infringement notices filed against it in Australia for alleged greenwashing.[42]

5. Rights of indigenous peoples

While not enforceable, New Zealand's Treaty of Waitangi has enabled Māori to agitate for a voice within the New Zealand democratic system directed to greater respect for Māori rights. In contrast, Australia has no treaty with First Nations people, nor has it enshrined recognition of the rights of First Nations peoples in the Constitution. While both nations have endorsed the United Nations Declaration on the Rights of Indigenous Peoples (UNDRIP) both are yet to implement it into domestic law. In this section we outline the key human rights issues in both countries.

5.1 Australia

(a) Aboriginal and Torres Strait Islanders denied the constitutional right to make representations to Parliament and the Executive Government

Australia's referendum to alter the Australian Constitution to recognise the First Peoples of Australia by establishing an Aboriginal and Torres Strait Islander Voice ('First Nations Voice') was held in late 2023 and was unsuccessful.[43] However, initiatives directed to achieving reconciliation with First Nations continue. One example is the State of Victoria's Yoorrook Justice Commission,

---

38 Financial Markets Authority, "Integrated financial products: Review of managed fund documentation" (Report, July 2022).
39 Renju Jose, "New Zealand regulator warns Vanguard over greenwashing notice", Reuters, 29 March 2023, www.reuters.com/business/sustainable-business/new-zealand-regulator-warns-vanguard-over-greenwashing-notice-2023-03-29/.
40 Financial Markets Authority, "Disclosure framework for integrated financial products" (Guidance Note, December 2020)
41 *Ibid*, p7.
42 Renju Jose, "New Zealand regulator warns Vanguard over greenwashing notice", *Reuters*, 29 March 2023, www.reuters.com/business/sustainable-business/new-zealand-regulator-warns-vanguard-over-greenwashing-notice-2023-03-29/.
43 Australian Government, "Aboriginal and Torres Strait Islander Voice", *Voice*, https://voice.gov.au/.

which is Australia's first formal truth-telling commission, examining historical and ongoing injustices experienced by First Peoples in Victoria. It is due to report in 2024.[44]

(b)   Recognising First Nations peoples' right to self-determination

The destruction of indigenous cultural heritage sites in Western Australia at Juukan Gorge in May 2020 exposed a significant gap in Australia's regulatory framework for the protection of cultural heritage. It has been the catalyst for demands from a cross-sector of the Australian community including First Nations people and institutional investors to respect the rights of First Nations people and in particular the right to give or withhold free, prior and informed consent (FPIC).

Critically, the government has committed to co-designing with Aboriginal and Torres Strait Islander peoples a new legislative framework for cultural heritage protection that specifies minimum standards for state and territory laws consistent with UNDRIP.[45]

Both the Australian Council of Superannuation Investors (ACSI)[46] and the Responsible Investment Association of Australasia[47] have released separate guidance on engaging with First Nations, setting the expectation that investors and investee companies commit to respecting First Nations peoples' rights and cultural heritage in accordance with the UN Guiding Principles on business and human rights and UNDRIP.

With First Nations rights and interests in lands and waters formally recognised over more than 50% of Australia, partnerships between Australia's renewable energy sector and First Nations peoples will be critical to Australia's transition to a low-carbon economy.[48]

5.2   New Zealand

New Zealand's parliament and the courts are continuing to recognise core principles of the Treaty of Waitangi – reciprocity, active protection, partnership, equity and equal treatment[49] – in legislation and development of the common law. New Zealand's highest court, the Supreme Court, unanimously confirmed

---

44   Letters Patent dated 12 May 2021 at https://yoorrookjusticecommission.org.au/wp-content/uploads/2021/09/Letters-Patent-Yoo-rrook-Justice-Commission-signed-10-1.pdf.

45   Australian Government, "Australian Government Response to the Joint Standing Committee on Northern Australia's: 'A Way Forward' and 'Never Again'" (Inquiry Report, November 2022) Recommendation 3.

46   Australian Council of Superannuation Investors, *ACSI Policy on Company Engagement With First Nations People* (Policy, December 2021).

47   Responsible Investment Association Australasia, *Investor Toolkit: An Investor Focus on Indigenous Peoples' Rights and Cultural Heritage Protection* (Toolkit, 2021).

48   Australian Government, National Indigenous Australians Agency, www.niaa.gov.au/indigenous-affairs/land-and-housing#:~:text=Aboriginal%20and%20Torres%20Strait%20Islander%20peoples'%20rights%20and%20interests%20in,importance%20to%20First%20Nations%20Australians.

49   Waitangi Tribunal, "Chapter 3: Treaty Principles and Standards", Publications & Resources web page, www.waitangitribunal.govt.nz/treaty-of-waitangi/principles-of-the-treaty/.

that tikanga (Māori customary practices or behaviours) has been and will continue to be recognised in the development of New Zealand's common law.[50]

New Zealand's Human Rights Commission has described the Treaty of Waitangi as New Zealand's own unique statement of human rights which is central to resolving indigenous rights issues in New Zealand. The Waitangi Tribunal was established in 1975 to hear Māori claims regarding Crown breaches of the treaty, and in 1989 formal processes were established to provide redress for historical claims for breaches of the treaty.[51]

New Zealand endorsed UNDRIP in 2010[52] and, like Australia, has yet to implement it into domestic law. However, the New Zealand Human Rights Commission describes the relationship between the Treaty and UNDRIP as strongly aligned and mutually consistent, with UNDRIP assisting with the interpretation and application of the Treaty of Waitangi principles including partnership, protection and participation.[53]

6. Respect for human rights in the workplace, supply chains and beyond

6.1 Australia

(a) Federal Bill of Rights

Australia is the only OECD country without a Federal Human Rights Act or Bill of Rights. Only three Australian States have statutory charters of rights. However, in December 2022 the Australian Human Rights Commission released its position paper on "A Human Rights Act for Australia".[54] Shortly after, Australia's Federal Attorney-General referred to Australia's Parliamentary Joint Committee on Human Rights various matters concerning Australia's human rights framework and is expected to examine whether Australia should implement a Charter of Human Rights.

(b) Workplace reforms: sex discrimination and harassment

In 2018, the Australian Human Rights Commission found that sexual harassment is prevalent and pervasive in Australian workplaces, with one in three workers having experienced workplace sexual harassment in the previous five years.[55] In 2020 the Australian Human Rights Commission published the

50   *Ellis v R* [2022] NZSC 114.
51   New Zealand Government, Treaty of Waitangi claims, www.govt.nz/browse/history-culture-and-heritage/treaty-of-waitangi-claims/; New Zealand Government, Te Tai Treaty Settlement Stories, https://teara.govt.nz/en/te-tai/about-treaty-settlements.
52   *Hansard* New Zealand Parliament vol 662 page 10229, 20 April 2010.
53   New Zealand Human Rights Commission, "The Rights of Indigenous Peoples: what you need to know", https://genderminorities.com/wp-content/uploads/2016/06/nzhr_booklet_12_web.pdf.
54   Australian Human Rights Commission (AHRC), "Free & Equal: A Human Rights Act for Australia" (Position Paper, 7 March 2023).

findings of its National Inquiry into Sexual Harassment in Australian Workplaces.[56] It recognised that the right of workers to be free from sexual harassment was a human right, workplace right and safety right[57] and recommended a new framework for workplaces to better prevent and respond to sexual harassment.

(c)   ***Gender pay gap***
Workplace Gender Equality Australia (WGEA) data analysis shows that progress on workplace gender equality in Australia has stalled and indicates employers are not necessarily following up with action to address their gender pay gaps. Accordingly, from early 2024, the WGEA will publish the gender pay gaps of reporting employers using the data from the 2022/2023 reporting period.[58]

(d)   ***Gender diversity***
Investors and stakeholders increasingly expect gender diversity on company boards. For example, ACSI expects companies to commit to achieving gender balance (40:40:20) on boards and in the meantime expects no gender to make up more than 70% of board positions in an ASX-listed company.[59] Recent statistics from the Australian Institute of Company Directors demonstrate that, as at February 2023, women represent 36% of ASX 200 boards and 35.5% of ASX 300 boards.[60]

(e)   ***Modern Slavery Act reforms may mean more than just reporting***
In its May 2023 Budget, the Federal Government committed to funding the appointment of an Anti-Slavery Commissioner. Subsequently the Government published the report of the statutory review of the Modern Slavery Act 2018 (Cth).[61] Thirty recommendations were made, which, if implemented, will see an increased number of reporting entities, a requirement to implement due diligence, reporting identified instances of modern slavery and penalties for failing to have a due diligence system in place or failing to report.

---

55   Australian Human Rights Commission, "Respect@Work: National Inquiry into Sexual Harassment in Australian Workplaces" (Report, January 2020), p17.
56   *Ibid.*
57   Australian Human Rights Commission, "Everyone's Business: Fourth national survey on sexual harassment in Australian workplaces" (Report, 2018).
58   Workplace Gender Equality Agency, "Get future ready: A guide to understanding changes to WGEA's legislation", www.wgea.gov.au/about/our-legislation/Closing-the-gender-pay-gap-bill-2023.
59   ACSI, "Governance Guidelines: A guide to investor expectations of listed Australian companies" (Guidelines, December 2021).
60   Australian Institute of Company Directors, "Gender Diversity Progress Report: December 2022 to February 2023" (Report, March 2023).
61   Australian Government, Attorney-General's Department, "Report of the Statutory Review of the Modern Slavery Act 2018 (Cth): The First Three Years", www.ag.gov.au/crime/publications/report-statutory-review-modern-slavery-act-2018-cth.

6.2   New Zealand

(a)   Modern Slavery Act to be introduced

New Zealand has actively contributed to measures against modern slavery and has proposed legislation that would impose reporting obligations on all types of entities with a graduated set of responsibilities based on an entity's annual revenue.[62]

7.   Governance of cyber risk, data protection and privacy law reform

7.1   Australia

High profile data breaches in Australia led to the expedited introduction of part of a raft of privacy law reforms being considered by the Federal Government. These include reforms to jurisdiction, with foreign entities carrying on business in Australia potentially caught by the reforms, expanding the enforcement powers of the Office of the Australian Information Commissioner and Australian Communications and Media Authority and significant increases in penalties.

Following the release of the Privacy Act Review Report,[63] further reforms are expected to significantly expand the regulatory burden for businesses operating in Australia that collect personal data.

7.2   New Zealand

New Zealand's Privacy Act 2020 introduced a range of privacy law reforms including extraterritorial application for organisations 'carrying on' business in New Zealand, mandatory notification of data breaches to New Zealand's Privacy Commissioner that are likely to result in serious harm to affected individuals and increased compliance and enforcement mechanisms.[64]

7.3   Private sector risks

Cyber security has recently emerged as a key ESG risk for Australian business. In 2022, cyber security was nominated as the top ESG priority for the Australian private sector,[65] with 77% of CEOs considering increasing investments in cyber security or data privacy to mitigate against exposure to geopolitical conflict.[66]

The increasing prevalence of cyber breaches together with recent and proposed reforms to privacy laws in Australia mean that governance of cyber

---

62   New Zealand Government, "A Legislative Response to Modern Slavery and Worker Exploitation – Towards freedom, fairness and dignity in operations and supply chains" (Report, 2020), p11.
63   Australian Government, Attorney-General's Department, "Privacy Act Review Report 2022".
64   Privacy Act 2020.
65   Perennial Partners, "Perennial Better Future Survey Report – Taking the ESG Pulse of ASX Listed Companies 2022", p4.
66   PwC, "PwC Australia's 26th CEO Survey", www.pwc.com.au/ceo-agenda/ceo-survey.html.

risk is a critical issue for Australian organisations. Cyber risk is perceived as the top risk for Australian business leaders[67] and estimated to cost the Australian economy A$42 billion a year.[68]

8. Directors' duties and ESG issues

Though no proceedings have been commenced against directors in Australia or New Zealand concerning ESG issues, legal opinions in both jurisdictions point to the potential for directors' duties to extend to financially material ESG risks.

8.1 Australia

Australian barristers Noel Hutley SC and Sebastian Hartford-Davis have opined that directors may be liable for a breach of their duty of care and diligence if they fail to consider the foreseeable risks that climate change poses to a company's interests.[69]

8.2 New Zealand

The Aotearoa Circle in New Zealand has partnered with a leading New Zealand law firm to provide clarity and direction on the legal duties of directors in managing climate-related and natural capital-related risks.[70] Informed by the directors' duty to act with reasonable care,[71] these opinions concluded that companies are generally permitted and, in some cases, required to take climate change into account when making business decisions where climate risks are foreseeable and material for the company.

9. Litigation trends

Climate change litigation has been increasing in Australia, New Zealand and globally, with the cumulative number of climate-related cases more than doubling since 2015.[72] Examples of key cases are identified below.

9.1 Australia

In Australia, more recent cases illustrate the convergence of human rights and environmental activism. For example:

---

67 PwC, "2022 Global Risk Survey: Australian highlights", (Report, 2022), p3.
68 Nigel Phair, UNSW Institute for Cyber Security, www.unsw.edu.au/news/2021/12/cybercrime-an-estimated—42-billion-cost-to-australian-economy.
69 Noel Hutley and Sebastian Hartford-Davis, "Memorandum of Opinion on Climate Change and Directors' Duties" (7 October 2016) and "Supplementary Memorandum of Opinion on Climate Change and Directors' Duties" (26 March 2019) and "Further Supplementary Memorandum of Opinion on Climate Change and Directors' Duties" (23 April 2021) published by the Centre for Policy Development.
70 Chapman Tripp Legal Opinion for The Aotearoa Circle 2019; Chapman Tripp Legal Opinion 2023 Instructed by The Aotearoa Circle – "New Zealand Directors Duties to Manage Nature-Related Risk and Impact on Natural Capital 2023".
71 Chapman Tripp Legal Opinion for The Aotearoa Circle 2019, p3.
72 Joana Setzer and Catherine Higham, "Global trends in climate change litigation: 2021 snapshot", Grantham Research Institute on Climate Change and the Environment and Centre for Climate Change Economics and Policy, London School of Economics and Political Science.

- Class action proceeding commenced by Pabai Pabai and Paul Kabai, First Nations' leaders from the Gudamalulgal nation of the Torres Strait Islands, on behalf of Torres Strait Islanders against the Australian government, alleging that the Commonwealth owes (and has breached) a duty of care to protect Torres Strait Islanders, their traditional way of life and their marine environment from climate change impacts.[73]
- In 2022, Mr Tipakalippa, an elder, senior lawman and traditional owner belonging to the Munupi clan on the Tiwi Islands successfully challenged the National Offshore Petroleum Safety and Environmental Management Authority's (NOPSEMA's) decision to accept an environment plan, which had been prepared by the proponent of an offshore gas project, approximately 300km north of Darwin. Mr Tipakalippa alleged that he and other traditional owners should have been directly consulted in relation to the environment plan because of their cultural connections to sea country and sea country resources. The Federal Court agreed with Mr Tipakalippa's claim, and the Full Federal Court dismissed an appeal from this decision.[74]
- A number of activist groups joined to object the grant of a mining lease and environmental authority to Waratah Coal in respect of a proposed thermal bituminous coal mine in the Galilee Basin in the State of Queensland. Objections included the environmental and human rights objections centred around the climate change implications of the Project in reliance on Queensland's Human Rights Act. President Kingham of the Land Court of Queensland recommended that the mining lease and environmental authority applications be refused, including on grounds that there would be unjustifiable limits to human rights by reason of ecological damage caused by the mine and the climate change implications of combustion of the coal.[75]

9.2 New Zealand

In New Zealand, cases have tended to be focused primarily on climate change. For example:

- In March 2022 New Zealand Supreme Court granted leave to Mr Smith, a Māori elder to hear his appeal of the Court of Appeal's decision to dismiss his claim that high emitting New Zealand companies[76] had breached a novel tortious duty of care to cease contributing to climate change.[77] The appeal is yet to be heard.

---

73   *Pabai Pabai v Commonwealth of Australia*, No: VID622/2021.
74   *Santos NA Barossa Pty Ltd v Tipakalippa* [2022] FCAFC 193.
75   *Waratah Coal Pty Ltd v Youth Verdict Ltd & Ors (No 6)* [2022] QLC 21.
76   Fonterra Co-Operative Group Limited, Genesis Energy Limited, Dairy Holdings Limited, New Zealand Steel Limited, Z Energy Limited, New Zealand Refining Company Limited, B T Mining Limited.
77   *Smith v Fonterra Co-Operative Group Limited* [2022] NZSC 35.

- Also in 2022, a group of law students commenced judicial review proceedings against the Minister for Energy and Resources, challenging the Minister's decisions to grant certain onshore petroleum exploration permits.[78] The students argued that the Minister had failed to substantively consider the climate change implications of his decisions and failed to have proper regard to the principles of the Treaty of Waitangi; for this reason the decision was unreasonable.[79] The High Court found that the Minister's decision was lawful, that climate change considerations were not legally relevant to the Minister's decision and the Minister had given proper consideration to the principles of the Treaty of Waitangi.[80]

The authors would like to thank Georgia Smith and Sam Walker, both lawyers at Corrs Chambers Westgarth for their significant assistance in preparing this chapter.

---

78   *Students for Climate Solutions Incorporated v The Minister of Energy and Resources* [2022] NZHC 2116.
79   *Ibid*, [2].
80   *Ibid*, [114]–[115].

Latin America: Chile, Brazil, Colombia and Mexico

Milenko Bertrand-Galindo
Paula Errázuriz Sotta
Bernardita Salvatierra Riquelme
Bertrand-Galindo Barrueto Barroilhet

1.   Introduction

The adoption of ESG practices has become an imperative to the business world, signifying a global shift towards responsible investment and sustainable development.

Latin America is a region where coordinated responses to environmental, social and political challenges are particularly urgent. However, the progress in the implementation of ESG criteria has been rocky due to a multiplicity of factors. Political instability and systemic corruption remain significant hurdles, as weak institutional frameworks and lack of accountability discourage long term ESG-focused endeavours. The persistence of problems such as social inequality and social conflicts related to land access, indigenous rights, water scarcity and climate change has led to local communities having very low trust in investment projects, even those that declare themselves as green or sustainable, which in turn discourages investment in ESG due to higher risks of green-washing accusations. Despite these and many other challenges, several countries in Latin America have gradually started to embrace the terminology and objectives of ESG, to a lesser extent through structured and systematic legislation, but mostly through pressures from the international market in which all countries in the region are, to a greater or lesser degree, integrated.

This chapter briefly studies the early manifestations of ESG legislation in the region, as well as the much greater penetration of ESG practices driven by the demands placed upon Latin American businesses and banks by international trade, international clients and public and private financing entities. Given the need for conciseness, we will focus on Chile, Brazil, Colombia and Mexico, as these nations, each at varying stages of ESG integration, provide instructive case studies into the advances and challenges of ESG implementation in Latin America.

2.   Chile

Probably due to the open nature of its economy, Chile has been a frontrunner in the region in terms of early adoption of ESG practices. As early as 2015, the

Santiago Exchange, in alliance with S&P Dow Jones Indices introduced the Dow Jones Sustainability Chile Index, promoting ESG criteria among listed companies. The Chilean Central Bank, in turn, incorporated climate risk assessments into its macroeconomic models as part of its 2018–2022 Strategic Plan, and the country was the first in Latin America to issue a sovereign green bond in June 2019.

As is often the case, well before any legislation mandated any reporting on ESG compliance, Chilean companies, particularly foreign-owned firms, large-scale raw materials and mineral exporters, as well as the banking sector, began incorporating sustainability information into their public reports. This practice has been driven by foreign commercial pressures, stemming from supply chain obligations, international financial and capital markets requirements, and heightened consumer consciousness regarding these issues.[1] As such, most large companies in Chile have voluntarily incorporated international reporting frameworks and standards such as those of the Sustainability Accounting Standards Board (SASB), the Global Reporting Initiative (GRI) and the United Nation's Global Compact.

In terms of binding legislation on ESG reporting, Chile was one of the pioneers in the region with the issuance of General Rule No 461 by the Financial Market Commission (FMC) in 2021.[2] In compliance with its duty to oversee the proper functioning, development and stability of the financial market, the FMC issued this rule, gradually expanding the scope of the report duties of all entities under its supervision (including insurance companies, issuers of publicly-offered securities, general fund managers, banks and stock exchanges) to sustainability and corporate governance issues (climate change, respect for human rights, adoption of gender-focused policies, and engagement with stakeholders, among others). Furthermore, in application of the recently enacted Law No 21.595 (Economic Crimes Law), if directors, managers, administrators or main executives of a corporation provide or approve the provision of false information in the company's annual report required by the FMC, they and the corporation could be subject to criminal liability.

Although General Rule No 461 has been a milestone in the Americas, its scope already exhibits limitations in the face of the new and forthcoming regulations regarding disclosure obligations in Europe, the United States and Canada. The limited reach of this regulation becomes apparent upon examining the incremental but still small number of companies subject to reporting

---

1   See for example, "In the midst of Chile's megadrought, anger turns towards avocados", www.lemonde.fr/en/m-le-mag/article/2022/10/20/in-the-midst-of-chile-s-megadrought-anger-turns-toward-avocados_6001156_117.html.

2   General Rule No 461 of the Financial Market Commission available at www.cmfchile.cl/normativa/ncg_461_2021.pdf.

obligations, the absence of mandatory external certification, and the omission of Scope 3 emissions reporting. While the mandatory reporting requirements remain somewhat timid, Chile has nonetheless experienced a rapid conventional incorporation of ESG criteria given its deep integration into the global market. Consequently, even though it will take some time for Chilean legislation to align with the new reporting standards under discussion in other jurisdictions, it is the demands of the international market and foreign credit and capital that will compel major Chilean businesses and the banking sector to proactively embrace the principles outlined in the European Sustainability Reporting Standards adopted by the Corporate Sustainability Reporting Directive, as well as the adopted Securities and Exchange Commission's Climate Related Disclosure Rules, which are suspended for the time being. This early and semi-voluntary adoption, well in advance of these standards becoming legally binding through strengthened domestic regulation, marks the strengths of international ESG as soft law.

3.   Brazil

The situation in Brazil with regard to ESG requires special attention, as this country is not only the largest in the region in terms of both economy and population, but also contains within its borders 65% of the Amazon rainforest, one of the most biodiverse regions on the planet, home of several indigenous tribes, and a key geographical area in relation to climate change mitigation.

Long-standing issues such as corruption, the occurrence of severe environmental disasters often linked to both climate change and illegal or unsafe extractive activities, as well as deforestation caused by the agro-industry in the Amazon, have engendered reluctance among ESG investors, precisely where it is most needed. In that regard, Brazil, especially in relation to who holds political power, has seen the emergence of ESG requirements as both a risk and a great opportunity. Despite the fluctuating attitude of successive governments regarding the adoption of regulation tied to ESG criteria, market actors, particularly in Brazil's huge financial sector – the Brazilian banking sector accounts for the 53% of all Latin America and the Caribbean assets[3] – have consistently progressed over recent years in integrating sustainability criteria into their risk analysis and financial products.

Since 2018, the Brazilian Monetary Council requires pension funds asset managers to include ESG risk assessment in their investment decision making.[4] In coordination with the aforementioned Council, the Central Bank of Brazil, following the recommendations of the Taskforce on Climate related Financial

---

3   (OECD 2022), p20.
4   Resolution CMN No 4.661, of 25 May 2018, available at: www.gov.br/economia/pt-br/orgaos/entidades-vinculadas/autarquias/previc/regulacao/normas/resolucoes/resolucoes-cmn/resolucao-cmn-no-4-661-de-25-de-maio-de-2018.pdf/view.

Disclosures, has also issued, starting in 2021, a set of new reporting rules for financial institutions.[5]

The Brazilian Federation of Banks has, since 2018, published guidance for lenders aimed at mitigating deforestation risks, especially with regard to critical industries such as cattle farming, soybean and palm culture, and pulp and paper production.[6] This same association also developed a Green Taxonomy in 2020 as well as an Explanatory Guide to its Green Taxonomy in 2021 aiming to clarify the 'green' credentials of sustainable investments and thus foster investors' confidence in the ESG market. For its part, Brazil's National Development Bank for Economic and Social Development (BNDES) issued its own Green Bond Framework in 2017, as well as a Sustainability Bond Framework according to the Green and Social Bond Principles, Sustainability Bond Guidelines and the United Nations Sustainable Development Goals in 2021. In 2022, BNDES signed a new cooperation agreement with the Climate Bonds Initiative looking to generate further mechanisms to bring international investment for sustainable projects.

The Brazilian Stock Exchange, in alliance with the S&P Dow Jones Indices, created in 2021 the S&P/B3 Brazil ESG Index, and the Brazilian Association of Financial and Capital Market Entities has expanded requirements for funds, allowing only funds which invest 100% in sustainable investment to use the suffix "IS".[7]

Finally, in January 2023 the Brazilian Securities Commission Resolution No 59 came into force, requiring ESG information disclosure criteria for publicly held companies, including its ESG key performance indicators, its materiality matrix, the companies' alignments with the United Nations Sustainable Development Goals, the applied ESG standards, as well as the inclusion or not of external audits and an inventory of greenhouse gas emissions.[8] In the same manner as the Chilean Financial Market Commission's General Rule No 461, Brazil's regulation does not require the use of a specific methodology or the involvement of external audits, and there are ultimately no clear penalties for non-compliance with the standard. As part of the plan to transition to a green economy nonetheless, at the end of 2023, Brazil made it mandatory for all public companies to submit annual sustainability and climate reports as of 2026, in accordance with the IFRS Sustainability Disclosure Standards developed by the International Sustainability Standards Board.

---

5   Brazilian Central Bank Resolution No 139/2021 mandates an annual report on Social, Environmental, and Climate Risks and Opportunities to financial institutions. Other relevant resolutions in relation to ESG disclosure are Brazilian Central Bank Resolution No 151/2021, Brazilian Central Bank Normative Instruction No 153/2021, and Brazilian Central Bank Normative Instruction No 222/2021.

6   (OECD 2022), p27.

7   See ANBIMA's "A Landscape of Sustainability in the Brazilian Capital Market", www.anbima.com.br/data/files/9D/11/CC/94/B1A8F710F62888F76B2BA2A8/A_landscape_of_sustainability_in_the_brazilian_capital_market.pdf.

8   Brazilian Securities Commission Resolution No 59, available at https://in.gov.br/en/web/dou/-/resolucao-cvm-n-59-de-22-de-dezembro-de-2021-369780708.

An ongoing development highly welcomed by human rights activists, is the current discussion of the Bill of Law No 572/2022, seeking to establish a framework for business and human rights, in which companies would be responsible for the integral reparation of the victims.

Beyond the expected increase in binding ESG regulation with the current government,[9] the creation of a comprehensive and official taxonomy is necessary to provide clarity to long-term investors across various sectors of Brazil's powerful economy. Currently, while state agencies catch up with international ESG standards, it is the same sheer power of Brazil's economy that has led to the incorporation of ESG criteria becoming a well-established reality, at least in the financial sector, for quite some time.

4.   Colombia

Colombia is undoubtedly one of the Latin-American countries that exhibits most significant success in the integration of a regulatory framework and sustainable growth policies compatible with ESG criteria. While Colombia leads the region's efforts to align the objectives of the Paris Agreement with its financial system, the country also stands out for its institutional efforts to generate a comprehensive national development policy that is not only compatible but synergistic with sustainable development.[10]

Having issued green sovereign bonds in accordance with the Green Bond Principles of the International Capital Market Association as early as 2021, Colombia, second only to Chile in the region, became the first American country to publish a comprehensive Green Taxonomy in collaboration with the World Bank and the International Finance Corporation in March 2022. This taxonomy encompasses all major productive sectors and enables the harmonisation of criteria for assessing assets and economic activities based on their alignment with sustainability objectives, particularly those related to decarbonisation.

The Financial Superintendence of Colombia (SFC) for its part, has established rules for integrating ESG risks in the investment analysis of pension funds and insurance companies. Furthermore, through External Circular No 28 of 2020, the SFC has regulated the issuance of ESG bonds in accordance with international standards and, in April 2022, through External Circular 008, regulated the sustainability-linked bond market in connection with the new taxonomy.

---

9   A trend that will also be strengthened by Brazil's Federal Supreme Court ruling ADPF No 708 which acknowledged international environmental treaties such as the Paris Agreement as human rights treaties, thus recognising their supra legal status and the State s constitutional obligation to act on climate change. See *PSB et al v Brazil* (on Climate Fund) (ADPF 708) available at: www.escr-net.org/caselaw/2023/psb-et-al-v-brazil-climate-fund-adpf-708#:~:text=The%20Court%20ordered%20the%20the %20Federal,the%20issue%20of%20climate%20change.

10   See for example the Colombian National Council on Economic and Social Policy (CONPES) Green Growth Policy (CONPES 3934), as well as its Strategy for the Implementation of Sustainable Development Objectives in Colombia (CONPES 3918).

Finally, with regard to reporting obligations for publicly traded companies, the SFC, through its External Circular 31/2021, has mandated that all issuers registered in the National Register of Securities and Issuers provide annual and quarterly ESG information. Starting in 2024, this information should include, at a minimum, a chapter dedicated to practices, policies, processes and indicators relating to social and environmental issues, including climate issues. Furthermore, quarterly reports should be provided for any material changes in these areas.[11]

Additionally, the Government published in 2021 the Guidelines for the Development of Sustainable Transportation Infrastructure Projects for the Fifth Generation of CONPES Concessions.[12]

However, not all initiatives have been successful, as some have encountered significant implementation difficulties or a lack of proper transparency and accountability. For example, the REDD+ project initiative, which allows companies needing to offset their carbon footprint to allocate resources to distant local communities working on projects aimed at curbing deforestation, has faced serious accusations in the Matavén Forest region. Specifically, questions have been raised regarding the accuracy and validity of the measurements used to calculate the contribution against deforestation, which is utilised for bonds linked to native forest preservation efforts in the area.[13]

In a similar vein, a widely celebrated initiative has been the Reduction of Greenhouse Gas Emissions Registry (RENARE). In 2015, Law 1,753 established the National Development Plan 2014–2018 for Colombia, which created RENARE as a registry for all reduction and removal of greenhouse gas initiatives, aiming to qualify for payments or compensations. However, this programme, designed to monitor and encourage the country's progress towards its Paris Agreement commitments, has faced multiple operative challenges – including technical failures at the project's registration. Moreover, several operational challenges, including technical failures in project registration and legal pitfalls such as the Colombian Government assigning the programme's operation to a different agency than the one established by law, resulted in the suspension of its operation by the Colombian Council of State. As of March 2024, it is still to be decided who will be in charge of the administration of RENARE.

5.   Mexico

Mexico, as the second largest country in the region in terms of economics and population, faces many of the same challenges as Brazil in advancing ESG

---

11   Colombia SFC External Circular 31/2021, https://cdn.actualicese.com/normatividad/2021/Circulares/
      CE031-21.pdf.
12   CONPES 4060/21, https://colaboracion.dnp.gov.co/CDT/Conpes/Econ%C3%B3micos/4060.pdf.
13   Report regarding this issue available at https://es.mongabay.com/2021/06/bonos-de-carbono-mataven-
      colombia-redd-investigacion/.

practices, including corruption and poor labour and migration conditions, as well as, in this particular case, drug trafficking violence.

Like Brazil, however, the Mexican market has a high appeal for foreign investment, despite some criticism of governmental actions against renewal energy investments in recent years. This openness of the Mexican market, especially after the entry into force in 2020 of the United States-Mexico-Canada Trade Agreement,[14] has favoured the adoption of measures and practices aimed at improving the social and environmental performance of investments in Mexico, so as not to lose and even enhance its appeal to foreign capital.

For example, the sustainability initiatives of the Mexican Stock Exchange date back to the launch in 2011 of the Business Sustainability and Well-being Index, which has been modified several times until the current Sustainability Guide with ESG recommendations for public listed companies according to the main international sustainability frameworks. In June 2020, the Mexican Stock Exchange launched its own sustainable index with the S&P/BMV Total Mexico ESG Index, and in 2022 its Carbon Neutrality Guide. For its part, the Institutional Stock Exchange has recently created a Chief Sustainability Officer Acceleration Program to facilitate the adoption of corporate sustainability principles by its Mexican market agents.

Other initiatives to highlight have been the General Provisions in Financial Matters applicable to the Retirement Savings Systems in 2022, which regulate the ESG investment of retirement fund managers (AFOREs), and the actions of the Green Finance Advisory Council tracking and promoting sustainable finance through the regulation of green bond issuers including third-party certification requirement.

On its part, the Ministry of Finance and Public Credit (SHCP) has undertaken actions such as aligning the Federal Expenditure Budget with the United Nations Sustainable Development Goals and designing the Sustainable Development Goals Sovereign Bond Framework.[15] More significantly, in March 2023, the SHCP introduced a Sustainable Taxonomy for the financial sector.[16] This will serve as a reference framework that will allow the identification of sustainable assets and projects under technical criteria (ie, assessment of substantial contribution to sustainability, criteria of no significant environmental harm and minimum safeguards, among others) and measure their impacts on environmental, social and governance variables. This taxonomy stands out for its transversal nature, covering 124 activities

---

14   United States-Mexico-Canada Trade Agreement available at: https://ustr.gov/trade-agreements/free-trade-agreements/united-states-mexico-canada-agreement.

15   Mexico's SDG Bond Allocation Impact Report 2021, www.finanzaspublicas.hacienda.gob.mx/work/models/Finanzas_Publicas/docs/ori/Espanol/SDG/Mexico_SDG_Bond_Allocation-Impact_Report_2021.pdf.

16   "Mexico's Sustainable Taxonomy" (1st edn), www.gob.mx/cms/uploads/attachment/file/809773/Taxonom_a_Sostenible_de_M_xico_.pdf.

distributed in six economic sectors. It also stands out for incorporating criteria for mitigation and adaptation to climate change, as well as objectives for gender equality and prevention of greenwashing. It is important to bear in mind nonetheless that Sustainable Taxonomy will not be applicable to small and medium-sized companies.

An important gap in Mexico's ESG regulatory framework is the lack of a proper mandatory comprehensive duty to report. Although publicly listed companies have some disclosure obligations related to ESG, they are scarce and extremely deficient in relation to international standards, and even compared to other Latin American jurisdictions. In 2023, the Mexican Council of Financial Information Standards announced the development of Sustainability Information Standards based on the International Sustainability Standards Board, which are expected to be in force from January 2025. The creation of obligations for public reporting of general ESG information under objective and standardised parameters is undoubtedly necessary to provide vital information not only for investors, but for all stakeholders of a company.

6. Conclusion

In conclusion, the advancement of ESG practices in Latin America is a complex and evolving landscape. While the region faces numerous challenges such as political instability, corruption, social conflicts and environmental degradation, there has been progress in embracing ESG principles. Countries like Chile, Brazil, Colombia and Mexico have made notable efforts to integrate ESG criteria into their regulatory frameworks and market practices. The influence of international commercial pressure, foreign financing and investment, as well as consumer awareness has played a significant role in driving the adoption of sustainable practices. However, there are still limitations and gaps in terms of reporting obligations and their scope, certification requirements, and comprehensive regulatory frameworks. Further developments are needed to ensure transparency, accountability and the alignment of domestic standards with global ESG standards. Latin America has the potential to become a leader in sustainable development, and ongoing efforts to strengthen ESG practices will be crucial to align the need for economic development with full respect and protection of the environment and the satisfaction of the region's social demands.

ESG in the insurance sector

Daniela Bergs
Thomas Kelly
Howden

1. Introduction

ESG is central to the insurance industry, arguably more so than any other. It provides a structure for assessing risks and identifying opportunities related to climate change, social issues and governance. These factors can have a significant impact on the long-term financial performance of insurers and society as a whole.

For example, insurers have been facing increased claims related to extreme weather events or natural disasters, which can affect their bottom line. By incorporating ESG considerations into their underwriting decisions, insurers can better assess and manage these risks. Insurers also need to assess ESG risks in their investments and identify opportunities for growth and innovation in a changing global landscape.

In addition, companies are increasingly being asked to demonstrate their commitment to sustainability and responsible business practices by stakeholders such as customers and investors. According to Bain & Company's 2023 customer behaviour and market survey, 80% of consumers said they want insurers to incorporate ESG initiatives into their offerings.[1] As a result, attracting and retaining customers and investors who share these values can be a competitive advantage for insurers that embrace ESG principles.

However, the insurance sector faces several challenges with respect to ESG.

- *Measuring ESG factors:* Insurers have difficulty with the measurement of ESG factors due to their complexity. Each insurer has different drivers for measuring ESG factors (eg, regulatory, stakeholder expectations, etc) and the challenge is to align all metrics according to the insurer's individual needs. Available metrics used in investment or underwriting decisions are inconsistent and often difficult to integrate. In most cases, smaller insurers struggle with limited human and financial resources to collect and analyse the data. Larger insurers may be able to collect the data, but it is often unclear how the data is then integrated.

---

[1] Henrik Naujoks, Andrew Scwedel and Tania Brettel, "Customer Behavior and Loyalty in Insurance: Global Edition", Bain & Company (16 February 2023), www.bain.com/insights/customer-behavior-and-loyalty-in-insurance-global-edition-2023/.

- *Consistency of ESG data:* A key obstacle is the lack of consistent data on ESG factors and the difficulty of assessing risk without a clear set of useful data. This makes it challenging for insurers to get an accurate picture of a company's sustainability performance and complicates comparing it with other companies. The data is not yet designed for use by the insurance industry, making it extremely difficult for the end user to aggregate the data; in essence, the data isn't yet trusted by the insurer.
- *Continuous change:* ESG standards are growing and changing quickly, often through societal or regulatory involvement. Insurers are facing challenges keeping up with the changing definition of ESG factors and it is difficult to navigate the landscape.

Nevertheless, changing ESG factors also present new opportunities for insurers.

- *Improved risk management:* Climate-related weather events have increased insurers' exposure to large losses. By integrating ESG factors into their underwriting and investment strategies, insurers can better prepare for and mitigate their climate-related risks. This will ultimately have a positive impact on their profitability.
- *Stakeholder demands:* Stakeholders are pressuring companies to demonstrate a commitment to longevity and sustainable business practices. Insurers create a competitive advantage by embracing stakeholder ESG values.
- *Product innovation:* ESG-related risks can provide new opportunities for product innovation and addressing emerging risks related to climate change, social issues and corporate governance.

In general, the insurance industry understands that ESG factors will continue to shape the perception of risk and are therefore a key factor for insurers to position themselves as market leaders. They are already implementing a wide range of opportunities as outlined above.

2.   ESG integration

ESG integration is already widespread in the insurance industry. Here are just a few examples of how they are included in their daily operations.

- *ESG and investments:* Insurers use non-financial ESG factors to screen potential investments and promote sustainability in their investment decision-making process. The insurance market is incorporating ESG factors not only for ethical reasons, but also because the sustainable investment market is predicted to quadruple from 2020 to 2030.[2]

---

2   Stout Insights, "The ROI of ESG", Stout (12 April 2024), www.stout.com/en/insights/article/roi-esg; Christopher Marchant, "Global ESG market predicted to quadruple by 2030", *Net Zero Investor* (19 June 2023).

- *ESG insurance products:* Several insurance companies are offering products that specifically address ESG issues. Examples include microinsurance, parametric insurance and cat bonds. Other innovations include lower premiums for certain customer groups or incentives for customers with certain internal measures in place.
- *Underwriting and disclosure requirements:* The implementation of ESG factors in the underwriting process has been an ongoing debate, particularly in the commercial and industrial lines. To date, there has not been a consistent approach among insurers. However, there have been initiatives to provide some guidance to insurers, such as the United Nations Environment Programme's (UNEP) Principles for Sustainable Insurance Initiative, which provides an ESG framework. It offers a guide to implementing risk assessment from "climate change, ecosystem degradation, pollution and animal welfare and testing; to child labour, controversial weapons, and bribery and corruption".[3]

3.   ESG and non-life insurance

ESG-related risks have had a significant impact on traditional insurance products, such as property and casualty (P&C) or directors and officers (D&O) insurance. The following paragraphs examine the different product lines and how ESG factors are influencing their underwriting process.

3.1   P&C insurance

P&C insurance is a general term and covers damages to or loss of property or liability claims. It protects businesses from financial losses caused by accident, theft, natural catastrophes or legal disputes.

3.2   D&O insurance

D&O insurance policies provide directors and officers with liability coverage to protect them from claims that may arise from decisions and actions they take as part of their duties as directors and officers.

3.3   Underwriting ESG

P&C and D&O insurance lines have suffered the highest amount of claims, given they have had to pay out high losses in recent years. These have related to increased weather impacted losses or high-profile cases affected by poor ESG implementation, such as if a company's board of directors fails to implement effective ESG policies and practices, which could lead to them facing legal action or regulatory penalties.

---

3   UN Environment Programme Finance Initiative, PSI ESG Guide for Non-Life Insurance, "Managing environmental, social and governance risks in non-life insurance business" (June 2020), www.unepfi.org/psi/wp-content/uploads/2020/06/PSI-ESG-guide-for-non-life-insurance.pdf.

An increase in 1 in 100-year weather events is one of the ways that climate change is affecting property insurance. These are events that have a 1% chance of occurring in any given year, but due to climate change are occurring more frequently than previously predicted.

Because of these growing risks, property insurers face higher losses, which may lead to higher premiums for policyholders. The (re)insurance market has suffered an unprecedented run of US$10 billion plus weather-related losses in real terms since 2017, with the number of events (12) more than double anything seen in previous five-year periods.[4]

In response to these challenges, property insurers are adapting their underwriting practices and risk management strategies to account for this change.

According to a 2023 analysis report from the World Business Council for Sustainable Development, lawsuits against companies concerning ESG issues have grown by 25% over the last three decades.[5] In addition, there has been a rise in shareholder activism related to ESG issues, with investors using their leverage to pressure companies to improve their ESG performance.

Poor ESG performance can also result in reputational damage and loss of shareholder value, which can lead to D&O insurance claims. Higher ESG ratings can lead to improved underwriting performance.

In response to these trends, D&O insurers are increasingly considering ESG factors in their underwriting and risk management practices. Some insurers are also offering ESG-related coverage and services, such as ESG advisory services.

Therefore, ESG factors are now being considered in the underwriting process, especially in areas that are vulnerable to climate-related risks, such as coastal areas, wildfire-prone regions and flood zones. Insurers are taking into account the potential costs associated with climate-related risks when underwriting policies, which may result in changes to policy terms or premiums or whether coverage can be offered.

Reinsurers are also factoring ESG considerations into their underwriting processes, which can impact the availability and cost of reinsurance for insurers. This can have a significant impact on the overall cost and profitability of P&C insurance products.

Insurers are increasingly being held accountable for the environmental and social impact of their underwriting decisions. Negative publicity surrounding a company's underwriting practices can harm its reputation and lead to decreased customer loyalty and investor confidence.

---

4   Howden Group Holdings, "Climate in peril", (2021), www.howdengroup.com/sites/g/files/mwfley566/files/2021-10/Howden-climate-in-peril-report-20211015-final.pdf.

5   World Business Council for Sustainable Development, "The Rise in ESG lawsuits highlights the need for companies to evaluate supply chain risks" (14 February 2023), www.wbcsd.org/Overview/News-Insights/General/News/The-rise-in-ESG-lawsuits-highlights-the-need-for-companies-to-evaluate-supply-chain-risks.

3.4   ESG losses

- The Wells Fargo 2016 fake accounts scandal resulted in a US$3 billion settlement.[6] The lack of corporate transparency and governance resulted in Wells Fargo opening up millions of fake bank and credit accounts in the names of their customers without their consent.
- European floods in July 2021 resulted in an estimated loss of US$13.8 billion.[7] The heavy rainfall caused severe flooding in Germany and Belgium.
- Sexual misconduct claims have increased in recent years with a number of high-profile cases resulting in significant losses. Insurers paid out approximately US$35 million in claims for Harvey Weinstein settlements.[8]

The response of the insurance market to losses as illustrated above has been inconsistent and most notably the insurers have responded by substantial premium increases or by pulling out of insuring companies or properties in certain geographical areas. To date, the most practical steps the insurance market has taken to mitigate ESG-related losses are the integration of improved risk assessment and management processes.

Insurance companies are investing in new technologies and data analytics tools to improve their risk assessment. This helps them to identify and monitor ESG-related risks and make informed decisions about underwriting and pricing.

Examples of these tools include ClimateWise, the UNEP Principles of Sustainable Insurance and Net-Zero Insurance Alliance.

4.   ClimateWise, UNEP Principles of Sustainable Insurance and The Net-Zero Insurance Alliance

Launched in 2007, ClimateWise is a global initiative of the insurance industry. It is a platform for sharing knowledge and best practices on climate change and sustainability. Members are required to report on their activities, which allows them to benchmark their progress against each other.[9]

The UNEP Principles for Sustainable Insurance (PSI) is a framework developed by the United Nations Environment Programme (UNEP) to promote

---

6   Office of Public Affairs, US Department of Justice, "Wells Fargo Agrees to Pay $3 Billion to Resolve Criminal and Civil Investigations into Sales Practices Involving the Opening of Millions of Accounts without Customer Authorization", Press Release (21 February 2020), www.justice.gov/opa/pr/wells-fargo-agrees-pay-3-billion-resolve-criminal-and-civil-investigations-sales-practices.

7   S Evans, "Cresta raises July 2021 European flood industry loss estimate to $13.8bn", Artemis (3 October 2022), www.artemis.bm/news/cresta-raises-july-2021-european-flood-industry-loss-estimate-to-13-8bn/.

8   T Winter and A Reiss, "Court approves $17 million payout for Harvey Weinstein's accusers", NBC News (26 January 2021), www.nbcnews.com/news/us-news/court-approves-17-million-payout-harvey-weinstein-s-accusers-n1255609.

9   University of Cambridge Institute for Sustainability Leadership (CISL), ClimateWise, www.cisl.cam.ac.uk/business-action/sustainable-finance/climatewise.

sustainable practices in the insurance industry. It helps insurance companies identify and manage risks and opportunities, and integrate best practices within the company and in the industry.[10]

The Net-Zero Insurance Alliance (NZIA) is a global initiative launched in 2021 by the United Nations PSI and leading insurance companies from around the world. The NZIA is a commitment by participating insurance companies to work towards net zero greenhouse gas emissions by 2050.[11]

The requirement for ESG to be at the heart of insurance frameworks is borne out clearly in the drive by the insurance industry to expand the scope of its coverage for disasters that are becoming more frequent and more severe due to climate change. For centuries, major corporations and governments have looked to the insurance industry to respond when there is a major natural catastrophe, with various major events in the Western world, from the 1905 San Francisco earthquake to Hurricane Katrina in 2005 being underwritten and covered within the insurance market. The insurance industry is relied upon because of its risk-modelling expertise and broad data set of historical losses, and if properly used, insurance can help to protect the real economy and help weather fortuitous, bad storms. Disaster relief insurance has grown out of the established 'natural catastrophe' insurance market. The natural catastrophe market has traditionally focused on areas which have a high concentration of valuable assets and are vulnerable to extreme natural events, such as in the Gulf of Mexico and Japan's eastern seaboard. There has been a trend in recent years to extend the insurance coverage to a broader spectrum of global society, using innovative structures such as parametric insurance and catastrophe bonds in order to provide cover for some of the world's most vulnerable communities. Innovation within the disaster relief insurance space resonates clearly with the three pillars of ESG, as the new structures and frameworks help to address and mitigate the environmental and societal problems that are caused by climate change. The convening power of various forums and organisations within the insurance market have also introduced a level of good governance across the market.

5.   Insurance innovation in the climate space

The climate crisis is redefining the role of insurance, making it a key player in mitigating financial losses due to the effects of climate change, and helping to build resilience to some of the worst effects of climate change. Commercial insurance is emerging as a key tool in building resilience, and is responding to the need for product development and constant evolution. The following

---

10   UN Environment Programme Finance Initiative, "Guidance on the integration of ESG risks into insurance underwriting", www.unepfi.org/insurance/insurance/projects/guidance-on-the-integration-of-esg-risks-into-insurance-underwriting/.
11   Principles for Responsible Investment, https://www.unpri.org/.

paragraphs provide an overview of disaster relief insurance, parametric insurance and voluntary carbon market insurance, as well as the use of climate analytics. These are some of the areas that are ripe for disruption by innovative insurance structures.

Insurance has an important role to play in helping to mitigate the damage from the climate crisis. The increase in natural catastrophes as a result of climate change is inevitable, given the damage that has already been done to the environment. In the IPCC's Sixth Assessment Report, "Climate Change 2022: Impacts, Adaptation and Vulnerability" there was a stark warning laid down that if significant changes weren't made, global temperatures would rise to over three degrees above pre-industrial levels, resulting in more frequent and extreme climatic events.[12] There were several different actions that the IPCC recommended, including a focus on transparency with regards to reporting, and a focus on ensuring carbon taxes are used correctly to enhance emission reduction.[13] The IPCC Report identifies commercial insurance as an important tool in an organisation's arsenal when it comes to building resilience. Parametric insurance products can be used as tools to help communities adapt to climate risks and support sustainable development. They can reduce both vulnerability and exposure, support post-disaster recovery and reduce financial burden on governments, households and business.

Insurance mechanisms enjoy wide legal and regulatory acceptability among policymakers and are institutionally feasible. However, socio-cultural and financial barriers make insurance spatially and temporally challenging to implement, even though it can improve the resilience and well-being of populations.[14] There is a significant risk that the programmes that are put in place do not generate the outcomes that they are designed to produce, which would be detrimental to the resilience of populations. There are also several hurdles that must be overcome. These include expanding the knowledge base on insurance, which is fundamental to successfully implementing insurance among all relevant stakeholders and determining where the funding will come from for the premium payments. Successful outcomes help to promote the use of insurance within populations that typically have not had access to it in the past, leading to more success, in a virtuous cycle. As discussed above, there is also a need to ensure equitable access to and benefits from innovative financial products such as parametric insurance products.

---

12 IPCC Sixth Assessment Report, "Climate Change 2022: Impacts, Adaptation and Vulnerability", www.ipcc.ch/report/ar6/wg2/.
13 S Mundy, P Temple-West and P Shimzuishi, "What we learned from the IPCC report", FT.com (2022), www.ft.com/content/b451075c-0ec1-4904-96c4-8ea0aa993a66.
14 IPCC Sixth Assessment Report, see n 12 above.

6. Parametric insurance

There are several ways that the insurance market can help support the provision of disaster risk insurance for vulnerable communities around the world. On the face of it, parametric insurance seems to be a fantastic opportunity for wider society, as traditional insurance capacity in both the insurance and reinsurance market is becoming more limited when it comes to natural catastrophes. There is wide acknowledgement in the market that more capacity is required in the natural catastrophe space, if the insurance sector is to continue to stay relevant as climate change increases both the severity and volatility of natural weather events. The market needs to continue to innovate in order to present new ways of transferring risk for the humanitarian organisations who are helping to build and maintain resilience in vulnerable communities around the world.

Parametric insurance, by its very nature, is able to provide humanitarian organisations with rapid funds that they require in the face of disaster. The availability of data is increasing the proliferation of parametric products, making them more accessible for organisations and individuals that had not previously accessed the parametric market. The importance of this rapid response should not be underestimated when it comes to allowing communities to recover quickly, which is a sign of good resilience. There are two ways that a parametric insurance programme can be structured; to provide rapid funds in the event of a disaster and to provide a different type of payout to a traditional indemnity policy. The rapid delivery of funds can help governments and organisations provide immediate relief, which dramatically increases the ability of communities to recover after a disaster. Parametric insurance allows for more scientific pricing of insurance products, and alongside lower claims management costs this can make them more viable.

The parametric market is poised to take advantage of the retreat of traditional (re)insurance capital in the natural catastrophe space, alongside other forms of alternative risk capital such as the insurance linked security market. In recent times, this has become more apparent for the wider reinsurance market as traditional catastrophe programmes have been battered by major catastrophes. In a recent report, it is claimed that the reinsurance sector has reached a 'tipping point' that has been caused by structural changes to the loss environment as well as macroeconomic forces that it labels the 'Three Cs' – conflict, climate and capital.[15] There is a parametric cycle of innovation and capital within the parametric market, and we are coming to a point of confluence where both will be aligned.

---

[15]   J Alovisi, "Reinsurance, A Tipping Point" (2022), www.howdengroup.com/sites/g/files/mwfley566/files/2022-09/howden-reinsurance-a-tipping-point-report.pdf.

7. Disaster relief insurance

For many decades, the insurance market sought to work with governments or groups of governments in order to facilitate the provision of disaster relief for vulnerable populations worldwide, and have utilised parametric structures to do so. There are several good examples of the successful structuring and implementation of these types of programmes: insurance companies have been assisting governmental and other state entities with the design and implementation of disaster relief programmes for decades.[16] Examples of this include Belize (Mesoamerican reef), Caribbean (Caribbean Catastrophe Risk Insurance Faculty (CCRIF)), Philippines (catastrophe bond) and New Zealand (earthquake protection).[17]

The CCRIF is particularly noteworthy, as it came about as a result of a major hurricane, Hurricane Ivan in 2004, and has provided consistent payouts to Caribbean nations since then, most notably Haiti during the devastating 2010 earthquake.[18] It is worth examining the New Zealand earthquake programme and Haiti's coverage within the CCRIF in more detail to understand the work that the insurance market has carried out so far in the disaster relief space. A paper written by the Bank of International Settlements in 2012 discusses the comparison between two large earthquakes that impacted Christchurch and Haiti in 2010/2011.[19] They were both of similar size, with a magnitude of 7.0, and occurred in close proximity to population centres, which were of similar economic importance to their respective countries.[20] The major difference identified within the paper is that the financial preparedness of the two cities, and countries, was poles apart. While Christchurch was well prepared, with an insurance programme that had been in place to protect against a disaster, Port-au-Prince in Haiti was underprepared and, as a result, suffered far greater losses, both financial and humanitarian. The Christchurch earthquake actually resulted in a mini-boom for the local economy, as insurance money flowed in and sparked growth in the construction industry. Insurance cannot prevent disasters happening; however, by using sovereign risk pools, countries in the emerging markets that are susceptible to natural disasters are able to channel payouts to vulnerable communities, allowing for a faster emergency response. The insurance payouts that have been made from these structures demonstrate

---

16 S Sowers and A Michel, "Parametric Insurance: Shaping the Future of Public Sector Resilience with Data and Technology", Wharton University of Pennsylvania (8 June 2022), https://esg.wharton.upenn.edu/climate-center/parametric-insurance-shaping-the-future-of-public-sector-resilience-with-data-and-technology/.

17 International Coral Reef Initiative, "First pay-out of Mesoamerican Reef Insurance Programme in Belize", 22 November 2022, https://icriforum.org/first-reef-insurance-payout-belize/.

18 C Kousky, *Understanding Disaster Insurance: New tools for a more resilient future* (Island Press, 2022).

19 G von Peter, S von Dahlen and S Saxena, BIS Working Papers: No 394 "Unmitigated disasters? New evidence on the macroeconomic cost of natural catastrophes", Bank for International Settlements (December 2012), www.bis.org/publ/work394.pdf.

20 *Ibid.*

the benefits that innovative insurance cover can provide against a changing climate. In addition, the countries that have participated in these sovereign risk pools have benefited as it reduces the cost of capital and the operating costs compared to if they were purchasing insurance individually.

8. The voluntary carbon market

The voluntary carbon market (VCM) is a marketplace where organisations and individuals can offset some of the emissions that they produce by purchasing carbon credits from project developers that design and implement projects that remove carbon from the atmosphere through sequestration. There are a variety of different project types, ranging from nature-based projects such as reforestation or mangrove restoration to engineering-based projects that include direct air capture mechanisms and carbon capture and storage. The methodologies that the project developers use within the VCM are set by the registries, typically non-profit entities that also act as the repository of the credits. Some of the larger ones include Verra, Gold Standard and American Carbon Registry.

Throughout the project life cycle, which leads to the generation of carbon credits, there are various risks that project developers and buyers of credits face. These range from traditional insurances such as third-party crime and political risks to natural weather events that could lead to the demise of a carbon project. Insurance has played a role in the voluntary carbon market from the beginning, as the registries established buffer pools to address some of the natural risks that carbon projects face. More recently, the entities that operate within the voluntary carbon market are increasingly looking for other insurance options to mitigate some of their risks and use insurance balance sheets as a means to boost confidence within the market as a whole.

There have been various different products developed within the insurance market that seek to address some of these risks. There are three approaches to the innovative development of new products within the carbon market. The first approach involves relying on existing insurance coverages within other business lines, with the innovation deriving from looking at a whole new asset class. A good example of this approach is a recently developed product with a carbon fund (Respira).[21] The cover was designed to protect Respira and its clients from fraud and negligence by the underlying project developers. In the event that a fraud was discovered, and the carbon credit that had been purchased was rendered worthless then the insured could claim against the insurance policy to recover its lost value and repurchase credits on the open market. This product helped to build buyer confidence in the marketplace.

---

21   Howden, "Howden launches 'World First' voluntary carbon credit insurance product to help scale the market" (6 September 2022), www.howdengroup.com/uk-en/Howden-launches-World-First-voluntary-carbon-credit-insurance-product-to-help-scale-the-market#:~:text=6%20September%202022%2C%20London%20%E2%80%93%20Howden,invalidation%20insurance%20solution%20to%20increase.

The second approach to innovation within the carbon market lies in the way that insurers are approaching how they indemnify their clients. While a cash payment is helpful for clients, as it allows them to repurchase carbon credits on the open market, what many of the corporates and other organisations need is to retire credits against their carbon emissions. Therefore, an insurance payment that was paid in like-for-like carbon credits would be very beneficial for clients, as they would not need to go back out into the market and repurchase credits. There have been two examples of this innovative new claims payment being arranged within the insurance market. The first was by AXA XL, a large European insurer, who in 2023 announced that it had partnered with a carbon business called Climate Seed to provide a carbon credit payment within the marine industry in the event that there was a delay in a cargo shipment that resulted in excess emissions.[22] The second example of this innovation was a recent announcement by Kita Earth, a managing general agent (MGA) that focuses solely on carbon insurance risks. MGAs are underwriting businesses, that operate in niche areas of the insurance market, typically underwriting specialist risks with underwriting authority given to them by other insurance carriers. Kita Earth has partnered with multiple different carbon entities to allow for clients to take the option of receiving a payment in carbon credits in the event that its flagship non-delivery cover is taken out.[23] The non-delivery cover protects buyers against a shortfall of delivery of credits, in the event that they have a forward purchase agreement in place with project developers.

The third approach to innovation is that there has been an increase in the number of MGAs that are being established to focus solely on the carbon market. This new capacity and expertise within the insurance market is a signal to entities within the carbon market that there is good appetite for taking on new risks, and that there is a long-term approach to innovation. There are three notable MGAs that have been set up recently, the first of which is Kita, mentioned above. Its focus is on non-delivery risks within the carbon market, and with its product, seeks to boost investor confidence within the market which will help it to scale. The second is a US-focused start-up called Oka, that has recently announced that it has approval to launch a syndicate-in-a-box at Lloyd's of London.[24] Oka's focus is on the reporting commitments that US businesses are going to be required to adhere to from 2024, regarding their climate commitments. Oka will provide cover for impaired carbon credits, which will insure the potential reputational losses that a corporate buyer might

22 AXA, "AXA XL launches carbon emissions product for marine clients", Press Release (18 July 2023), https://axaxl.com/press-releases/axa-xl-launches-carbon-emissions-product-for-marine-clients.
23 Kita, "Kita announces pioneering approach for paying claims in carbon" (12 October 2023), www.kita.earth/blog/press-release-kita-announces-pioneering-approach-for-paying-claims-in-carbon.
24 Saumya Jain, "Oka granted in principle approval for Asta-managed SIAB 1922 by Lloyd's", *Reinsurance News* (18 October 2023), www.reinsurancene.ws/oka-granted-in-principle-approval-for-asta-managed-siab-1922-by-lloyds/.

face within the carbon market.[25] Finally, a business called CarbonPool is seeking to provide cover for a fall in the expected yield of carbon credits. CarbonPool is based in Switzerland and seeks to provide an indemnity payment in carbon credits in the event that the yield is lower than expected due to natural disasters, such as fire, disease and windstorm.[26]

The amount of new capacity flowing into the insurance market, coupled with the ability to make payments in carbon credits, is driving innovation for insurance products that help to de-risk some of the transactions within the carbon market. This innovation has its foundation within well-tested and understood insurance coverages, that ensure that the insurance market can continue to model and price the risks appropriately.

9. Climate analytics

Climate analytics is an essential tool for assessing current and future climate exposures for physical assets under various Representative Concentration Pathway (RCP) scenarios. Traditional insurance pricing for physical risks operates on an annual basis, with premiums set based on the perceived risks for the following year. However, this approach does not adequately reflect how climate exposures may evolve over the longer term, for example to 2030, 2050 or even 2100.

To address this gap, climate advisory services are designed to provide clients with long-term projections. These projections support informed decisions on investment, insurance, mitigation strategies and disclosure reporting, including compliance with frameworks such as the Task Force on Climate-Related Financial Disclosures (TCFD) and the EU Taxonomy.

This innovative approach provides clients with a comprehensive understanding of how their climate risks may change, particularly for assets and regions that are expected to be resilient in the long term. For those in the pre-construction phase, it also provides an opportunity to efficiently incorporate physical resilience measures into their plans, avoiding the need for costly retroactive measures.

In addition, the transparency provided by up-to-the-minute risk analysis is enabling some clients to re-evaluate their current insurance programmes, and it gives companies insight into which risks to prioritise and focus on and ultimately to find the appropriate risk transfer tool.

Predictive loss modelling can also provide companies with an indication of how their technical insurance premiums may evolve in the future, giving them a holistic view of their evolving risk landscape.

---

25   Press Release, "Oka receives Lloyd's in principle approval for Asta-managed syndicate in a box 1922", Oka (17 October 2023), https://carboninsurance.co/oka-receives-lloyds-in-principle-approval-for-asta-managed-syndicate-in-a-box-1922/.
26   CarbonPool, www.carbonpool.earth (2023).

10.   Forums and initiatives

The insurance market is now looking to build upon these innovative structures by supporting the resilience of vulnerable populations in other ways, most notably by helping the humanitarian organisations that respond to disasters and help communities recover in places where governments do not have the resources to do so. Several different forums and organisations have been established in order to convene the market to address some of these risks. Some of the most notable include Insurance Development Forum (IDF), the Sustainable Markets Initiative (SMI) and the Risk Informed Early Action Partnership (REAP).

The IDF is a public/private partnership led by the insurance industry and supported by various international organisations, including the United Nations Development Programme (UNDP) and the German Government.[27] It helps to organise the insurance sector to respond to the climate challenges that are being faced by vulnerable societies around the world, by providing risk modelling expertise and capacity. The then Prince Charles and Lloyd's of London convened the SMI with the aim of driving progress towards the pace of the energy transition and building a more resilient future.[28] These forums and partnerships have a great convening power, bring together the insurance market to produce innovative ideas and solutions to the problems that communities are facing as a result of climate change.

The forums and organisations that are helping to drive innovative disaster relief structures, have largely focused on supporting governmental actors. However, the next evolution of these types of structures is starting to play out within the insurance market, through partnerships with humanitarian organisations. The humanitarian sector spends billions of dollars each year on disaster relief, and yet still faces a significant funding gap, which was estimated to be over US$35 billion by the United Nations Office for the Coordination of Humanitarian Affairs (OCHA).[29] Humanitarian organisations operate in many parts of the world where national governments fail to reach, and are often the first responders to disasters as they unfold. Traditionally, the sector has been underserved by the insurance markets, and there is now a growing recognition within the insurance market that this needs to be addressed. There have been several new innovations such as a volcano bond that paid out based on a parametric trigger of plume height and wind direction, covering ten different volcanos worldwide.[30] Another example was an initiative to fund the

---

27   IDF, www.insdevforum.org/.

28   Sustainable Markets Initiative, www.sustainable-markets.org/taskforces/insurance-taskforce/.

29   OCHA, "Global Humanitarian Overview 2023, December update", 19 January 2024, www.unocha.org/publications/report/world/global-humanitarian-overview-2023-december-update-snapshot-31-december-2023.

30   Julian Alovisi *et al*, "Climate in Peril", Howden (2021), www.howdengroup.com/sites/g/files/mwfley566/files/2021-10/Howden-climate-in-peril-report-20211015-final.pdf.

structuring costs, of establishing a disaster relief bond, which allowed a non-profit to fully fund the premium payment.

Insurance can be a powerful tool for encouraging good resilience practices, and helping communities to respond to increasingly severe and frequent weather events. While insurance cannot prevent social or environmental catastrophes from happening, it can help to promote good governance and risk mitigation strategies, whether at a governmental, non-governmental or community level.

How technology is transforming ESG reporting

Kristina Wyatt
Persefoni

1. Introduction

Discussions about ESG reporting frequently drift to abstraction.[1] Environmental, social and governance (ESG) captures a swath of complex issues that are not easily compressed into neat discussion points. Nor are these matters intuitive. To caption them under a three-letter acronym drops a veil over their economic significance, complexity and importance to companies and their investors. We have witnessed significant movement in the direction of harmonisation of ESG reporting laws, rules and standards, which will certainly bring greater clarity to investors and other stakeholders using the ESG information that companies report. Now that the parameters around what companies will be required to report are becoming clearer, the question of how they will prepare their ESG information for reporting in a regulated environment is squarely in focus. Technology will play a critical role in helping companies to gather ESG data in a manner that enables them to evaluate their ESG risks and opportunities, build ESG into their corporate strategy, measure progress against goals and report out with confidence. The threshold we are crossing is one in which ESG data are increasingly treated like financial data and the rigours and controls around that data must mirror those around a company's financial reporting. Technology will play a key role in facilitating the gathering and reporting of ESG data with the rigour of financial reporting. This chapter focuses principally on climate data and climate reporting software as the process of calculating a company's greenhouse gas emissions for climate reporting is particularly challenging without software. This is because companies must conduct conversions that translate their myriad corporate activities into a common language of greenhouse gas (GHG) emissions. As such, with this added layer of complexity, the need for software is most pronounced in the context of climate. Software is, however, playing a critical role in broader

---

1   PWC, "The ESG Execution Gap: What Investors Think of Companies' Sustainability Efforts" (2022) ("I think it is really telling if you look through some sustainability reports. I'm going to start counting up the number of times that a company says 'sustainability' versus using actual descriptors. The more a company talks about sustainability in a vague way and the less information I walk away with, the bigger the red flag gets from my perspective – US-based investor.")

ESG reporting on issues related to nature, biodiversity, human capital, supply chain human rights and other ESG issues, all of which require strong systems of record and accountability to serve investors and other stakeholders using the information.

While there now is greater clarity as to what standards and frameworks should be applied to climate disclosures, the processes of carbon accounting and climate reporting remain complex. If you were to ask companies "What is your carbon footprint? What does that mean for your company? Does it create financial risks and opportunities? Are your customers asking you for lower carbon products? Are lower carbon substitutes threatening your top-line growth? Will carbon taxes or tariffs diminish your profits? Do you stand to benefit from the development of lower carbon products? What strategies are you employing to address those risks and opportunities? Have you established carbon reduction goals? How will you meet those goals and how are you tracking progress?", many will not have ready answers. These are some of the more granular questions investors are asking related to climate change. When shrouded under the ESG moniker, these concrete and important issues are frequently obscured or glossed over. Answering them requires data to inform an understanding of how climate change impacts a company's business today and into the future. The same thing can be said for the host of other issues under the ESG umbrella. Technology is playing an increasingly significant role in helping companies to address these issues.

Gathering information on one's carbon footprint, making sense of it and planning for the future are complex processes. They depend on reliable data that can inform corporate decisions and, in turn, the information they report to their shareholders and other stakeholders. At one time, companies might have viewed ESG issues as a monolithic, 'check the box' exercise that could be addressed through the adoption of policies and collecting high-level data on spreadsheets. As ESG reporting (starting with climate reporting) has moved from a fragmented, voluntary reporting environment to a harmonised and regulated one, it has become clear that companies need technology to help them to calculate the data required to understand, manage and report on their climate-related risks and opportunities.

Technology has emerged that is transforming companies' processes for calculating their carbon footprints, making well-informed business decisions, tracking progress toward their goals and reporting out to their stakeholders. Technology also facilitates the sharing of climate data throughout value chains across the economy. The pace of technological development is rapid and will likely continue to improve the transparency and reliability of carbon data across the global economy over the coming months and years. These same technological developments will facilitate the gathering and sharing of data related to other ESG issues, including biodiversity, nature, water consumption,

supply chain human rights and a host of other issues, as rules and standards are developed to define the information to be reported. Finally, emerging technologies such as artificial intelligence, machine learning and generative artificial intelligence (AI) are further transforming the ESG reporting landscape and will continue to foster access to the data companies and investors need to incorporate environmental and social considerations into their business and investment decisions.

2.   The carbon data challenge

2.1   Carbon accounting
Carbon accounting is essential to enabling the measurement of emissions in a uniform manner. Carbon accounting is the process of translating activities to greenhouse gas emissions, most often represented in the carbon currency of carbon dioxide equivalent (CO_2e). The most broadly accepted framework defining how carbon accounting is conducted is the Greenhouse Gas Protocol, which was developed by the World Business Council for Sustainable Development and the World Resources Institute. The GHG Protocol is used around the world, including by the International Sustainability Standards Board, the European Union's standards under the Corporate Sustainability Reporting Directive, and most voluntary reporting frameworks. The GHG Protocol defines how to convert the many economic activities engaged in throughout the world to CO_2e. It is the carbon analogue to a monetary system. It is also the mechanism that enables comparison of GHG emissions across companies, geographies and activities and it is essential to managing GHG emissions and climate-related transition risks.

2.2   The translation of activities to GHG data
The GHG Protocol categorises emissions in three scopes. Scope 1 emissions are those emissions from an entity's direct operations. This might include emissions from clearing land, driving vehicles, processing raw materials and refrigerant or methane leaks from company equipment. Scope 2 emissions are the emissions associated with the production of purchased electricity, steam, heating and cooling, for example, to operate a company's buildings. Scope 3 emissions are the indirect emissions associated with the upstream and downstream activities that relate to a reporting entity's activities. These might include the goods and services that the entity purchases, waste generated in the production process, the transportation of those goods, business travel, use of a company's sold products and activities financed by a financial institution. The GHG Protocol defines 15 categories of Scope 3 emissions, including emissions from both upstream and downstream activities.

In order to determine the emissions associated with the various activities in which different companies engage, the GHG Protocol defines a process whereby the activities are multiplied by emission factors that reflect the emissions associated with specified activities. The GHG Protocol includes emissions from the gases identified in the Kyoto Protocol: carbon dioxide, methane, nitrous oxide, hydrofluorocarbons, perfluorocarbons, sulphur hexafluoride and nitrogen trifluoride. The GHG Protocol accounts for the fact that each of these gases has a different global warming potential – that is, capacity to trap heat in the atmosphere – to calculate emissions in the common carbon currency of CO_2e.

The complexity a reporting entity faces in calculating its GHG emissions is compounded by the fact that it might have thousands of different activities that must be multiplied by appropriate emission factors to derive the CO_2e associated with those activities. Those emission factors in turn vary based on the location and other attributes of the specific activity.

Historically, GHG inventories were maintained on spreadsheets that produced broad emissions estimates and depended on assumptions that were not easily traced and recorded over time. As carbon reporting has gone from a voluntary exercise to a regulated one, reporting entities have begun to shift from the use of spreadsheets to technologies that facilitate the calculation and reporting of emissions.

3.   The role of technology in facilitating carbon accounting at company level

3.1   Facilitating the granular collection of data and matching to appropriate emission factors

Software technology has transformed the process of collecting companies' activity data that feeds into carbon calculations. Software reduces complexity and the need for manual intervention, thereby reducing the cost of data collection and the incidence of data entry errors. For example, technology platforms connect to company financial, procurement, facilities management and other systems to ingest the activity data that forms the basis for the company's carbon inventory.[2] Processes that formerly took months to complete are automated, completed efficiently and with errors minimised.

Current technology also plays a critical role in matching activities to appropriate emission factors to ensure accurate GHG calculations. To illustrate the importance of using appropriate emission factors, and the potential difficulty of doing so using manual processes, consider that software can hold and appropriately match location and activity specific emission factors to a company's activities around the world. The software might ingest hundreds of

---

2   See, eg, www.persefoni.com.

thousands of separate pieces of activity data and match them up to emission factors specific to those activities. Software enables the ingestion, organisation and management of large amounts of activity data and the accurate calculation of GHG emissions associated with those activities based on factors tailored to the specific activities. The source of the emission factors applied and the specific factors used in the calculation are documented and maintained in the system as a ledger – much like a financial ledger that tracks company financial information. This level of detail and accountability cannot be achieved without a proper software tool.

Gaining the ability to measure GHG emissions at a granular level is critical to managing emissions and meeting GHG reduction goals. If a company were to estimate its emissions using only broad industry emissions averages, it would derive a rough emissions figure but it would not have useful data to inform strategy and reduction efforts. For example, a company could estimate the emissions associated with the purchase of certain goods used in its products (Scope 3, Category 1 emissions under the GHG Protocol) by multiplying the amount of goods purchased or the money spent on such goods by an industry average emissions factor for such types of goods. However, painting with such a broad brush would deprive the company of the ability to reduce the emissions associated with the purchase of such goods, except by means of reducing the amount of goods purchased. For most companies, such an approach is inconsistent with growth and therefore infeasible. Those companies then would be limited in their ability to meet their carbon reduction goals, except through the purchase of carbon offsets, which for many companies is an unappealing option due to cost, investor expectations and customer demands. Moreover, companies that have set science-based targets pursuant to the Science Based Targets Initiative would not be able to meet those targets by simply relying on offsets.

Software unlocks the ability to calculate emissions at a granular level with specificity and thereby enables companies to manage their emissions and meet their stakeholder demands.

3.2 Real-time carbon data

Only software allows for real-time carbon footprint calculations, as opposed to once-a-year manual calculations performed on spreadsheets, which are outdated by the time they are published. Ultimately, the objective for most companies and investors is not to derive a simple number that reflects the company's carbon footprint as of a single point in time. Rather, the emissions data is a starting point for the important work of assessing and managing companies' risks and opportunities associated with their carbon footprint.

As companies build strategies to meet their decarbonisation goals, software enables them to understand their emission sources and to model carbon reduction plans. Software facilitates the integration of carbon reduction goals into broader company strategy. Carbon data that at one time was only available at the company level can be seen in detail at every point in a company's operations, making it feasible to map their carbon reduction pathways and align those with the company's business operations.

3.3 Accountability

Software has dramatically enhanced the reliability and traceability of companies' reported data. As companies have moved from a voluntary reporting environment to a regulated one, ensuring the reported numbers can be supported with recorded data has become critically important. Software systems with an open ledger maximise the ability of third parties to perform audit and assurance on the emissions calculations included in reported data. Technology has emerged that has significantly changed the manner in which carbon emissions data is not only calculated but also tracked. Open software systems maintain a detailed ledger showing each activity and associated emission factor that contributes to the company's carbon footprint. This data is fully traceable and visible in a carbon ledger that shows the activities, the emissions factors applied, the source of the emissions factors, the constituent gases emitted and the CO_2 equivalent measurement. This form of record keeping enables assurance of the emissions data to meet regulatory requirements and investor demand. Companies, in turn, have a record of their calculations in the event of regulatory or other challenge.

3.4 Internal controls

As GHG reporting moves from a voluntary exercise to a regulated one, carbon data is treated in a manner similar to the treatment of financial data. The activities that contribute to the calculations must be subject to rigorous internal controls to ensure their accuracy. Software tools facilitate the identification and tracing of data sources and allow for certification of data at appropriate points of control. Carbon management software plays the same role in carbon accounting that financial management software plays in financial accounting. The process of establishing and recording internal controls over climate reporting is still quite new and is necessitated by the regulatory mandates requiring disclosure of climate data in regulatory filings. The internal controls that are currently being developed to ensure the integrity of climate data are not dissimilar to the internal controls over financial reporting that companies developed after certification of such controls was mandated by the US Congress in the Sarbanes-Oxley Act of 2002 and enforced by the Securities and Exchange Commission (SEC) in its implementing regulations. Software enabled those systems of internal controls over financial reporting, and those systems of internal controls improved the integrity and reliability of companies' financial reports. The same dynamic is unfolding with software that enables the development of internal controls over climate and broader ESG reporting.

4. Network effects

Technology not only facilitates the gathering of activity data and calculation of emissions at the level of the individual reporting company, it also enables the sharing of data among companies within the reporting company's value chain.[3] This data exchange is critical to the development of robust, granular and reliable Scope 3 emissions calculations. Technology is critical to enabling the sharing of data among companies and their business partners in much the same way that technology facilitates the automation of carbon accounting within the company's four walls. Companies are able to request data from their suppliers and other business partners and can establish automated connections with their suppliers and customers to share GHG data. This data feeds into the technology's system of record to create Scope 3 data that can be traced and verified.

As technology facilitates companies' reporting of their Scopes 1 and 2 GHG emissions, more data will be available to feed into other companies' Scope 3 emissions calculations. The availability and easy exchange of data among companies will create a flywheel that will promote more granular reporting across the economy. As a result, the percentage of carbon emissions data that is based on reported calculations rather than spend-based industry averages will increase. This more granular data will facilitate corporate decision making and support companies' decarbonisation efforts.

In time, GHG emissions data calculated using different technology platforms will be interoperable, enabling the sharing of data broadly across the economy. Initiatives such as the Partnership for Carbon Transparency, created by the World Business Council for Sustainable Development (WBCSD), hold significant promise for the scaling of network effects throughout the global economy.[4] The WBCSD describes the rationale behind the development of the Partnership for Carbon Transparency's Pathfinder Network as follows: "Without access to primary data, full transparency and hence decarbonization are difficult to achieve. The Pathfinder Network facilitates the peer-to-peer exchange of such data by creating a standardized approach and ensuring interoperability between tech solutions."[5]

Other data exchanges and networks are being developed that will foster the sharing of carbon data. Provided these networks adhere to principles that assure

---

3   For examples of this data exchange, see Persefoni's Scope 3 Data Exchange for supplier engagement at www.persefoni.com/use-cases/supplier-engagement and Scope 3 Data Exchange for investment portfolios at www.persefoni.com/use-cases/inve;ipk/stment-portfolio-engagement.
4   See more information on the WBCSD's Pathfinder Network at www.carbon-transparency.com/.
5   *Ibid.*

transparency, interoperability and data fidelity, the availability of useful carbon data should rapidly accelerate. As these data networks scale, more primary data will be available throughout the economy. This will promote a virtuous cycle wherein the increase in availability of primary data will facilitate reporting, which in turn will feed more data into the network. Access to high quality carbon data across the economy is essential to achieving decarbonisation goals at the company, national and global levels. High-quality data will help capital to flow to the most promising and cost-effective decarbonisation strategies necessary to achieve a rapid and orderly transition to a lower carbon economy.

5.   AI, machine learning and generative AI

We are witnessing a technological revolution driven by artificial intelligence, machine learning and generative AI. These technologies will accelerate the developments described earlier. The specific contours of the changes to come are still to be defined. Some of the applications of these technologies already employed include the use of AI to identify the types of activities that contribute to a company's carbon footprint, based on the company's industry. AI can help to identify data anomalies or gaps and help to resolve them. Predictive analytics can use historical and broader industry, scientific and other data to make forecasts that can be used in corporate decision making, such as physical climate risk modelling and scenario analysis. Another use case is the identification of the most cost-effective carbon reduction strategies.

There is significant discussion of the potential of generative AI tools such as ChatGPT, which was released in prototype form in November 2022 and saw stable release in February 2023.[6] Generative AI uses learning technology and natural language systems to answer questions. In response to the question "what is ChatGPT", ChatGPT itself explained that: "ChatGPT, like other language models based on the GPT architecture, uses a technique called deep learning to understand and generate human-like text. Here's a simplified overview of how it works." The response proceeded to explain how the system trains data on large datasets from a wide range of sources, uses "deep neural networks with a transformer architecture, conducts pretraining on language to predict what words will be used together and fine tunes on specific tasks under the supervision of human AI trainers". All of this enables the AI platform to process human questions and generate a response in natural language based on its training.[7]

When asked whether Hong Kong will be under water in 2050, ChatGPT described the factors contributing to the sea level rise, including melting polar

---

6   See chat.openai.com.
7   Response to query conducted on chat.openai.com, 14 July 2023 using question "how does chatgpt work?".

ice caps and expansion of ocean water. It noted that Hong Kong is a coastal city and therefore faces risk due to sea level rise. It also hedged, appropriately, by noting that it cannot see the future and that many factors, such as the pace of climate change, climate resilience, mitigation and adaptation strategies will impact whether in fact the city will be flooded.

The potential impact of AI, machine learning, predictive analytics and generative AI has not been lost on regulators. In a statement to the SEC's Investor Advisory Committee in June 2023, SEC Chair, Gary Gensler, observed that: "Predictive data analytics and artificial intelligence are transforming so much of our economy. Finance is no exception."[8] Further, Gensler is quoted as declaring that "AI may prove to be more transformative than the internet itself".[9]

Gensler has expressed concern, however, over the use of AI in the brokerage industry. "As to artificial intelligence, this technology already is playing a part in call centres, account openings, compliance programs, trading algorithms, sentiment analysis, robo-advisers, and brokerage apps. Such applications can bring benefits in market access, efficiency and returns."[10] However, he cautioned that "the use of predictive data analytics also can lead to potential conflicts. In particular, conflicts may arise to the extent that advisers or brokers are optimizing for their own interests as well as others". As such, the SEC has asked its staff to draft rule proposals for consideration related to potential conflicts of interest that might be exacerbated by the use of AI and predictive analytics.[11]

Gensler posed the question of the emerging role of technology in capital formation to the SEC's Small Business Advisory Committee: "It would be good to hear your thoughts on the increasing use of predictive data analytics, including artificial intelligence, in the capital markets and by financial companies. I ask the committee members for your thoughts regarding how the growing use of these technologies has changed funding practices and availability with regard to small businesses."[12]

As generative AI accelerates, its promise will become clearer. A McKinsey report in June 2023 predicted that generative AI will add more than $4 trillion to the global economy annually.[13] It is likely that risks will emerge as well. President Biden articulated his optimism and apprehension: "AI can help deal with some very difficult challenges like disease and climate change, but we also

---

8   SEC Chair Gary Gensler, "Prepared Remarks Before the Investor Advisory Committee" (22 June 2023).
9   Paul Mulholland, "SEC's Gensler Confirms AI is Regulatory Priority", *Plan Advisor* (19 May 2023), citing Gensler's statements at a 19 May 2023 conference on emerging trends in asset management.
10   SEC Chair Gary Gensler, "Honest and Unbiased Investment Management": Remarks before the Inaugural Conference on Emerging Trends in Asset Management (19 May 2023).
11   *Ibid.*
12   SEC Chair Gary Gensler, "Prepared Remarks before the Small Business Capital Formation Advisory Committee" (14 June 2023).
13   McKinsey & Co, "The economic potential of generative AI: The next productivity frontier" (14 June 2023).

have to address the potential risks to our society, to our economy, to our national security."[14] Similar concerns led the European Commission to propose an EU regulatory framework for AI. AI systems for different applications are evaluated and classified according to their potential risk to users. "As part of its digital strategy, the EU wants to regulate artificial intelligence to ensure better conditions for the development and use of this innovative technology. AI can create many benefits, such as better healthcare; safer and cleaner transport; more efficient manufacturing; and cheaper and more sustainable energy."[15] The World Economic Forum launched its AI Governance Alliance in June 2023, a "pioneering multi-stakeholder initiative that unites industry leaders, governments, academic institutions and civil society organizations, to champion responsible global design and release of transparent and inclusive AI systems".[16] Its goals include "shaping the future of AI governance, fostering innovation and ensuring that the potential of AI is harnessed for the betterment of society while upholding ethical considerations and inclusivity at every step".[17]

It is clear that the promise of generative AI is significant. It is also clear that the companies developing such technology will do well to apply thoughtful governance processes around where and how they source data, how they train the learning systems and how they communicate their processes to users. While a great deal about the future of AI is unknown at this point, some best practices, including transparency, candour and integrity of data sources will be useful guideposts. Corporate users should maintain a clear focus on the role emerging technologies should play in their corporate planning and decision making. AI appears to hold significant promise in helping to inform companies about their ESG risks, the sources of their carbon footprint and profitable strategies for carbon reduction. However, if generative AI were used to replace corporate decision making or if disclosures to investors were automatically generated by AI without management consideration, the outcomes would seem far less positive. This space will evolve and will bear close monitoring.

6. Technology and broader ESG issues

Much of the discussion in this chapter has focused on carbon emissions calculation and reporting, which is necessary to the analysis of climate transition risks. Technology systems are also critical to understanding and planning for physical climate risks. Software systems, satellite imagery and predictive analytics are crucial to projecting the physical risks associated with

---

14   President Joe Biden, "Remarks by President Biden in Meeting with the President's Council of Advisors on Science and Technology" (14 April 2023).

15   "EU AI Act: first regulation on artificial intelligence", *European Parliament News* (8 June 2023).

16   World Economic Forum, "AI Governance Alliance" available at https://initiatives.weforum.org/ai-governance-alliance/home.

17   *Ibid.*

climate change under different future temperature scenarios.[18] These systems are important to helping companies, particularly those with significant operations in areas exposed to physical climate risks, to plan for those risks.

Many of the same technological developments described here regarding GHG emissions will apply to broader ESG issues, particularly as the standards for those issues are fleshed out by the ISSB and the European Financial Reporting Advisory Group (EFRAG) as they move to other issues after climate. These include human rights, water consumption, deforestation, waste management, biodiversity, human capital and other topics. Factors that will help to enable the scaling of technology to address these broader issues include the development of standardised methods of measuring and reporting (which the ISSB and EFRAG is developing), and an openness to sharing information. As with climate, investor demand as well as regulatory requirements are likely to drive transparency.

Even though we have seen significant convergence and harmonisation of regulatory requirements and standards in the early 2020s, it is inevitable that differences among regulatory requirements will persist. For example, the EU requires reporting using a double materiality lens while the United States and ISSB apply a single materiality filter with the US focusing on information that is important to investors and the ISSB focusing on the information that is important to the primary users of the information. Moreover, the topics addressed by the SEC, ISSB and EFRAG form a Venn diagram with some overlapping requirements but without perfect alignment. These different reporting requirements create challenges for companies in gathering, analysing and reporting data to satisfy the requirements of different jurisdictions. Software systems will be critical in helping companies to collect their data and track their reporting in satisfaction of different requirements.

7.   Conclusion

ESG reporting is hard. It is not a 'tick box' exercise. Rather, it requires the generation and analysis of large amounts of data that inform company decisions. Shareholders and other stakeholders have an expectation of transparency as to the financial risks and opportunities ESG issues pose for companies as well as companies' impacts on society. This expectation of transparency reached an inflection point in 2021 with the creation of the ISSB and over the ensuing years as the US SEC, ISSB and EFRAG have embarked on standard setting and rule writing to more clearly define the information that companies must report. The disclosure expectations are becoming clearer and

---

18   See, eg, the Climate Impact Map, available at https://impactlab.org/map/#usmeas=absolute&usyear=1986-2005&gmeas=absolute&gyear=1986-2005; and GIS Geography, "10 Climate Change Maps – The Climate Explained" available at https://gisgeography.com/climate-change-effects-maps/.

companies' focus on the quality of the information they report is intensifying as we move from voluntary to mandatory reporting.

The SEC, ISSB and EFRAG have begun their rule writing and standard setting with a focus on climate change. In time, they will move on to other topics. EFRAG will address additional environmental issues (eg, pollution, water and marine resources, biodiversity and ecosystems, resource use and circular economy), social issues (eg, own workers, workers in the value chain, affected communities and consumers/end users) and governance issues (eg, governance, risk management and internal control and business conduct).[19] The ISSB will address additional sustainability topics likely to include biodiversity, ecosystems and ecosystem services, human capital, human rights and connectivity in reporting.[20]

As these reporting standards develop, reliable, actionable data will be ever more essential to corporate compliance and, beyond simple compliance, to addressing the complex sustainability challenges we face. Technology, from software to AI, machine learning and generative AI, will play an increasingly critical role in facilitating the access to the data companies and investors need to address the impacts of this range of ESG issues on company performance, communities and global financial stability.

---

19   See www.efrag.org/lab6.
20   See www.ifrs.org/groups/international-sustainability-standards-board/.

What's next for ESG? Leading perspectives on the future development of ESG

In this chapter we seek the views of a number of leading ESG practitioners from a cross-section of sectors and roles as to what will be the leading trends with respect to ESG over the next 10 years and beyond, and how this will shape the legal sector and the broader development of industry and investments.

1. ESG and the legal practice

Reena SenGupta

RSGI Limited

Considering the impact of ESG on the legal practice, it could be said that the profession is still leaning into the ESG agenda, albeit the global picture is quite complex. Just as ESG has been implemented in a fragmented manner across geographies and sectors by governments and private actors, the same is true for the legal profession, especially in the face of the ESG backlash in the United States.

A letter from five Republican senators to 51 law firms in November 2022, warning them to be aware of anti-competitive practices in their ESG advisory work was a shock to many law firm leaders.[1] As a result, some law firms have dialled down their ESG language in their public reporting, as can be seen in the RSGI Greenprint report, published in December 2023.[2]

Along with some asset managers recently pulling out of collaborative fora to tackle climate change,[3] the legal profession faces a conundrum in its approach to ESG, particularly with regard to its own sustainable business activities. Some commentators suggest that the blow to ESG's momentum is largely US based. And it is true that there are widely different geographical approaches to ESG activities and reporting, with UK law firms leading the way, followed by European and then American law firms. Asia-Pacific firms, with the exception of Australia, are not so equally focused.

In private practice, many law firms do field client advisory ESG practices. A

---

1   Thomson Reuters, letter from the US Senate to 51 law firms, 3 November 2022, https://fingfx. thomsonreuters.com/gfx/legaldocs/znvnbdgxnvl/ESG%20letters%20to%20law%20firms.pdf.
2   RSGI, "Greenprint 2023", 1 December 2023, https://rsgi.co/greenprint-2023/.
3   Climate Action 100, "Climate Action 100+ Reaction to Recent Departures" 26 February 2024, www.climateaction100.org/news/climate-action-100-reaction-to-recent-departures/#:~:text=Climate%20 Action%20100%2B%20can%20confirm,Action%20100%2B%20to%20BlackRock%20International.

majority (65%) of RSGI's assessment of 180 firms said they advised clients on ESG obligations and related issues.[4]

But while businesses are generally more responsive to the demands of different stakeholders, achieving widespread integration of ESG considerations into law firm practices is challenging. Nigel Brook, a reinsurance specialist who co-founded Clyde & Co's global Resilience and Climate Risk practice, told the author: "I strongly believe lawyers have a profound role to play here. But if you ask them what the implications for climate risk in your sector or area are, a lot of lawyers would struggle."

Private practice practitioners also have a role to play in the decision-making process. The Law Society of England and Wales issued guidance in April 2023[5] that, among other things, noted that law firms may elect to refuse to act for clients whose ESG values contradict their own.

For many law firms, the ideal of giving legal assistance to all who need it is an enshrined tenet. Law firm practitioners may prefer to categorise their role as 'transitional' lawyers, who are there to help multinationals succeed commercially in their move to renewable energy. In fact, some lawyers say they prefer to use the acronym 'ESE', standing for 'environment, society and economy'. Their role, they feel, is intrinsic to helping their clients grow sustainable but profitable businesses.

Their counterparts working in-house – general counsel (GC) – are often more vociferous in their support for the ESG agenda and are increasingly central to corporate ESG decisions. Many GCs are the board sponsor for ESG in their companies and have taken on wider remits. The agenda could be said to have played right into the bailiwick of the GC. The emergence of the 'supra-risks' – geopolitical tensions, supply chains, climate risk including energy transition, societal issues and governance, cyber and data security – all have significant legal components. Few other corporate functions have the legal department's overview or touch so many parts of the organisation that are dealing with these risks.

Measuring the impact a lawyer can have on the ESG agenda is critical to galvanising the industry from both a grassroots and leadership perspective. Unfortunately, measuring the value a lawyer brings on any matter has historically been challenging because it is hard to assess the criticality of legal advice in enabling commercial outcomes.

Private practice law firms are expanding their ESG client advisory work, even if they now prefer to use a different nomenclature for their own activities. In-house legal teams are increasing their demands to see sustainability credentials

---

4   RSGI, "Greenprint 2023", see above, n 2.
5   The Law Society, "The impact of climate change on solicitors", 19 April 2023, www.lawsociety.org.uk/topics/climate-change/impact-of-climate-change-on-solicitors.

from their law firms in their request for proposals. GCs want to work with firms whose values are aligned to those of their organisations. Across the profession, there is an acceptance that every commercial lawyer needs a 'sustainability sense' and the ability to approach legal problems with a wide but integrated and practical approach to risk both now and in the future.

2. ESG in law

Ruth Knox
Sabrina Zhang
Paul Hastings

As we reflect upon the major developments and trends we saw in management and maximisation of ESG risks and opportunities respectively in 2023, 2024 holds perhaps even more potential for the ESG (and anti-ESG) megatrends to have a lasting impact on society. While more than 40 countries prepare for elections, the world will inevitably experience the ripple effects of divergent perspectives on ESG being forced to the surface through both public and private debate. As such, in no particular order, we outline our top predictions for 2024 on ESG.

2.1 We will continue to see growth in the scrutiny by stakeholders of respect for human rights

Since 2016, we have seen what used to be a smattering of human rights laws, standards and commitments grow into an increasingly controversial and dynamic legal landscape. The EU Corporate Sustainability Due Diligence Directive (CSDDD) is a landmark proposal which would require companies to: (i) undertake due diligence to identify potential human rights risks and impacts; (ii) take steps to address those risks; and (iii) monitor the steps that are being taken through reporting requirements. At the time of writing in March 2024, the adoption of the proposal by the EU has been stalled due to political infighting about multiple controversial elements of the text released in early 2024, including but not limited to the definition of supply chain, the civil liability regime and the impact of the regime on SMEs. Could this deceleration represent the beginning of the anti-ESG backlash in the EU?

Regardless of whether or not the CSDDD breaks the current impasse, we are seeing movement across multiple jurisdictions towards enhanced transparency, public procurement and regulatory compliance requirements for sponsors, asset managers, public and private companies alike. In 2023, we saw Germany's Supply Chain Due Diligence Act come into force, along with the EU's Deforestation Regulation, Canada's Fighting Against Forced Labour and Child Labour in Supply Chains Act, and substantial steps were taken towards the enactment of New Zealand's modern slavery legislation, adding to an existing list of jurisdictions including the US with its California Transparency in Supply Chains Act. As new disclosure regimes emerge across the globe, stakeholders increasingly have the ability to scrutinise not just the actions taken to address potential human rights issues, but now also the effectiveness of such strategies up and down the value chain of duty holders.

2.2 We predict an uptick in climate-related disclosures and transition planning as public and private sectors alike pull their socks up on scenario analysis

In 2023, we saw increasing momentum in climate-related disclosure requirements in leading jurisdictions such as California. In October 2023, California signed into law Senate Bill 253 and Senate Bill 261, imposing climate-related disclosures for companies doing business in California with total annual revenues over US$1 billion and US$500 million respectively. Senate Bill 253 requires large companies generating over US$1 billion in revenue a year to track and publicly disclose greenhouse gas emissions, while Senate Bill 261 requires large companies generating over $500 million in revenue a year to prepare climate-related financial risk reports for publication on their company websites. California also signed into law Assembly Bill 1305 – the Voluntary Carbon Market Disclosures Act – setting out disclosure requirements in respect of entities that make claims of 'net zero' emissions, 'carbon neutrality', or other similar claims that imply environmental effects. The bill mandates that if any company operating in California makes any claim that the entity and/or any of its products do not add greenhouse gases to the climate or that it has significantly reduced its emissions, then the company must meet detailed reporting requirements. These reforms are just a sliver in a long line of state, national and international disclosure rules mandating broad and deep disclosures with respect to the carbon footprint of (and climate adaptation steps taken by) businesses. As such disclosure requirements begin to bite and, as regulatory initiatives begin to flesh out thinking on the means and real-world impacts of robust transition planning,[6] we predict an uptick in the breadth and depth of climate-related financial disclosures around the globe.

2.3 The US will continue to be the hotbed for ESG litigation, with a slight increase in the EU

As the EU's sustainability and transparency regimes continue to settle and become embedded (eg, the EU Sustainable Finance Disclosure Regulation, Corporate Sustainability Reporting Directive and Deforestation Regulation), ESG litigation risks will sharpen in the EU but not necessarily materialise to a material extent in 2024. Agencies within the member states, for example, may

---

6   Transition Plan Taskforce, "Developing a gold standard", https://transitiontaskforce.net/about/.

be reluctant to enforce regulation which has only just been enacted or which may change in the near future. In the US, by contrast, we expect potential further investigations and enforcement proceedings arising out of the anti-ESG backlash and enhanced focus on emerging risks,[7] including but not limited to the rapidly evolving landscape on diversity, equity and inclusion.[8] In addition, as the 2024 presidential election approaches, we expect to see continued growth of anti-ESG legislative proposals that have gained tremendous momentum across the US, whether in the form of new prohibitions on the consideration of ESG factors in investment decisions, 'anti-boycott' restrictions which prohibit boycotts of firearms, ammunition, energy and/or energy infrastructure-related investments, and restrictions related to the role of ESG or non-pecuniary factors in discharging a state instrumentality's fiduciary duty. In the non-election year of 2023, the US saw over 165 anti-ESG proposals in 37 states in the first half of the year alone. While the majority of these proposals did not successfully pass, we anticipate a higher volume of anti-ESG legislation against the politically-charged backdrop of the election as we move into 2024.

3.   ESG in finance
Helene R Banks
Gregory J Battista
Cahill Gordon & Reindel LLP

With a global focus on the urgency to ramp up funding to meet global climate change targets, we expect the private ESG finance industry to continue to make progress toward becoming an important part of the solution. We have outlined below three areas of this evolution.

3.1   ESG criticism will lead away from labels to a focus on long-term value
The rise of ESG principles and ESG's inclusion in corporate business strategies and investment portfolio considerations has met with a substantial wave of criticism. Opponents claim ESG standards lead to allocation of resources based on political agendas rather than on value creation for stakeholders. While this dialectical battle may continue far into the future, smart business leaders will continue to steer their organisations to focus on the individual components of ESG without making grand proclamations that might attract negative attention.

Going forward, while too much emphasis on ESG labels could become a hindrance, the substance of ESG initiatives can still provide long-term value for corporations. For example, investments in fossil fuel reduction/energy

---

7   US Securities and Exchange Commission, "SEC Division of Examinations Announces 2024 Priorities", 16 October 2023, www.sec.gov/news/press-release/2023-222.
8   *Students for Fair Admissions v Harvard University* 600 US 181 (2023).

efficiency (E), employee satisfaction (S) and rooting out corruption in the supply chain (G) can result in meaningful and measurable impacts regardless of labels under ESG.

3.2 Climate-related initiatives will drive a majority of ESG finance

What gets measured, gets managed. The regulatory demand for corporate reporting on greenhouse gas (GHG) emissions and the stated goal of 'net zero' by 2050 will force GHG reductions and ESG financial vehicles will provide the capital necessary to make the transition to a low-carbon economy. Climate-related projects will dwarf all other areas of ESG finance. This will include not only GHG reductions and renewable energy investments but also infrastructure hardening plans to resist severe weather events.

3.3 ESG finance will become easier and cheaper, with better incentives

A green or sustainability-linked loan or bond can be a significant undertaking. Establishing frameworks, benchmarks, key performance indicators and monitoring systems for these instruments has a steep learning curve. The cost of sustainability coordinators, tracking and reporting may be difficult to justify even in comparison to the relatively lower cost of capital for ESG finance instruments. Nevertheless, over time the ESG finance markets will evolve from bespoke engagements to a more standardised format, especially by industry. The International Capital Markets Association (ICMA), for instance, will help lead the move towards accepted standards and best practices that will result in a more streamlined, less expensive experience for borrowers, issuers and lenders alike.

In addition, carrot and stick incentives will be improved to encourage the achievement of timely ESG goals. For example, sustainability-linked bonds (SLBs) tie interest rates to sustainability goals but the current structure is generally weak. Sustainability goals are stated in very broad terms. Call options, which enable a loan pay off before interest rates are increased, are a feature of a large majority of current SLBs. Interest rate step-ups for missing targets are typically only about 25 basis points. All of these features will be improved to create a tighter link between issuers' stated goals and investors' desire to see results. These improvements should help unlock the trillions of dollars needed for a worldwide energy transition.

4. ESG in insurance
Glenn O'Halloran
Howden

In the next decade, the continued integration of ESG factors into financial decision making will fundamentally change the landscape of underwriting, risk assessment and management within the insurance market. This transformation will bring opportunities and have implications for those on the risk transfer side of the insurance balance sheet, as well as investors and the broader economy.

The incorporation of ESG considerations into financial risk assessment will lead to a more comprehensive understanding of the long-term risks facing businesses and industries. Insurers will increasingly factor in environmental risks such as climate-related natural hazards, social risks such as labour practices and diversity, and governance risks such as board composition and executive compensation. Whilst certain factors such as weather-related climate risks will bring unpredictability to this aspect of the risk profile, a holistic approach that incorporates additional governance datapoints will allow the market to better price risk, resulting in more accurate premiums and improved underwriting profitability in certain lines of insurance.

The growing emphasis on ESG factors will drive demand for innovative insurance products tailored to address emerging risks. The insurance market will develop new products to cover ESG-related exposures. Examples already cited today based on demand signals from clients include innovative credit insurance solutions to unlock financing of new green technologies, an expanded use of parametric weather-linked insurance and liability coverage for ESG-related lawsuits. By providing coverage for these risks, the market will facilitate capital allocation to sustainable initiatives and help enable the transition to a net zero future.

As ESG factors become increasingly influential, directors and officers (D&O) liability claims are expected to surge. Heightened scrutiny on ESG practices means directors and officers may face litigation over mismanagement. Insurers must revise D&O policies to address emerging ESG-related risks and offer robust risk management assistance. Proactive engagement in ESG issues can help mitigate liabilities, safeguard corporate reputation, and align with broader sustainability goals.

Additionally, the adoption of ESG criteria by investors and regulators will exert pressure on insurers to both disclose and improve their own ESG performance. Insurers will face scrutiny from stakeholders regarding their environmental footprint, social impact and corporate governance practices. Those that fail to meet ESG expectations may face reputational damage, regulatory penalties, or constraints on capital availability. Consequently, insurers will increasingly integrate ESG considerations into their own operations, from investment decisions to supply chain management.

In summary, the widespread adoption of ESG principles within the financial sector will significantly impact the insurance market over the next decade. Insurers will need to adapt their risk management strategies, develop innovative products, enhance their own ESG performance and improve transparency to remain relevant in this evolving landscape. By embracing ESG considerations, insurers can not only mitigate financial risks but also contribute to a more sustainable and resilient economy.

5.   ESG in consulting
Jonathan Friedman
Anthesis Group

Our view is that the ESG landscape will be transformed by three key factors within 10 years: data, technology and regulation.

Sustainability data will be like financial data: collected, reported, credible, audited and analysed on an on-going basis. Sustainable performance metrics will be discussed on earnings calls and affect pay of C-Suite managers. Data will enable better modelling of materiality, quantitatively linking ESG impacts to earnings before interest, taxes, depreciation and amortisation (EBITDA) and enterprise risk. Investors and consumers will have access to credible, regulated sustainability data and ratings when making investments and when buying goods and services.

Technology will revolutionise the ESG space. Software solutions backed by artificial intelligence will make it affordable for companies to increase efficiency in their value chains on a significant scale. Advanced computer modelling will spur the development of new materials and processes needed to power the energy transition, from better batteries to super-efficient solar panels with short supply chains. However, the risk that the rapid pace of AI-fuelled technological change will outstrip our ability to manage its impacts on society is present. This will bring social and governance factors to the fore and force policy makers, investors, companies and advisers to address the issue of how we exert oversight and apply morality to an intelligence that becomes greater than our own.

We anticipate that differences in policy making and adoption of new technologies will cause countries and industries to materially diverge on their decarbonisation trajectories. Many developed markets will green their grids and regulate carbon intensive industries to advance on their own net zero pathways. Further, employee activism and consumer preferences in these markets will also change how companies see their role in society. Other parts of the world will be slower to transition away from a carbon-intensive growth model, due to differing access to technology, perceived development needs and political preferences.

We expect the world to continue missing targets to decarbonise fast enough to limit increases in temperature to 1.5 degrees Celsius. This causes extreme weather events to be more frequent and habitats to decline, prompting mass human migration and loss of wildlife. Governments and companies will be called on to preserve natural capital in support of a new human right – the right to live in a habitable climate – which will lead to a great focus on the need to preserve natural capital. Among industries, the food sector will face significant pressure from physical climate risks and informed consumers demanding healthy, low-carbon products that respect animal rights.

In short, the coming decade will see parts of world economy having entered a future of sustainable performance, benefitting from technological breakthroughs, credible ESG data and effective regulation. However, an accelerating pace of change, together with differing impacts from climate change, will present new risks and opportunities, and increase the urgency of good governance to protect vulnerable people and ecosystems.

6. ESG in consulting

Aiste Brackley
ERM Sustainability Institute

The concept of ESG has been in use for a couple of decades and recently has become the subject of polarising debates. It will continue to evolve, and it would not be very surprising if ESG as we know it ceases to exist. However, regardless of the terms and definitions, ESG issues will continue to serve as a powerful tool for companies to measure their footprint in society and for investors to direct capital to sustainable activities. Three developments in particular will shape the future of ESG.

Mandatory ESG disclosure will become the new reality for most companies, public and private. Companies with operations in the EU must start reporting on ESG performance in 2026. Many other jurisdictions have also adopted or are in the process of making reporting of non-financial data mandatory. Convergence of financial and non-financial reporting and alignment of frameworks means that ESG data will become more comprehensive, reliable and comparable. ESG disclosure will have to meet high standards for assurance and regulatory compliance.

Digitisation is another powerful force that will shape the future of ESG. The time for manual processing of GHG emissions and other types of ESG data is over. The need to meet regulatory requirements and rising investor expectations is forcing companies to automate the collection, analysis and processing of ESG data, adopting new digital solutions and integrating enterprise information systems. Big data and artificial intelligence are paving the way for new climate solutions while data collection is rapidly expanding further up and down the value chains.

Finally, the 'S' pillar of ESG will grow in prominence and urgency. So far, companies' understanding of why social issues matter and how they shape the success of their business has been limited, especially in comparison to environmental and governance topics. This will change. The systemic nature of global challenges means that solutions to climate change will not be successful unless just transition is taken into consideration, society (and, in turn, consumers) will not thrive if inequality deepens, and companies will not be successful if they don't respect human rights. Our understanding of social issues and how to measure success addressing them will evolve along with rising regulatory and investor expectations.

7.   ESG in private equity
Cornelia Gomez
General Atlantic

7.1   What will ESG in private equity look like in 10 years' time?
On the basis of its scale alone, the private equity industry – an estimated 10,000 managers overseeing 40,000 portfolio companies and 20 million employees[9] – is a critical stakeholder in advancing ESG. With assets under management forecast to exceed US$11 trillion by 2026,[10] the stakes are only rising for firms, but so is their ability to counter climate, societal and governance challenges at scale.

Based on my experience as a practitioner in the space over the past 15 years, I expect three meaningful evolutions to unfold around ESG over the next decade.

7.2   The themes in which we invest time, dedicate resources and regulate may be territories that are yet to be considered
A decade ago, when I was assessing labour and environmental conditions in Bangladesh and Chinese factories, health and safety, child labour, retention of papers and soil contamination were central. Today, corporates actively engage their suppliers in the measurement of their carbon footprint (as this often comprises the bulk of scope 3 emissions). In 10 years, we might be hyper-focused on the green workforce, a just transition, the working conditions of employees in the digital sector and/or the impact of AI.[11]

7.3   Different cooks in the kitchen
ESG is already progressing to a board-level topic of discussion[12] and finding its way to the office of the chief financial officer (CFO) through the evolution of financial and non-financial reporting directives – from the Corporate

---

9   Robert G Eccles, Vinay Shandal, David Young and Benedicte Montgomery, "Private Equity Should Take the Lead in Sustainability", *Harvard Business Review*, July–August 2022, https://hbr.org/2022/07/private-equity-should-take-the-lead-in-sustainability.

10   *Ibid.*

11   PwC's 27 Annual Global CEO Survey, "Thriving in an age of continuous reinvention", 15 January 2024, www.pwc.com/gx/en/issues/c-suite-insights/ceo-survey.html#.

12   Jessica Rodgers and James Gannon, "How to make sense of the ESG conversation", EY, 11 May 2023, www.ey.com/en_us/banking-capital-markets/making-sense-of-the-esg-conversation.

Sustainability Reporting Directive (CSRD) and Task Force on Climate-related Financial Disclosures (TCFD) to the Sustainable Finance Disclosures Regulation (SFDR).

Corporates and private equity players will always need a centre of expertise to tackle new topics and regulations, but oversight will likely be reconfigured as part of senior risk management or head of Strategy function. Today, Heads of ESG in private market firms are already taking on more operational roles, either within impact investment funds, the corporate structure (corporate affairs, strategy department), or on boards as non-executive directors (NEDs). Current practitioners would be well advised to expand their skillsets within corporate affairs, strategy and/or finance areas.

7.4   The changing nature of private markets will impact ESG

Historically, many founders and management teams may have chosen to stay private, at least in part, to pursue growth objectives away from the onerous transparency requirements of public listings.

Going forward, as the scope of reporting requirements potentially expands to incorporate a greater number of private companies – whether under the SEC's Federal Supplier Climate Risks and Resilience Rule or the EU's CSRD requirements – staying private will no longer present this advantage.

Instead, we may see an increase in the number of companies delisting or choosing to go private due to the superior operational and financial resources, and leadership being committed to advancing ESG practices.

Consolidation across the private markets arena may also drive notable dynamics for the future of ESG. Recognising and responding to the role that ESG risks play in the creation and protection of value for rapidly growing portfolio companies, and to firms' own licence to operate, is a competitive advantage in a consolidating market.

First, it enables managers to achieve greater alignment with sustainability-aware founders. However, it is also an important differentiator for limited partners as they adopt more sophisticated approaches to assessing the ESG capabilities of their managers.

Over time, consolidation may result in a more institutionalised, uniform approach to ESG across private markets, resulting in an 'uplevelling' of approaches across an industry with the investment time horizon, resources and intellectual capabilities to lead ESG approaches over the next decade.

8.   Conclusion

The concept of ESG is now widely recognised and no longer requires explanation to most stakeholders. ESG has become a staple in the corporate landscape, regularly discussed in board meetings, executive offices, investor gatherings and regulatory speeches.

ESG as a discipline is at an exciting and critical time, having rapidly increased in prominence among different stakeholder groups in a relatively short period of time and is now a key consideration in many boardrooms. Moving forward, across sectors including law, finance, insurance, consulting and private equity, among others, the extent and pace at which ESG considerations become inherently incorporated in everyday decision making, as opposed to being a standalone consideration, will be notable to watch in the coming years. This potential for a more organic incorporation of ESG within companies marks the next phase in its evolution from a concept championed by activists to a fixture on the agendas of boards and regulators.

At this inflexion point in the development of ESG, it is clear for many that the core principles are no longer peripheral concerns but are increasingly becoming the bedrock of strategic business decision-making. However, the journey thus far has not been without its challenges, and the backlash against ESG underscores the complexity of balancing diverse stakeholder interests in a rapidly changing world.

As we look ahead, it is clear that the path forward will require innovation and collaboration, where ESG is not just a criterion for assessment but a driving force for growth, risk management and potentially competitive advantage.

Throughout this handbook we have considered the concept of ESG from a myriad of perspectives. The question is, where do we go from here? Looking to the next 10 years it is likely that new concepts and frameworks will emerge that build on ESG principles, potentially leading to a new lexicon and set of practices that take us beyond ESG as we currently view it.

Regardless of the future trajectory of ESG, we trust that you have found the exploration of ESG concepts in this handbook both insightful and thought-provoking.

About the authors

Mariana Abreu

Global lead, human rights, Anthesis Group

mariana.abreu@anthesisgroup.com

Mariana Abreu is a human rights lawyer with over 12 years of experience working on human rights and social impact. Prior to her work as a consultant, Mariana led field and desk-based investigations into human rights in Brazil and sub-Saharan Africa at Amnesty International and Global Witness.

Mariana leads an international team of human rights experts who support leading investors and businesses on human rights due diligence, designing and implementing risk and impact assessments, and advising on best practices globally. Major projects she has worked on include managing a year-long human rights impact assessment in the chemical sector across Brazil, the United States, Mexico and Germany; overseeing training of over 200 suppliers in the manufacturing sector in Malaysia; and supervising human rights risk assessments across Africa, the Middle East and Turkey for a tech client. Mariana was individually ranked as a top ESG adviser by *Chambers & Partners*, being described as having a "very strong sense of responsibility" and "an excellent manager, leader and consultant".

Mariana holds an MA in Human Rights from the Paris School of International Affairs – Sciences Po, and a BA in Law from Pontifícia Universidade Católica de São Paulo. She is admitted to practice law in Brazil.

Andrew Angle

Research and networks manager, ERM Sustainability Institute

andrew.angle@erm.com

Andrew Angle is a managing consultant with the ERM Sustainability Institute. Based in Washington DC, he authors reports, briefings and blogs designed to provide business leaders with actionable insights and a deeper understanding of the rapidly evolving sustainability landscape. He has produced numerous works, including the Institute's "Annual Trends Report" and "Quarterly Trends Report", "Renewables Conundrums" report series and *The Decarbonization Imperative: An Executive Primer*. In addition to his thought leadership work, Andrew provides corporate sustainability consulting services for clients across numerous industries and geographies.

He holds a master's degree in Climate and Society from the Climate School at Columbia University and a bachelor's degree in Physical Geography from the College of Earth and Mineral Sciences at The Pennsylvania State University.

Desi Baca

Senior associate, Vinson & Elkins

dbaca@velaw.com

Desi Baca's principal areas of practice are corporate and securities law, including securities offerings, general corporate representation, private equity and mergers and acquisitions. As a senior member of Vinson & Elkins' shareholder activism practice, she has significant experience representing clients, including in more than 75 activism campaigns over the past seven years. Desi routinely advises public companies in competitive proxy solicitations, withhold campaigns, merger contests, consent solicitations, settlement negotiations, hostile takeover and other unsolicited bids, strategic investor relations, and corporate governance. In 2023, Desi was recognised by *The Legal 500 US* in the "Shareholder Activism – Advice to Boards" category.

Helene R Banks

Partner, Cahill Gordon & Reindel LLP

hbanks@cahill.com

Helene R Banks is chair of Cahill's M&A and corporate advisory practice group and a thought leader in the increasingly complex ESG arena. Helene advises publicly held and private companies in significant corporate and securities matters, with particular emphasis on mergers and acquisitions, corporate governance and capital markets transactions. Her work ranges from managing complex international transactions for large public companies to guiding owners through investments in their privately held businesses to advising companies as they progress on their ESG journeys.

Helene is recognised as a leading M&A and Corporate Governance lawyer by *The Legal 500* and in 2023 was recognised as a Notable Leader in Sustainability by *Crain's New York Business*. Helene frequently speaks and writes on ESG, M&A, corporate governance and board diversity issues. She has been published in *Practical Law, NACD BoardTalk, NACD Directorship, Law360, The Deal, New York Law Journal* and *Corporate Secretary* and has spoken on these topics at numerous industry events.

Ian Barclay

Board member, Anthesis Group

ian.barclay@anthesisgroup.com

Ian Barclay is a board member of Anthesis and a co-founder of Wallbrook, a global ESG advisory firm that merged with Anthesis in 2023. He previously worked as executive managing director at Stroz Friedberg and Aon from 2013 to 2018 and was part of the management team that oversaw the acquisition and integration of the cyber risk manager Stroz Friedberg by Aon Plc in 2016.

Ian was previously a director of Billiter, a leading due diligence and investigations firm which was acquired by Stroz Friedberg in 2013. While at Billiter, Ian oversaw the establishment of the firm's London and Hong Kong offices. Ian started his career at UBS and has degrees from Queen Mary College and the University of Cambridge.

Rachel Barrett

Partner, Linklaters

rachel.barrett@linklaters.com

Rachel Barrett leads the Linklaters global ESG practice. She has deep expertise and exceptional breadth of experience advising on existing and incoming ESG regulation and soft law standards, ESG strategy and disclosures, sustainable finance products and frameworks, ESG governance and risk management and on stakeholder activism, litigation risk and crisis management.

Rachel has been recognised in the Fifty Most Influential in Sustainable Finance 2023 list by *Financial News*, as the go-to adviser on ESG matters by *The Lawyer Hot 100* list as well as "Next Generation Partner" in the Environment and Corporate Governance category by *The Legal 500*. She was previously a member of the UK Government's Green Technical Advisory Group.

Gregory J Battista

Counsel, Cahill Gordon & Reindel LLP

gbattista@cahill.com

Gregory J Battista leads Cahill's environmental practice group. Greg advises clients on environmental/ESG matters relating to mergers and acquisitions, financing transactions, and debt and equity offerings. Greg has over 35 years of experience handling environmental matters, including risk analysis, federal and state compliance, remediation and corporate transactions. He regularly advises clients in a variety of areas including: EHS compliance and litigation matters; site investigation and clean-up; SEC disclosure; sustainability strategy and reporting; climate change regulation; government enforcement and administrative proceedings; OSHA matters; auditing; supply chain and ESG risk; real estate development projects and due diligence with respect to financing; and M&A and other corporate matters. Greg has been recognised as a leading environmental lawyer by *Chambers USA, The Legal 500, International Who's Who of Environmental Lawyers, Lawdragon Green 500* and *Euromoney's Expert Guides*.

James Bee

Associate, Latham & Watkins

james.bee@lw.com

James Bee is an associate in the ESG practice of Latham & Watkins' London office. James primarily advises clients on ESG, environmental, health and safety and energy matters, across a range of transactional, regulatory and contentious issues.

Daniela Bergs

Director, Howden

daniela.bergs@howdengroup.com

Daniela Bergs is a director at Howden M&A. Prior to joining she worked as a senior environmental insurance underwriter at Liberty Mutual Insurance in New York. Together with the environmental team, her focus is finding insurance solutions for complex environmental liability structures for both real estate and operational transactions. Her focus extends to ensuring environmental compliance across multiple jurisdictions, aiding companies in mitigating nature-related risks and advancing sustainability initiatives. Daniela holds a master's degree in Business Marketing from the Freie Universität Berlin.

Milenko Bertrand-Galindo

Partner, Bertrand-Galindo Barrueto Barroilhet

mbertrand@bertrand-galindo.cl

Milenko Bertrand-Galindo is the head of the international law and ESG departments at Bertrand-Galindo Barrueto Barroilhet. Milenko holds a law degree from Universidad Católica, an LLM from Harvard Law School and an SJD from the Washington College of Law. He specialises in international law, ESG compliance and finance, corporate compliance, indigenous law, community relations and human rights.

He has been part of Chile's legal team before The Hague International Court of Justice, and a member of the Interamerican Judicial Committee of the Organization of American States. He has been legal adviser for the Presidency, the Ministries of Foreign Affairs and Justice and the National Human Rights Institute in Chile.

Milenko has been recognised as a "Leading Lawyer in ESG" by *Leading Lawyers* in 2021 and is the author of the Chilean chapter for *The Legal 500*'s Country Comparative Guide on ESG, among other several publications in the field.

About the authors

Aiste Brackley
Partner, ERM Sustainability Institute
aiste.brackley@erm.com

Aiste Brackley is a partner at ERM and director at the ERM Sustainability Institute. She leads advisory projects on corporate sustainability and climate change strategy with a focus on energy, pharma and technology sectors. Aiste also oversees research projects at the Sustainability Institute and manages the production of research briefs, surveys and insights articles. Most of Aiste's research has focused on climate change, sustainability strategy and natural climate solutions, and she has been the lead author of many of the Institute's flagship publications.

Aiste frequently appears as a speaker at webinars and conferences and has been published in *GreenBiz*, *The Guardian*, *Huffington Post* and other publications. She has taught at Vilnius University and the Haas School of Business at the University of California, Berkeley. Prior to joining ERM, Aiste spent more than 15 years working at the intersection of private, non-profit and public sectors in the US, UK, Germany, Lithuania, Sweden and Russia.

Amandine Bressand
Manager, business and human rights, ISEAL
amandine@isealalliance.org

Amandine Bressand is the business and human rights manager at ISEAL, the global membership organisation for ambitious and transparent sustainability systems. Amandine oversees ISEAL's work on human rights and decent work. She also manages projects advancing equity and producer empowerment in global supply chains.

Amandine's human rights expertise stems from her work in the advocacy, humanitarian and ESG consultancy sectors. Her thematic focuses have included forced labour, human trafficking and poor working conditions. She was previously senior associate at Wallbrook (Anthesis Group) where she helped businesses address human rights risks in their value chains. Before that, Amandine was chief of staff at Battery Associates, a company advancing sustainable battery innovation. She also worked with iNGOs like International Crisis Group and the International Federation for Human Rights.

Amandine holds an MSc in Violence, Conflict and Development from SOAS University of London, and a BA in Political Science and Human Rights from Barnard College of Columbia University in New York. She has lived in Syria, Tunisia, Lebanon, Vietnam, France, the US, and the UK where she is based.

Dearbhla Cantwell
Managing associate, Linklaters
dearbhla.cantwell@linklaters.com

Dearbhla Cantwell is a managing associate in the Linklaters ESG practice, where she advises clients on a wide range of environment, social and governance matters. In particular, she advises on the ESG aspects of complex international corporate transactions across multiple sectors, including in relation to the UK contaminated land, environmental permitting and operational health and safety regimes. Dearbhla also advises on various sustainability-related regulatory reporting regimes, including TCFD, CSRD and UK SECR. She also has experience advising clients on a variety of innovative voluntary carbon market transactions and on the development of carbon insetting and offsetting projects, including in relation to blue carbon.

Christine Covington

Partner, Corrs Chambers Westgarth

christine.covington@corrs.com.au

Christine Covington has over 38 years' experience as a specialist environment and planning lawyer and member of Corrs' responsible business practice group. She advises public and private sector clients across energy and resources, education, real estate, state and local government and retail sectors. For some of Australia's largest institutional real estate investment trusts, including the Stockland, Mirvac and Frasers Property Group, Christine advises on a range of environmental issues including environmental impact assessment, planning and environmental litigation.

Australia's energy transition has been a recent focus, including energy transmission client Transgrid and generator AGL Energy. ESG is a key area of practice across a range of public and private sector clients together with advice on biodiversity conservation agreements, credit transfers and climate-related reporting obligations. Christine is a former board member of the New South Wales Environment Protection Authority and is currently the deputy chair of the New South Wales Biodiversity Conservation Trust.

Paul Davies

Partner, Latham & Watkins

paul.davies@lw.com

Paul Davies is global co-chair of Latham's environmental, social and governance (ESG) practice and a member of Latham & Watkins' sustainability committee. He advises clients on a broad range of ESG issues involving contentious, regulatory and transactional matters. He is recognised as a "world-leading ESG lawyer" (*Chambers UK* 2022). He is also acknowledged for his innovative approach, twice being named among Europe's Top Innovative Individuals (*FT Innovative Lawyers Report*). For his long-term contribution to ESG, Paul was acknowledged with a lifetime achievement award with recognition as "a truly exceptional individual" (*The Legal 500* 2024).

Lawrence Elbaum

Partner and co-head of the shareholder activism practice, Vinson & Elkins

lelbaum@velaw.com

Lawrence Elbaum is the co-head of Vinson & Elkins' shareholder activism practice and a member of the firm's management committee. He leverages nearly two decades of experience as a securities attorney and business adviser to counsel senior management and boards of public companies with respect to proxy fights, merger contests, consent solicitations, "Withhold the Vote" or "Vote No" campaigns, precatory proposals and short attacks, as well as an array of complex corporate governance matters.

Over the past 10 proxy seasons, Lawrence has led over 300 activism defence engagements for public companies of all sizes and across all industries. He regularly defends clients against high-profile shareholder activists such as Starboard Value, Elliott Management, Carl Icahn, Engaged Capital, Jana Partners, Value Act Legion Partners, Corvex Management and D.E. Shaw & Co.

Throughout Lawrence's leadership of the shareholder activism practice, the team has been ranked the top firm for shareholder activism defence for company and board representation by Bloomberg, Refinitiv, Activist Insight and FactSet. *Chambers USA* 2021–2023 lists Lawrence as a leading practitioner in its category for "Corporate/M&A: Takeover Defense (New York)" and *The Legal 500 US* ranked the shareholder activism practice among the top law firms from 2019–2023 in the "Shareholder Activism – Advice to Boards" category.

Paula Errázuriz Sotta

Associate, Bertrand-Galindo Barrueto Barroilhet

p.errazuriz@bertrand-galindo.cl

Paula Errázuriz Sotta is an associate lawyer at Bertrand-Galindo Barrueto Barroilhet and holds a law degree from Universidad Católica. Paula has concentrated her practice in the areas of ESG, communities and corporate compliance. At Bertrand-Galindo Barrueto Barroilhet she has advised multiple clients in the development and review of ESG policies, the preparation of collaboration agreements with indigenous communities and the accompaniment of resettlement processes, among others.

Sarah E Fortt

Partner, Latham & Watkins

sarah.fortt@lw.com

Sarah E Fortt, global co-chair of Latham's environmental, social and governance (ESG) practice, is the mind behind one of the first ESG legal practices in the United States. In her role, she acts as a trusted adviser of her clients, navigating with them risks and opportunities relating to climate change, human rights and corporate culture. Sarah advises public and private companies and their boards on corporate governance and strategic transparency. She also counsels clients in high-stakes governance situations, including public and political ESG-related campaigns, stakeholder engagement and corporate crises.

Sarah draws on her background in corporate governance, compliance, securities, executive compensation and sophisticated understanding of cross-organisational structures to help clients create consistent, effective and meaningful ESG strategies and communications.

Jonathan Friedman

Global lead, client strategy and solutions: ESG advisory, Anthesis Group

jonathan.friedman@anthesisgroup.com

Jonathan Friedman leads global client engagement for the ESG advisory business line at Anthesis, the Carlyle Group-backed sustainability consultancy. He previously co-founded Wallbrook, an international ESG due diligence and human rights consultancy, which was sold to Anthesis in 2023. Before entering consultancy, he worked on Capitol Hill.

Jonathan's analysis and forecasts of global developments have been widely featured in broadcast and print media, including the BBC, Bloomberg, the *Financial Times* and *The Wall Street Journal*. He holds a bachelor's degree in Middle Eastern Studies from the University of Pennsylvania, and a master's degree in Comparative Politics (States and Markets) from the London School of Economics.

Patrick Gadson

Partner and co-head of the shareholder activism practice, Vinson & Elkins

pgadson@velaw.com

Patrick Gadson's principal areas of practice are private equity, mergers and acquisitions and shareholder activism. Patrick is co-head of Vinson & Elkins' shareholder activism practice, which advises public companies in competitive proxy solicitations, strategic investor relations and corporate governance. He also counsels senior management, boards of directors, investment managers and both private equity and strategic investors in a wide variety of complex business transactions, corporate governance matters, strategic investor relations and other special situations. His experience includes advising clients in connection with shareholder activism related investments, hostile takeovers, public and private M&A transactions, strategic minority investments and corporate capital investments. Prior to joining Vinson & Elkins, Patrick practised law at a leading shareholder activism law firm and a preeminent corporate law firm in New York City.

From 2021–2023 Patrick was featured on *Lawdragon*'s "500 Leading Dealmakers in America" list. From 2021–2023, Patrick was recognised as "Next Generation Partner" by *The Legal 500 US* in the Shareholder Activism – Advice to Boards category and ranked "Up and Coming" by *Chambers USA* in the Corporate/M&A: Takeover Defense (New York) category. He has also been recognised on Thomson Reuters' "Super Lawyers" rising star list for 2022.

Kate Gill-Herdman

Special counsel, Corrs Chambers Westgarth
kate.gill-herdman@corrs.com.au

Kate Gill-Herdman is an experienced legal practitioner in Corrs' responsible business and ESG practice group who specialises in contentious and non-contentious responsible business and ESG matters. She advises financial institutions, other corporate and public sector clients on a range of complex and sensitive issues including supply chain investigations, greenwashing allegations, human rights risk management frameworks and responsibilities under the UN Guiding Principles on Business and Human Rights. Kate has also acted in many of Australia's significant public inquiries, including the Royal Commission into the Casino Operator and Licence, the Victorian Hotel Quarantine Board of Inquiry, the Victorian Royal Commission into the Management of Police Informants and the Financial Services Royal Commission. She is a member of the Responsible Investment Association of Australasia and leads Corrs' membership of the Australian Sustainable Finance Institute.

Cornelia Gomez

Global head of sustainability, General Atlantic
cogomez@generalatlantic.com

Cornelia Gomez is the global head of sustainability at General Atlantic. In her role, Cornelia oversees the firm's sustainability strategy and efforts to advance ESG policies, procedures and value-creation initiatives for its global operations, asset classes and across its portfolio. Before joining GA, Cornelia was head of ESG and sustainability at PAI Partners, and she also served as the global coordinator for the International Climate Initiative, an industry group that is sponsored by the United Nations' Principles for Responsible Investment. Previously, Cornelia led the supply chain sustainability work at Casino Group.

Patrick Gordon

Partner, Cahill Gordon & Reindel LLP
pgordon@cahill.com

Patrick Gordon represents leading investment banking firms, direct lenders, private credit funds and other institutional investors in a broad range of corporate financing transactions. He has extensive experience representing the financing sources in privately placed and syndicated secured term loan financings, secured and unsecured bridge loan and debt securities financings, and public and private equity and equity-linked issuances. Pat specialises in financings supporting leveraged buyouts and acquisition financings across a wide variety of industries, including telecommunications and media, entertainment, healthcare, financial services, retail and food services, gaming and industrials. Pat also represented the financing sources in the recent ground-breaking sustainability-linked loans supporting the acquisition of Novolex by Apollo Global Management, which were the first sustainability-linked loans placed in connection with the financing of a leveraged buyout.

Michael D Green
Counsel, Latham & Watkins
michael.green@lw.com

Michael D Green is a counsel and member of Latham's environmental, social and governance (ESG) practice and environment, land and resources practice. He advises clients on a range of ESG and environmental, health and safety matters in the context of transactional work, the management of risks and opportunities and litigation matters. Michael is consistently recognised by *Chambers UK* and clients say that "Michael is an incredibly able and consistently very focused lawyer" who "brings attention to detail and real intellectual rigour to the process", with another noting "I trust his judgement hugely". Michael is named a Recommended Global Leader for Environment by *Who's Who Legal* 2019. He is also described by clients as their "go-to lawyer" who stands out for his "excellent practical advice" and "impeccable level of service".

Vanessa Havard-Williams
Consultant, Linklaters
vanessa.havard-williams@linklaters.com

Vanessa Havard-Williams is a consultant at Linklaters, focusing on ESG and sustainability. She was previously the head of the firm's global environmental and climate change practice, founded the firm's ESG practice and co-headed the risk and resilience and crisis management teams.

She advises financial institutions, corporates and funds around the world across the spectrum of emerging ESG requirements. She is currently leading the UK Government's Transition Finance Market Review and is part of the UK's Transition Plan Taskforce. She is also a board member of UK Export Finance and chair of the UK Export Guarantee Advisory Group.

Nicola Higgs
Partner, Latham & Watkins
nicola.higgs@lw.com

Nicola Higgs is a partner in the London office of Latham & Watkins and global co-chair of the firm's financial institutions industry group. Nicola specialises in offering ESG regulatory advice across the financial services ecosystem. Nicola advises public companies, global investment banks, institutional investors and ESG index and data services providers on a variety of ESG legal and regulatory risk management matters, with particular expertise in the anti-greenwashing expectations of securities laws regulators.

Betty M Huber
Partner, Latham & Watkins
betty.huber@lw.com

Betty M Huber, global co-chair of Latham's environmental, social and governance (ESG) practice, shapes business-critical corporate sustainability initiatives, policy and reporting for leading companies, funds and their boards. Betty also advises on sustainable finance products, M&A transactions and capital markets offerings. She provides pragmatic, commercial guidance across a broad spectrum of industries and market caps, driving value through strategy, oversight, reporting and other programmes while carefully addressing, managing and mitigating risk. Betty draws on over twenty-five years of experience providing a sophisticated understanding of her clients' businesses to meet their emerging demands in today's rapidly evolving regulatory climate.

Robin M Hulshizer

Partner, Latham & Watkins

robin.hulshizer@lw.com

Robin M Hulshizer is a US-based trial lawyer practising out of Chicago, Illinois with more than 25 years of experience litigating complex commercial and environmental matters. She is a member of Latham & Watkins' complex commercial litigation and environmental, social and governance (ESG) practices, focusing on environmental litigation, greenwashing claims, environmental justice-based claims and general regulatory compliance. Her experience is multi-disciplinary, including toxic torts, product liability, consumer fraud, business contract, insurance coverage, class actions and securities litigation.

She has represented clients across various sectors such as manufacturing, oil and gas, consumer products, energy and industrial hygiene. In the environmental arena, Robin's experience has spanned every major US environmental statute and includes not only litigation but compliance strategies, regulatory work, investigation/enforcement actions and ESG/environmental counselling in connection with large-scale financial and corporate transactions.

Thomas Kelly

Senior associate, Howden

thomas.kelly@howdengrp.com

Thomas Kelly is a senior associate in the climate, risk and resilience team at Howden. Thomas's main focus within the climate, risk and resilience team is on the intersection between the insurance and the carbon markets. He recently completed a dissertation at Advanced Chartered Insurance Institute level on how the collaboration between the humanitarian and insurance sector can help increase the resilience of vulnerable communities

around the world. Before joining the climate team, Thomas worked in the M&A, reinsurance and financial lines teams at Howden. During this time, Thomas completed a secondment to the Department for International Trade where he worked in the insurance and climate resilience team, helping to build its resilience campaign and engagement with the insurance sector. Thomas has a BA honours degree in History from the University of Bristol and an MSc in History of International Relations from the London School of Economics.

Edward Kempson

Partner, Latham & Watkins

edward.kempson@lw.com

Edward Kempson is an English law-qualified partner based in the Riyadh office of Latham & Watkins. Edward is the global coordinator of the firm's sustainable finance practice. He has considerable experience advising clients on a wide variety of debt and equity capital markets transactions and ESG, sustainable finance and corporate related matters.

Ruth Knox

Partner, Paul Hastings

ruthknox@paulhastings.com

Ruth Knox is a partner and global co-chair of the ESG and sustainable finance practice at Paul Hastings and is based in the firm's London office.

Ruth advises some of the world's most sophisticated private equity firms, corporations and project sponsors and lenders on complex and evolving legal issues relating to ESG and climate-related regulatory requirements, investor demands, strategic opportunities (including transition strategies), and voluntary reporting frameworks and coalitions.

Ruth has spent more than a decade advising on

ESG regulations and soft law standards, including the EU Sustainable Finance package, the Corporate Sustainability Reporting Directive and the Task Force on Climate-related Financial Disclosure (TCFD) standard.

Ruth provides commercial, solutions-oriented advice in sustainable fund formation, large-scale international M&A, sustainable finance transactions and ESG-related corporate crises, as well as climate and nature-based finance. She also advises on a wide range of product regulatory regimes across different sectors.

Sophie Lamb KC

Partner, Latham & Watkins

sophie.lamb.KC@lw.com

Sophie Lamb KC is an accomplished advocate who draws on an exceptionally diverse international case load and more than 20 years of international tribunal and trial experience including in the UK Supreme Court. Her experience extends across the full range of significant corporate and commercial arrangements, international investment law, public law and climate litigation. Leveraging strong expertise in class action litigation targeting multinational groups, Sophie is increasingly engaged on sensitive and strategic mandates which engage the ESG agenda, covering such issues as directors' duties, reporting risks, climate change and public interest litigation, global supply chain integrity, human rights-related exposure and OECD National Contact Point processes. She also counsels more generally on navigating the risks and opportunities arising from heightened focus on ESG, net zero ambitions and corporate purpose.

Mark Lee

Global director, ERM Sustainability Institute

mark.lee@erm.com

Mark Lee is the global director of the ERM Sustainability Institute and an ERM partner. His work helps companies make better and fast progress on sustainable development. Mark has over 25 years' experience in leadership positions in the sustainability field and is an expert in sustainability strategy and implementation. He is the co-author of *All In: The Future of Business Leadership* (Routledge, 2018) and *The Sustainable Business Handbook* (Kogan Page, 2022). Mark was previously the executive director of SustainAbility, vice president at Business for Social Responsibility, and manager, CSR at Vancity Savings. He is a graduate of the University of British Columbia, an *alumnus* of the Cambridge Institute for Sustainability Leadership, and he completed the Berkeley Executive Program at the Center for Executive Leadership at the Haas School of Business at UC Berkeley.

Carmen XW Lu

Counsel, Wachtell, Lipton, Rosen & Katz

cxwlu@wlrk.com

Carmen XW Lu is counsel in Wachtell Lipton's corporate department where she advises companies and boards of directors across industries on corporate governance, shareholder activism and ESG matters, evolving market and regulatory trends and practices, and effective stakeholder engagement.

Carmen advises companies and boards of directors on a range of governance issues, including: governance structure, policies and practices; board fiduciary duties and oversight responsibilities, including with respect to ESG matters; shareholder, proxy adviser and stakeholder engagement; shareholder activism and proxy contests; shareholder proposals; identification and evaluation of ESG risks and opportunities; board and committee composition, structure and evaluations; evolving market, industry and stakeholder expectations; and compliance with legislative, regulatory and list rule requirements.

Carmen received her JD from Yale Law School in 2016, where she was articles and essays editor of the Yale Law Journal and executive editor of the *Yale Journal on Regulation*.

Anne Mainwaring
Counsel, Latham & Watkins
anne.mainwaring@lw.com

Anne Mainwaring is counsel in Latham's financial regulatory practice in London. She has extensive experience advising clients on UK and EU regulatory developments relevant to ESG matters, including advising clients in relation to compliance with ongoing ESG regulatory developments across multiple regulatory regimes.

Meghan McDermott
Partner, Cahill Gordon & Reindel LLP
mmcdermott@cahill.com

Meghan McDermott represents leading investment banking firms and commercial banks in a brand range of financing transactions involving syndicated institutional loans, leveraged buyouts, secured and unsecured debt securities and equity securities, including initial public offerings and follow-on equity offerings. Meghan has experience practising in a variety of industries, including telecommunications and media, entertainment, healthcare, financial services, retail and food services, gaming and industrials. Meghan has also represented the financing sources in the sustainability-linked senior notes offering by Covert Mergeco, Inc that was used to fund the acquisition by EQT Infrastructure V fund of Covanta Holding Corporation.

In 2024, Meghan was shortlisted for the Women in Business Law Awards Americas, Debt Capital Markets Lawyer of the Year. Meghan was also recognised as a Rising Star Partner by *IFLR1000*, a 2022 Rising Star in the area of Capital Markets by *Law360*, and a Rising Star in Equity Capital Markets as a part of *IFLR*'s Rising Stars Awards 2022 Americas.

Stuart McLachlan
Chief executive officer, Anthesis Group
stuart.mclachlan@anthesisgroup.com

Stuart McLachlan is co-founder and CEO of Anthesis Group, which started trading in 2013 and has grown to over 1,000 people across several continents, with a client portfolio that includes many FTSE 100 and Fortune 500 companies. Since commencement, the company has acquired 15 sustainability firms and in 2021 they entered a partnership with private equity firm, Palatine. Anthesis has featured on numerous occasions in the FastTrack100 and the FT1000 as one of the fastest growing private companies in the UK and Europe.

Prior to Anthesis, Stuart spent 16 years developing the WSP Environment and Energy business, building it from a start up in WSP Group PLC to one of the leading global consultancies in the sector. For six years from 2006 to the merger with GENIVAR, Stuart also served as a PLC director on the board of WSP Group, a FTSE 250 company. In addition to his focus on business leadership, he has a passion for sustainable development and is a speaker on market trends and the relationship between sustainable futures and business success. In 2019, Stuart featured as the LDC "One to Watch" and in 2021 was listed in the Top 32 ESG pioneers by *Business Leader* magazine.

Glenn O'Halloran

Executive director, Howden

glenn.ohalloran@howdengroup.com

Glenn O'Halloran has over 10 years' experience in the environmental liability insurance market, most recently developing and leading the environmental team within Howden's M&A practice. Prior to joining Howden, he led the environmental liability team within a global insurer, after a career working on remote mining and construction projects across Australia as an environmental engineer. Glenn holds an honours degree in Environmental Engineering and a Master of Business Administration degree. Within the climate risk and resilience team, Glenn focuses on developing risk transaction products in order to support clients through the energy transition and with acquisitions made in the carbon markets.

Chidi Onyeche

Associate, Latham & Watkins

chidi.onyeche@lw.com

Chidi Onyeche is an associate in the project development and finance practice of Latham & Watkins' London office and is a member of the firm's Africa practice. Chidi advises financial institutions, multilateral organisations, governments and project sponsors on a wide range of financing transactions in the ESG and sustainable finance space.

Bernardita Salvatierra Riquelme

Associate, Bertrand-Galindo Barrueto Barroilhet

bsalvatierra@bertrand-galindo.cl

Bernardita Salvatierra Riquelme holds a law degree from Pontificia Universidad Católica de Chile and a postgraduate diploma in natural resources and sustainable development from Universidad de Chile. Bernardita focuses her professional practice on ESG, indigenous law, communities, sustainability, mining, energy and natural resources. Bernardita works as an associate lawyer at Bertrand-Galindo Barrueto Barroilhet, where she has advised a wide range of local and foreign clients from various economic sectors, mainly energy and mining, in the development of their projects in Chile, from an ESG perspective.

Reena SenGupta

Executive director, RSGI Limited

reena.sengupta@rsgi.co

Reena SenGupta is a leading thought leader in the global legal profession, with a 30-year track record of innovation. From creating the *Chambers & Partners* research, ranking and editorial methodology and approach in the mid-1990s to the FT Innovative Lawyers programme in the mid-noughties, Reena has designed and authored leading studies and assessments on how lawyers are evolving to remain relevant. Her company RSGI Limited, the global legal think tank, consults to top law firms and in-house legal teams as well as legal technology companies and alternative legal service providers on strategy, innovation and sustainable growth. Its latest rating system, the RSGI Greenprint, assesses the responsible business reporting and policies of 180 international law firms.

Farhana Sharmeen

Partner, Latham & Watkins

farhana.sharmeen@lw.com

Farhana Sharmeen is co-deputy Asia managing partner in the corporate department of Latham & Watkins' Singapore office and heads the firm's Singapore law practice. Farhana primarily handles corporate and finance transactions. She also advises on general corporate matters, including regulatory compliance and corporate governance issues. Farhana has particular experience representing clients in real estate, financial institutions and the luxury goods industry.

Farhana is recognised as a leading lawyer for corporate M&A in Singapore by *Chambers Asia-Pacific*, which highlights her "active public takeovers practice with expertise regarding fund formation and regulatory work". In addition, she is noted by *Best Lawyers* in Singapore for her work in corporate law. She is the chair of the ESG Asia Working Group at Latham & Watkins and has experience with a range of clients across Asia advising on a number of ESG issues.

Kathleen Teo
Trainee solicitor, Latham & Watkins
kathleen.teo@lw.com

Kathleen Teo is a trainee solicitor in the London office of Latham & Watkins. Kathleen has assisted in advising financial institutions, multilateral organisations, major international energy companies, governments and project sponsors on a wide range of financing transactions.

Elina Tetelbaum
Partner, Wachtell, Lipton, Rosen & Katz
etetelbaum@wlrk.com

Elina Tetelbaum is a corporate partner at Wachtell Lipton, where she leads the firm's efforts on shareholder activism defence and proxy fights. Elina also frequently counsels, lectures and publishes on corporate governance, shareholder activism and M&A. Elina has been named a Dealmaker of the Year by *The American Lawyer*, was recognised as one of *The Deal*'s Top Women in Dealmaking and a *Law360* Rising Star for M&A, among other honours. Elina is the president of the Stuyvesant High School Alumni Association, an advisory board member of the John L Weinberg Center for Corporate Governance at the

University of Delaware and a board member of the Yale Law School Center for the Study of Corporate Law. She received an AB *magna cum laude* in Economics from Harvard University and completed a JD from Yale Law School.

Gary Whitehead
Associate, Latham & Watkins
gary.whitehead@lw.com

Gary Whitehead is an associate in the London office of Latham & Watkins and a member of the global financial institutions industry group. Gary advises on a range of financial services regulation and has experience advising a wide range of financial institutions in relation to their regulatory compliance.

Kristina Wyatt
Deputy general counsel and chief sustainability officer, Persefoni
kristina.wyatt@persefoni.com

Kristina Wyatt is Persefoni's deputy general counsel and chief sustainability officer. She joined Persefoni from the Securities and Exchange Commission (SEC) where she was senior counsel to the director of the division of corporation finance, focused on climate and ESG. Before joining the SEC, Kristina was director of sustainability at Latham & Watkins. Kristina holds a BA from Duke University, a JD from the University of Colorado and an MBA in Sustainability from Yale University.

Sabrina Zhang
Associate, corporate department, Paul Hastings
sabrinazhang@paulhastings.com

Sabrina Zhang is an associate in the investment funds and private capital practice at Paul Hastings and is based in the firm's New York office. Her practice focuses on private investment funds. Sabrina has a bachelor's degree from the University of California Davis and a JD from Harvard Law School.

David J Ziyambi
Partner, Latham & Watkins
david.ziyambi@lw.com

David J Ziyambi is a member of Latham & Watkins' finance department and the vice chair of the firm's Africa practice. His practice focuses primarily on project, structured and leveraged financing in the energy and infrastructure sectors within both mature and developing markets, particularly throughout Africa. He represents sponsors, lenders and governments on a range of matters, from project development and project finance deals to structured financing, prepayments and reserve-based lending.

About Globe Law and Business

Globe Law and Business was established in 2005. From the very beginning, we set out to create legal books that are sufficiently high level to be of real use to the experienced professional, yet still accessible and easy to navigate. Most of our authors are drawn from Magic Circle and other top commercial firms, both in the United Kingdom and internationally.

Our titles are carefully produced, with the utmost attention paid to editorial, design and production processes. We hope this results in high-quality publications that are easy to read and a pleasure to own.

In 2021, we were very pleased to announce the start of a new chapter for Globe Law and Business following the acquisition of law books under the imprint Ark Publishing. Our law firm management list is now significantly expanded with many well-known and loved Ark Publishing titles.

We are also pleased to announce the launch of our online content platform, Globe Law Online, which allows for easy access across firms. Details of all titles included can be found at www.globelawonline.com. Email glo@ globelawandbusiness.com for further details and to arrange a free trial for you or your firm.

We'd very much like to hear from you with your thoughts and ideas for improving what we offer. Please do feel free to email me on sian@ globelawandbusiness.com. Happy reading and thank you for your time.

Sian O'Neill
Managing director
Globe Law and Business
www.globelawandbusiness.com

Milton Keynes UK
Ingram Content Group UK Ltd.
UKHW021030260924
448679UK00002B/7

9 781787 429765